Language and a Sense of Place

Place has always been central to studies of language variation and change. Since the eighteenth century, dialectologists have been mapping language features according to boundaries – both physical and institutional. In the twentieth century, variationist sociolinguists developed techniques to correlate language use with speakers' orientations to place. More recently, perceptual dialectologists are examining the cognitive and ideological processes involved in language–place correlations and working on ways to understand how speakers mentally process space.

Bringing together research from across the field of language variation, this volume explores the extent of twenty-first-century approaches to place. It features work from both established and influential scholars, and up and coming researchers, and brings language variation research up-to-date.

The volume focuses on four key areas of research: processes of language variation and change across time and space; methods and datasets for regional analysis; perceptions of the local in language research; and ideological representations of place.

CHRIS MONTGOMERY is a SENIOR LECTURER in Dialectology at the University of Sheffield. His research focuses on non-linguists' perceptions of dialects. He has published articles in the *Journal of Sociolinguistics* and *Studies in Variation, Contacts and Change in English*. He was the editor (with Dr Jennifer Cramer, University of Kentucky) of *Cityscapes and Perceptual Dialectology* (2016) and, with Professor Karen Corrigan, of a special issue of *English Language and Linguistics* (2015) focussing on the role of place in historical linguistics.

EMMA MOORE is a READER in Sociolinguistics at the University of Sheffield. Her research explores how individuals and communities use language to construct social styles and create social meaning. Emma's most recent project is an AHRC-funded project exploring language variation and change in a rather unique place: the Isles of Scilly. She has published in the *Journal of Sociolinguistics*, *Language Variation and Change*, and *Language in Society*, and is on the editorial board of *Language in Society* and *Gender and Language*.

D1346292

Language and a Sense of Place

Studies in Language and Region

Chris Montgomery

University of Sheffield

Emma Moore

University of Sheffield

CAMBRIDGE
UNIVERSITY PRESS

University Printing House, Cambridge CB2 8BS, United Kingdom

One Liberty Plaza, 20th Floor, New York, NY 10006, USA

477 Williamstown Road, Port Melbourne, VIC 3207, Australia

4843/24, 2nd Floor, Ansari Road, Daryaganj, Delhi – 110002, India

79 Anson Road, #06–04/06, Singapore 079906

Cambridge University Press is part of the University of Cambridge.

It furthers the University's mission by disseminating knowledge in the pursuit of education, learning, and research at the highest international levels of excellence.

www.cambridge.org
Information on this title: www.cambridge.org/9781107098718
DOI: 10.1017/9781316162477

First published 2017

Printed in the United Kingdom by TJ International Ltd. Padstow Cornwall

A catalogue record for this publication is available from the British Library.

ISBN 978-1-107-09871-8 Hardback

Contents

List of Figures   *page* vii
List of Tables   xi
List of Contributors   xiii
Preface and Acknowledgements   xv

Introduction: 'Place' in Studies of Language Variation and Change   1
EMMA MOORE AND CHRIS MONTGOMERY

Part I   Changing Places   13

1   Changing Places: Tracking Innovation and Obsolescence across
    Generations   15
    SALI A. TAGLIAMONTE

2   Changing Sounds in a Changing City: An Acoustic Phonetic
    Investigation of Real-Time Change over a Century of Glaswegian   38
    JANE STUART-SMITH, BRIAN JOSÉ, TAMARA RATHCKE,
    RACHEL MACDONALD AND ELEANOR LAWSON

3   Local vs. Supralocal: Preserving Language and Identity in
    Newfoundland   65
    SANDRA CLARKE

4   Variation and Change in the Realisation of /r/ in an Isolated
    Northumbrian Dialect   87
    WARREN MAGUIRE

Part II   Describing Places   105

5   Corpora for Regional and Social Analysis   107
    KAREN P. CORRIGAN

6 Using Archives to Conduct Collaborative Research on
   Language and Region   128
   FIONA DOUGLAS

7 Maps and Mapping in (Perceptual) Dialect Geography   147
   CHRIS MONTGOMERY

8 Which Way to Look?: Perspectives on 'Urban' and 'Rural'
   in Dialectology   171
   DAVID BRITAIN

Part III   Identifying Places   189

9 Identifying Places: The Role of Borders   191
   DOMINIC WATT AND CARMEN LLAMAS

10 'I Stole It from a Letter, off Your Tongue It Rolled.'
    The Performance of Dialect in Glasgow's Indie Music Scene   215
    MIRIAM KRAUSE AND JENNIFER SMITH

11 Where the Black Country Meets 'Black Barnsley': Dialect
    Variation and Identity in an Ex-Mining Community of Barnsley 234
    KATE BURLAND

12 'The Land Steward Wouldn't Have a Woman Farmer':
    The Interaction between Language, Life Trajectory and
    Gender in an Island Community   258
    EMMA MOORE AND PAUL CARTER

Part IV   Enregistering Places   281

13 Characterological Figures and Expressive Style in
    the Enregisterment of Linguistic Variety   283
    BARBARA JOHNSTONE

14 Enregisterment, Indexicality and the Social Meaning
    of Howay: Dialect and Identity in North-East England   301
    JULIA SNELL

15 Indexing Acadian Identities   325
    RUTH KING

16 'Turtlely Amazing': The Enregisterment of "Yorkshire" Dialect
    and the Possibility of GOAT Fronting as a Newly Enregistered
    Feature   348
    PAUL COOPER

Index   368

Figures

1.1 Map of Yorkshire *page* 16
1.2 Overall frequency of alveolar variants in York by age group 20
1.3 Frequency of alveolar variants in York by age and sex 20
1.4 Frequency of alveolar variants in York by job type and age group 21
1.5 Frequency of alveolar variants in York by grammatical category and age 22
1.6 Frequency of alveolar variants in nouns and verbs according to preceding phonological segment 22
1.7 Frequency of alveolar variants in nouns according to preceding phonological segment by age group 23
1.8 Number of tokens of come in each age group 25
1.9 Overall frequency of the variants of variable (come) in York by age and sex 26
1.10 Overall frequency of the variants of variable (come) in York by age and education level 26
1.11 Patterning of preterit *come* by grammatical person and age group 27
1.12 Overall frequency of DAR variants by age and sex 29
1.13 Distribution of DAR by women, by age and education 30
1.14 Distribution of DAR variants by preceding phonological segment and age 31
1.15 Distribution of DAR variants by grammatical category and age 31
2.1 Wilhelm Doegen (right) recording a speaker in a German Prisoner of War camp (from The Doegen Records Web Project, http://doegen.ie/about; © Humboldt-Universität, Berlin) 41
2.2 Vowel plots for stressed monophthongs /i ɪ e ɛ a ʌ ɔ o ʉ/ <i I e E a V O o u>, showing means of Lobanov-normalised F1 and F2 for (a) the three BL speakers recorded in 1916/17 (n = 794), and the speakers from (b) Glasgow (n = 289), (c) Maryhill (n = 239) and (d) Newarthil (n = 266) 44

2.3 Plots of observed means of Lobanov-normalised F1 and
     F2 measures for stressed monophthongs /i e a ɔ o ʉ/
     <i e a O o u>, showing the relative position for each speaker
     group for (a) BOOT(n = 1426), (b) COT (n = 1261), and
     (c) COAT (n = 913)   47
2.4 LME estimates of vowel durations in milliseconds for the
     BL speakers for vowels in (a) nuclear syllables and (b)
     non-nuclear syllables   52
2.5 Plots of mean F1 and F2 (Hz) measured at 25%, 50%, and
     75% of the vowel duration for /ai/ according to SVLR short
     contexts (PRICE) and long contexts (PRIZE), for (a) all three
     speakers, (b) Glasgow, (c) Maryhill, and (d) Newarthill (n = 37) 53
2.6 LME estimates in milliseconds for /i ʉ/ in SVLR contexts in
     five speaker groups, in nuclear syllables (top) and non-nuclear
     syllables (bottom)   55
2.7 Mean F2 Hz values for word-initial /l/ across all phonetic contexts
     in the BL sample (1890s/1910s) and the male speaker groups
     from the SoC sample (n = 845)   57
3.1 Newfoundland and the various communities mentioned
     in this chapter   67
3.2 Palatal postvocalic /l/ by age group   72
3.3 Slit fricative /t/ by age group   73
3.4 Palatal postvocalic /l/ by age and ethno-religious background 73
3.5 Palatal postvocalic /l/ by age and sex   74
3.6 Slit fricative /t/ by sex   76
3.7 Slit fricative /t/ by SES level   76
3.8 Post-tonic /t/ flapping by age group   77
3.9 Post-tonic /t/ flapping by sex   78
3.10 /Θ/-stopping in SSSJE by age and sex, informal style   81
3.11 H-deletion by age and sex (based on Newhook 2002: 84)   83
4.1 The frequency of uvular /r/ in the Holy Island corpus   95
4.2 The pronunciation of /r/ by the *Diary of an Island* speakers 95
5.1 Transcript from the original NFCSAC archive   113
5.2 Truncated transcript from the digitised NFCSAC   114
5.3 Occurrence of vernacular verbs for all informants (N = Frequency
     of occurrence per 1,000 words per year)   115
5.4 North East Map indicating the locations of DECTE interviews   116
5.5 Concordance list identifying discourse markers in NECTE   119
5.6 Relative marking in NECTE by birth decade   121
5.7 Rates of intensifier usage in DECTE (1960s–2000s)   122

7.1 Realisation of vowel in House(s) in SED data, from Kolb
(1966: 257). Reproduced with permission from Narr Franke
Attempto Verlag GmbH + Co. KG.   150
7.2 17-year-old female respondent's completed draw-a-map task   154
7.3 Survey locations   157
7.4 Perception of Scottish dialect areas. Permisson granted by
John Wiley and Sons.   160
7.5 Perception of English dialect areas. Permisson granted by
John Wiley and Sons.   161
7.6 Commuting flows along the Scottish-English border   163
8.1 The percentage of the population of three small Fenland towns
born outside of the United Kingdom (in pre-2004 member
states, in the new post-2004 accession states, and elsewhere)
from the 2001 and 2011 census   183
9.1 Map of Scottish-English border region, showing the four
fieldwork sites   197
9.2 VOT values (represented by probability density functions)
across the four AISEB fieldwork sites, split by speaker
age group   201
9.3 Example of a Relational Analogue Scale (RAS) completed
by an 18-year-old woman from Gretna   204
9.4 Relational Analogue Scale (RAS) data for the four fieldwork
sites, showing individual and mean group distances (%)
between the British and national (Scottish or English) labels,
split by speaker age group   206
10.1 Postvocalic /r/ by speaker across song and speech   226
11.1 Location of Barnsley relative to the north of England   236
11.2 Location of Royston in relation to the Metropolitan Boroughs
of Barnsley and Wakefield   237
11.3 Population totals for Royston 1801 to 1911 (UK Census data) 239
11.4 Location of The Black Country in relation to Barnsley
and Royston   240
11.5 A comment from an online article about the Royston accent   242
11.6 Degree of diphthongisation in ERB of FACE and GOAT
tokens for Royston speakers   245
11.7 Degree of diphthongisation in ERB of FACE and GOAT
tokens for Barnsley speakers   245
11.8 Degree of diphthongisation in ERB of FACE and GOAT
for Wakefield speakers   246
12.1 Location of the Isles of Scilly relative to the south-west
of England   259

12.2 Density plot showing raw formant data for TRAP and BATH,
     according to education-type (horizontal axis) and gender
     (vertical axis)   264
12.3 Variable importance plots predicting the relative importance
     of F1, F2 and duration in the TRAP/BATH split for each
     speaker group   265
13.1 The Yappin' Yinzers   288
13.2 The 'sayings' of the Yappin' Yinzers   291
14.1 Map of the north-east   303
14.2 Commodification of *howay*   305
14.3 Statue of Andy Capp   311
15.1 The areas of Acadian settlement in 1750   327
15.2 The four Atlantic Provinces and part of neighbouring
     Quebec today.   328
15.3 Acadieman (LeBlanc 2007), Rogers TV 2007 and
     Productions Mudworld 2007   338
15.4 Acadieman: Ses origines (LeBlanc 2007), Rogers TV 2009
     and Productions Mudworld 2009   338
16.1 Geographical location of Yorkshire showing historic country
     boundary   349
16.2 'Yorkshire It's Turtlely Amazing' t-shirt   360

Tables

1.1 The York English Corpus   *page* 17
1.2 Overall distribution of variants of the definite article   29
1.3 Summary of findings across three variables   33
2.1 Stratification of the Glaswegian *Sounds of the City* (SoC) corpus
    by age and decade of birth   40
2.2 Mean F2 in Hz for word-initial /l/ in the BL sample, ordered by
    following vowel height   58
4.1 Speakers from the Holy Island corpus   92
4.2 Speakers from *Diary of an Island*   93
5.1 Number of words and percentage occurrence of words in
    the Murphy corpus by gender (1942–1974)   111
5.2 DECTE's composition   118
7.1 Recognition of dialect areas by respondents' country,
    non-Scottish dialect areas shaded   159
7.2 'Out-of-area' commuting data, with recognition levels for
    Scottish and English dialect areas   164
10.1 Continuum of use for postvocalic /r/   222
10.2 Overall distribution of variants   224
10.3 Postvocalic /r/ by speaker   225
10.4 Postvocalic /r/ by speaker across speech and song   225
10.5 James's use of postvocalic /r/ across the different linguistic
    contexts   227
11.1 Stratification of age and gender across the Royston, Barnsley,
    and Wakefield samples   243
11.2 Vowel qualities of FACE and GOAT in the Royston, Barnsley
    and Wakefield dialects   247
11.3 Vowel qualities of FACE and GOAT in RP and
    Yorkshire dialects   247
11.4 Vowel qualities of FACE and GOAT in the Royston,
    Black Country, and Derbyshire dialects   248
11.5 A sampling summary of the younger Royston speakers   250

11.6 A sampling summary of the older Royston speakers   250
12.1 Participant sample used in the analysis   262
12.2 The roles and responsibilities of the male participants and
      the topics covered in their interviews   268
12.3 The roles and responsibilities of the female participants and
      the topics covered in their interviews   270
14.1 Corpus 1 (2005–7) – Distribution of *howay* across topic in
      national and regional newspapers   308
14.2 Corpus 2 (2012–13) – Distribution of *howay* across topic in
      national and regional newspapers   308
14.3 Occurrences of *howay* in tabloid and broadsheet newspapers   309
15.1 Linguistic features by source   342
16.1 Yorkshire dialect commentary texts   352
16.2 Corpus of Yorkshire Dialect Literature and Literary
      Dialect texts sampled for quantitative analysis   353
16.3 Common Yorkshire features provided by both Yorkshire
      and non-Yorkshire respondents   356
16.4 Enregistered Repertoire of Yorkshire dialect   356

Contributors

DAVID BRITAIN, University of Bern

KATE BURLAND, University of Leeds

PAUL CARTER, University of Sheffield

SANDRA CLARKE, Memorial University

PAUL COOPER, University of Liverpool

KAREN CORRIGAN, Newcastle University

FIONA DOUGLAS, University of Leeds

BARBARA JOHNSTONE, Carnegie Mellon
University

BRIAN JOSÉ, Indiana State University

RUTH KING, York University

MIRIAM KRAUSE, University of Glasgow

ELEANOR LAWSON, Queen Margaret University
Edinburgh

CARMEN LLAMAS, University of York

RACHEL MACDONALD, University of
Glasgow

WARREN MAGUIRE, University of Edinburgh

CHRIS MONTGOMERY, University of Sheffield

EMMA MOORE, University of Sheffield

TAMARA RATHCKE, University of Kent

JENNIFER SMITH, University of Glasgow

JULIA SNELL, University of Leeds

JANE STUART-SMITH, University of Glasgow

SALI TAGLIAMONTE, University of Toronto

DOMINIC WATT, University of York

Preface and Acknowledgements

This volume followed from a colloquium held at the University of Sheffield in April 2013. The event was in honour of our colleague and mentor, Professor Joan Beal, who retired from academia that same year. The regard in which Joan is held was evident from the enthusiasm for the one-day event; some contributors travelled thousands of miles to celebrate her career. This volume is not a *Festschrift*, but it was inspired by the debate that arose from the colloquium that celebrated Joan's work. It reflects her influence on the field and the regard in which she is held. Joan is cited in every single paper, across every section, with reference to every topic covered.

The structure of the volume also reflects Joan as an academic. Despite being an internationally renowned historical linguist and dialectologist, Joan is a down-to-earth, warm, generous, and supportive mentor. The volume contains contributions from established and influential scholars, but it also includes the work of up and coming research stars. Both editors benefitted enormously from Joan's mentoring and we hope that, by giving voice to some early career researchers, we are emulating the way in which Joan has always championed and supported junior colleagues.

Our first thank you of this volume, then, must be to Professor Joan Beal. Joan, we are grateful for your support, your wisdom, and – most importantly for this volume – your inspiration.

We would also like to thank the contributors to this volume. The volume was not the editors' only joint project: our daughter, Lara, was born as we were nearing completion of the final manuscript. The contributors have been exceedingly patient with two sleep-deprived editors making last minute demands on their time. Thanks to you all for your efficiency and responsiveness. Thanks too, to Helen Barton, at Cambridge University Press, as well as our Content Managers, Neil Ryan and Sarah Lambert, and our Project Manager, Yassar Arafat for their calm and helpful support throughout the project. We also want to thank Kate Lovatt for her careful copy editing and help preparing the final manuscript.

Finally, we would also like to thank several colleagues who helped with the reviewing process. Their knowledge and insight has helped to ensure the integrity of the volume (although, of course, any outstanding errors are the fault of the contributors and editors). Thanks go to: Lynn Clark, Sylvie Dubois, Susan Fitzmaurice, Lauren Hall-Lew, Paul Kerswill, Sam Kirk-ham, Robert Lawson, Claire Nance, Kate Pahl, Dennis Preston, Susanne Wagner, Katie Wales, and Gareth Walker. Thanks, also, to the anonymous reader who evaluated the entire volume and passed on a constructive and positive review. Finally, Emma is grateful to the AHRC for funding grant AH/I026243, which enabled her to focus her attention on the study of language and place.

Introduction

'Place' in Studies of Language Variation and Change

Emma Moore and Chris Montgomery

Place has always been central to studies of language variation and change. Since the eighteenth century, dialectologists have been mapping language features according to boundaries – both physical (rivers, hills) and institutional (districts and regions). In the twentieth century, variationist sociolinguists developed techniques to correlate language use with speakers' alignment to place (considering the effects of social practice and identity processes on their orientations). Complimenting this work, perceptual dialectologists examined the cognitive and ideological processes involved in language–place correlations and began to consider how speakers mentally process space, and evaluate it in metalinguistic commentary.

Given the role that place has played in studies of language variation and change, this volume seeks to consider how place is being defined and utilised by sociolinguists in the twenty-first century. Our aim is not to present one unified approach to the study of language and place, but to consider the various approaches that have been taken, and to evaluate their utility in answering specific questions about the nature of language variation and change. As one of us has argued in collaborative work elsewhere (Moore and Carter 2015: 3–4), whilst it is tempting to prioritise one kind of approach to variationist research over others, different types of research bring their own drawbacks and benefits. For instance, in what Eckert (2012) has referred to as the 'first-wave' of variationist research, the emphasis is on studying the broad demographic patterns of language variation and change across a geographically bounded community. Whilst variationists working in this tradition use the concept of the 'speech community' to define their sampling universe, Coupland (2010: 101) notes that 'place' and 'speech community' have been conflated in this type of research. So although Labov (1972) theorises that speech community is more accurately defined as being about shared interpretative norms, the way in which communities have been delimited for the purposes of this kind of variationist analysis has been (and continues to be) geographical in practice. Coupland (2010: 101) terms this 'community-as-demography'. In this type of work, then, place has been defined straightforwardly as 'location', as

1

determined by the placement of boundaries upon a map. To put it another way, the individual regions, cities and towns studied in traditional variationist research have been 'largely reduced to that of a canvas onto which dialectological findings could be painted' (Britain 2009: 144).

It is easy to dismiss this kind of research for its essentialism and, indeed, within this volume, there are several chapters which engage in precisely this kind of critique. However, it is important to remember that a degree of essentialism can be beneficial to our understanding of broad-scale patterns of variation and change. By abstracting from complex sociocultural contexts, it is possible to provide a general overview of how language change progresses across time and space. The long-term trajectories of language variation and change can only really be observed using such a wide-angled lens. Furthermore, whilst we may critique definitions of place that are limited to demography and geography, there is also ample evidence that the ways in which places are defined institutionally have consequences on language use and perceptions of language variation. This has been shown by Llamas (2007) in a study of Middlesbrough, England, where the language behaviour of different generations of speakers correlates with the town's official designation as being in the counties of Yorkshire, Teeside or Cleveland, or as its own unitary authority. As Beal (2010: 225) has observed, we should not underestimate the effects of 'the stroke of a bureaucrat's pen' on a speaker's sense of place and, consequently, their experience and use, of language variation.

The chapters in Part I of our volume exemplify the best of first wave variationist research, which considers how language is affected by its use within a particular locale, as designated by 'the bureaucrat's pen'. By using a wide-angled lens, these kinds of studies are able to consider which aspects of language variation are locally specific and which reflect the 'remarkable uniformity' (Labov 2011: 374) of some kinds of language change. For instance, in Chapter 1, Tagliamonte demonstrates how the trajectories of three distinct morphosyntactic variables in the city of York, England, are affected by their status as local or universal markers of vernacular English. In this example, the sociolinguistic setting of York is key to understanding how and why some variables pattern as they do. Similarly, in Chapter 2, Stuart-Smith et al. show how phonological variables vary and change in the city of Glasgow, Scotland, in ways that reflect social changes within the city itself. Although some of the changes they observe could be interpreted as a consequence of the type of sweeping sound changes observed elsewhere, they hypothesise that the changes are not just the consequence of dialect contact and supralocal innovations. Rather, these changes are driven by linguistic constraints, but supported by social changes within the city itself, including the increasing need to mark out different forms of social meaning amongst the city's inhabitants.

Clarke's contribution (Chapter 3) also considers how language marks social meaning within a region. Recent studies of dialect levelling have highlighted the loss of locally marked features, and this is explained as a consequence of increased mobility and the disruption of local networks (see, for instance, Kerswill 2003). However, Clarke demonstrates that whilst locally marked variants may be generally declining within a region, it does not necessarily follow that they are being lost altogether. Her work on Newfoundland English presents an instance where locally marked variants are decreasing over all, but not equally in all segments of the population. She explains this as a consequence of their shifting social associations over time, which result in there being different correlations with varied aspects of regional identity. Like the other chapters in Part I, Clarke's chapter emphasises the need to consider the social associations of features, not just their relative frequency, within a given locale.

First wave studies are particularly good at exposing the changing fortunes of language across time. Maguire's chapter (Chapter 4) is no exception. This study focuses on the small island community on Holy Island, off the north-east coast of England. The use of uvular /r/ (the 'Northumberland Burr') in this community does seem to represent a genuine case of dialect levelling. However, by carefully amassing a range of historical recordings, Maguire is able to interrogate the trajectory of this decline, exposing limitations in the methodological practices of earlier dialect surveys. He demonstrates that the loss of this feature is uneven across Holy Island speakers and hypothesises that the variability is, once again, linked to the local social meanings of the form and their distributions amongst islanders.

All of the studies in Part I offer longitudinal insights into processes of language variation and change – something that is not possible with more micro and nuanced analyses of individual locales. They present data from a range of communities (mainland cities and island populations) and, in doing so, demonstrate that processes of language variation and change operate in similar ways, irrespective of the precise logistics of the locations involved.

The studies in Part I also provide evidence of the benefits of working with archive data, which is enabling researchers to collate regional corpora in ways not previously available due to the time-depth involved. This is significantly changing our ability to study linguistic variation in specific locales by offering real-time data for studies of language change. Consideration of these methodological advances is addressed more specifically in Part II of the volume, which focuses on the methods and kinds of data available to researchers interested in the relationship between language and region. Corrigan's contribution (Chapter 5) explicitly demonstrates how we might apply, define, and organise regional corpora for sociolinguistic analyses. It provides practical advice on creating and using corpora (old and new) by discussing the nature of data which might comprise a regional corpus, and comparing small-scale personal collections with larger institutionally amassed resources. The chapter addresses the utility of data sources, and the relevant aspects that might require coding and tagging to be of optimal use to a linguist, as well as providing case studies of this data in use.

In addition to providing a resource for the sociolinguist, archive data also offers opportunities to engage communities in the linguistic heritage of their regions. This, in turn, can be used to obtain metalinguistic commentary on place and history – a benefit considered in depth by Douglas in Chapter 6. This piece evaluates the advantages of collaborating with museums to disseminate archive materials and generate new language resources and research opportunities. It explores how, in engaging individuals in a particular locale, we can obtain a more richly informed account of the specific experiences of these individuals and their relationship to the language forms found within their region.

Whilst Corrigan and Douglas focus on the practical issues surrounding the creation and use of archive materials, the remaining two chapters in Part II consider how our methodological approaches lead us to interpret sociolinguistic patterns in regional data in particular ways. In Chapter 7, Montgomery provides an overview of how linguistic data has been related to space over the history of traditional dialectology and language perception studies. Drawing upon interdisciplinary resources, it outlines advances in mapping techniques which have enabled us to think in more sophisticated ways about how speakers experience geographical space. Using evidence from a case study investigating perceptions of language in locations around the Scottish–English border, this chapter demonstrates the benefits of using Geographical Information Systems (GIS) and georeferenced data to interpret and understand patterns in linguistic data. More specifically, Montgomery's chapter shows how visualisation of data can enable sociolinguists to 'layer' social and linguistic information in ways which make the 'canvas' onto which we paint dialectological findings (described earlier) more three-dimensional.

The final chapter (Chapter 8) in Part II considers how our gaze as sociolinguists has been limited by our tendency to fetishise certain spatial domains over others. This, Britain argues, has had the consequence of us too narrowly defining the places in which certain processes of language variation and change can occur. More specifically, Britain's chapter considers how discourses around the 'urban' and the 'rural' have affected how we approach linguistic variation in particular locales. He argues that there has been a bias towards the 'urban' in variationist sociolinguistics, which has implied that regular and established processes of language variation and change do not occur in rural locations. Rather than assuming that different methodologies are required to study rural locations, Britain argues that it is necessary to consider the typologies of language change and to evaluate the conditions required for different kinds of changes to occur. This allows us to evaluate whether the same processes of language variation and change occur in a diverse range of locations.

Britain's chapter links back to an issue we raised at the beginning of this chapter – the tendency in certain kinds of language variation and change work to narrowly define 'community-as-demography'. Britain's work suggests that this model has been considered to work best in urban locations, due to their generally increased population sizes and, thus, their increased potential to generate sufficient data upon which to test statistical correlations between language use and demographic factors such as gender, ethnicity, and age. The ability to make statistical correlations between language use and demo-graphic categories is beneficial to our understanding of the spread of language change across space (as we have argued earlier, and as evidenced by the chapters in the first part of our volume), but it is also true that this approach limits our ability to understand the more local, interactionally relevant, and diverse social meanings that linguistic features can acquire. Therefore, where a sociolinguist's goal is not to define the long-term trajectory of a language change, but to understand how speakers use language to construct and create social meanings around place at a particular point in time (as in the second- and third-wave variationist work, described by Eckert 2012), it is necessary to develop a more nuanced appreciation of the social and cultural meanings of place. The chapters in the second half of our volume demonstrate the benefits of this type of research.

The techniques used in these chapters tend to build upon interdisciplinary methods and techniques because, as observed by Johnstone (2004) and Coupland (2010), outside sociolinguistics, community is rarely defined in the narrow terms utilised in first wave variationist research. For instance, contemporary work in human geography or anthropology tends to align definitions of place with social and moral values 'as well as with more material and pragmatic considerations of people occupying a defined space and taking part in conjoined activity' (Coupland 2010: 101). Therefore, to gain a more nuanced understanding of the relationship between language and place, sociolinguists need to consider place to be symbolic, socially con-structed, and culturally defined, as much as it is physically delimited. That is to say, to begin to develop more nuanced studies of regional dialect, we need to be more carefully attuned to the possibility that terminology referring to regions and localities is ideologically loaded and, as such, differentially understood and experienced by different people. This means we need to take care in applying regional labels to the communities we study. As Beal (2010: 266) has noted '"place" is not a given, to be taken for granted in our research designs; what appears to be a town or a city delimited by boundaries on a map may actually be several different places to different groups of speakers, whose allegiances to these "places" may be indexed by linguistic variables.' The notion of *indexicality* is key here. The term is utilised and contextualised in many of the chapters in this volume, so we do not consider it in depth here. But, put simply, it refers to an ideological association between a linguistic feature and a socially defined stance, alignment, persona or identity type (see Ochs 1992; Silverstein 2003; Eckert 2008; Moore and Podesva 2009). If linguistic variants can index alternative senses of place for different speakers, then we must be cautious in how we identify features with places. We are often encouraged to think about variants as exclusively 'belonging to' certain regions (see for instance, the British phenomena of the 'Bristol /l/' (Trudgill 1999: 76), or, even, the 'Northumberland Burr' (Maguire, this volume's Chapter 4)), but the reality is that the features may nominally index a place that is conceptually ambiguous to those living in it. The features may have no indexical value for some residents, despite those individuals having a strong orientation to the locale that the features are labelled as reifying (see, in particular, Johnstone and Kiesling 2008, on the variable social meanings associated with /aw/ by users and non-users in Pittsburgh). This suggests that serious consideration needs to be given to which speakers (and, indeed, what variables) are considered by linguists. Put another way, 'a study of regional dialect that is open to the possibility that vernacular conceptions of place and localness may help explain patterns of variation has to be attuned from the start to how the region in question is locally understood and talked about' (Johnstone 2004: 76).

The chapters in Part III of our volume explore how speakers use language to construct social meanings which are tied to locations where identities, and the linguistic features associated with them, are contested. In Chapter 9, Watt and Llamas consider how a state boundary (that between England and Scotland) affects the way that speakers orient towards and experience competing national identities, as evidenced by their language production and perceptions. They examine locations that are in close proximity to the border (and each other), and demonstrate that speakers make use of a linguistic feature (Voice Onset Time (VOT) of the stop consonants /p t k b d g/) in ways which reflect their regional affiliations (as evidenced by use of national identity labels in a self-identification exercise). They also find differences in identity perceptions on the basis of age, and predict that, over the course of time, these might lead to differences in pronunciation, even in a variable as subtle as VOT. Llamas and Watt's chapter shows that proximity to the border or to surrounding areas is not the only factor to determine language use; how speakers understand and orient towards the border is key to their language use. They find that younger and older speakers identify themselves differently, suggesting that shifts are occurring in the 'sense of place' assigned to border locations.

In Chapter 10, Krause and Smith also consider the notion of national identity, but focus solely on the Scottish side of the border considered by Llamas and Watt. They explore how the language used in popular music can be manipulated to demonstrate variable kinds of Scottish identity by Glaswegian artists. More specifically, they show how rhoticity has fluctuated as a marker of Scots, and how this fluidity has led to variability in its use in performative contexts. Whilst rhoticity may be traditionally perceived as a prototypical feature of Scots English, Krause and Smith show that this linguistic form encodes variable social meanings, dependent on speaker and context. So, whilst the form may continue to be emblematic of Scots, it can also be used to articulate different values and attitudes towards place and social identity in the evolving Scottish music industry.

Burland's work (Chapter 11) also focuses on the subtle nuances of meaning associated with particular linguistic features. Her research shows how different generations within the same ex-mining town, Royston in South Yorkshire, England, attribute different social explanations to the variants of FACE and GOAT vowels that are shown (via production analysis and comparison with nearby dialects) to uniquely identify town residents. Her work demonstrates that the older generation perceive these features as unique because of dialect contact caused by the in-migration of miners, whereas the younger generation, who grew up after mine closures, consider the features to be unique because of the town's semi-isolated location. This shows how the associations and definitions of a place can shift over time, even if the use of linguistic features remains stable across a community. Burland's work also reveals that, where features are strongly associated with place, they may resist the processes of dialect levelling found elsewhere: there is no evidence of attrition in the uniquely Royston dialect forms in her study, despite pan-regional levelling of FACE and GOAT vowels in Yorkshire more generally.

The last chapter (Chapter 12) in Part III also considers the potential effects of dialect contact on the social meanings allocated to linguistic features. Moore and Carter's work, which considers language variation in the Isles of Scilly (a group of islands off the south-west coast of England), also demonstrates that bounded communities do not necessarily have one homogeneous identity to which all speakers orient. They consider how variants of the TRAP and BATH vowels are used to index subtly different identities associated with certain ways of being 'Scillonian', and how life trajectory and gender interact with the styles adopted by certain groups on the island. Whereas other chapters in this part tend to focus on features which are considered to be distinctly local, Moore and Carter show that it is not necessarily the case that only vernacular features can index place. Some Scillonians use more standard-like pronunciations to index a particular kind of Scillonian identity, and this is explained as a consequence of the islands' unique sociocultural history and the ideology of Scillonian privilege, compared with mainland locales.

Taken together, the chapters in Part III demonstrate how context-dependent identity can be, and how language may do different kinds of identity work dependent upon the specific location in which it occurs. Questions still remain, however, about how the social meanings linking language to place are ideologically encoded amongst populations. These issues are considered in Part IV of our volume, which focuses on the enregisterment of language features. As discussed in these papers, Agha's (2003) term *enregisterment* is used to refer to the process by which linguistic features become associated and assigned to particular modes of speech (for our purposes, those associated with particular locales). In Chapter 13, Johnstone shows how particular, iconic representations of personae, or 'characterological figures' (in the form of speaking, plush toy dolls), are used to reflect and construct these associations in Pittsburgh, Pennsylvania (USA). Her chapter shows how place and social class can interact in the enregisterment of certain forms over others. This can result in a mismatch between what speakers actually do in their production of a particular form within a region, and what is perceived to be stereotypically meaningful linguistic practice within that region. In this way, Johnstone exposes the ideological nature of enregisterment, such that the 'concept' of a variety may be more pervasive than the reality of that variety in use.

Snell's analysis (Chapter 14) also considers the complicated relationship that language has to region and class. Her chapter explores how these two factors interact in the production and perception of the emblematic dialect term 'howay', found in Middlesbrough, in the north-east of England. Snell compares metalinguistic commentary about 'howay' with the distribution and use of the form in day-to-day interaction within the region. Like Johnstone's chapter, Snell's work highlights the difference between how a place-feature indexical link functions for those both outside and within the region in question. An analysis of *howay*'s commodification in novelty items like mugs and greetings cards, and its links to a particular social persona found in UK newspapers, suggests that the form has general social meanings linked to working-class culture. However, her micro-level discourse analysis demonstrates that, in local interactions, the form takes on much more subtle pragmatic functions. In this way, Snell suggests that the enregisterment of a form in one context does not prevent that form from acquiring and contributing to more nuanced meanings when it is used in spoken interaction within the region in which it is found.

Of course, the relationship between language and place is not restricted to English, and in Chapter 15 King focuses on Acadian French, the variety traditionally spoken in eastern Canada (in the four Atlantic Provinces and in parts of eastern Quebec). She considers how the trajectories of enregistered features may fluctuate over time, examining how features of the variety have persisted or changed, and considers what these changes suggest about the indexical and ideological value of the variety across time. Like other chapters in our volume, King's work suggests that different generations of speakers attach different social meanings to the same linguistic features, with younger speakers re-configuring social meanings in line with the changing social and demographic status of Acadian communities. Of particular importance here are the ways in which contemporary artistic and media representations of the variety facilitate these reconfigurations, as in Johnstone's chapter earlier in the volume.

King's chapter considers a range of texts in her longitudinal account of Acadian French, and the matter of which texts can be utilised to investigate the enregisterment of linguistic forms is also considered in our final chapter in Part IV. Cooper's chapter (Chapter 16), which focuses on the variety of English associated with the English region of Yorkshire, utilises dialect literature, dialect representation in written texts, and metalinguistic commentary in an online survey to explore how indexical links between language forms and the Yorkshire dialect emerge and change over time. This chapter shows how certain features are used to enregister 'Yorkshire' across different historical periods. Like Johnstone's chapter, Cooper's work examines the role of particular emblematic features used in products and advertising, and considers the commodification of language as an identifier of place (for a discussion of dialect commodification, see Beal 2009). Cooper's work also provides evidence of ongoing change in the enregisterment of Yorkshire English, by focusing on the feature of GOAT-fronting (a particularly fronted pronunciation of the vowels in the GOAT lexical set), and considering how this change corresponds with other variationist research into the changing distribution of this feature.

The chapters in Parts III and IV of our volume show that, whilst some associations may govern how we think about the correlation between language and place, there are often fluctuating and ambiguous social meanings associated with linguistic features and their relationship with particular locales. In order to uncover the range of potential meanings (if, indeed, that is our research goal), it is necessary to go beyond broad demographic correlations. As suggested earlier, the idea that we might want to focus on different kinds of speakers and their diffuse experiences of place is antithetical to many of the practices that have been typically employed in traditional variationist research. Whereas longitudinal surveys have tended to focus primarily on prototypical or 'central' inhabitants of a place (rejecting data from speakers considered to be 'lames' (Labov 1973) in relation to an abstract notion of the 'vernacular culture'), the studies in the second half of our volume demonstrate the value of exploring liminal or atypical spaces. This has important consequences, not just in terms of representativeness, but also for our ability to explain how and why language change occurs. As Eckert (2004: 109) has observed, '[d]ifferent people in a given community view the boundaries differently, use different parts of the community, and participate in the surroundings differently. These differences will result in different patterns of contact, which have implications for linguistic influence'. Thus, whilst large-scale survey studies, exemplified by the work in Part I, inform us of diachronic patterns of language change, the smaller-scale studies of Parts III and IV provide clues about the diversity within a locale, which may help to explain why and how changes may be activated. Both types of work are key to the full understanding of the linguistic histories of specific locales. We hope that, alongside the methodological insights offered in Part II, the full range of work in this volume demonstrates the utility of taking multiple approaches to the study of language and place and, in doing so, provides a useful and well-rounded account of the current state of the field.

REFERENCES

Agha, Asif 2003. 'The social life of cultural value'. *Language and Communication* 23: 231–73.

Beal, Joan C. 2009. 'Enregisterment, commodification and historical context: "Geordie" versus "Sheffieldish"'. *American Speech* 84: 138–56.

 2010. 'Shifting borders and shifting regional identities', in Llamas, Carmen and Dominic Watt (eds.) *Language and Identities*. Edinburgh: Edinburgh University Press. pp. 217–26.

Britain, David 2009. 'Language and space: the variationist approach', in Auer, Peter and Jürgen E. Schmidt (eds.) *Language and Space: An International Handbook of Linguistic Variation*. Berlin: Mouton de Gruyter. pp. 142–62.

Coupland, Nikolas 2010. 'The authentic speaker and the speech community', in Llamas, Carmen and Dominic Watt (eds.) *Language and Identities*. Edinburgh: Edinburgh University Press. pp. 99–112.

Eckert, Penelope 2004. 'Variation and a sense of place', in Fought, Carmen (ed.) *Sociolinguistic Variation: Critical Reflections*. Oxford: Oxford University Press. pp. 107–20.

 2008. 'Variation and the indexical field'. *Journal of Sociolinguistics* 12: 453–76.

 2012. 'Three waves of variation study: The emergence of meaning in the study of sociolinguistic variation'. *Annual Review of Anthropology* 41: 87–100.

Johnstone, Barbara 2004. 'Place, globalization and linguistic variation', in Fought, Carmen (ed.) *Sociolinguistic Variation: Critical Reflections*. Oxford: Oxford University Press. pp. 65–83.

Johnstone, Barbara and Scott Kiesling 2008. 'Indexicality and experience: exploring the meanings of /aw/-monophthongization in Pittsburgh'. *Journal of Sociolinguistics* 12: 5–33.

Kerswill, Paul 2003. 'Dialect levelling and geographical diffusion in British English', in Britain, David and Jenny Cheshire (eds.) *Social Dialectology: In Honour of Peter Trudgill*. Amsterdam: John Benjamins. pp. 223–43.

Labov, William 1972. *Sociolinguistic Patterns*. Philadelphia: University of Pennsylvania Press.

    1973. 'The linguistic consequences of being a lame'. *Language in Society* 2: 81–115.

    2011. *Principles of Linguistic Change, Cognitive and Cultural Factors*. West Sussex: John Wiley and Sons.

Llamas, Carmen 2007. '"A place between places": Language and identities in a border town'. *Language in Society* 36: 579–604.

Moore, Emma and Paul Carter 2015. 'Dialect contact and distinctiveness: The social meaning of language variation in an island community'. *Journal of Sociolinguistics* 19: 3–36.

Moore, Emma and Robert Podesva 2009. 'Style, indexicality, and the social meaning of tag questions'. *Language in Society* 38: 447–85.

Ochs, Elinor 1992. 'Indexing Gender', in Duranti, Alessandro and Charles Goodwin (eds.) *Language as Interactive Phenomenon*. Cambridge: Cambridge University Press. pp. 335–58.

Silverstein, Michael 2003. 'Indexical order and the dialectics of sociolinguistic life'. *Language and Communication* 23: 193–229.

Trudgill, Peter 1999. *The Dialects of England*. Oxford: Wiley-Blackwell.

Part I

Changing Places

1 Changing Places
Tracking Innovation and Obsolescence across Generations

Sali A. Tagliamonte

1. Introduction

Studies of language variation and change are able to capture the history, changing culture and linguistic ebb and flow of a community. In fact, the tracks of change across generations can expose innumerable 'stories' about a place. The particular place under scrutiny here is the city of York in the centre of Yorkshire, as shown in Figure 1.1.

One of the hottest contemporary issues in sociolinguistics is whether or not local distinctions are being swept away in the face of widespread urbanisation, even in the United Kingdom where dialects are prevalent: 'Those of us who work in the area of language variation and change in the United Kingdom are only too aware of the ubiquity ... sweeping away local distinctions' (Beal 2009: 138). Despite this, northern England is a place where local vernaculars are vigorous, which attests to a vibrant championing of northern features (Watt 2002: 58), particularly in Newcastle (Foulkes et al. 1999; Watt 2000, 2002; Allen et al. 2007), Berwick-upon-Tweed (Pichler 2009, 2013; Pichler and Levey 2011), Middlesbrough (Llamas 2000, 2007), and Yorkshire, as 'in the midst of widespread geographical changes among all the dialects of England and amid the "unstable nature of UK geography", Yorkshire ... maintain[s] its salience and perceptual prominence' (Beal 2010: 221).

In this chapter, I present highlights of three studies on York English with the goal of illustrating another northern perspective on how intimately tied dialect, variation, and linguistic change can be in the context of place. The linguistic features investigated are variable (ing), preterit *come* and definite article reduction (DAR). In each case, I focus on the patterns of use by age and sex and the most salient linguistic factors known to constrain the variation. More in-depth analyses of social and linguistic factors can be found in earlier

I gratefully acknowledge the support of the Economic and Social Science Research Council of the United Kingdom for research grants on British places from Northern Scotland to Devon between 1995 and 2003. I am also indebted to several reviewers whose comments were very helpful in the revision process.

Location of Yorkshire

Figure 1.1: Map of Yorkshire.[1]

[1] This work is based on data provided through EDINA UKBORDERS with the support of the ESRC and JISC and uses boundary material which is copyright of the Crown and the ED-LINE Consortium and the Post Office. Location information provided via Edina Digimap. ©Crown Copyright/database right 2013. An Ordnance Survey/EDINA supplied service.

publications (Tagliamonte 2001, 2004; Tagliamonte and Roeder 2009). First, I introduce the corpus from which the analyses come.

2.   The York English Corpus

The York English Corpus (Tagliamonte 1996–8, 1998) was collected in 1997, was designed to furnish a description of a dialect that had not (at that time) been subject to systematic analysis. As described by Beal earlier, Yorkshire as well as the city of York is a place with a unique dialect heritage.

Interviewer: Why do you think it is, that York is so different?

I think it is because people came from Tadcaster, Leeds, same as they come from Scarborough. There's South Yorkshire and there's East Yorkshire and they seem to come and they mixed.[2] (Lilly Jackson, age 64)

Individuals born and raised in York were audio recorded in casual conversations, summarised in Table 1.1. All of the people had been educated to the age of 14, many to 16. Of the speakers educated beyond the age of 16, their educational level ranges from technical college to university, although those in the latter category are a minority. Given these characteristics, the York English Corpus can be taken to represent the vernacular of the city in the late twentieth century.[3]

The city of York is unique amongst English cities for at least two reasons. According to historians, the industrial revolution somewhat passed it by (Armstrong 1974: 19). York did not undergo the massive economic upheaval – population growth, rebuilding, post-industrial social turmoil – found in other

Table 1.1: *The York English Corpus.*

	Male	Female	Total
15–30	12	13	25
35–69	19	24	42
70 and over	12	17	29
Total	43	54	97

---

[2] Tadcaster is a small town 10 miles southwest of York, not represented on the map. Leeds is a city to the southwest and Scarborough is a small town on the north-east shoreline (see map in Figure 1.1).

[3] In the York English Corpus, education level was categorised according to the current minimum education age, 16. Speakers who had been educated up to this point were categorised as 'less educated' while those who had had more education were categorised as 'more educated'.

English towns and cities, such as Manchester and Liverpool. Moreover, the predominant in-migrations in the 19th century were from local (north-eastern and Yorkshire) dialects (Armstrong 1974: 145). For these reasons, York is conservative with and a general Yorkshire character as described in (1).[4]

1. Because it's made up of everything around about. And you know when I've been down south or abroad and met other people there's only been one guy that – of course everybody knows we're from Yorkshire – good grief, you tried spelling like we speak, you'd have a continuous word, wouldn't you? And this guy, he was in Cornwall[5] of all places and we was only on about it the other night. We're sat in this pub and he sat down, was talking to him. Cornish chap. And he says 'Oh you're from Yorkshire.' Which is pretty obvious, you know. So yeah, I won't go on to another thing, but he went on and I could see him working in his mind. And he says, 'You're not from Barnsley, you're not from Leeds.' he said 'But you're not far off Leeds.' He says, 'You're from t'Dales side, and you're not from t'Moors side,' he says, 'All I can say is er-' and he got it, he says, 'You're from York.' And he's only one that I know who's actually got us bang on where we're from. (Robin Jones, age 50[6])

Among the innumerable linguistic phenomena that have been investigated in the York English Corpus, I focus here on: 1. a pervasive and well-known feature, variable (ing) (Tagliamonte 2004); 2. a ubiquitous morphological form, variable (come) (Tagliamonte 2001); and 3. a highly localised dialect phenomena, definite article reduction (DAR) (Tagliamonte and Roeder 2009). Variationist sociolinguistics (Tagliamonte 2012) uses the linguistic variable as a litmus test for what is going on in the speech community. If we can find out how these features are used and how they pattern across generations we may discover their social nature and history. Depending on how they pattern according to speaker age, we can find out whether or not they are 'fading into antiquity' (Tidholm 1979: 125) or stable. Another possibility is that there is ongoing recycling. As one form increases another rises and the cycle repeats itself, sometimes leading to an earlier form rising again, as with Cajun French in the southern United States (Dubois and Horvath 2000). Alternatively, certain dialect variants could be strengthening, as in recent developments in other northern communities, Newcastle (Watt 2002) and Middlesbrough (Llamas 2007), as well as in the United States (Schilling-Estes and Wolfram 1999). Which of these possibilities exists in the city of York?

---

[4] The 1851, 1901, and 1951 census reports list residents having a birthplace in Yorkshire at 83%, 82%, and 72% respectively. The 1851 census reports that 51% of the household heads had been born in Durham and Northumberland (Armstrong 1974: 94, 98).

[5] Cornwall is a county in the far south-east of England. Barnsley is a town in South Yorkshire, Leeds is a city in West Yorkshire. The Dales are in the north-west of Yorkshire and the Moors are in the north-east.

[6] The names of individuals are pseudonyms appropriate to the local population as inferred from the phone directory c. 1997.

There are many different approaches to the interface between language and community. While traditional dialectology focused on lexis and modern syntactical theory focuses on structure, sociolinguistics attends to forms and patterns. Furthermore, the use of quantitative techniques and accountable methodologies ensures that analysis targets systems of the language rather than intuition or anecdote. Broad-scale social correlates, such as age, sex, education, and job type, expose the sociolinguistic patterns of a place. Linguistic correlates, such as grammatical person, syntactic structure, and discourse patterning, reveal the underlying linguistic mechanisms. Together with synthetic linguistic knowledge and informed social interpretation, these offer key insights into the nature of the variation. A story of place emerges in the context of variation and change.

Building and corroborating other recent work on language, place, and identity in the United Kingdom (Beal 2004, 2010; Kerswill 1996; MacFarlane and Stuart-Smith 2012; Watt 2002), I argue that social and intergenerational patterns of language use expose the (recent) socio-history of the community and lead to a greater understanding of language and society.

3.   Variable (ing)

Variation in the pronunciation of the suffix -*ing* in English, as in (2), is a feature that has figured prominently in studies of linguistic variation and change (e.g. Fischer 1958; Labov 1966; Trudgill 1974). It is the well-known 'dropping of g's' axiom:

2.   a. We were *having* a good time out in what we were *doin'*. (Bradley Lowe, age 62)
            b. I'm just *startin'* at the *beginning* of this episode. (Samuel Clark, age 75)

Speakers alternate between an alveolar variant [n] and a velar variant [ŋ][7] and the quality of the vowel may also vary. This variation is reported to be ubiquitous across varieties of English around the world. It is one of the prototypical cases of stable linguistic variation, namely one that is not undergoing change. Furthermore, the variation appears to have relatively stable and consistent social and linguistic correlates wherever it has previously been studied. As enshrined in the famous figures from Labov (1972), but also corroborated by many studies (Houston 1985; Labov 1989; Trudgill 1974), women tend to use the standard (velar) variant, as do more highly educated speakers in formal contexts. From a system-internal perspective, the variation is also highly conditioned: words that are noun-like (such as nouns, pronouns,

---

[7] While a velar nasal followed by a voiced velar plosive is also possible in North and Midlands dialects, it was rare in the York English data.

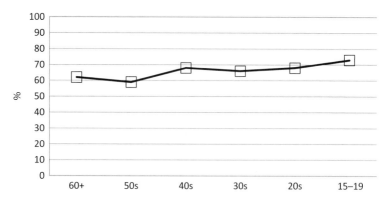

Figure 1.2: Overall frequency of alveolar variants in York by age group.

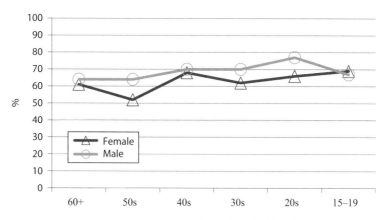

Figure 1.3: Frequency of alveolar variants in York by age and sex.

adjectives) favour the standard variant. Given these well-documented trends, let us probe the nature of this variable in York. Figure 1.2 displays the proportion of alveolar variants by age group.

Figure 1.2 shows that variable (ing) is frequent and stable just as it has been reported in many other localities. In this view York does not appear to be any different from any other place.

The alveolar variant is often found to have socio-symbolic value, for instance in Norwich (Trudgill 1974), and North America (Hazen 2008). Indeed, according to Labov's Principles of Linguistic Change, Principle 2 (Labov 2001: 166) dictates that men will have a higher rate of non-standard variants than women. Figure 1.3 tests for this possibility by contrasting the frequency of alveolar variants by age and sex in York.

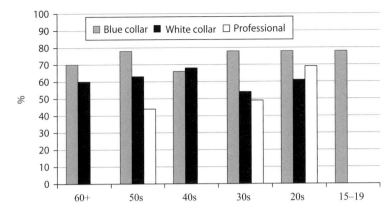

Figure 1.4: Frequency of alveolar variants in York by job type and age group.

Figure 1.3 shows that there is little or no male/female contrast in any age group. This is unusual for a variant that is known to be stigmatised. If the alveolar variant is indeed stigmatised, we would also expect other social contrasts (Chambers 2002). The York data was not collected with a controlled stylistic dimension; however, the data are substantial enough by age group to test for the effect of job type, which not only taps into linguistic marketplace behaviours, but also an educational element, as in Figure 1.4.

Figure 1.4 shows that blue-collar workers use more of the alveolar variant, whereas white-collar workers and professionals use it less. This is particularly evident in the two age groups (50–9 and 30–9) were there is sufficient representation across the three categories. Despite stability overall and no visible sex effect, this result shows that the use of the alveolar variant is tied to the social organisation of the community.

The most pervasive linguistic pattern underlying variable (ing) is the difference between nominal and verbal categories (Labov 1989). Figure 1.5 tests for this constraint in each age group.[8]

Figure 1.5 shows that verbs (shown by the grey columns) have a much higher frequency of the alveolar variant and this frequency is stable by speaker age. In contrast, the frequency of the same variant with nouns appears to be a change in progress. Among the older speakers nouns have half the rate of alveolar variants as the verbs (38 per cent vs. 73 per cent); however, among the youngest generation the frequency of alveolar variants

---

[8] In this comparison, I abstract away from the fine distinctions among gerunds, adjectives, prepositions, and different types of nouns.

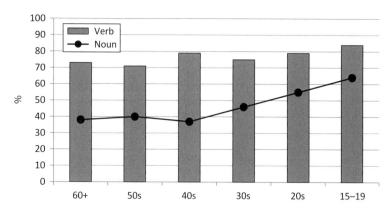

Figure 1.5: Frequency of alveolar variants in York by grammatical category and age.

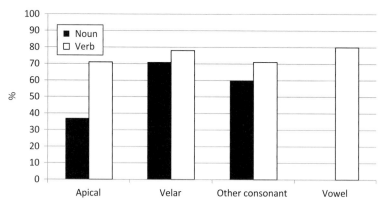

Figure 1.6: Frequency of alveolar variants in nouns and verbs according to preceding phonological segment.

for nouns has increased to 64 per cent. In other words, the gap between verbs and nouns narrows as individuals get younger.

This result demonstrates that the noun–verb contrast is paramount, corroborating earlier research. The explanation for this is the independent historical roots of these parts of the system (see e.g. Labov 1989; Tagliamonte 2004). However, the difference between the two categories in York exposes a nuance that has not been reported before, linguistic change in progress. To confirm a qualitative difference between nouns and verbs, Figure 1.6 tests for the effect of another linguistic factor that has been found to significantly constrain the use of the alveolar variant: preceding phonological segment.

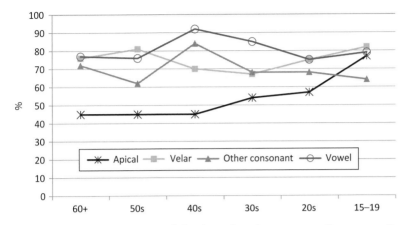

Figure 1.7: Frequency of alveolar variants in nouns according to preceding phonological segment by age group.

This perspective reveals that the two grammatical categories have quite distinct conditioning. The preceding phonological segment has no effect on verbs, yet nouns with a preceding apical segment are resistant to the alveolar variant. It now remains to determine whether this phonological effect can help to explain the shifting pattern of nouns. Figure 1.7 shows the frequency of alveolar variants in nouns according to preceding phonological segment by age group.

The results in Figure 1.7 demonstrate a rising frequency of the alveolar variant in the environment of apical consonants. This is the context that is changing.

To summarise, in York, the pronunciation of word final -*ing* is rooted in the functional differences of words that had a similar phonological suffix in earlier stages of English: one nominal, one verbal. This difference endures in the variable patterns of variable (ing) along with phonological conditioning on the nominal forms, which likely developed as the nominal forms coalesced into the same morpheme and variation between pronunciations of the ending developed. Overall, the variable is stable in York, yet underlying the steady frequency (Figure 1.2) is ongoing continuity of historical grammatical patterns. A place such as York, in the northern climes of England, retains this historical contrast over centuries to the point that the two variants are still partitioned by grammatical category. Perhaps this is because in York the variation is an entrenched class marker, as evidenced from the patterning by job type (Figure 1.4) but not the gendered and stylistic values reported in other places (Campbell-Kibler 2010; Hazen 2008; Labov 1972; Trudgill 1974). Instead, the alveolar variant prevails in York as the way to pronounce word final *-ing*, especially for verbal forms and even in words such as *participatin'*, *interestin'*. As Marsh (1866: 462) described, '[t]he ancient termination in *–end* survived in popular speech as the pronunciation [In] long after the form became extinct in literature, and the vulgar pronunciation *goin'*, *livin'* and the like, is a relic of that form.' However, the findings I have presented here demonstrate that the contrast between verbs and nouns is fading away in York. Nouns ending in *-ing* are increasingly being pronounced with the alveolar variant and levelling across phonological configurations (Figure 1.6), so that pronunciations such as *mornin'*, *evenin'* and *weddin'* are becoming the norm. It remains for future research to establish whether this shift is happening in other places.

4.   Variable (come)

One of the most familiar non-standard features of English is the use of *come* in past reference contexts, also known as 'preterit *come'*. Preterit *come* is reported in many places, Britain, North America, Australia, and Tristan da Cunha, for instance. Indeed, this use is so common that Chambers (1995: 240–1) classifies it as 'ubiquitous' and 'mainstream' and includes it among the group of features he calls Vernacular Roots. This feature is also found in York (Tagliamonte 2001). Notice that not only do individuals in the city use both *come* and *came*, but the use of the non-standard variant *come* occurs among both older and younger speakers (compare the speakers in (3) and (4)).

Male, age 91, educated to 14

3.   a. When I *came* home that day, it was a different world.
      b. Yeah, well when war *come* out they pulled me in.

Female, age 20, educated beyond 16

4.   a. She was like taking the piss out of them, but she *come* back.
      b. But she went last year and then left after a term and *came* back.

Traditionally, preterit *come* was explained as levelling of the verbal paradigm, such that all forms of the verb are trending towards a single form. At the same time the use of preterit *come* is said to be decreasing in the younger gener-ations, apparently due to standardisation and increasing literacy. In fact, researchers working in Yorkshire have suggested that the standard form *came*, 'will probably be used exclusively in a generation or so' (Tidholm 1979: 147).

Given these claims about the behaviour of variable ('come'), I consider its distribution and patterning in York. Figure 1.8 displays the use of the non-standard variant, *come,* by speaker age. The proportion of individuals in each age group that use this variant (if only once) are also indicated as well as the total number of instances of the variable (total tokens of both *come/came*).

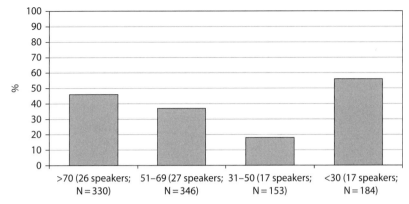

Figure 1.8: Number of tokens of come in each age group.[9]

Figure 1.8 exposes a distributional pattern that has been referred to as a u-shaped curve (Tagliamonte 2012: 46–55). Approximately half of the individuals in the youngest and oldest generations use preterit *come*. In contrast, very few of the 31–50-year-olds use it (only 18 per cent) and over a third of the 51–69- year-olds. This pattern has all the hallmarks of age-grading, although real time data are not available to confirm this interpretation. Further evidence can be gleaned from the patterning of forms by sex of the speaker. Figure 1.9 shows the frequency of use of preterit *come* by individual age and sex.[10]

The proportion of preterit *come* is now shown as a proportion of all tokens of preterit 'come'. This offers a different perspective on the variable. While Figure 1.8 showed us that 46 per cent of the >70-year-old speakers used *come*, Figure 1.9 reveals that the rate of the non-standard form in that age group is relatively rare, approximately 10 per cent. In so doing, it is now evident that the male population is maintaining it, albeit at low levels. In contrast, the female population (mostly) avoids this form.

To probe this further we can contrast the population by other social factors. Due to the fact that there are insufficient numbers across age groups for occupational categories, Figure 1.10 shows the contrast between individuals educated to age 16 versus those educated beyond the age of 16 by age group.

Figure 1.10 reveals that education impacts the use of preterit *come*. Most age groups show that less educated speakers have more preterit *come*. This is

---

[9] The data in Figure 1.8 are taken from a later study than the one reported above. The age groupings differ across studies for many different reasons, including nature of the distributions, number of tokens, and other practicalities.

[10] In some cases, paucity of token dictated merging the data from 20-year- olds and teenagers.

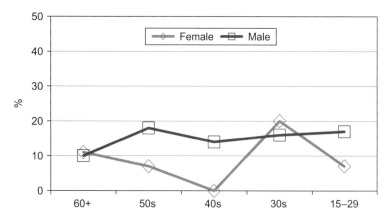

Figure 1.9: Overall frequency of the variants of variable (come) in York by age and sex.

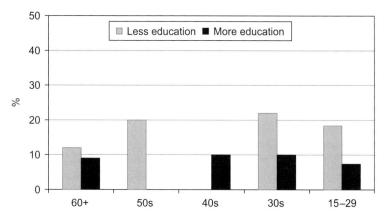

Figure 1.10: Overall frequency of the variants of variable (come) in York by age and education level.

consistent with the results from variable (ing) and exposes a typical profile whereby less standard features are used more by blue-collar and less educated members of a community. A question that arises is: if the use of preterit *come* is maintained among a stable population of individuals, is it possible that it retains an imprint of its ancestry?

Variable morphological marking on verbs can be conditioned by linguistic context. Sometimes this is the result of retention of earlier patterns, for

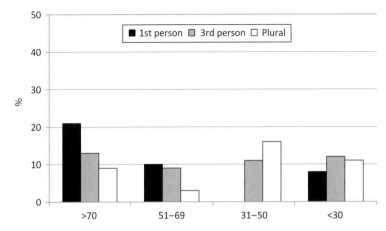

Figure 1.11: Patterning of preterit *come* by grammatical person and age group.

example the Northern Subject Rule (Klemola 2000; McCafferty 2003). Sometimes it is the result of the disambiguating effects of temporal indicators, a type of local disambiguation (Mufwene 1986). Statistical modelling of these effects overall and in each age group showed that none were present, save for one internal factor among the oldest generation (Tagliamonte 2001).

Preterit *come* occurs with relatively high frequency with third person and less frequently with other persons, as in (5).

5.   a. Well I *come* home with a few cuts and bruises but then I used to think nowt to them. (Bobby Hamilton, age 92)
         b. She only *come* when she thought she wanted to *come*. (Gladys Walton, age 87)
         c. When lads *come* back out of war, they wouldn't work with him (Red Fielding, age 81)

Figure 1.11 reveals that the constraint ranking 1st > 3rd > plural is distinct in the oldest cohort (> 70). However, this pattern changes by speaker age. A similar contrast is maintained among the 51–69-year-olds although it changes to a contrast between singular and plural. Among the under 50-year-olds this degenerates further until among the <30-year-old generation the constraint has levelled.

The favouring effect of first- and third-person singular for preterit *come* may have historical antecedents. In Old Norse the preterit singular for the verb 'come', was the form *kom* (Brunner 1963; Tidholm 1979). The city of York was once a Scandanavian settlement (Yorvik). The fact that preterit *come* is used more in singular subjects amongst the oldest generations suggests that it is a retention.

In summary, the use of preterit *come* is indelibly linked to the social hierarchy in York. The female population exhibits a progressive decline in the use of preterit *come* suggesting obsolescence. However, amongst males, it persists. This suggests that although it has lost its linguistic patterning in the younger generations, it is retained as a socio-symbolic feature. This type of contrast between males and females is a well-attested age–gender pattern. Younger males tend to have a stronger sense of place and identify with traditional values (Labov 1964; Trudgill 1972). In so doing, they employ conservative features, such as preterit *come*. However, the use of preterit *come* in York, unlike other places where it has been studied, is also rooted to the distant past, demonstrating longitudinal continuity of age-old patterns.

5.   Variable (DAR)

The dialects of northern England have an incredible array of different variants of the definite article that are not found anywhere else. In York, glottalised variants such as [ʔ] and alveolar variants such as [t], can be heard among the standard pronunciations of 'the', as in (6a–c).

6.   a. t'only thing – only way you'd fin' [ʔ] well would be to follow [ʔ] pipe
           from where [ʔ] pump was. (male born 1906, age 81 in 1997)
        b. We both went t [ʔ] chip shop. Next thing I know, these fellas are picking
           me up off the floor (laughs). (female: born 1959, age 38 in 1997)
        c. I remember handin' t' ten pound note over and that was it . . . Gone onto
           [ʔ] concrete floor. (female born 1959, age 38 in 1997)

Not surprisingly this phenomenon has been the subject of long-standing fascination, with much early dialectological research focusing on it (Hedevind 1967; Jones, W. E. 1952; Morris 1911; Nicholson 1889; Tidholm 1979). It has been submitted to phonological analyses (Barry 1972; Melchers 1972; Petyt 1977; Shorrocks 1991, 1992); in-depth phonetic, as well as pragmatic, analyses have been conducted (Jones, M. J. 2002; Rupp and Page-Verhoeff 2005).

One of the most challenging aspects of studying DAR is that the possible phonetic variants of the reduced definite article fall along a continuum, making them difficult to categorise (Barry 1972; Jones, M. J. 1999, 2002, 2005; Shorrocks 1991, 1992). In this analysis, every token of a definite noun that could take the definite article in Standard English was included. This provided at least 100 nouns per individual covering all possible phonological and grammatical environments with a grand total of nearly 10,000 tokens. Each context was also coded for a series of additional linguistic factors that were culled from the existing literature as being possible conditioning effects on the realisation of forms. (For detail on variants, coding strategies and

Table 1.2: *Overall distribution of variants of the definite article.*

	%	N
Full form	80.9	7438
Glottalised	13.2	1215
[Ø]	3.4	316
[w, v]	1.4	126
[d]	0.5	47
[t]	0.3	24
[ə]	0.3	28
TOTAL N	-	9195

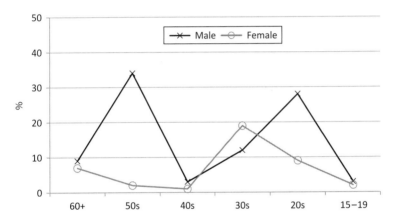

Figure 1.12: Overall frequency of DAR variants by age and sex.

other information see Tagliamonte and Roeder 2009). Table 1.2 shows the overall distribution of variants.

The full forms of the definite article represent the majority form in York; however, 13 per cent of the time the unique glottalised pronunciations occur (shaded), encompassing the variety of pronunciations called DAR. Figure 1.12 shows the distribution of these forms by age and sex.

Figure 1.12 reveals that there is a strong male/female contrast, such that males use DAR variants in certain age groups: 50s, 30s and 20s. The fact that males have a much higher frequency of the non-standard form follows in line with Principle 2 (Labov 2001). As with variable (come) the pattern is such that the middle-age generation of men (40s) is conservative, suggesting age-grading. In contrast, the women in the community are for the most part

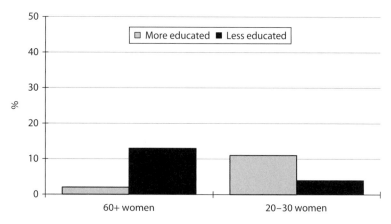

Figure 1.13: Distribution of DAR by women, by age and education.

standard, also in line with the results for preterit *come*. Notice, however, the upswing in usage among women aged 20–30, exceeding the rate of women aged 60+. Note too that in this age group both males and females have a heightened rate of DAR. This is a curiosity. Further scrutiny of the women from the older and younger age groups according to education level, is shown in Figure 1.13.

The comparison of older and younger women by education in Figure 1.13 shows an unusual result. The educated young women are using DAR more than the less educated ones. This result is unlike Labov's (1990, 2001) well-known Principle 2 of linguistic change, where women are predicted to favour standard forms. However, younger speakers may recycle non-standard traditional features. In research on Cajun English, Dubois and Horvath (2000) found that older (local) Cajun French variants were increasing among the youngest male speakers. They argued that this development was the result of recycling and reallocation of the sociolinguistic value of Cajun forms to prestige markers of Cajun identity, a male-oriented development. The patterns for DAR in York show the same trend: the young male speakers have recycled an older feature of the language. However, the nuance of note here is that in York the females are also implicated in this process.

At least two linguistic constraints have been found to underlie the use of DAR (Tagliamonte and Roeder 2009). The most important of these is the contrast between sibilants and other consonants, and prepositional and other contexts. Figures 1.14 and 1.15 display how these constraints pattern according to speaker age.

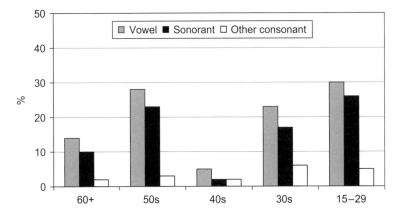

Figure 1.14: Distribution of DAR variants by preceding phonological segment and age.

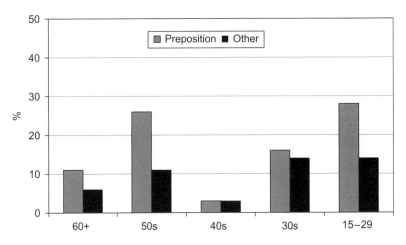

Figure 1.15: Distribution of DAR variants by grammatical category and age.

Figure 1.14 confirms that the DAR variants are conditioned by the preceding phonological context in every age group. It is even visible among the 40-year-olds who rarely use the DAR forms.

Figure 1.15 confirms that the DAR variants are also conditioned by the grammatical category in every age group, with the exception of 40 year olds who barely use them. DAR variants are much more likely after prepositions, as in (7).

7.   a. Which is early enough to still go out to [?] pub and stuff. (Sandra George, age 22)
        b. They were only there to go during [?] day. (Samuel Watkins, age 37)

The results in Figures 1.14 and 1.15 support the idea that variation in the forms of the definite article is the product of linguistic conditioning that has been reported throughout the history of the English language (Tagliamonte and Roeder 2009). This suggests that, while the use of DAR in York is not robust, it is systemically patterned. Moreover, although DAR is used more by young men, young women are also participating in its resurgence showing evidence of recycling.

6.   Summary

I have now provided an overview of three linguistic variables that are part of the contemporary vernacular of York. The variables are drawn from different levels of grammar and have contrasting pedigree in terms of local/universal status. Each one elucidates a story of vernacular usage that is visible in apparent time (generation) and social categories (sex, job type, education), as summarised in Table 1.3.

Amongst the most intriguing findings is the extent to which historical patterns remain visible in the contemporary variation. While in some cases patterns are visibly waning (e.g. preterit *come*), it is remarkable that features that are relatively rare maintain linguistic constraints, phonological and grammatical, in some cases (for instance, DAR) across the population. It is important to emphasise that there is no universal explanation of male conservatism/female alignment with prestige norms in these findings. Each phenomenon has its own story. While preterit *come* exhibits the classic pattern: retention by males and eschewed by females, variable (ing) is not distinguished by gender and there is a notable change in progress occurring. For DAR, there is a visible upswing among young adults, both male and female. The latter suggests identification with local norms. It is also important to emphasise that, even in the face of rampant standardisation and levelling in the United Kingdom, the conservative variants in these three variables endure in York and can be heard on the streets and snickleways in casual conversation.

The comments from the York interviews support the development of positive affect related to place, as in (8).

8.   a. I love York. I could wander 'round York forever. I many a time go and sit outside the Minster and I look up at it and I think, 'nobody could build that today!' (Elsie Burritt, age 82)

Table 1.3: *Summary of findings across three variables.*

Variable	Apparent Time	Sex	Job/ Edu	Linguistic Patterns
(ing)	Overall, stable nouns, change in progress	No difference	√	Verb > noun
(come)	Stable	Male	√	1st p. > 3rd > plural
DAR	Recycling	Male > female	√	Sonorants > other Prepositions > other

b. *Interviewer: Do you like living here?* Yeah. I love York. I think it's brilliant, really like it. (Nancy Heath, age 20)

c. Peter and I were both born in York and my parents were born in York ... If anybody asks me where I come from, I come from York. (May Simpson, age 63)

Together with the results from the three variables, such comments converge in suggesting a particular allegiance to the city. I propose that the young men (and in some cases the women) are maintaining certain non-standard variants because they serve to encode the identities they wish to portray, consistent with concepts of identity (Le Page and Tabouret-Keller 1985), linguistic marketplace, and capital (Bourdieu 1999). These ideas are emblematically enshrined in this dialect of northern England and corroborate research on other dialects in the vicinity (Beal 2004; Llamas 2000; Watt 2002; Watt et al. 2009), as well as in Europe and North America. For the young people in York, standard norms are not sufficiently strong to trump the desire to align with the local scenario. As Poplack and Dion (2012: 581–2) have suggested 'where prescription is diametrically opposed to community patterns ... the cost of aligning with the standard would be too great for the speaker ... who must confirm to the norms of her speech community'.

More generally, these findings demonstrate the key contribution that studies of language variation and change offer for understanding the history, culture and identity of communities. Linguistic features – either ubiquitous, such as variable (ing), old-fashioned, such as variable (come), or local, such as DAR – can expose a story of place and time in the underlying patterns of variation. The interpretation of linguistic usage must be situated in geographic context and in terms of speakers' positions in a particular generation, and their gender. Within this framework, the concept of place becomes not only useful but explanatory. Place and time encode the grammar of centuries as well as the alignment and orientation of speakers to their place. In the sage words of Beal (2004: 45): 'The future of dialects is that they will evolve: some features will disappear, others will be fossilised or lexicalised others will be levelled, but there will still be a distinctive voice.'

REFERENCES

Allen, William, Joan C. Beal, Karen Corrigan, Warren Maguire and Hermann Moisl 2007. *Creating and Digitizing Language Corpora: Diachronic Databases.* Basingstoke: Palgrave Macmillan.

Armstrong, Alan 1974. *Stability and Change in an English County town: A Social Study of York, 1801–51.* Cambridge: Cambridge University Press.

Barry, M. 1972. 'The morphemic distribution of the definite article in contemporary regional English', Wakelin, Martyn (ed.) 1972. *Patterns of the Folk Speech in the British Isles.* London: Athlone Press. pp. 164–81.

Beal, Joan C. 2004. 'Geordie nation: Language and identity in the north-east of England'. *Lore and Language* 17: 33–48.

2009. 'Three hundred years of prescriptivism (and counting)', in Tieken Boon van Ostade, Ingrid and William Van der Wurff (eds.) *Current Issues in Late Modern English.* Bern: Peter Lang. pp. 35–56.

2010. 'Shifting borders and shifting regional identities', in Llamas, Carmen and Dominic Watt (eds.) *Language and Identities.* Edinburgh: Edinburgh University Press. pp. 217–26.

Bourdieu, Pierre 1999. *Language and Symbolic Power.* Cambridge: Polity Press.

Brunner, Karl 1963. *An Outline of Middle English Grammar.* Oxford: Blackwell Publishers.

Campbell-Kibler, Kathryn 2010. 'The sociolinguistic variant as a carrier of social meaning'. *Language Variation and Change* 22: 423–41.

Chambers, J. K. 1995. *Sociolinguistic Theory: Linguistic Variation and Its Social Significance.* Oxford: Blackwell Publishers.

2002. 'Patterns of variation including change', in Chambers, J. K., Peter Trudgill, and Natalie Schilling-Estes (eds.) 2002. *The Handbook of Language Variation and Change.* Malden and Oxford: Blackwell Publishers. pp. 349–72.

Dubois, Sylvie and Barbara Horvath 2000. 'When the music changes, you change too: Gender and language change in Cajun English'. *Language Variation and Change* 11(2): 287–313.

Fischer, John L. 1958. 'Social influences on the choice of a linguistic variant'. *Word* 14: 47–56.

Foulkes, Paul, Gerard Docherty, and Dominic Watt 1999. 'Tracking the emergence of structured variation: Realisations of (t) by Newcastle children'. *Leeds Working Papers in Linguistics*: 1–18.

Hazen, Kirk 2008. '(ING): a Vernacular baseline for English in Appalachia'. *American Speech* 83: 116–40.

Hedevind, Bertil 1967. *The Dialect of Dentdale in the West Riding of Yorkshire.* Stockholm: Almquist and Wiksell.

Houston, Anne 1985. 'Continuity and change in English morphology: The variable (ing)'. Unpublished PhD thesis, University of Pennsylvania.

Jones, Mark J. 1999. 'The phonology of definite article reduction', in Upton, Clive and Katie Wales (eds.) *Dialectal Variation in English. Proceedings of the Harold Orton Centenary Conference 1998*. Leeds: Leeds Studies in English. pp. 103–21.

2002. 'The origin of definite article reduction in northern English dialects: Evidence from dialect allomorphy'. *English Language and Linguistics* 6: 325–45.

2005. *The Phonetics and Phonology of Definite Article Reduction in Northern English Dialects*. PhD dissertation, University of Cambridge.

Jones, W. E. 1952. 'The definite article in living Yorkshire dialect'. *Leeds Studies in English*: 81–91.

Kerswill, Paul 1996. 'Children, adolescents, and language change'. *Language Variation and Change* 8: 177–202.

Klemola, Juhani 2000. 'The origins of the northern subject rule: A case of early contact?', in Tristam, Hildegard L.C. (ed.) *The Celtic Englishes II*. Heidelberg: Carl Winter. pp. 329–46.

Labov, William 1964. 'Phonological correlates of social stratification'. *American Anthropologist* 66: 164–76.

1966. *The Social Stratification of English in New York City*. Washington, D.C.: Center for Applied Linguistics.

1972. *Sociolinguistic Patterns*. Philadelphia: University of Pennsylvania Press.

1989. 'The child as linguistic historian'. *Language Variation and Change* 1: 85–97.

1990. 'The intersection of sex and social class in the course of linguistic change'. *Language Variation and Change* 2: 205–54.

2001. *Principles of Linguistic Change: Volume 2: Social Factors*. Malden, MA: Blackwell Publishers.

Le Page, Robert B. and Andrée Tabouret-Keller 1985. *Acts of Identity: Creole-Based Approaches to Language and Ethnicity*. Cambridge, MA: Cambridge University Press.

Llamas, Carmen 2000. 'Middlesbrough English: Convergent and divergent trends in a part of Britain with no identity', *Newcastle and Durham Working Papers in Linguistics* 8: 123–48.

2007. '"A place between places": Language and identities in a border town'. *Language in Society* 36: 579–604.

MacFarlane, Anne and Jane Stuart-Smith 2012. '"One of them sounds sort of Glasgow Uni-ish": Social judgements and fine phonetic variation in Glasgow'. *Lingua* 122: 764–78.

Marsh, George P. 1866. *Lectures on the English Language*. London: Murray.

McCafferty, Kevin 2003. 'The northern subject rule in Ulster: How Scots, how English?'. *Language Variation and Change* 15: 105–39.

Melchers, Gunnel 1972. 'Studies in Yorkshire Dialects'. Unpublished PhD thesis, Stockholm University.

Morris, Marmaduke C. F. 1911. *Yorkshire Folk-Talk: With Characteristics of Those Who Speak It in the North and East Ridings*. London: Brown.

Mufwene, Salikoko S. 1986. 'Number delimitation in Gullah'. *American Speech* 61: 33–60.

Nicholson, John 1889. *Folk Speech of East Yorkshire*. Driffield: London.

Petyt, Malcolm K. 1977. '"Dialect" and "accent" in the industrial West Riding: A study of the changing speech of an urban area'. Unpublished PhD thesis, University of Reading.

Pichler, Heike 2009. 'The functional and social reality of discourse variants in a northern English dialect: I don't know and I don't think compared'. *Intercultural Pragmatics* 6: 561–96.

2013. *The Structure of Discourse-Pragmatic Variation*. Amsterdam: John Benjamins.

Pichler, Heike and Stephen Levey 2011. 'In search of grammaticalization in synchronic dialect data: General extenders in north-east England'. *English Language and Linguistics* 15: 441–71.

Poplack, Shana and Nathalie Dion 2012. 'Myths and facts about loanword development'. *Language Variation and Change* 24: 279–315.

Rupp, Laura and Hanne Page-Verhoeff 2005. 'Pragmatic and historical aspects of definite article reduction in northern English dialects'. *English World-Wide* 26: 325–46.

Schilling-Estes, Natalie and Walt Wolfram 1999. 'Alternative models of dialect death: Dissipation vs. Contraction'. *Language* 75: 486–521.

Shorrocks, Graham 1991. 'The phonetic form of the definite article and some other linguistic features in parts of Lancashire and Greater Manchester County: A reply to John Kerins'. *Lore & Language* 10: 3–9.

1992. 'The definite article in the dialect of Farnworth and district, Greater Manchester County, Formerly Lancashire'. *Orbis* 34: 173–86.

Tagliamonte, Sali A. 1996–8. *Roots of Identity: Variation and Grammaticization in Contemporary British English*. Economic and Social Sciences Research Council (ESRC) of Great Britain.

1998. 'Was/were variation across the generations: View from the city of York'. *Language Variation and Change* 10: 153–91.

2001. 'Come/came variation in English dialects'. *American Speech* 76: 42–61.

2004. 'Someth[in]'s go[ing] on!: Variable ing at ground zero', in Gunnarsson, B. L., L. Bergstrom, G. Eklund, S. Fidell, L. H. Hansen, A. Karstadt, B. Nordberg, E. Sundergren, and M. Thelander (eds.) *'Language Variation in Europe'. Paper presented at the Second International Conference on Language Variation in Europe, ICLAVE 2*. Uppsala: Uppsala University. pp. 390–403.

2012. *Variationist Sociolinguistics: Change, Observation, Interpretation*. Malden and Oxford: Wiley-Blackwell.

Tagliamonte, Sali A. and Rebecca V. Roeder 2009. 'Variation in the English definite article: Socio-historical linguistics in t'speech community'. *Journal of Sociolinguistics* 13: 435–71.

Tidholm, Hans 1979. *The Dialect of Egton in North Yorkshire*. Gothenburg: Bokmaskine.

Trudgill, Peter 1972. 'Sex, covert prestige, and linguistic change in urban British English'. *Language in Society* 1: 179–95.

1974. *The Social Differentiation of English in Norwich*. Cambridge: University of Cambridge Press.

Watt, Dominic 2000. "Phonetic Parallels between the close-mid vowels of Tyneside English: Are they internally or externally motivated?". *Language Variation and Change* 12(1): 69–101.

    2002. "'I don't speak with a Geordie accent, I speak, like, the Northern accent": Contact-induced levelling in the Tynesdie vowel system'. *Journal of Sociolinguistics* 6: 22–63.

Watt, Dominic, Carmen Llamas, and Daniel E. Johnson 2009. 'Linguistic accommodation and the salience of national identity markers in a border town'. *Journal of Language and Social Psychology* 28: 381–407.

2   Changing Sounds in a Changing City

An Acoustic Phonetic Investigation of Real-Time Change over a Century of Glaswegian

*Jane Stuart-Smith, Brian José, Tamara Rathcke,
Rachel Macdonald and Eleanor Lawson*

1.   Introduction

Language change in progress has been shown to be as intricately linked with particular peoples and places, as it is with the linguistic systems within which they exist (Milroy 1992; Labov 1994, 2001; Eckert 2000, 2012; Beal 2006; 2010). This is clear from numerous apparent-time studies of change in progress; real-time views of language change are less common (Labov 1994; Sankoff 2006). For example, if we consider sound change in Scottish English, previous apparent-time studies of Glaswegian vernacular have shown increases in TH-fronting and L-vocalisation alongside reduction in local Scottish variants such as /x/ and /ʍ/ (Stuart-Smith *et al.* 2007). At first sight, these changes seem to suggest the traditional connections between a dialect (urban Scots) and its place (Glasgow) are being weakened in favour of supralocal norms (Kerswill 2003). Closer inspection of the relationships between linguistic variation and linguistic constraints on the one hand, and recent urban regeneration, social practices, and local language ideologies on the other, suggests that these sound changes are tightly bound to the dialect and the city itself (Stuart-Smith *et al.* 2007; Stuart-Smith *et al.* 2013; Beal 2006, 2010). But questions remain, both with respect to this dialect and, more generally, as to whether place is always so closely connected with sound changes, for example, those characterised by continuous acoustic phonetic variation, like vowel quality, and whether such an impression would be gained from real-time views of change within a particular place.

Jane Stuart-Smith is very grateful to the Leverhulme Trust for funding the *Sounds of the City* project (*The role of fine phonetic variation in sound change*; RPG-142). This paper is dedicated to Joan Beal, who probably knows far more about all of this than we do, and whose erudite and cheerful support has always been an inspiration for our work on phonological variation and change, and in particular, the *Sounds of the City* project. She is also extremely grateful to the editors of this volume for their outstanding and unusual patience with this contribution.

This paper contributes new findings which help to answer these theoretical questions about real-time sound change and place. Our study exploits the possibilities offered by a longer-term perspective on real-time change by combining archive recordings from the First World War with those from a real- and apparent-time corpus from the 1970s. We consider three aspects of urban Scots: vowel quality, duration, and the realisation of word-initial /l/, using acoustic phonetic measures. The real-time comparisons reveal change in progress in all three features. The direction of these changes is intriguing, since despite the substantial geographical and social changes which have taken place across the United Kingdom (especially during the second half of the twentieth century) and their impact in terms of contact-induced changes on urban British accents (Foulkes and Docherty 1999), it appears that linguistic and social factors relating to the dialect and its location have played a stronger role.

2.   Materials and Resources

2.1   The Sounds of the City (SoC) Corpus (1970–2010)

The *Sounds of the City* (*SoC*) corpus (http://soundsofthecity.arts.gla.ac.uk/; accessed 25 August 2015) is a controlled-access, force-aligned, electronic corpus of audio recordings and orthographic transcripts, stored in a *LaBB-CAT* database (Fromont and Hay 2012). The recordings are of spontaneous speech, and include oral history and sociolinguistic interviews, conversations between friends, and extracts of broadcast speech. The informants are all working-class speakers of Glasgow dialect, as determined by factors such as socio-economic background, education, and occupation. The corpus currently holds recordings of different lengths from 142 male and female speakers (around 730,000 words), and is structured by decade of recording and generation of the speaker (see Table 2.1). The real- and apparent-time structure of the corpus allows investigation of stability and change effectively across the entire twentieth century.

2.2   The Berliner Lautarchiv (BL) Sample (1916/17)

The *Berliner Lautarchiv* (*BL*) recordings,[1] now held in digital form at the British Library, were made by language teacher and sound pioneer Wilhelm Doegen and Professor of English Alois Brandl, during visits to Prisoner of War camps in various parts of Germany between 1916 and 1917, to

---

[1] For more information, see Stuart-Smith and Lawson (in press).

Table 2.1: *Stratification of the Glaswegian* Sounds of the City *(SoC) corpus by age and decade of birth (decade of recording is given in square brackets and shaded columns indicate the period of Glasgow's urban regeneration).*

Decade of Birth Speaker Age	1890s	1900s	1910s	1920s	1930s	1940s	1950s	1960s	1970s	1980s	1990s
Older 67–90	[70s]	[80s]	[90s]	[00s]							
Middle 40–55				[70s]	[80s]	[90s]	[00s]				
Young 10–15								[70s]	[80s]	[90s]	[00s]

document soldiers' languages and dialects. There are seventeen recordings of Scottish soldiers, eight from the Central Belt (there is no recording from Edinburgh). Here we consider the speech of two men from Glasgow and one from a small village, Newarthill, in the countryside of Lanarkshire about 15 miles east of Glasgow (a few personal notes were recorded for each speaker):

Glasgow William Bryce states that he and his parents were from Glasgow. He was born on 14 January 1891, and was recorded aged 25, on 21 July 1916 in Sennelager. He was educated in a 'public' (probably state-funded) school and was in the army from the age of 18. He gives 'Scottish' as his mother tongue and regards English as an 'additional language'.

Maryhill John Johnstone appears to be more aspirational middle class. He states that he was educated at a boarding school in Glasgow, and describes himself as an 'accountant', after previously being a clerk in a railway company. We include him in our sample because his recording is clearly in Scots, though unlike Bryce and Fulton, he only admits to speaking in 'English'. Johnstone was born on 4 April 1896, and was aged 21 when he was recorded on 15 June 1917 in Quedlinburg. Johnstone's father is from Dumfries and his mother from Stirlingshire.

Newarthill Hugh Fulton, a 'van man', was slightly older than the other two men when he was recorded, aged 34 (born 4 March 1883) on 3 July 1917, at Gustrow. Fulton and his parents were both from Newarthill. He states that he was educated at a 'public' (state) school and that he could read and write in both 'English' and 'Scottish'.

Short recordings were made from each speaker. Here we present analyses of the men reciting the passage, the *Parable of the Prodigal Son* (Luke chapter XV, verses 11–32). The few photographs of the recordings in progress, as shown in Figure 2.1, suggest that speakers had a text in front of them as they

Figure 2.1: Wilhelm Doegen (right) recording a speaker in a German Prisoner
of War camp
(from The Doegen Records Web Project, http://doegen.ie/about; © Humboldt-
Universität, Berlin).

spoke (Doegen is holding the text above the recording horn for the speaker).
They also had a rather diverse audience.

3.   Method

For both corpora, time-aligned transcriptions were made for each
recording in Praat (Boersma and Weenick 2013), breaking the speech
down into shorter utterances, usually intonational phrases aligning with
major or minor syntactic boundaries. Transcripts and .wav files were then
uploaded to *LaBB-CAT*, and an automatic phonemic transcription was
generated by *LaBB-CAT*'s link with CELEX (a lexical database, which
comprises general lexicons for British English, German and Dutch). After
correction and addition of any new words, the recordings were then force-
aligned using HTK in *LaBB-CAT*, providing an automatic phonemic seg-
mentation of the waveform. Segments were located for measurement by
using orthographic or phonemic search strings, against other parameters
such as lexical stress.

The sound quality of the recordings is variable in the *SoC* corpus, but all can
be analysed acoustically. Given that the *BL* materials are digitised versions of
audio recordings made around a hundred years ago on shellac discs, their
quality is poorer. The recordings were lowpass filtered to remove high-
frequency hiss above 7KHz; thereafter noise-cancelling was carried out using
Audacity (Audacity Project 2005). All automatic segment boundaries for the
BL recordings were handcorrected using the filtered and noise-cancelled sound
files. A broad transcription of stressed and unstressed vowel qualities was also

carried out, replacing those produced automatically through the links with the CELEX databases, to ensure more accurate searches.

Our selection of variables for considering the evidence for real-time change using continuous acoustic phonetic measures was motivated by three factors. The first was practical: the quality of the *BL* recordings means that sounds characterised by higher energy regions, such as formants, are more amenable to acoustic analysis than others. The second was their possible status in terms of variation and change in Glaswegian over the course of the twentieth century. The third was that each had already been investigated in a *SoC* subproject. This led us to select vowel quality (José *et al.* 2013), vowel duration (Rathcke and Stuart-Smith, 2016), and the realisation of word-initial /l/ (Macdonald *et al.* 2014). Here we only give an outline of the *SoC* studies since they are reported in detail in the references listed earlier.

4.   Vowel Quality

4.1   *Vowel Quality in Scottish English*

Scots and Scottish Standard English generally share a vowel inventory, for example, they typically have one vowel where Anglo-English has two for TRAP/BATH, FOOT/GOOSE, and COT/CAUGHT (Wells 1982), but deploy it differently for systematic lexical alternations (*aff/off* /a ɔ/, *heid/head* /i ɛ/, *oot/out* /ʉ ʌʉ/, see Stuart-Smith 2003), and show some socially stratified differences in phonetic realisation (fronter /a ʉ/ in vernacular than standard; found in Macaulay 1977). Earlier descriptions of particular vowel qualities in particular dialects, especially by contrast with Scottish Standard English, Anglo-English, and Received Pronunciation (RP), can be gleaned from the elocution manuals (Grant 2012; McAllister 1938), and from studies on Glaswegian by Macaulay (1977) and Macafee (1994). Johnston (1997) provides the most comprehensive account of vowel variation in Scots, based on auditory analysis of the materials from the *Linguistic Survey of Scotland*.

Following Johnston (1997) and Macaulay (1977), we expected that over time, the acoustic qualities of the stressed vowels /i e a ɔ o ʉ/ might be fairly stable, with the possible exception of /ʉ/. The /ʉ/ vowel corresponds to Anglo-English GOOSE and FOOT, both of which are known to have undergone fronting during the twentieth century, most especially GOOSE (Harrington *et al.* 2011). Our question is whether the Scottish vowel quality, which was already much fronter than that of Anglo-English, would also be fronting, or whether it might have lowered over time, as suggested by Scobbie *et al.* (2012).

4.2   *Vowel Quality in the Sounds of the City Corpus*

José *et al.* (2013) analysed the six unchecked monophthongs /i e a ɔ o ʉ/ (MEET/BEAT, MATE/BAIT, CAT, COT, COAT, BOOT) in a subset of four speaker groups from the *SoC* corpus: (1) older men born in the 1890s and recorded in the 1970s, (2) older men born in the 1920s and recorded in the 2000s, (3) adolescents born in the 1960s and recorded in the 1970s and (4) adolescents born in the 1990s and recorded in the 2000s. José *et al.* (2013) used automatic search, extraction, and measurement of first and second formants, followed by data pruning to remove outliers and problematic measures (Labov *et al.* 2013). The formant measures were then normalised using the Lobanov method, for comparison, and also because Rathcke and Stuart-Smith (2014) have shown that Lobanov normalisation is useful for reducing the effects of noise and poor spectral balance on formant measures. Statistical analysis used Linear Mixed Effects modelling using the lme4 package in R to investigate the evidence for change over time in each vowel. F1 and F2 were the dependent variables, with fixed factors of Preceding and Following Context, and Group, and random factors of Speaker and Word. The results showed significant patterns consistent with change across apparent- and real-time for three vowels, BOOT, COT, and COAT; we discuss these results together with the extended real-time comparison afforded by the BL recordings in Section 4.4 (see Figure 2.3).

4.3   *Vowel Quality in the Berliner Lautarchiv Speakers*

All instances of the stressed vowel monophthongs were identified in the *BL* recordings, so /i ɪ e ɛ a ʌ ɔ o ʉ/ (MEET/BEAT, BIT, MATE/BAIT, BET, CAT, CUT, COT/CAUGHT, COAT, BOOT); n = 794. Vowels before /r/ were excluded because they constitute a separate subsystem in terms of quality (Lawson et al 2013). While we coded for Scots lexis, for example /i/ selected for Scots *heid* 'head' and /a/ for Scots *aff* 'off', to see if vowel quality might vary in Scots words, the small numbers made it difficult to test for this statistically. Following José *et al.* (2013), the first three vowel formants were measured at 25, 50 and 75 per cent through the vowel duration in *LaBB-CAT*, which uses Praat's default settings. All measures were inspected and hand-corrected by consulting the spectrogram and/or vowel spectra. We also coded for the place of articulation of preceding and following segments.

Formant measures were taken from sound files which had not undergone filtering or noise cancellation, because the subsequent real-time comparison was made against measures from José *et al.* (2013), which also had not been altered. As a precaution, a sample of formant measures was taken from the

Glasgow speaker for stressed /i o ʉ/ from the sound files with and without noise cancellation and filtering. The measures from the two sound files were highly correlated, suggesting that the additional noise in the unaltered file may be less problematic for higher energy resonances in the lower formants: F1 ($t = 31.25$, df = 142, $p < 0.001$, $R = 0.93$); F2 ($t = 28.24$, df = 142, $p < 0.001$, $R = 0.92$). To facilitate the real-time comparison and minimise further the effects of noise, we normalised the measures using the Lobanov method.

Figure 2.2 shows the Lobanov-normalized first and second formants of these vowels for all three speakers together (a), and for each speaker separately (Glasgow (b), Maryhill (c) and Newarthill (d)). We used LME modelling, as in

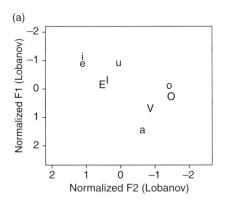

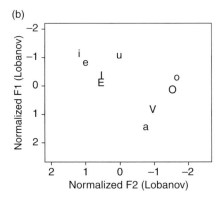

Figure 2.2: Vowel plots for stressed monophthongs /i ɪ e ɛ a ʌ ɔ o ʉ/ <i I e E a V O o u>, showing means of Lobanov-normalised F1 and F2 for (a) the three BL speakers recorded in 1916/17 (n = 794), and the speakers from (b) Glasgow (n = 289), (c) Maryhill (n = 239), and (d) Newarthil (n = 266).

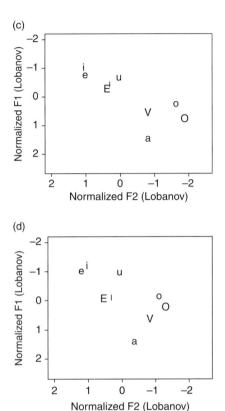

Figure 2.2: (*cont.*)

José *et al.* (2013), in order to ascertain the relative relationships of the vowels in the F2-F1 vowel space, so here the dependent variable was F1 or F2, and the fixed factors were Vowel, Preceding, and Following Segment (interactions could not be included given the low numbers of tokens).

Vowel was a significant factor for both F1 and F2 (F1: $F = 126.26$, df = 8, $p < 0.001$; F2: $F = 131.34$, df = 8, $p = 0.001$). Place of articulation of the following segment was only significant for F2 (Preceding: $F = 2.96$, df = 3, p = 0.03; Following: $F= 4.79$, df = 3, p = 0.003). We report comparisons as significant after applying the appropriate Bonferroni correction to account for multiple comparisons.

Overall, in terms of normalised F1, reflecting vowel height, the vowels fall into four groups from low to high: /a/, /ʌ/, /ɛ ɪ o ɔ/, and /i e ʉ/; /ɛ ɪ o/ are marginally higher than /ɔ/. In terms of normalised F2, reflecting vowel front-backness, there are effectively four groups from back to front: back /o ɔ/ and /a ʌ/, central/front /ʉ/, and the front vowels, which cluster as /ɛ ɪ/ and /i e/. So the vowel space for the *BL* speakers shows the following configuration: /a/ is a low vowel, retracted and close to /ʌ/; /o ɔ/ are back vowels, statistically almost merged in terms of height; /ʉ/ is a high vowel, which is fronter than /a ʌ ɔ o/, but not as front as /i e ɪ ɛ/; /i e/ are front high vowels; /ɪ/ is mid and retracted, similar to /ɛ/. These qualities align with some observations from contemporary descriptions.

/ɪ/ Grant (1912: 49) notes that in 'Scotch dialect . . . *hill* is often pronounced as if it were *hull* or *hell* or something between these two'; see also McAllister (1938: 134). Here we find retraction of /ɪ/, also noted by Johnston (1997: 470), but not the stereotypical lowering to /ʌ/ found by Macaulay (1977).

/e/ The very raised quality of /e/ in our speakers is similar to Johnston's (1997: 459) 'Raised MATE', which he finds in some Mid-Scots speakers, alongside more usual 'Mid e:' for this vowel.

/ʉ/ Grant (1912: 56) also refers to the fronting of **u** (the vowel in *food*) 'from the full back position in normal speech', noting that 'in some parts of Scotland, viz. Gaelic districts and in and around Glasgow, this advancing is very marked and should be corrected.' McAllister (1938: 161) also notes an 'advanced' quality of /u/ in 'Clydeside' speakers, also found in working-class speakers in Macaulay's study, and is designated 'OUT-fronting' by Johnston (1997: 475).

/o ɔ/ Johnston (1997: 480) notes that merger of COT with COAT is 'more or less complete in vernacular Scots '.

/a/ Both McAllister (1938) and Macaulay (1977) found retracted /a/ to be typical of 'local' and 'working-class' speakers respectively.

We can only make qualitative observations about the vowel qualities of the individual speakers. The country speaker from Newarthill shows the most lowered and retracted /ɪ ɛ/. The more aspirational Maryhill speaker shows the highest BIT and the most separation between COT and COAT, possibly reflecting some hypercorrection towards the standard. But he shares central /ʉ/ and retracted /a/ qualities with the other two men.

4.4   *Vowel Quality over the Twentieth Century*

The *SoC* findings of José *et al.* (2013) indicate real-time lowering of BOOT and raising of COT and COAT since the 1970s. The apparent-time evidence of the elderly speakers suggests that these changes may have started much earlier in the century. The average decade of birth of the *BL* men and the older *SoC* men recorded in the 1970s is the same, the 1890s. The *BL* recordings enable us to check our inference of change with an extended, albeit cautious, real-time comparison. We remain cautious given

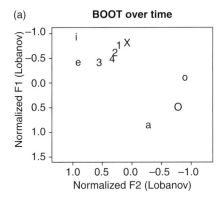

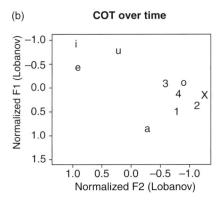

Figure 2.3: Plots of observed means of Lobanov-normalised F1 and F2 measures for stressed monophthongs /i e a ɔ o ʉ/ <i e a O o u>, showing the relative position for each speaker group for (a) BOOT(n = 1426), (b) COT (n = 1261), and (c) COAT (n = 913).[2]

the small number of speakers, the stylistic differences between the corpora, and the possibility of life-span shifts in the speakers recorded in the 1970s (Sankoff and Blondeau 2007).

The *BL* speakers were included as an additional group in the statistical modelling as described in José *et al.* (2013) (see Section 4.2), for each of the six vowels. Indications of real-time change are confirmed for the three vowels, (see Figure 2.3).

---

[2] 1 = older men born in the 1890s, recorded in the 1970s; 2 = older men born in the 1920s, recorded in the 2000s; 3 = adolescents born in the 1960s, recorded in the 1970s; 4 = adolescents born in the 1990s, recorded in the 2000s; X = the *BL* men born in the 1890s, recorded in the 1910s.

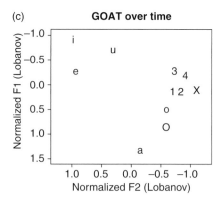

(c) **GOAT over time**

Figure 2.3: (*cont.*)

The clearest result is found for BOOT, which does indeed seem to be lowering over time (Group for F1: $F = 12.56$, df = 4, $p = 0.0002127$). This finding is robust in the *SoC* sample, and is suggested by Scobbie *et al.*'s (2012) articulatory data. This new real-time comparison shows that the *BL* men demonstrate higher BOOT than all of the other groups, except the older speakers who were also born in the 1890s, but recorded much later in their lives, in the 1970s. Thus, the lowering of /ʉ/ may have started after the First World War.

The results for COT and COAT are weaker, which probably also relates to the specific relationship between these two vowels. In Scots, COT is reported to be a higher vowel, often fully merged with COAT (Johnston 1997). The *BL* speakers also show a raised COT, which is almost merged with COAT in terms of vowel height. But if we look at the relative means of COT and COAT for the *SoC* speaker groups 1 to 4 (Figure 2.3 (b) and (c)), we can see that COAT is higher than COT for all groups, indicating that this merger is not apparent for these speakers. Across real- and apparent-time, the *SoC* speakers show COT to be a higher vowel, whilst the *BL* speakers sit between them. Group is significant for F1: $F = 3.38$, df = 4, $p = 0.04$, but this reflects differences between Groups 1, 3, and 4. The *BL* men – with their almost merged COT/COAT – do not show differences in vowel height from any of the groups recorded later. We infer from this that COT probably has raised across the century, but that lowered variants of unmerged COT were also possible in vernacular speech even early in the twentieth century. What is more striking, and unexpected, is the fronting: Group is also significant for F2: $F = 8.77$, df = 4, $p = 0.003$, such that the *BL* men show backer COT than all of the other speaker groups.

COAT, on the other hand, shows significant real- and apparent-time raising in the *SoC* speaker groups, but the tendency for raising only becomes apparent when comparing with the *BL* speakers, possibly because of the low number of tokens for this vowel. Having said that, the distribution is more focussed in the F2 dimension, and the *BL* men do show a marginally more retracted COAT vowel than the adolescents born in the 1960s and recorded in the 1970s ($F = 3.37$, df = 4, $p = 0.04$).

5.   Vowel Duration – the Scottish Vowel Length Rule

Scottish English shows a distinctive pattern of phonologically and morphologically conditioned vowel duration with respect to many varieties of Anglo-English, known as the Scottish Vowel Length Rule (SVLR). This is thought to have applied to all vowel monophthongs in the history of Scots (Aitken 1981; Johnston 1997). Grant's (1912: 84) earlier comments on the shortening of tense vowels before plosive consonants in 'Standard Scottish' is followed by the observation that '[t]his shortening is specially marked in the high vowels, but is less noticeable with lower vowels'. He gives examples for /i/, /ʉ/, and /o/, for instance *greed/agreed; brood/brewed, brew; road/rowed*. More recent durational analyses have found evidence for SVLR only for the vowels /i ʉ ai/ (Scobbie *et al.* 1999). Further erosion in the direction of the Anglo-English pattern of vowel duration, conditioned purely by voicing of the following consonant (the Voicing Effect), has also been found in varieties of Scottish English with higher levels of contact with Anglo-English, for example in Edinburgh (Hewlett *et al.* 1999).

We expected that the SVLR would be robustly maintained in Glasgow over the twentieth century, though the impact of contact with Anglo-English through increased geographical and social mobility might also predict some contact-induced weakening, especially for the second half of the twentieth century. We also wanted to see whether the *BL* recordings would show the SVLR in more vowels than /i ʉ ai/. Phonetic research into the effects of prosody on vowel duration points to weakening of durational patterns in particular prosodic contexts (Beckman *et al.* 1992; Nakai 2013). Previous studies of the SVLR have only considered citation forms in read speech. Both our corpora comprise connected speech, and so we were also able to investigate prosodic factors on the SVLR over time.

5.1   The SVLR in the Sounds of the City Corpus

Rathcke and Stuart-Smith (2014) examined the SVLR in /i/, /ʉ/, and /a/ in a real- and apparent-time subsample of sixteen speakers from the *SoC* corpus in four groups: 70M: middle-aged men born in the 1920s and recorded in the 1970s;

00M: middle-aged men born in the 1950s and recorded in the 2000s; 70Y: adolescent boys born in the 1960s and recorded in the 1970s; and 00Y: adolescent boys born in the 1990s and recorded in the 2000s. All possible tokens of the three vowels were extracted and the vowel durations were hand-corrected in EMU (Harrington 2010). Contexts were coded as SVLR 'short' unless the vowels were followed by a voiced fricative or /r/ (phonologically 'long') or a morpheme boundary (morphologically 'long'). Lack of difference between the two 'long' categories led to a single 'long' category. Voicing Effect contexts were coded according to the following context: 'short' if followed by a mono-morphemic voiceless obstruent, 'long' if followed by a mono-morphemic voiced obstruent, and 'unspecified' if morpheme final. Because vowel duration is sensitive to a range of other factors, tokens were also coded for properties of the word (number of segments in the word, number of syllables in the word) and prosodic factors (position of the word in the phrase: initial, medial, final, and prominence: stressed, accented, nuclear).

Previous phonetic studies of the SVLR have considered citation forms in read speech which make direct comparison of durations in SVLR and Voicing Effect contexts more straightforward (e.g. SVLR: *fleece* vs. *please,* voicing effect: *seat* vs. *seed* in Hewlett *et al.* 1999). Given that the *SoC* data were from spontaneous conversational speech, we needed a statistical analytical strategy that would allow comparison of vowel durations according to the relevant contexts for SVLR and Voicing Effect, but that would also take account of other key factors. Rathcke and Stuart-Smith therefore used Linear Mixed Effects Modelling in lme4 in R to find the best-fitting model. The dependent variable was vowel duration and the fixed factors were SVLR, Voicing Effect, and factors capturing prosodic and word-level factors. We also included random factors of Speaker and Word to control for lexical and speaker-specific effects, such as global speaking rate.

The results confirmed the SVLR for /i/ and /ʉ/ (see Figure 2.6), but not for /a/. Rathcke and Stuart-Smith also found evidence for weakening of the SVLR, both in a general reduction of the SVLR contrast in less prominent syllables (Beckman *et al.* 1992), and in the shortening of SVLR long syllables in prominent syllables over time (Nakai 2013). Interestingly, this suggests that dialect-internal factors, especially prosodic ones, are promoting this change. There was only weak evidence to suggest that contact with Anglo-English varieties may be triggering a shift to the Voicing Effect patterning, and no significant Voicing Effect, contrary to Edinburgh English (Hewlett *et al.* 1999).

5.2   *The SVLR in the Berliner Lautarchiv Recordings*

We used the protocol developed by Rathcke and Stuart-Smith to analyse the *BL* recordings. Corrected segment boundaries were used to extract durations for the stressed monophthongs /i e a o ɔ ʉ/ and /ai/ to assess evidence for the SVLR in these three speakers (n = 517). The same coding for SVLR, Voicing Effect, and all prosodic and word-level factors was applied. We also used the same strategy for our statistical analysis, with modifications to account for the nature of the *BL* dataset. The fixed factors were SVLR, Voicing Effect, Number of segments, Vowel, Phrase position and Prominence, and the random factors were Speaker and Word. Possible interactions were limited by small numbers, but we were able to test for the three-way interaction of SVLR*Vowel*Prominence. We had hoped to be able to consider SVLR in all vowel qualities, but low numbers of tokens for GOAT and CAT in some contexts meant that our analysis was restricted to /i ʉ ai e ɔ/.

As expected, vowel durations were significantly longer in phrase-final position (by 26ms, $F = 17.55$, df = 1, $p < 0.001$), and in nuclear syllables (by 22ms, $F = 17.62$, df = 1, $p < 0.001$), but were shorter as the number of segments in the word increased ($F = 6.9$, df = 1, $p = 0.009$). Vowel was also a significant factor ($F = 3.007$, df = 4, $p = 0.02$), reflecting shorter durations of /i/ and /ʉ/ than /ɔ/ and /ai/. Durations were longer in general in SVLR long contexts by 27ms ($F = 21.45$, df = 1, $p < 0.001$), but particularly for certain vowels in nuclear syllables (Prominence*SVLR*Vowel: $F = 7.89$, df = 1, $p < 0.001$). The results of this three-way interaction are shown in the two charts in Figure 2.4. Overall, much longer durations are found in nuclear syllables (see upper chart), especially for /i ʉ/. SVLR is found for three vowels, /i ʉ ai/, though to differing degrees. /ʉ/ shows the greatest lengthening (by 53ms, $t = 25.85$, $p < 0.001$), followed by /i/ (by 31ms, $t = 9.42$, $p < 0.005$) and /ai/, though only just statistically longer (by 34ms, $t = 1.37$, $p < 0.04$). Neither /e/ nor /ɔ/ shows statistical evidence for SVLR in these speakers, though /e/ is numerically longer by 12ms in nuclear SVLR contexts. There is no evidence for the Anglo-English Voicing Effect.

Our results confirm Grant's observations for /i ʉ/, and align with those of Scobbie *et al.* (1999) for Glasgow for /i ʉ ai/. We were unable to consider /o/ properly, given the low number of SVLR long tokens in the nuclear position. Comparison of raw means shows that /o/ in SVLR long contexts is 12ms longer than in short contexts. It is possible that these results, taken together with those of /e/, may reflect an erosion of the SVLR for /e/ and/o/, such that by the turn of the nineteenth century, consistent SVLR patterning no longer occurred for these vowels in Glasgow.

The situation for /ai/ seems to be different. PRIZE is longer in SVLR contexts, but the difference is only just significant. Scobbie *et al.* (1999) found /ai/ to be proportionally longer than /o ɔ/, but shorter than /i ʉ/. In a subsequent study on the same Glasgow data, Scobbie and Stuart-Smith (2012) found vowel quality to be important, with the 'short' diphthongs produced as [ʌi/ɪi/əi], while the 'longer' diphthong is produced as [ai/ae].

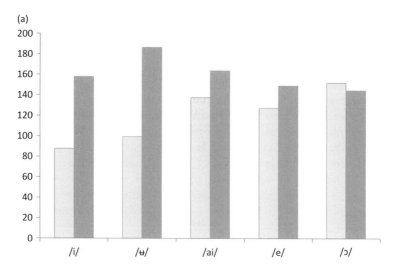

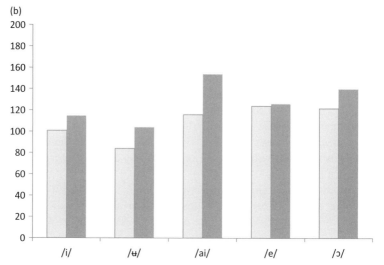

Figure 2.4: LME estimates of vowel durations in milliseconds for the BL speakers for vowels in (a) nuclear syllables and (b) non-nuclear syllables. Light bars show SVLR short contexts, dark bars display long contexts (n = 148).

Differentiation between short and long versions of the diphthong with these changes in quality also varies depending on differences in socio-economic background. We therefore also measured F1 and F2 across the duration of the diphthong, taking measures at 25, 50 and 75 per cent across the vowel. Mean Hz tracks for /ai/ are shown in Figure 2.5. Consideration of the acoustic vowel quality suggests that, for these speakers at least, the main difference between the SVLR long and short contexts is one of vowel quality, as shown later by Scobbie and Stuart-Smith (2012). Interestingly, Grant (1912: 63) even seems to prescribe the SVLR-conditioned difference. He notes first that 'many speakers use ɔ as the first element in the diphthong in *rice, light,* etc. instead of **a**', reflecting the 'local' pronunciation observed by McAllister (1938: 184). But he then goes on to state that 'this is allowable except when the diphthong ends the syllable or stands before **r, z, v, ð**'.

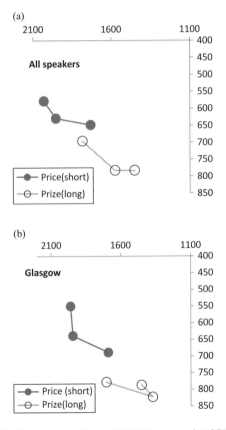

Figure 2.5: Plots of mean F1 and F2 (Hz) measured at 25%, 50% and 75% of the vowel duration for /ai/ according to SVLR short contexts (PRICE) and long contexts (PRIZE), for (a) all three speakers, (b) Glasgow, (c) Maryhill and (d) Newarthill (n = 37).

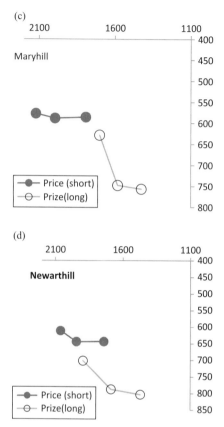

Figure 2.5: (*cont.*)

5.3   *The SVLR over the Twentieth Century*

In order to carry out the real-time comparison across the *SoC* and *BL* data for SVLR, we ran Linear Mixed Effects models for the duration for /i ʉ/ for all five speaker groups, with fixed factors of SVLR, Voicing Effect, Group, Number of Segments and Prominence, together with a three-way interaction of Prominence*SVLR*Group, and random factors of Speaker and Word (Figure 2.6).The expected general prosodic effects were found to hold for the real-time dataset as a whole. Vowels were longer in phrase-final position ($F = 124.23$; df = 1; $p < 0.001$) and in nuclear syllables: $F = 41.6$; df = 1, $p < 0.001$), and a little shorter the more segments there were in the word ($F = 10.23$; df = 1, $p = 0.002$). SVLR long contexts also conditioned

(a)

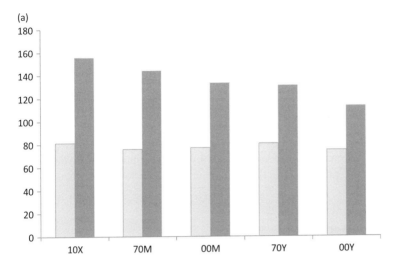

(b)

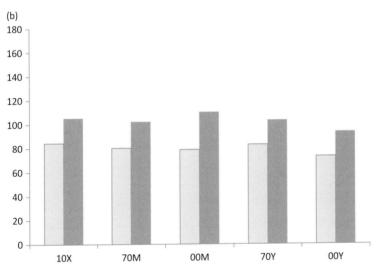

Figure 2.6: LME estimates in milliseconds for /i ʉ/ in SVLR contexts in five speaker groups, in nuclear syllables (top) and non-nuclear syllables (bottom).[3]

---

[3] Light bars show SVLR short contexts, dark bars display long contexts (n = 1130). 10X = *BL* sample born in 1890s and recorded in 1910s; 70M = middle-aged men born in the 1920s and recorded in the 1970s; 00M = middle-aged men born in the 1950s and recorded in the 2000s; 70Y = adolescent

longer durations (F = 211.32; df = 1, p < 0.001). No evidence of the Anglo-English Voicing Effect was found.

The three-way interaction was also significant (F = 3.12, df = 4, p = 0.02); as can be seen from Figure 2.6, durations are longer in nuclear syllables, but those of the *BL* speaker group (10X) are longer than those of all speaker groups, other than 70M, who were born in the 1920s and recorded in the 1970s. It looks as if the weakening of the SVLR in this prosodic position may have begun during or after the Second World War, which is consistent with the suggestion put forward by Rathcke and Stuart-Smith (2014) that weakening of the SVLR may have been promoted by changes in social network structure during the process and aftermath of urban regeneration between the 1950s and 1990s.

6.   Word-initial /l/

6.1   *Word-initial /l/ in Scottish English*

Much attention has been paid to coda /l/ which is known to have vocalised historically in Scots, and more recently across urban British accents (Stuart-Smith *et al.* 2006). Less is known about the realisation of onset /l/, which is typically clear in many varieties of Anglo-English, and dark in most varieties of Scottish English, especially Glaswegian (Johnston 1997: 510; Stuart-Smith *et al.* 2011). At the same time, while Johnston emphasises the pharyngealised quality of Scots /l/, he also suggests that dark /l/ is – in the long term – the innovative variant ('the dark /l/ variant has won out except around the periphery'). The question is, then, whether there has been any shift in resonance over the twentieth century.

6.2   *Word-initial /l/ in the Sounds of the City Corpus*

Macdonald and Stuart-Smith (2014) analysed the acoustic characteristics of word-initial /l/ according to preceding and following phonetic context, and real-time in a subsample of the *SoC* corpus. Three older men and three older women (aged 67–90) were recorded in the 1970s, 1980s, 1990s and 2000s. Darkness of /l/ was considered in terms of relative F2 values, assuming darker /l/ shows lower values (Carter and Local 2007). All possible instances of /l/ were segmented following Carter and Local (2007). Hand-corrected F2 measures of the steady state were subjected to Linear Mixed Effects

boys born in the 1960s and recorded in the 1970s; and 00Y = adolescent boys born in the 1990s and recorded in the 2000s.

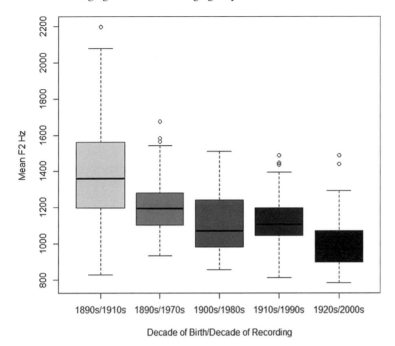

Figure 2.7: Mean F2 Hz values for word-initial /l/ across all phonetic contexts in the BL sample (1890s/1910s) and the male speaker groups from the SoC sample (n = 845).

modelling using the lme4 package in R, looking for the best-fitting model with fixed factors of Decade, Preceding and Following Context, and random factors of Speaker and Word. The results showed expected significant conditioning effects of adjacent phonetic context. They also showed a significant effect depending on the decade of birth/recording, with F2 being darker in speakers born in the 1920s (and recorded in the 2000s) than the other three speaker groups (Figure 2.7).

6.3   Word-initial /l/ in the Berliner Lautarchiv Recordings

All instances of stressed word-initial /l/ were located (n = 23), and the first three formant measures were taken at the midpoint of the steady state of the lateral. Obtaining reliable formant measures for /l/ was more difficult in the original sound files so, for these tokens, formant measures were taken from the noise-cancelled files, where visual inspection showed that that formant tracking was more accurate. Even so, every measure was hand-checked.

Table 2.2: *Mean F2 in Hz for word-initial /l/ in the BL sample, ordered by following vowel height.*

Speaker	Before High Vowels	Before Non-High Vowels	All Contexts	N
Glasgow	1143	1009	1054	9
Maryhill	n/a	1294	1294	6
Newarthill	1410	1288	1319	8
Mean	1250	1197	1208	23

Preceding and Following Context was also coded. The second formant values of possible instances of word-initial /l/ in the *BL* speakers are shown in Table 2.2.

The overall average F2 Hz value falls into the higher end of Recasens and Espinosa's (2005) 'dark' lateral group, or the lower end of their 'clear' group. The speaker from Glasgow shows the lowest values, the rural speaker in Newarthill shows the highest values. The Maryhill accountant has high F2 values even before non-high vowels. This accords with the later advice from McAllister (1938: 115): 'Scottish speakers who aim at shedding cruder local characters from their speech [for instance dark l] should make the use of clear l habitual'.

6.4   Word-initial /l/ over the Twentieth Century

Our real-time comparison for /l/ can only be qualitative. We show the average F2 Hz values for each of the five speaker groups in Figure 2.7.

The lowering of F2 values across the decade of birth/recording over the entire real-time sample clearly evident, with the older men born in the 1920s and recorded in the 2000s showing values similar to those of the dark, velarised laterals found in Russian and Portuguese (Recasens and Espinosa 2005). At the same time, whilst the mean value for the *BL* sample is higher than those of the *SoC* speaker groups, the range for these twenty-three tokens is also extensive, both overlapping with the much darker /l/s of the later *SoC* speaker groups, but also showing some much higher F2 values (clearer instances). The general pattern looks consistent with the assumption of the darkening of /l/ over the twentieth century, as implied by Johnston (1997). But we also note that the *BL* Glasgow speaker (Table 2.2) shows a lower average F2 Hz value than the older *SoC* men, who were also born in the 1890s, but recorded much later in their lives, in the 1970s. It therefore seems possible that this change may also have shown age-grading, with younger speakers leading the darkening (the Glasgow soldier was 25).

7.   Perspectives on Real-Time Change and Place from Scottish English

Our analysis of acoustic variation across the twentieth century in Glasgow dialect yields the following findings:

1. BOOT has lowered over time. The *SoC* data also show that COT and COAT are raising, but the Scots merger of COT/COAT, evident in the *BL* speakers, prevents further inference from the early recordings. This is consistent with assumptions made from articulatory data by Scobbie *et al.* (2012). But it seems to be a different kind of change from those observed in the fronting of Anglo-English GOOSE and BOOT (Harrington *et al.* 2011). This looks more like evidence of a chain-shift (Labov 1994), which is progressing within this dialect, and may have begun after the First World War.

2. The SVLR is now restricted to /i ʉ ai/ and is reduced in prosodically weaker syllables (Beckman *et al.* 1992). It has also weakened over time in prosodically strong positions, consistent with Nakai's (2013) observation that quantity differences can give way to prosodic timing effects. At the same time, there is no clear shift to the Anglo-English Voicing Effect. This also appears to be a dialect-internal change, promoted by prosodic factors, which – given the available time sampling – may have begun during or after the Second World War, possibly promoted by fragmentation of tight-knit social networks during the process of urban regeneration from the 1950s to 1970s (Milroy and Milroy 1985).

3. Word-initial /l/ has become darker, confirming Johnston's (1997) observation about the early twentieth century for this variety of Scottish English. This change may also be dialect-internal because the trend for such a dark onset /l/ is in the opposite direction to clear onset /l/s in many Anglo-English varieties (Carter and Local 2007).

Together these changes inform our perspective on change, in terms of time depth and analytical resolution, and consideration of the role of place in sound change.

Increasing the resolution of our real-time window by including the *BL* archival evidence confirms these changes as progressing diachronically across the twentieth century. Our view of their progress over this period is necessarily affected by our sampling, but suggests that shifts in vowel and lateral quality may have preceded those in vowel duration. Stability and shift is also observed if we consider the real-comparison for the auditory derhoticisation of coda /r/ in words like *car,* also made across *BL* and *SoC* corpora by Stuart-Smith and Lawson (in press). There, the six *BL* speakers show similar levels of derhoticisation to the middle-aged men born in the 1940s and 1950s and recorded in the 1990s and 2000s, indicating stability in this feature for the first half of the century. It is difficult to know whether the impression of stability, in derhoti-cisation, versus change, in the features considered here, is simply a result of the time resolution of our 'window' and/or the sampling within that window (Milroy 2003).

It may also relate to the change itself. Stuart-Smith and Lawson (in press) also show that derhoticisation did increase, in Glaswegian at least, towards the end of the century. The Glaswegian adolescents born in the 1980s and 1990s show much higher usage of weak /r/, suggesting either an age-graded increase, or that the change may have taken off somewhat later than supposed. This took place in conjunction with the other consonantal changes, TH-fronting and L-vocalisation, and all three seem to have acquired locally salient social meanings. These changes seem to have accelerated around the same time through the interplay of several factors, such as social practices and personal psychological engagement with TV (Stuart-Smith *et al.* 2007; Stuart-Smith *et al.* 2013; Jansen 2014). These consonantal changes look like instances of supralocal diffusion (Kerswill 2003), but show weaker evidence for dialect contact, and stronger indications that the changes are strongly constrained by the 'local', the city, and its dialect (Stuart-Smith *et al.* 2013). This is high-lighted by derhoticisation, which has been established by Lawson and Stuart-Smith (in press) as a local variant at the start of the twentieth century; however, it is also promoted by 'external' influence of the broadcast media, yet it has not been subject to dialect contact, by the end of the century. These changes appear to have long trajectories which relate to their locales (Beal 2006, 2010).

This brings us back to the questions posed at the outset. We have found evidence consistent with long-term real-time change for these three features. But despite the substantial geographical and social changes known to have taken place across the United Kingdom, particularly during the second half of the twentieth century, we do not appear to have evidence for the influence of Anglo-English norms on any of the changes considered here. While this may be an erroneous impression in the absence of relevant data, these changes appear to have been promoted by dialect-internal factors, both linguistic and social, relating to the city of Glasgow itself.

Exactly how changes to the local context over the twentieth century relate to these fine-grained shifts in speech remains a question for future research, though we have some hints from previous studies and the data themselves. Stuart-Smith *et al.* (2007) argued that the social-spatial changes undergone by Glasgow, during the period of urban regeneration between the 1950s and 1970s, led to the fragmentation of previously dense social networks which was then followed by the re-formation of new tight-knit networks in the inner city districts from the mid-1970s on. The suggested impact on consonantal variation, following Milroy and Milroy (1985), was twofold: firstly, the weakening and reduction of the maintenance of some local variants, such as the Scottish consonants /x/ and /ʍ/ and the admission of new non-local variants, such as TH-fronting and L-vocalisation. Secondly, the acceleration of the new array of variation fuelled by local language ideologies (Andersen 1988).

Of the changes considered by comparing the *BL* and *SoC* corpora, the time frame for the subtle erosion of the SVLR and derhoticisation of coda /r/ also seems consistent with this version of events, though both processes are evident in the dialect from the turn of the twentieth century. The lowering of BOOT (and possibly then the raising of COAT and COT) and darkening of word-initial /l/ also seems to have started early in the twentieth century, but may well have been accelerated by the social and linguistic impact of urban regeneration and its aftermath. Future work will help us to refine and revise these sugges-tions, both by filling in the gaps through sampling more of the *SoC* corpus for these changes, and by considering the development of a standard variety which accompanied the vernacular across the same period.

To finish, we pose a question: how important is the lens through which we observe change, for example via auditory (discrete) versus acoustic (continu-ous) data? The changes considered here are all phonetically gradient, even word-initial /l/, and all look thoroughly local in their trajectories for change and structural embedding. The consonantal changes which took off in the 1980s are considered in terms of discrete auditory data, and look supralocal, especially TH-fronting and L-vocalisation (Kerswill 2003). But we also know that, in this dialect, structural linguistic factors were the strongest factors influencing these changes too (Stuart-Smith *et al.* 2013). The distinction does not seem to relate to whether the features are vocalic or consonantal, or whether they are structurally embedded (as they all seem to be), nor is it easily related to the nature of the evidence (discrete/continuous; auditory/acoustic). We suspect it lies rather in the ways in which linguistic variation and locally relevant social meanings may or may not become connected and established (Agha 2003; Eckert 2008). Much more research is needed to understand why some aspects of the linguistic system seem to develop ideological associations relating to place more easily than others.

REFERENCES

Abercrombie, David 1979. The accents of Standard English in Scotland. In Aitken, A. J. and Tom McArthur (eds.) *The Languages of Scotland*. Edinburgh: Chambers. pp. 68–84.

Agha, Asif 2003. The social life of cultural value. *Language and Communication* 23: 231–73.

Aitken, A.J. 1981. The Scottish Vowel Length Rule. In Benskin Michael and Michael Samuels, eds. *So meny People, Longages and Tonges: Philological Essays in Scots and Mediaeval English presented to Angus McIntosh*. Edinburgh: The Middle English Dialect Project. pp. 131–157.

Andersen, Henning 1988. Center and periphery: Adoption, diffusion and spread. In Fisiak (ed.) *Historical Dialectology: Regional and Social*. Berlin: Mouton de Gruyter. pp. 39–63.

Audacity Project. 2005. *Audacity*. 2.0.5 ed. Pittsburgh: Carnegie Mellon University, October 21, 2013.

Beal, Joan 2006. *Language and Region*. London: Taylor Francis.

   2010. *An Introduction to Regional Englishes*. Edinburgh: Edinburgh University Press.

Beckman, Mary, Ken de Jong, Sun-Ah Jun and S-H. Lee 1992. The interaction of coarticulation and prosody in sound change. *Language and Speech 35*: 45–58.

Boersma, Paul and David Weenink 2013. Praat: Doing phonetics by computer. 5.3.47. www.praat.org.

Carter, Paul and John Local 2007. F2 variation in Newcastle and Leeds English liquid systems. *Journal of the International Phonetic Association* 37: 183–99.

Eckert, Penelope 2000. *Linguistic Variation as Social Practice*. Oxford: Blackwell.

   2008. Variation and the indexical field. *Journal of Sociolinguistics* 12: 453–76.

   2012. Three waves of variation study: The emergence of meaning in the study of variation. *Annual Review of Anthropology* 41: 87–100.

Foulkes, Paul and Gerard Docherty (eds.) 1999. *Urban Voices: Variation and Change in British accents*, London: Edward Arnold.

Fromont, Robert and Jennifer Hay 2012. *LaBB-CAT: An annotation Store*. University of Otago, Dunedin, New Zealand: Australasian Language Technology Workshop (ALTA), 4–6 Dec 2012. *In Proceedings* 10: 113–17.

Grant, William 1912. *The Pronunciation of English in Scotland*. Cambridge: Cambridge University Press.

Harrington, Jonathan 2010. *The Phonetic Analysis of Speech Corpora*. Oxford: Blackwell.

Harrington, Jonathan, Felicitas Kleber, and Ulrich Reubold 2011. The contributions of the lips and the tongue to the diachronic fronting of high back vowels in Standard Southern British English. *Journal of the International Phonetic Association* 41: 137–56.

Hewlett, Nigel, Ben Matthews, and Jim Scobbie 1999. Vowel duration in Scottish English speaking children. *Proceedings of the XVth ICPhS, San Francisco*. pp. 2157–60.

Jansen, Sandra 2014. Salience effects in the north-west of England. Die Vermessung der Salienz(forschung)/Measuring (the Research on) Salience. *Linguistik Online* 66(4): 91–110. https://bop.unibe.ch/linguistik-online/index.

Johnston, Paul 1997. Regional variation. In Jones, Charles (ed.) *The Edinburgh History of Scots*. Edinburgh: Edinburgh University Press. pp. 433–513.

José, Brian, Jane Stuart-Smith, Claire Timmins and Ben Torsney 2013. Material and methodological advances in sociolinguistics as applied to a study of Glaswegian Vernacular English vowels. Paper presented at NWAV42, Pittsburgh. 17–20 October 2013. http://soundsofthecity.arts.gla.ac.uk/NWAV%2042-paper-BJetal.pdf.

Kerswill, Paul. 2003. Models of linguistic change and diffusion: New evidence from dialect levelling in British English. In Britain, David and Jenny Cheshire (eds.) *Social Dialectology: In Honour of Peter Trudgill*. Amsterdam: Benjamins. pp. 223–43.

Labov, William 1994. *Principles of Linguistic Change. Volume 1: Internal Factors.* Oxford: Blackwell.

2001. *Principles of Linguistic Change. Volume 2: Social Factors.* Oxford: Blackwell.

Labov, William, Ingrid Rosenfelder and Josef Fruehwald 2013. One hundred years of sound change in Philadelphia: linear incrementation, reversal, and reanalysis. *Language* 89: 30–65.

Lawson, Eleanor, James M. Scobbie, and Jane Stuart-Smith 2013. Bunched /r/ promotes vowel merger to schwar: An ultrasound tongue imaging study of Scottish sociophonetic variation. *Journal of Phonetics* 41: 198–210.

Macafee, Caroline 1994. *Traditional Dialect in the Modern World: A Glasgow Case Study.* Frankfurt: Lang.

Macaulay, Ronald. 1977. *Language, Social Class and Education: A Glasgow Study.* Edinburgh: Edinburgh University Press.

Macdonald, Rachel and Jane Stuart-Smith 2014. Real-time change in onset /l/ over four decades of Glaswegian. Poster presented at the Second Workshop on Sound Change, UCLA Berkeley, 28–31 May 2014. http://soundsofthecity.arts.gla.ac.uk/SCIHS2014-poster-RM+JSS.pdf.

McAllister, Anne 1938. *A Year's Course in Speech Training.* London: University of London Press Ltd.

Milroy, James 1992. *Linguistic Variation and Change.* Oxford: Blackwell.

2003. When is a sound change? On the role of external factors in language change, in Britain, David and Jenny Cheshire (eds.) *Social Dialectology: In Honour of Peter Trudgill.* Amsterdam: Benjamins. pp. 209–21.

Milroy, Lesley and James Milroy 1985. Linguistic change, social network and speaker innovation. *Journal of Linguistics* 21: 339–84.

Nakai, Satsuki 2013. An explanation for phonological word-final vowel shortening: Evidence from Tokyo Japanese. *Laboratory Phonology* 4: 513–53.

Rathcke, Tamara and Jane Stuart-Smith, 2016. On the tail of the Scottish Vowel Length Rule in Glasgow. *Language and Speech*, 59: 404–30.

2014. On the impact of noise on vowel formants. Paper presented at the 15th Methods in Dialectology Conference, Groningen, 12 August 2014. (http://soundsofthecity.arts.gla.ac.uk/Methods2014-paper-TR+JSS.pdf)

Recasens, Daniel and Aina Espinosa 2005. Articulatory, positional and coarticulatory characteristics for clear /l/ and dark /l/: evidence from two Catalan dialects. *Journal of the International Phonetic Association*, 35: 1–25.

Sankoff, Gillian 2006. Age: Apparent time and real time. *Encyclopedia of Language and Linguistics*, Second Edition, Article Number: LALI: 01479.

Sankoff, Gillian and Hélène Blondeau. 2007. Language change across the lifespan: /r/ in Montreal French. *Language* 83: 560–88.

Scobbie, James, M., Nigel Hewlett and Alice Turk 1999. Standard English in Edinburgh and Glasgow: The Scottish vowel length rule revealed, in Foulkes, Paul and Gerard Docherty (eds.) *Urban Voices: Accent Studies in the British Isles.* London: Arnold. pp. 230–45.

Scobbie, James, M., Eleanor Lawson, and Jane Stuart-Smith 2012. Back to front: A socially-stratified ultrasound tongue imaging study of Scottish English /u/. *Rivista di Linguistica/Italian Journal of Linguistics* 241: 103–48.

Scobbie, James, M. and Jane Stuart-Smith 2012. Socially-stratified sampling in laboratory-based phonological experimentation, in Cohn, A., C. Fougeron, and M. Huffman (eds.) *The Oxford Handbook of Laboratory Phonology*, Oxford: Oxford University Press. pp. 607–21.

Stuart-Smith, Jane 2003. The phonology of Modern Urban Scots, in Corbett, John, J. Derrick McClure and Jane Stuart-Smith (eds.) *The Edinburgh Companion to Scots*. Edinburgh: Edinburgh University Press. pp. 110–37.

Stuart-Smith, Jane and Eleanor Lawson, in press. Glasgow/Scotland, in Hickey, Ray (ed.) *Listening to the Past*. Cambridge: Cambridge University Press.

Stuart-Smith, Jane, Eleanor Lawson and James M. Scobbie, 2014. Derhoticisation in Scottish English: A sociophonetic journey, in Celata, Chiara and Silvia Calmai (eds.) *Advances in Sociophonetics*. Amsterdam: Benjamins. pp. 57–94.

Stuart-Smith, Jane, Claire Timmins and Farhana Alam (2011), Hybridity and ethnic accents: A sociophonetic analysis of 'Glaswasian', in Gregersen, F., J. Parrott and P. Quist (eds.) *Language Variation – European Perspectives III*. Amsterdam: Benjamins. pp. 43–57.

Stuart-Smith, Jane, C. Timmins, G. Pryce and B. Gunter (2013). Television is also a factor in language change: Evidence from an urban dialect. *Language 89*: 1–36.

Stuart-Smith, J., C. Timmins and F. Tweedie. 2006. Conservation and innovation in a traditional dialect: L-vocalization in Glaswegian. *English World Wide 27*: 71–87.

Stuart-Smith, Jane, Claire Timmins and Fiona Tweedie 2007. 'Talkin' Jockney: Accent change in Glaswegian. *Journal of Sociolinguistics 11*: 221–61.

Wells, John 1982. *Accents of English. Vol. 2: The British Isles*. Cambridge: Cambridge University Press.

3   Local vs. Supralocal
Preserving Language and Identity in Newfoundland

Sandra Clarke

1.   Introduction

A sense of place is central to Newfoundland identity. Not only is Newfoundland, as an island, physically separated from the nearby North American continent, its unique European settler origins, along with its distinct cultural and linguistic heritage, has instilled in Newfoundlanders a sense of difference, and even alienation, relative to what is generally referred to as 'the Mainland'.[1] This status is reinforced by its independent political status throughout most of four centuries of European settlement.

It was not until 1949 that Newfoundland transitioned from British Dominion to province of Canada, a development that, for many, was far from welcome. A view held by some older Newfoundlanders is captured in the words of a 62-year-old female resident of the capital city, St. John's, in a 1982 interview: 'you know I'm not really Canadian, see. I'm a Newfoundlander (laughing). I'm a Newfoundlander right through [to] the backbone. Don't no one ever call me a Canadian! . . . I'll never be a Canadian.'[2] While few present-day residents of the province might share this highly nationalistic stance, many Newfoundlanders born in the post-Confederation era maintain a strong sense of Newfoundland identity and allegiance to place (Delisle 2013: 23).

In this age of increased globalisation, the themes of accelerated linguistic change, standardisation and regional dialect loss frequently play out in the

---

[1] This chapter deals only with the insular portion of the province; since 2011, the latter has been officially known as Newfoundland and Labrador. The province's continental portion, Labrador, is ethnically and linguistically more complex as a result of its considerable aboriginal input (see Clarke 2010: 14–16). Like the island of Newfoundland, Labrador has its own distinct identity, deriving at least in part from its sense of alienation, its view of having been 'neglected and short-changed in its relationship with the much more densely-populated and politically powerful island portion of the province' (MacDonald 2014: 27). A similar sense of alienation, though from mainland Canada, has played an important ideological role in shaping Newfoundland identity.

[2] This informal interview (with speaker WF71_RT23, p. 15) forms part of the Sociolinguistic Survey of St. John's English, reported on in more detail later in this chapter. The Survey was supported by Grants No. 410-81-1386 and 410-83-0351 from the Social Sciences and Humanities Research Council of Canada, as well as by the Institute of Social and Economic Research, Memorial University.

popular media, and such perceptions are widespread among the general public. A recurring topic in the work of Joan Beal (Beal 2006, 2010) is the question of whether geographic differences remain as strong as ever in the face of increased social pressures, which favour dialect levelling. It is this question, of primary importance for Newfoundland English (NE), which forms the focus of this chapter. I address this issue in the following sections, by analysing several linguistic features that differentiate NE from varieties spoken in much of mainland North America. Prior to this, however, I attempt to contextualise ongoing change in NE by situating it within the broader social context.

2.   Background: Newfoundland in a Changing Economy

Until the mid-twentieth century, the Newfoundland economy was almost entirely grounded in the inshore cod fishery, and much of its small population was scattered in hundreds of tiny rural 'outport' coastal communities (see Clarke 2010: ch. 1). The tenuous nature of this industry led to little in-migration after the mid-nineteenth century. In fact, the island's population remains sufficiently homogeneous – many residents can trace their south-west English and south-eastern Irish roots back two centuries or more – that those not born there, including recent immigrants and visitors, are still viewed as coming 'from away'.

The Second World War, along with Confederation with Canada, ushered in a new social and economic era for Newfoundland, and massive change has occurred over the past seventy years. Many rural Newfoundlanders who grew up just prior to Confederation experienced a lifestyle that had changed little in the previous century, without such modern conveniences as electricity, indoor plumbing or even road connections to nearby coastal communities. Beginning in the 1950s, government attempts to diversify the economy led to the forced resettlement of hundreds of small outports, through the creation of regional 'growth centres', in which rural populations could be serviced more economically. Yet, for well over half a century after union with Canada, the province remained the poorest in the nation, perhaps best known for its high unemployment rates and seasonal welfare programs. This situation was to change in the 1990s with the exploitation of offshore oil. Yet the province's newfound prosperity has primarily benefitted the urbanised Avalon Peninsula in the south-eastern corner of the island, particularly the greater St. John's area (Figure 3.1 provides a map illustrating the various Newfoundland communities mentioned in this chapter). Elsewhere, the economic situation remains grim. The inshore cod fishery, in decline for years largely as a result of overfishing, experienced a total collapse and a subsequent moratorium in 1992, leaving many small outports without a viable future.

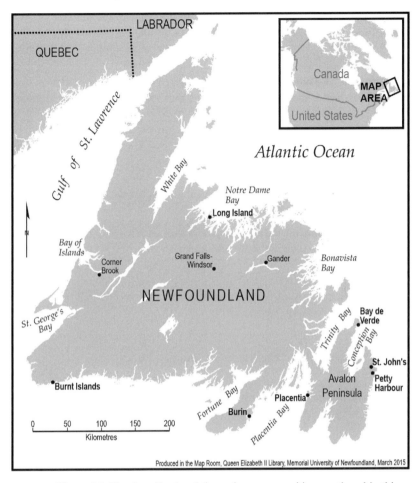

Figure 3.1: Newfoundland and the various communities mentioned in this chapter. (Map designed by David Mercer)

While out-migration, whether temporary or permanent, has been an eco-nomic necessity for Newfoundlanders since the late nineteenth century, its pace has accelerated in recent years. Delisle (2013: 2) cites sources indicating that the province lost some 100,000 people (about 20 per cent of its total population) between 1971 and 1998; she also points out that, by 2003, New-foundland's expatriate community (estimated at approximately 220,000 at the time) represented more than 40 per cent of the province's resident population. The sense of cultural marginalisation felt by many out-migrants is aptly summed up by Anonsen (1999: 49), whose family settled in Ontario in 1969:

And you never ever felt like a Canadian. You were from Newfoundland. Other kids you knew had moved to Ontario from Saskatchewan or British Columbia and no one noted it. But you were marked. You were different. You might as well have been from another country.

Writing in a national Canadian newspaper, *The Globe and Mail*, on 16 August 2014, acclaimed Newfoundland novelist Michael Crummey observes:

Traditional Newfoundland – a world of isolated, tightly knit communities that relied on the fishery and each other for survival – is still at the heart of our conception of ourselves, of how we present ourselves to the world. But with every passing year, that conception has less to do with the reality on the ground. A generation from now, what it means to be a Newfoundlander will be something altogether different.

None the less, the construction of Newfoundland identity described by Crummey lies at the heart of the official image that the province offers up to the outside world, particularly with respect to its tourism sector. 'Authentic' Newfoundland continues to be imagined as a place whose essence is defined by its rurality, to the point that urban or urbanised Newfoundlanders (who now constitute the majority of the population) may come to feel that they are not 'real' Newfoundlanders (Delisle 2013: 90).

3.   Newfoundland English in a Changing Landscape

An important component of the cultural marginalisation felt by many Newfoundlanders relative to mainland North America (Anonsen 1999) is the province's highly distinctive regional speech. Geographic isolation has helped to preserve many of the features inherited from founder varieties, which themselves represent regional non-standard dialects within the British Isles and Ireland. Along with these linguistic features, the island has inherited a distinct cultural identity, most obviously expressed in its music, folklore, and literature. Yet while the latter have undergone a post-Confederation renaissance, this has not typically been the case for Newfoundland's regional varieties, at least not until quite recently. On the contrary, many Newfoundlanders have tended to internalise the negative stereotyping of Newfoundland speech common throughout Canada – stereotyping reinforced by the province's educational system (Clarke 2010: 138 ff.) – given Newfoundland's long-standing situation as the poor cousin within the Canadian federation.

The enormous social and economic changes of the past half century have led to new concerns. Among these is the potential loss of local symbols of cultural identity, including the province's distinctive regional dialects. A number of NE sociolinguistic studies over the past thirty years do indeed suggest linguistic change in the direction of adoption of supralocal norms, in both rural and urban areas of the province (Colbourne 1982; Clarke 1991; Newhook 2002). Yet, while out-migration continues to threaten the long-term viability of small rural communities, there are many indications that the speech of such communities remains extremely robust. Author Michael Crummey (2014: F5) observes 'even as more and more Newfoundlanders move to the mainland or to urban centres on the island, the culture and character of the people remains remarkably unchanged'. He continues, 'Even now, 60 years into standardized education, in a time when every child is raised on 200 mainland cable channels, it's still possible to identify where someone is from by the particular idiosyncracies of their speech'.

Despite the general sociolinguistic findings, there is considerable evidence to support Crummey's conclusions. Take for example the Discovery Channel's 2014 Canadian television series 'Cold Water Cowboys', which documents the daily lives of rural Newfoundland fishing crews. This series provides an excellent illustration of the linguistic divide that continues to separate rural Newfoundland from most of the North American continent. In a blog from 24 February 2014, the *Calgary Herald*'s Ruth Myles comments on the producers' decision to insert subtitles ('Viewers expect subtitles when they're watching the Oscar nominees for Best Foreign Film, but a series filmed in Canada?'). Her surprise was, however, not shared by one of the fishing captains featured in the series, who was obviously accustomed to not being understood by outsiders. He observes, 'If you were here when my dad and I were talking, you would say, "What language are they talking?"'. [3]

This chapter examines a small set of NE features that have close associations with place. While not unique to NE, they are far from widespread in North American English. Most appear to be undergoing decline, at least in so far as their apparent time profiles suggest. Yet closer investigation uncovers several different patterns. Some features no longer primarily index 'place', but rather have come to be associated with particular social groups. Others have taken on second-order indexicality (Johnstone, Andrus and Danielson 2006), and can engage in complex social semiotic work, often marking local affiliation. And some prove remarkably resistant to change, despite obvious overt stigmatisation. In short, the situation is considerably more nuanced than mere dialect levelling, whereby more geographically widespread forms push out local variants. Moreover, the picture would be incomplete without consideration of local demographic and migration patterns.

---

[3] Information on the series is available at www.discovery.ca/Shows/Cold-Water-Cowboys. The *Calgary Herald* blog can be found at http://blogs.calgaryherald.com/2014/02/24/ruth-myles-cold-water-cowboys-ride-the-risky-waters-off-newfoundland-on-new-tv-series/. The quote attributed to the fishing captain is linguistically suspect, given such unexpectedly standard features as the use of *were* rather than vernacular *was* ('if you were here', 'when my dad and I were talking') and the pronominal subject form in a conjoined subject NP ('my dad and I').

All features to be examined here are consonantal. Two are of unambiguously Irish origin: 'clear' (palatal) pronunciations of postvocalic /l/ in words like *fill* or *full*; and so-called 'slit fricative' (lenited) pronunciations of postvocalic /t/ in words like *bit* or *better*. A third is found only in varieties of NE originating in south-west England: variable deletion of initial /h/ in words like *hat* or *whole*. The final feature – the stopping of the voiced and voiceless interdental fricatives /ð/ and /θ/ in words like *this, whether, think*, and *with* – occurs throughout the province, in regions originally settled by both the Irish and the south-west English.

4.   Features in Apparent Decline: Palatal Postvocalic /l/ and Slit Fricative /t/

In traditional rural NE recorded in the 1960s and 1970s, both palatal postvocalic /l/ and slit fricative /t/ [4] remained closely correlated with place, in that their regional distribution in Newfoundland echoed Irish versus south-west English settler origins. This is attested by the new online Dialect Atlas of Newfoundland and Labrador (Clarke and Hiscock 2013), which documents the features of traditional rural speakers born in the late 1800s and early 1900s. The pronunciation feature 'L after vowels' indicates palatal /l/ to be the norm in the Irish-settled southern Avalon Peninsula (along with the island's south-western corner, which had considerable Scottish and French input). In other coastal regions, however, where south-west English settlement predominated, the usual realisation is the standard-like dark or velar /l/ (with vocalised variants occurring in some sub-regions). Regarding postvocalic /t/, while /t/ allophones were not investigated in the Atlas, an alveolar slit fricative pronunciation does surface as a variant of the voiceless interdental fricative /θ/, often realised as [t] in NE. The Atlas contains this variant in words like *cloth, nothing* and *month* in the chiefly Irish-settled southern Avalon Peninsula (where fricated pronunciations in words such as these are often found today). Apart from a handful of communities adjacent to this area, English-settled regions do not display lenited /t/.

   Palatal postvocalic /l/ and slit fricative /t/ also characterise the speech of the province's capital, St. John's, given the city's historical Irish roots. I outline later in this chapter the social profiles associated with these two features, as revealed by the Sociolinguistic Survey of St. John's English (SSSJE), conducted in the early 1980s. This study uses a traditional Labovian framework

---

[4] Note that in NE the lenited or 'slit fricative' variant of /t/, just as in Irish and other Irish-origin varieties, is restricted to postvocalic environment (to be understood as also including post-sonorant, as in *punt* or *part*). Lenition of /t/ tends to be most frequent in pre-pause (utterance final) position, but is also common intervocalically, whether within (for example *ditto, better*) or across (*bit of*) word boundaries (Clarke 2010: 54).

(Labov 1966) to obtain a sample of 120 native speakers of St. John's English (SJE), stratified by age, sex, socio-economic status (SES) and ethno-religious background (the last factor used Roman Catholic vs. Protestant religious affiliation as a proxy for Irish vs. English ancestry; see Clarke 2012 for more information on all these variables). Of the four age cohorts examined (15–19, 20–34, 35–54, 55+), only members of the first two would have grown up entirely in post-Confederation Newfoundland. SSSJE also attempted to capture a range of stylistic registers, from informal ('casual') conversational interview style to more formal registers obtained via a series of reading tasks, including the word list style reported on here. SPSS Analysis of Variance (ANOVA) was applied to relative frequencies of usage, per speaker, of each linguistic variant, in each style, to assess the significance of the speaker-related factors.

SSSJE reveals that by the early 1980s neither palatal /l/ nor lenited /t/ constituted the broad community norm. Across the entire sample, the palatal variant of /l/ occurs in casual (conversational) style at an overall rate of 35 per cent, considerably less than the standard-like velar contoid pronunciation (64 per cent). Slit fricative /t/ likewise represents a minority variant, occurring at an overall rate of only 12 per cent in casual style, and from 24 to 40 per cent in word list style, depending on linguistic environment (intervocalic vs. prepausal, respectively).

Figures 3.2 and 3.3 provide an age breakdown of percentage usage rates for the two features, in casual and formal styles (for slit fricative /t/, formal style is represented in intervocalic environment). In both registers, for both features, age level proved statistically significant. The apparent time profiles revealed by Figures 3.2 and 3.3 are typical of change in progress: they show a linear (monotonic) pattern, representing a decline in use across generations. This decline is particularly dramatic in the case of postvocalic /l/, with teenagers on average using the palatal pronunciation between 48 and 57 per cent less than the 55+ generation, depending on style.

These age profiles are highly suggestive of dialect levelling, whereby local variants are receding in the face of increased competition from supralocal North American features. However, a closer look at the social profiles associated with these two features – interpreted in the context of the city's changing demographics since 1940 – indicates that a more nuanced interpretation is warranted. The following two subsections examine each feature in greater depth.

4.1   Palatal Postvocalic /l/

Figure 3.2 reveals a fairly flat stylistic profile for palatal postvocalic /l/, which tends to suggest little overall awareness on the part of speakers. However, the social patterns associated with this variant echo those displayed by stigmatised local features. Thus palatal /l/ is used significantly more by St. John's males

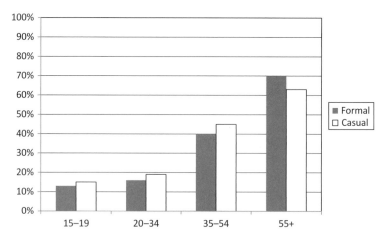

Figure 3.2: Palatal postvocalic /l/ by age group. (F (3,82) = 38.07, p < .001, casual style (6526 tokens); F (3,82) = 38.24, p < .001, formal (4968 tokens).[5]

than females, and by groups toward the lower rather than the upper end of the socio-economic spectrum.[6]

Yet unlike most of the two dozen or so phonetic features investigated by SSSJE, palatal /l/ also shows a close correlation with ethno-religious background: it is utilised significantly more often by St. John's residents of Irish than non-Irish ancestry, particularly in formal register (F (1,83) = 9.62, $p < .01$ in conversational style; F (1,83) = 13.10, $p < .001$ in word list style). When age level is examined in combination with ethno-religious background (see Figure 3.4), it is evident that Irish versus non-Irish origin plays out in all age groups. However, differences are least marked among St. John's residents aged 55+. For this group, all of whom were born prior to 1927 and grew up

---

[5] ANOVA investigates whether variation (mean variance) between groups (in Figure 3.2, between age levels) is significantly greater than within-group variation (here, within each age level). The larger the F-ratio (the ratio of between-group variation divided by within-group variation), the greater the likelihood of significant differences between groups. The probability (p value) of the F-ratio being due to chance is determined in conjunction with the degrees of freedom associated with both the numerator and denominator of this ratio (degrees of freedom appear here, and elsewhere, within brackets, immediately before the F value). A p of $< .001$ indicates that the F-value is likely to have resulted from chance in less than one case out of 1000. Here and elsewhere, separate ANOVAs were run for each of the two styles investigated. Post-hoc tests which would indicate exactly where the between-group significance lies are not reported on in this chapter.

[6] For speaker sex, F (1,82) = 4.88, $p < .05$ (casual style); formal style not significant. For SES, F (4,82) = 12.36, $p < .001$ (casual); F (4,82) = 9.64, $p < .001$ (formal).

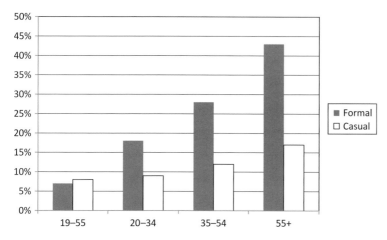

Figure 3.3: Slit fricative /t/ by age group. (F (3,82) = 9.50, p < .001, casual style (18870 tokens); F (3,82) = 23.53, p < .001, formal style (1440 tokens).

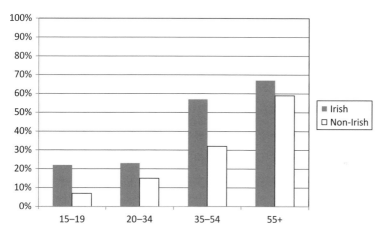

Figure 3.4: Palatal postvocalic /l/ by age and ethno-religious background (for casual style no significant interaction is evident between the two social variables).[7]

---

[7] In simplified terms, the lack of a significant interaction between the two social factors examined means that they act independently – that is, the impact of one is not significantly dependent on the level (namely the subgroup) of the other. Thus, in Figure 3.4, the (direction of the) effect of ethno-religious background on the realisation of postvocalic /l/ is sufficiently similar from one age level to another to conclude that these two social factors produce no significantly different results among subgroups when acting in combination.

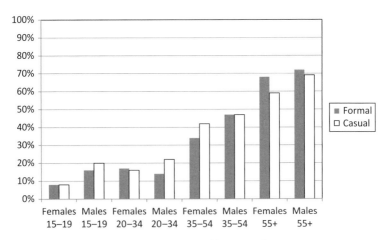

Figure 3.5: Palatal postvocalic /l/ by age and sex.

in pre-Confederation Newfoundland, the palatal variant obviously constitutes the regional norm. Further insight is provided by examining age and sex simultaneously. Figure 3.5 shows that, among men and women in the 55+ age level, the palatal variant displays the profile of a prestige norm, since both groups use it more frequently in formal than in casual style. This pattern is not generally replicated among the three younger age groups, for whom the standard-like dark (velar) variant is more common in formal style.

Here, then, we see the transformation of a feature which originally indexed region (place) into a marker whose primary associations are social. In addition to the continued link to speaker ancestry (as represented by ethno-religious background), these include, as noted earlier, associations with younger rather than older speakers, men rather than women, and lower rather than higher SES levels. It is tempting to interpret this situation as a case of dialect levelling, in which the competing supralocal 'mainland-like' velar postvocalic /l/ is gaining ground among more upwardly mobile and outward-looking segments of the St. John's population, to the detriment of the traditional pronunciation. This is, in fact, the interpretation offered by Clarke (1991) (see also Chambers [2012]). The situation is more complex, however, since this interpretation fails to take into account twentieth century population dynamics and internal migration within the province. As Clarke (2012) points out, the period since 1940 (particularly the decade 1940–50) represents a time of particularly intense in-migration from rural Newfoundland to urban St. John's. Rural in-migrants, who hailed chiefly from the English-settled north-east coast of the island, would have brought with them their velar /l/ pronunciation. Clarke (2012: 510) suggests that the ultimate reason for the decline of palatal /l/ 'may well lie in the non-reinforcement of the urban 'founder' variant (Irish-origin clear l/) on the part of Newfoundland in-migrants from SWE [south-west English]-settled areas of the province'. As Figure 3.4 shows, this is evidenced by the large drop in use of the palatal variant among speakers of non-Irish origin in the 35–54-year-old cohort.

4.2   Lenited /t/

As we have seen, SSSJE indicates that the feature of /t/ lenition in words like *bit* and *bitter* is also undergoing decline in apparent time. Prior to examining the social profiles associated with /t/ lenition in SJE, however, a brief word is in order on findings for other speech varieties in which this fairly unusual Irish-originating articulation has been documented.

To date, research on stop lenition[8] in English has tended to focus on its articulatory and acoustic properties (see, e.g., Sangster 2001 for Liverpool; Jones and Llamas 2008 for Dublin and the northern English city of Middles-brough; Gardner 2013 for Nova Scotia, Canada). Few studies have investi-gated its social correlates, and those that have do not report uniform findings. Wells (1982: 429) notes that /t/ lenition occurs at all social levels in Irish English. Likewise, Sangster (2001) has found it not to be socio-economically stratified in adolescent Liverpool English, though she speculates that it origin-ated in working-class speech. In Australian English, on the contrary, Tollfree (2001) has observed an association between fricated /t/ and middle rather than lower socio-economic levels. Similar findings have emerged from other Aus-tralian studies (Jones and McDougall 2006; Loakes and McDougall 2007). Regarding register, while Hickey (1984) has suggested that /t/ frication in Irish English is a feature of casual rather than more formal (reading) styles, Tollfree (2001) has come to the opposite conclusion for Australian English. In any case, its use in citation forms is well documented (Sangster 2001; Jones and Llamas 2008).

Social meanings are of course often locally constructed, so the aformen-tioned disparities are not particularly surprising. But what, if anything, do these findings have to offer with respect to the Newfoundland situation? Despite its similarity to palatal /l/ in apparent time, the social profiles displayed by lenited /t/ in SJE are otherwise quite different.[9] As Figure 3.6

---

[8] While stop lenition (fricativisation) tends to be most common for /t/, it can also occur for /p/ and /k/ (as in Liverpool English), along with /d/. In Irish-originating NE, lenition also occurs for /p k d/, though less frequently than for /t/.

[9] In the NE varieties reported on here, 'lenited' /t/ refers uniquely to the 'slit fricative' alveolar/alveodental variant of postvocalic /t/, represented by Wells (1982: 429–30) with the IPA symbol [t̞]. It does not include such realisations as a highly aspirated stop (which is discussed near the end of this section). Slit fricative /t/ involves a relatively flat tongue position, rather than the front-to-back tongue 'groove' associated with such fricatives as /θ/ and /s/.

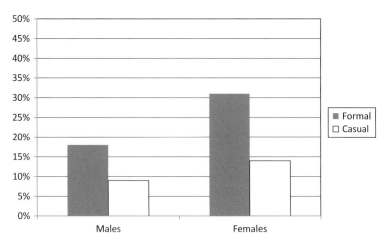

Figure 3.6: Slit fricative /t/ by sex. (F (1,82) = 10.45, p < .01, casual style; F (1,82) = 10.16, p < .01, formal style).

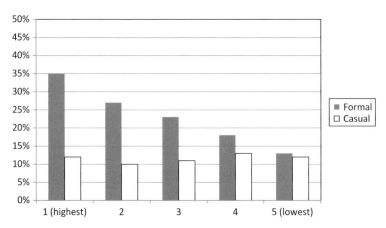

Figure 3.7: Slit fricative /t/ by SES level. (F (4,82) = 6.66, p < .001, formal style; SES not significant in casual style).

indicates, the local variant is favoured significantly more by women than by men. In fact, in casual style, the greatest users by far of lenited /t/ are women in the oldest (55+) age group: their 20 per cent usage rate is a full 7 per cent more than that of men of comparable age, whose rate is almost identical to that of women in the next highest (35–54) age cohort (for age x sex, *F* (3/83) = 3.49, *p* < .05). Figure 3.7 reveals that, in formal style at

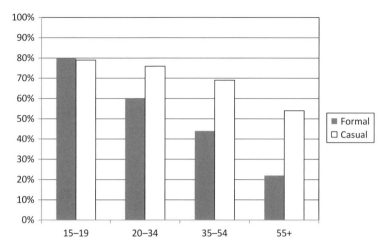

Figure 3.8: Post-tonic /t/ flapping by age group. (F (3,82) = 25.61, p < .001, casual style (9944 tokens); F (3,82) = 40.13, p < .001, formal style (2160 tokens)).

least, the lenited pronunciation is favoured by groups towards the upper rather than lower extremities of the socio-economic hierarchy. Figures 3.6 and 3.7 also show that sex and SES differences are considerably more marked in formal than casual style. In short, the local lenited variant bears the stamp of a prestige feature. Yet, if we glance back at the overall age profile shown in Figure 3.3, we see evidence of a change in social evaluation. Style-shifting in the direction of lenited /t/ in formal style is by far most evident in the 55+ age group, and entirely absent among teenagers. For teens, then, the slit fricative variant no longer represents a formal style target.

The social patterning associated with lenited /t/ is in fact best understood in the context of a variant with which it competes in postvocalic post-tonic position, whether medially (as in *better*) or across word boundaries (as in *set-up*). This is the voiced flap (tap), which in SSSJE represents both the casual and formal style norms in this environment, occurring at overall cross-sample rates of 70 and 52 per cent, respectively. Figures 3.8 and 3.9 show significant age and sex differences, respectively, for the flap pronunciation; these prove to be the mirror image of the patterns associated with the lenited variant. Thus men display significantly higher flap ratios than women, a difference particularly obvious in formal style. As to age, choice of the flap is inversely proportional to age level.

Figure 3.8 also sheds light on the change in social evaluation noted earlier: for the teenage group alone, the flap is selected as much in formal as in casual

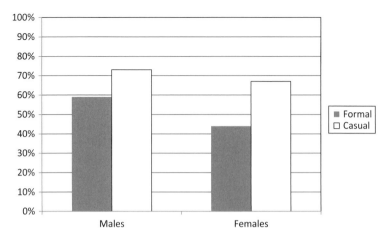

Figure 3.9: Post-tonic /t/ flapping by sex. (F (1,82) = 4.23, p < .05, casual style; F (1,82) = 7.07, p < .01, formal style).

style. In short, the social profile associated with the flap variant in SJE suggests a male-led change in progress.[10]

The incremental change in apparent time towards adoption of the flap echoes the situation documented in supralocal varieties (see, e.g., the urban Canadian sociolinguistic studies of de Wolf 1992 and Woods 1999). Its incursion into SJE again suggests dialect levelling, as a form associated with 'mainland' North American English gradually displaces the local lenited variant. Yet, as in the case of postvocalic /l/, a confluence of factors may be involved. Flap adoption in SJE may well have been reinforced by the post-1940 trend towards increased in-migration from rural Newfoundland to the capital city. For migrants from south-west English-settled coastal Newfoundland, the flap would have been the usual pronunciation in words like *better* or *ditto* (Clarke 2010: 53).

The social profiles outlined earlier for both fricated and flapped /t/ in SJE closely parallel findings reported for Australian English. Loakes and McDougall (2007: 1448), for example, indicate that in Melbourne lenited /t/ seems to be 'favoured by female speakers from higher socio-economic backgrounds, and less preferred by male speakers and speakers from lower socio-economic

---

[10] This pattern of a classic Labovian 'change from below' finds some support in the SES profile associated with the flap variant: while in both styles SES differences are not significant, the flap is used more by groups towards the lower end of the socio-economic hierarchy. Yet SSSJE also incorporated a '(Minimal) Pairs' reading style, which focused participants' attention on intervocalic /t/ via such contrasting pairs as *matter/madder*. Only here did SES prove statistically significant (see later in this chapter for ideologies associated with 'hypo/hyperarticulated' /t/).

backgrounds'. Males, on the contrary, seem more likely than females to use a tap pronunciation of /t/. Is this high degree of similarity in two locations halfway across the globe from each other due purely to chance? While the answer to this question remains elusive, there are tantalising clues. The flap pronunciation, representing a hypoarticulation in the form of a natural phonetic assimilation to the intervocalic environment, may be perceived as 'sloppy,' or, as Eckert (2008: 468) puts it, may evoke such stereotypes as 'anti-intellectual and loutish'. The 'hyperarticulated' (that is, released) /t/, on the contrary, evokes the opposite stereotype, by virtue of 'a broader national ideology that links hyperarticulation to clarity and clarity to education and power' (Eckert 2008: 470). In its acoustic and perceptual similarity to aspirated released /t/, the fricated /t/ pronunciation may likewise index careful and 'proper' speech – hence the close parallels in its social profile between SJE and Australian English.

The above does not suggest, of course, that a generalised ideology will trump other factors in any given locale: individual variants can be expected to index different social meanings and perform different social functions from community to community. For example, in her study of stop frication in the community of Placentia, on Newfoundland's Irish-settled southern Avalon Peninsula, Power (2011) does not find this feature to be associated with careful speech and the typical users thereof (notably women and upper SES levels). Rather, stop frication is most characteristic of younger community residents. Parris (2009) documents a similar situation in Cape Breton, Nova Scotia. Both researchers attribute this development to local conditions – in the latter case, economic decline and out-migration appear to have led to increasing adoption of a marker of local affiliation on the part of younger speakers. For these speakers, then, stop frication indexes localness (place), and all that this connotes.

The ability of local features to do social semiotic work relates to their degree of indexicality. While both palatal /l/ and lenited /t/ may be metapragmatically linked to the social meanings outlined earlier, for many, if not most, Newfoundlanders these two features are far from salient, and in fact seem to lie beneath the level of consciousness. They are not typically manipulated in the performance of local identity, nor are they generally linked to it discursively. In this regard, they differ from the features examined in the following section.

5.   Enregistered Symbols of Place: TH-stopping and H-deletion

One of the most iconic of Newfoundland features is TH-stopping, the variable substitution of (usually alveolar) stops for the interdental fricatives /θ/ and /ð/, so that *thin* sounds like *tin*, and *other* sounds like *udder*. TH-stopping, particularly frequent for voiced /ð/, occurs in every community in the province

(Clarke and Hiscock 2013), and has been documented in NE for well over two hundred years (Clarke 2010: 45, 160). A highly salient and stereotyped feature (which unlike many others is easily represented in writing, as in 'tree' for *three*, 'dis' for *this*), TH-stopping functions at the metadiscursive level, and has become fully 'enregistered' (Johnstone *et al.* 2006) in its ideological link to Newfoundland identity.

TH-stopping is of course by no means unique to Newfoundland – it occurs in such varieties as Irish, African American, and Caribbean English (see e.g., the many mentions of this feature in Schneider *et al.* 2004). It is also found in some American English varieties of European origin. For these, Eckert (2008: 471) suggests that, in its association with immigrant groups, this feature has taken on a range of ideological meanings, an 'indexical field', which includes lack of education and, in some urban contexts, toughness. Given the pragmatic salience of TH-stopping in many varieties of English, Woolard (2008: 443) speculates that this results from the indexical association of /ð/ with definiteness and deixis (as in *these, them* and *those*); it is thus 'especially ripe for social semiotic and stylistic work', including acting as a driver for linguistic change.[11]

In sociolinguistic studies which deal with rural Newfoundland (see, for instance, Colbourne 1982 for communities on Long Island, just off Newfoundland's northeast coast; Van Herk et al. 2007 and Childs *et al.* 2010, for the small village of Petty Harbour near St. John's), TH-stopping frequently exhibits an age profile indicative of a feature in decline. It also bears the hallmark of a variant that carries overt stigmatisation, via its association with men rather than women, and with casual rather than formal speech styles. SSSJE results for TH-stopping echo these rural findings for gender and style. Particularly noteworthy in the SJE study is the fact that stop variants display some of the most dramatic rates of style shifting of any of the features investigated. Moreover, TH-stopping also exhibits a higher degree of SES stratification than most SJE features. These findings attest to the high public profile of this feature, as an enregistered symbol of local identity (see Clarke 2012 for more information).

Despite the decline in apparent-time that emerges from some studies, and which is assumed by others (such as Childs and Van Herk 2013), the long history of TH-stopping in NE raises the question of whether it is a relatively stable feature, whose age gradations reflect intra-community fluctuations

---

[11] Woolard's hypothesis, however, would not explain why voiceless /θ/ behaves in much the same way as /ð/ within the English-speaking world, despite its lack of association with deixis. It also does not explain why in British English the change towards a labiodental articulation of the interdental fricatives (TH-fronting) is more advanced for /θ/ than for /ð/; while fronting of the former occurs in all environments, for the latter it is restricted to non-word-initial contexts.

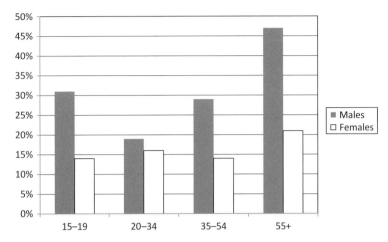

Figure 3.10: /Ɵ/-stopping in SSSJE by age and sex, informal style. (Age x sex interaction: F (3/83) = 2.66, p = .05; 4880 tokens).

associated with its use as a salient marker of local identity, rather than change in realtime. There are indications of this, in the form of non-linear age profiles, from both SSSJE and several rural Newfoundland sociolinguistic studies (Reid 1981; Lanari 1994). Reid's (1981) study of the small fishing community of Bay de Verde shows that, in casual style, rural speakers in the 17–30 age group select the stop variant of /ð/ at approximately the same rate as do speakers a generation older; this results from an unexpectedly high stopping rate on the part of younger women. In the south coast community of (greater) Burin, Lanari (1994) describes a similar situation for younger adults (aged 25–35, both male and female) with close ties to the fishing industry and strong local networks. In each of these cases, TH-stopping serves as an iconic symbol of local orientation and affiliation. With regards to urban St. John's, voiceless /θ/ stopping proved to be one of the very few features that does not exhibit a linear age distribution. As Figure 3.10 shows, this results from the exceptionally high use of stop variants by male teenagers (particularly, it should be added, from the lower end of the socio-economic spectrum), whose rate is surpassed only by the oldest (55+) male group. For these St. John's teens of the 1980s, TH-stopping represents a salient marker of masculine working-class identity.

Given its iconic nature, it is not surprising that TH-stopping can be called upon in various ways to project, and perform, highly localised – and variable – social meanings. This point emerges forcefully for NE in the work of Van Herk and colleagues (Van Herk *et al.* 2007; Childs *et al.* 2010). Childs and Van Herk (2013: 147) observe that '[t]he more locally-enregistered a variant becomes … the more speakers manipulate it to do social work for them'.

Yet this statement does not appear to hold for all highly enregistered features in NE – indexical field also plays a central role.

By way of example, take the feature of word-initial /h/ deletion (as in *heave* pronounced 'eave' or *hold* pronounced 'old'), along with its less frequent counterpart, non-etymological /h/ insertion (as in *eave* pronounced 'heave' or *old* pronounced 'hold'). Non-standard /h/ receives overt commentary both within and outside the province, is the butt of jokes, is exploited by dialect imitators and in dialect performance, and has even generated such local folk sayings as 'Drop your aitches in 'Olyrood ("Holyrood") and pick them up in Havondale ("Avondale")'.[12] In British varieties, H-deletion is highly stigmatised; Beal (2006: 48) indicates that it is 'one of the strongest shibboleths of lower-class and/or uneducated speech in England'. In NE, likewise, this feature carries strongly negative stereotypes. But more than this, it is a highly salient marker of region, or place. Inherited from south-west English founder populations, H-deletion (along with H-insertion) continues to correlate closely with areas of the island settled by the south-west English, and is absent from Irish-settled areas (Clarke 2010: 47–8; Clarke and Hiscock 2013). As such, it exists as a stereotype, epitomising a 'bay' identity for Newfoundlanders, in the 'townie' (urban St. John's) versus 'bay' (rural outport) ideological divide.

While non-standard /h/ patterning may be exploited with humorous intent by those who do not regularly use it, the few sociolinguistic studies that have analysed this feature in NE do not suggest that H-deletion is typically manipulated as a marker of local identity. Newhook (2002), in an investigation of a small south coast outport community, shows initial /h/ deletion to be the overwhelming community norm, in both casual and formal speech styles (see Figure 3.11). The overall casual style rate in Newhook's study (85 per cent) closely approximates the 84 per cent deletion rate found by Clarke *et al.* (2005) for a small sample of traditional rural NE speakers born between 1870 and 1930. This remarkable similarity over an apparent time span of more than a century suggests that this local feature displays a high degree of stability in NE. Figure 3.11 also shows little in the way of style-shifting, which might indicate a lack of awareness unusual for a stereotyped feature. This may result, at least in part, from the fact that /h/ does not appear to constitute an underlying phoneme for some speakers of south-west English-origin NE, but rather represents a sandhi phenomenon conditioned primarily by syllable stress (Clarke 2010: 47).

---

[12] Holyrood and Avondale are two rural communities under an hour's drive from St. John's. The saying is unintentionally ironic, since the area in question is largely Irish-settled and consequently does not display non-standard /h/ patterning, apart from the pronunciation of the letter *h* as 'haitch' (the case throughout Irish-settled Newfoundland, including St. John's). Perhaps, however, for 'townies', any area outside the capital is conceptualised as sufficiently rural as to be stereotyped as 'bay'.

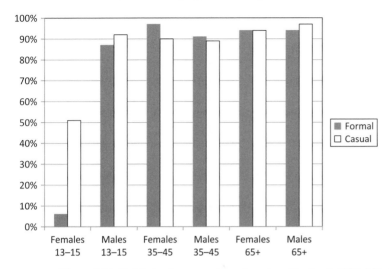

Figure 3.11: H-deletion by age and sex (based on Newhook 2002: 84). (Age, sex and age x sex statistically significant in both styles; in all cases, p < .001. N of tokens: 1306 [informal style]; 192 [formal style]).

Figure 3.11 indicates a very slight decline across the three age groups in Newhook's study, with one obvious exception: the dramatic reduction in use of this local feature on the part of teenage girls. Newhook attributes this to the supralocal orientation of this group. Unlike other members of her sample, including the teenage boys, these girls are socially mobile, and intend to pursue educational and employment opportunities outside the community. While H-deletion may signal local orientation (as possibly exhibited by a higher-than-expected formal style deletion rate among middle-aged women), the ideological association of this feature with rural outport Newfoundland leads to its suppression on the part of the teenage girls, particularly in formal (word list) style. This suggests that, while rurality may lie at the core of the widely disseminated construct of 'authentic' Newfoundland (see Section 2), this ideology does not resonate with all rural Newfoundlanders.

6.   Conclusion

In assessing the role played by dialect levelling (Beal 2006, 2010) in what the sociolinguistic literature has generally depicted as rapid linguistic change in Newfoundland English, this chapter has investigated a number of phonetic features which, according to apparent time profiles, are undergoing linguistic decline.

These consonant features, emblematic of place, reveal several different social patterns. Yet none appear to represent simple cases of dialect levelling, in the sense of replacement of local variants by supralocal mainland Canadian forms. Some features are in transition from generalised 'markers of place' (that is, community norms) towards greater specialisation, as they have come to index particular social groups. While this retraction might suggest a greater incursion of standard-like supralocal variants, the situation is considerably more complex, since local migration and demographic patterns must also be taken into account. Other features display a degree of stability – or perhaps more accurately, an 'ebb and flow' – in that their enregisterment as salient markers of local identity enables them to be utilised for purposes of regional affiliation on the part of younger speakers from one generation to another. Still, other local features appear remarkably robust, regardless of enregisterment and overtly negative stereotyping.

Yet it cannot be denied that at least some features closely associated with region are in decline. Many younger Newfoundlanders sound less local than their parents and grandparents, especially in formal styles. Features which were integral components of the urban speech of St. John's two or three generations ago (palatal postvocalic /l/, lenited /t/) have not diffused to form part of a Newfoundland regional standard. Yet perhaps the greatest threat comes not from external supralocal varieties, but from non-linguistic factors. The fragile economy in many areas of the province means that outport communities continue to disappear as rural populations decline, and with them their characteristic forms of speech. For the moment, however, local varieties remain strong, interwoven as they are with Newfoundland identity.

REFERENCES

Anonsen, Kay 1999. 'Confederation'. *TickleAce* 37: 48–51.

Beal, Joan C. 2006. *Language and Region*. London: Routledge.
    2010. *Introduction to Regional Englishes*. Edinburgh: Edinburgh University Press.

Chambers, Jack. K. 2012. 'Homogeneity as a sociolinguistic motive in Canadian English'. *World Englishes* 31: 467–77.

Childs, Becky, Paul De Decker, Rachel Deal, Tyler Kendall, Jennifer Thorburn, Maya Williamson, and Gerard Van Herk. 2010. 'Stop signs: The intersection of interdental fricatives and identity in Newfoundland'. *University of Pennsylvania Working Papers in Linguistics*, 16: 25–35.

Childs, Becky and Gerard Van Herk 2013. 'Superstars and bit players: Salience and the fate of local dialect features', in Barysevich, Alena, Alexandra D'Arcy, and David Heap (eds.), *Proceedings of Methods XIV. Papers from the Fourteenth International Conference on Methods in Dialectology,* Frankfurt: Peter Lang. pp. 139–48.

Clarke, Sandra 1991. 'Phonological variation and recent language change in St. John's English', in Cheshire, Jenny (ed.) 1991. *English around the World: Sociolinguistic Perspectives*. Cambridge: Cambridge University Press. pp. 108–22.

    2010. *Newfoundland and Labrador English*. Edinburgh: Edinburgh University Press.

    2012. 'From autonomy to heteronomy? Phonetic change in Newfoundland English'. *World Englishes* 31: 503–18.

Clarke, Sandra and Philip Hiscock 2013. The Dialect Atlas of Newfoundland and Labrador. www.dialectatlas.mun.ca.

Clarke, Sandra, Pauline Hollett, and Robert Hollett 2005. 'The story of /h/: A Newfoundland perspective'. Paper presented at the 12th International Conference on Methods in Dialectology, Moncton, New Brunswick.

Colbourne, B. Wade 1982. A sociolinguistic study of Long Island, Notre Dame Bay, Newfoundland. Unpublished M.A. thesis, Memorial University of Newfoundland.

Crummey, Michael. 2014. 'Where you 'longs to?' *The Globe and Mail*, 16 August 2014, F1, F5.

Delisle, Jennifer B. 2013. *The Newfoundland Diaspora: Mapping the Literature of Out-Migration*. Ontario: Wilfred Laurier University Press.

de Wolf, Gaelan D.1992. *Social and Regional Factors in Canadian English: A Study of Phonological Variables and Grammatical Items in Ottawa and Vancouver*. Toronto: Canadian Scholar's Press.

Eckert, Penelope 2008. 'Variation and the indexical field'. *Journal of Sociolinguistics* 12: 453–76.

Gardner, Matt H. 2013. 'The acoustic and articulatory characteristics of Cape Breton fricative /t/'. *Dialectologia et Geolinguistica* 21: 3–20.

Hickey, Raymond 1984. 'Coronal segments in Irish English'. *Journal of Linguistics* 20: 233–50.

Johnstone, Barbara, Jennifer Andrus, and Andrew E. Danielson 2006. 'Mobility, indexicality, and the enregisterment of "Pittsburghese"'. *Journal of English Linguistics* 34: 77–104.

Jones, Mark J. and Carmen Llamas 2008. 'Fricated realisations of /t/ in Dublin and Middlesbrough English: An acoustic analysis of plosive frication and surface fricative contrasts'. *English Language and Linguistics* 12: 419–43.

Jones, Mark and Kirsty McDougall 2006. 'A comparative acoustic study of Australian English fricated /t/: Assessing the Irish (English) link', in Warren, Paul and Catherine I. Watson (eds.), *Proceedings of the Eleventh Australasian International Conference on Speech Science and Technology,* Auckland, NZ: Australasian Speech Science and Technology Association. pp. 6–12.

Labov, William 1966. *The Social Stratification of English in New York City*. Washington, D.C.: Center for Applied Linguistics.

Lanari, Catherine E. P. 1994. A sociolinguistic study of the Burin region of Newfoundland. Unpublished M.A. thesis, Memorial University of Newfoundland.

Loakes, Deborah and Kirsty McDougall 2007. 'Frication of Australian English /p,t,k/: Group tendencies and individual differences'. *Proceedings of the 16t[h] International Conference of Phonetic Sciences* (ICPhS XVI) Saarbrucken, Germany.

MacDonald, Martha 2014. 'English in Labrador: Demonstrating difference'. *Regional Language Studies ... Newfoundland (RLS)* 25: 23–32.

Newhook, Amanda 2002. A sociolinguistic study of Burnt Islands, Newfoundland. Unpublished M.A. thesis, Memorial University of Newfoundland.

Parris, Samantha 2009. 'The reanalysis of a traditional feature in industrial Cape Breton'. Paper presented at Change and Variation in Canada III conference, Ottawa, Ontario.

Power, Suzanne 2011. 'The linguistic trace of an American Base: Identity practices and sociophonetic variation in word-final oral stop frication in Placentia, Newfoundland'. Paper presented at the 35th annual meeting, Atlantic Provinces Linguistic Association, Sydney, Nova Scotia.

Reid, Gerald 1981. The sociolinguistic patterns of the Bay de Verde speech community. Unpublished M.Phil.paper, Memorial University of Newfoundland.

Sangster, Catherine 2001. 'Lenition of alveolar stops in Liverpool English'. *Journal of Sociolinguistics* 5: 401–12.

Schneider, Edgar W., Kate Burridge, Bernd Kortmann, Rajend Mesthrie, and Clive Upton (eds.) 2004. *A Handbook of Varieties of English, vol I: Phonology*. Berlin: Mouton de Gruyter.

Tollfree, Laura 2001. 'Variation and change in Australian English consonants: Reduction of /t/', in Blair, David and Peter Collins (eds.) *English in Australia*. Amsterdam: John Benjamins. pp. 45–67.

Van Herk, Gerard, Becky Childs, and Jennifer Thorburn. 2007. 'Identity marking and affiliation in an urbanizing Newfoundland community', in Cichocki, Wladyslaw (ed.) 2007. *Papers from the 31st Annual Meeting of the Atlantic Provinces Linguistic Association*. Fredericton, NB: University of New Brunswick. pp. 85–94.

Wells, John C. 1982. *Accents of English*, vol 2. Cambridge: Cambridge University Press.

Woods, Howard B. 1999. *The Ottawa Survey of Canadian English*. Ontario: Strathy Language Unit, Queen's University.

Woolard, Kathryn A. 2008. 'Why *dat* now?: Linguistic-anthropological contributions to the explanation of sociolinguistic icons and change'. *Journal of Sociolinguistics* 12: 432–52.

4 Variation and Change in the Realisation of /r/ in an Isolated Northumbrian Dialect

Warren Maguire

1. Introduction

One of the most distinctive traits of the traditional dialects of north-east England is the pronunciation of /r/ as a uvular fricative [ʁ], a pronunciation known as the '(Northumbrian) Burr' (Wells 1982: 368–9, Beal 2000). This pronunciation of /r/ in north-east England is almost unique amongst dialects of English, even though it is common (and increasing) in languages all over Europe (Chambers and Trudgill 1980: 186–9), and it has been around for at least the last 300 years. Although many geographical regions are indexically linked to linguistic features, as the chapters in this volume demonstrate, the limited geographical scope of uvular /r/ results in a distinctive language-place association seldom found for other linguistic features. In late nineteenth and early to mid-twentieth century descriptions of dialects from the north-east of England (Ellis 1889, Ryland 1998, Orton and Dieth 1962–71), uvular /r/ was the only pronunciation recorded across most of Northumberland and north Durham, including the area in and around Tyneside. But something dramatic appears to have happened to the pronunciation of /r/ in the north-east of England in more recent times. If you travel or live there today, you will struggle to hear a single person utter a single instance of the Northumbrian Burr. This is certainly true of urban centres such as Newcastle, where, in twenty years of living and working there, I never heard it once from a native of the city. It is also increasingly true of rural Northumberland. In fact, in places such as Newcastle many people may be shocked to discover that such an exotic sound, more likely to be associated with French and German in the classroom, was used by their ancestors in the not-so-distant past.

But what is the reason for the striking difference between the pronunciation of /r/ in early twentieth century north-east English dialects, and its pronunciation in the region today? Have people in the north-east of England abandoned, over the space of a few decades, a pronunciation which was once synonymous with their region? Or do traditional dialect records give us a misleading impression of the state of affairs in north-east English dialects, over-emphasising the degree to which speakers and communities in the past used the Northumbrian Burr? And is it true that, even in remotest Northumberland, people no longer pronounce /r/ this way? This chapter seeks to answer these questions by examining in detail the pronunciation habits of a range of speakers in a corpus of recordings from one isolated rural location in Northumberland – the Holy Island of Lindisfarne.

In the next section of this chapter, I set the necessary background for this study, examining previous data for, and studies of, the Northumbrian Burr, and introducing Holy Island and the corpus of recordings the analysis in this chapter is based on. In Section 3, I describe the analysis of /r/ in this corpus, and present the results that arise from it. In Section 4, I discuss the relevance of these results for understanding the diachronic and synchronic status of the Northumbrian Burr in Holy Island, and what this tells us about the questions raised earlier. It will be seen that the Holy Island corpus sheds considerable light on this little understood phenomenon which is, it would seem, about to disappear as a feature of everyday speech from the dialects of the north-east of England.

2.   Background

In his early eighteenth century *Tour Through the Whole Island of Great Britain*, Daniel Defoe (1724–7, vol. iii: 232–3) made the following comment about Northumberland:

I must not quit *Northumberland* without taking notice, that the Natives of this Country, of the antient original Race or Families, are distinguished by a *Shibboleth* upon their Tongues in pronouncing the letter *R*, which they cannot utter without a hollow Jarring in the Throat, by which they are as plainly known, as a Foreigner is in pronouncing the *Th*: this they call the *Northumberland R*, or *Wharle*; and the Natives value themselves upon that Imperfection, because, forsooth, it shews the Antiquity of their Blood.

Here we have one of the earliest mentions of this peculiarity of Northumberland speech,[1] which has thus been around for at least the last 300 years, and was considered a defining feature of the region and a source of pride and identity by its users.[2]

By the time we get to the first linguistic descriptions of north-east English dialects in the late nineteenth century (in particular Ellis 1889: 637–80, note especially pp. 641–4), the Northumbrian Burr was recorded as the only pronunciation of /r/ in the dialects of Northumberland (excluding the far

---

[1] Wales (2006: 101) notes one other slightly earlier brief reference to the phenomenon, from 1724.
[2] Note that Heslop (1892: xxiv) refers to a suggestion by famed Scottish dialectologist and lexicographer, Dr. J. A. H. Murray, that Shakespeare indirectly referred to the phenomenon as a characteristic of the speech of Harry Hotspur in King Henry IV, 2nd part, Act II, Scene 3. Whether Hotspur's 'speaking thick' actually refers to the Burr is of course unknown.

south-west, and with variation between it and [r] at Berwick-upon-Tweed, right next to the Scottish Border), Tyneside, and north County Durham. This is likewise the case in the dialects documented in the *Orton Corpus* (Rydland 1998, data collected between 1928 and 1939), though [ɹ] for /r/ is fairly common at Newburn, just west of Newcastle (and again, Berwick varies between [ʁ] and [r]). And in the last exhaustive survey of the traditional dialects of England, the *Survey of English Dialects* (SED) in the 1950s (Orton and Dieth 1962–71), uvular /r/ was the only pronunciation recorded for all of the Northumberland locations away from the southwest of the county and for the two northernmost locations in County Durham, including the three locations surrounding Tyneside: Earsdon (Nb6) and Heddon (Nb8) in Northumberland, and Washington (Du1) in Durham. It looks as if the Burr was a consistent feature of north-east English dialects until about 60 years ago, though there is some evidence of its decline in and around the Tyneside conurbation – note the case of Newburn referred to earlier and Viereck (1966: 72), who, in his study of the dialect of Gateshead, found that [ʁ] and [ɹ] were in variation with each other in this urban area.

The story of the Burr since the mid-twentieth century has continued to be one of decline, though we are lacking evidence for most areas in north-east England. Påhlsson (1972) is the classic study of the feature in rural Northumberland (the village of Thropton, SED location Nb3), and he finds that 'the Burr seems to be faced with fairly bleak prospects for the future, although it constitutes a prominent and vigorous feature of the dialect of the community at present' (Påhlsson 1972: 222), since it is common in the speech of his older speakers but almost entirely absent from the speech of the younger members of the community (though it was also found in the speech of young children who were still under the direct linguistic influence of their parents). This appears to represent a striking change in the fortunes of this shibboleth of Northumberland speech, given that the Burr was recorded as the only pronunciation of /r/ in Thropton in the SED, just sixteen years before Påhlsson carried out his fieldwork.

More recently, the Burr appears to have disappeared from most of the north-east of England entirely, especially in urban areas and the speech of the young. Beal *et al.* (2012: 40) note that 'The "Northumbrian Burr" [ʁ] is nowadays completely absent from urban areas and indeed very rare in rural areas, so much so that its use by speakers is said by Beal (2008: 140) to be little more than a "party trick"'. In the far north Northumberland town of Berwick-upon-Tweed, Llamas *et al.* (2009) and Llamas (2010) find that uvular articulations of /r/ are in the minority and are essentially absent in the speech of young speakers. There is certainly some truth in Beal's reference to the Burr as a 'party trick'; it is possible to find people in Northumberland who do not use the Burr, but who have a folk memory of it (cf. Trudgill 1999) and who can produce phrases such as 'Round and round the rugged rock the ragged rascal runs' with a series of (often hyperarticulated) uvular fricatives. This is reminiscent of the use of trilled [r] by middle-class speakers in Scotland as an overt Scotticism in the production of set Scots phrases and poetry (Aitken 1984: 107–8). In other words, the Burr appears to have changed, in the terminology of Labov (1994: 78), from being a sociolinguistic 'indicator' (an unmarked linguistic variant not subject to stylistic stratification) or a 'marker' (a regular feature in the speech community subject to stylistic variation) to a 'stereotype' (a feature which is subject to overt comment and metalinguistic usage), which can be used for purposes such as signalling identity and regionality without having any real linguistic life in the community (see Beal 2009, and chapters in this volume, for discussion of such enregisterment of linguistic features). If the evidence in traditional dialect studies and Påhlsson (1972) is anything to go by, this has been a very quick change, at least in rural Northumberland, where the Burr appears to have been a regular pronunciation feature until at least the middle of the twentieth century.

But as I pointed out in the introduction to this chapter, there are many questions that remain unanswered about the history of the Northumbrian Burr since that time. Just to reiterate, was it really the case that traditional dialect speaking communities had such high levels of the Burr in the mid-twentieth century as traditional studies suggest? Was there, in fact, variation in these communities and, if so, of what type? Do traditional dialect studies, through their rather arcane methodologies (see the discussions in Trudgill and Chambers 1980, and Petyt 1980), give us a false impression of the frequency of the Burr at the time? And what has happened since then? Has the Burr disappeared from the rural dialects of northeast England as Påhlsson (1972) predicts and as Beal (2008) suggests?

In order to address these questions, the rest of this chapter examines a corpus of recordings from the Holy Island of Lindisfarne in north-east England. Holy Island lies off the far north-east coast of Northumberland, 14 miles by road from Berwick and 60 miles from Newcastle. At 'high water', the Island is cut off from the mainland, but at 'low water' it is connected to the rest of Northumberland by a tarmacked causeway, which was constructed in the mid-1950s (prior to that access to the Island was over sand and mudflats, or by boat). Holy Island was, until the mid-twentieth century, a traditional community of farmers and fishermen, but in the last sixty years the economy of the Island has been transformed to one based on tourism and hospitality (though fishing and farming still continue to a small extent). The population of the Island is currently about 180 people,[3] less than half of which are native,

---

[3] Office for National Statistics, www.neighbourhood.statistics.gov.uk/dissemination/LeadTableView .do?a=7&b=11124733&c=holy+island&d=16&e=13&g=6452883&i=1001x1003x1004&m=0&r= 1&s=1417515923392&enc=1&dsFamilyId=2491.

representing a significant decline overall and in the number of natives from the middle of the twentieth century onwards (Berger 1980 records a population of 230, 190 of which were native, in the early 1970s). In addition to the dramatic changes in its population and economy, education practices on the Island have changed considerably since the mid-twentieth century, from a situation where children were educated solely at the primary school on the Island, to one where the few remaining children on the Island attend infant school on the Island and (tide allowing) at Lowick on the mainland, followed by middle and high school in Berwick-upon-Tweed, requiring them to board in the town through the week. In other words, young people on the Island have, for the last few decades, had a rather different upbringing than their parents and grandparents, growing up in an Island dominated by tourists and spending much of their time away from the Island itself. This relatively fast change in Holy Island society mirrors the apparently rapid change in the pronunciation of /r/ in Northumberland discussed earlier, making Holy Island a fascinating place to study this important feature of north-east English dialects.

The dialect of Holy Island remained unrecorded until the early 1970s, despite its distinct character compared with other Northumberland varieties. But between 1971 and 1973, a Swiss PhD student, Jörg Berger, visited the Island and made a collection of reel-to-reel audio recordings of natives from the Island (see Berger 1980). This corpus of recordings consists of about 23 hours of conversations and of dialect questionnaire sessions (especially the SED questionnaire and the Fishing Questionnaire as detailed in Wright 1964 and Elmer 1973 respectively) between Berger and the Islanders. Berger gave me these recordings in 2003, and I have added further recordings to the corpus, two from the *Millennium Memory Bank* (MMB) collection and four made by myself on Holy Island between 2006 and 2013.[4] It is this corpus of recordings which is analysed in this chapter. In addition, I have analysed the speech of a selection of natives of the Island in the Tyne Tees (2007) television documentary *Diary of an Island*, which contains short stretches of speech by a number of males born in the 1940s, 1960s and 1970s, and one male born in the early 1990s (see Section 3 for further details).

A key feature of Berger's data is that it contains recordings of speakers not only in 'normal' conversation with Berger and other Islanders, but also of

---

[4] Thanks to Jonathan Robinson from the British Library for providing me with copies of the MMB recordings. Berger's original recordings, along with two hours of the new recordings made by me, now form the *Dialect of the Holy Island of Lindisfarne* (DHIL) corpus, a corpus of time-aligned orthographic transcriptions and audio recordings hosted, via a password-protected interface, on the *Diachronic Electronic Corpus of Tyneside English* website (http://research.ncl .ac.uk/decte/dhil.htm). Potential users may request access to the DHIL corpus via the website. I would like to thank the British Academy (grant no. SG-112357) for providing the funds to construct the DHIL corpus.

Table 4.1: *Speakers from the Holy Island corpus.*

Speaker	Occupation	Source	Speech Types	/r/ Tokens
1893F	'Herring girl'	Berger	Q + N	256
1900M*	Fisherman, railway worker	Berger	Q + N	22
1901M*	Fisherman	Berger	Q + N	67
1902F	Shop keeper	Berger	Q + N	151
1903M	Fisherman	Berger	Q + N	92
1904M	Wireless operator	Berger	Q + N	295
1905M	Various jobs locally	Berger	Q + N	125
1906M	Fisherman	Berger	N	174
1908M	Driver	Berger	Q + N	221
1908F	Housewife	Berger	N	289
1910M	Fisherman, lifeboat man	Berger	Q + N	310
1910F*	Housewife	Berger	Q + N	46
1911M*	Farmer	Berger	Q + N	27
1913M*	Farmer	Berger	Q + N	36
1914M	Various, inc. Navy	Berger	Q + N	82
1926M	Merchant Navy, painter and decorator	MMB	N	463
1942M*	Fisherman	Berger	N	18
1945Ma	Fisherman	Berger	Q + N	497
1945Mb	Fisherman	WM 2006	Q + N	234
1947M	Fisherman, bus driver (on the Island)	WM 2013	N	384
1963F	Hotelier	WM 2013	N	100
1965F	Priory attendant	MMB	N	100
1967M	Navy, publican	WM 2013	N	100

many of those speakers giving answers to dialect questionnaires, such as the SED. This means that we can get an insight into how speakers act, linguistically, when subject to traditional dialect elicitation procedures compared with how they speak otherwise. This is important, given the concerns expressed earlier about the nature of traditional dialect data, and these recordings provide an important check on the representativeness of traditional accounts, and the extent to which speakers styleshift under such questioning. In this chapter, I divide the speech of the speakers in the corpus into N (or 'normal') speech, which represents their speech when they are not specifically answering dialect questionnaire questions, and Q (or 'questionnaire') speech, when they are giving the answers to those questionnaires. Although N speech is available for all speakers in the corpus, Q speech is not. For full details of all of the speakers analysed in this paper, and the speech types that they produce, see Tables 4.1 and 4.2.

Speakers in Table 4.1 are identified by a code consisting of four numbers (their year of birth) and a letter (M for 'male', F for 'female'). The number of tokens of /r/ analysed for each speaker is indicated (see further in Section 3;

Table 4.2: *Speakers from* Diary of an Island.

Speaker	Decade of Birth	Occupation
OM1	1940s	Unknown
OM2	1940s	Businessman
OM3	1940s	Farmer
OM4	1940s	Farmer
OM5 (=1942M)	1940s	Fisherman
YM1	1960s	Tour guide
YM2	1960s	Shopkeeper
YM3	1960s	Fisherman
YM4	1970s	Publican
YM5	1990s	School pupil

note that speakers marked *, though included in the analysis, only contribute a small amount to Berger's recordings and the number of tokens they produce is consequently somewhat low compared to the other speakers). Note also that 1945Ma and 1945Mb are the same individual, who was recorded by Berger in the early 1970s and by myself in 2006. I have kept the analyses of these two data sets separate for the purposes of this investigation.[5]

The precise dates of birth of the speakers in Table 4.2 are mostly unknown, but their decades of birth are reasonably secure. Note that OM5 is the same speaker as speaker 1942M in Table 4.1.

In addition to the speakers in Tables 4.1 and 4.2, the analysis in Section 3 includes the phonetic transcriptions and the accompanying short audio recording data from the nearest SED location, Lowick (Nb1), which is 7 miles west of Holy Island in mainland Northumberland. In this case, the phonetic transcriptions from the SED are taken to represent Q speech, while the data from the recording are of free conversation (N speech). Although there are differences between the Lowick and Holy Island dialects, they, like most other places in Northumberland, are traditionally characterised by the Northumbrian Burr, and the inclusion of the SED, and its comparison with the speakers in the Holy Island corpus, allows us to determine the extent to which this traditional dialect survey reflects what rural communities were really like with respect to this feature. The SED data for Lowick was supplied by three speakers whose average year of birth was 1881. For the purposes of this analysis, they are

---

[5] The recordings of 1945M made by me in 2006 include an added wordlist task designed to elicit traditional Holy Island dialect pronunciations, as per the method described in Maguire *et al.* (2010). These elicited pronunciations are grouped with Q speech for the purposes of this analysis.

treated as one data point, as they do not differ from each other with respect to this feature (or indeed significantly for others features).[6]

3.   The Analysis

The purpose of this section is to explain the analysis of the pronunciation of /r/ in the Holy Island corpus, and to present the results of this analysis. Given that the Holy Island dialect is partially and variably rhotic, the pronunciation of /r/ is analysed in onset position only. Up to an hour of speech was analysed for each of the speakers in Table 4.1, with the pronunciation of /r/ in N and Q speech assessed separately (only the first 100 tokens were analysed for the three speakers born in the 1960s, as they had no uvular pronunciations of /r/ whatsoever in their speech). In the case of the *Diary of an Island* speakers, however, all data were analysed owing to the short stretches of speech involved. The analysis of /r/ divides pronunciations into the following three categories:

1. Uvular (e.g. [ʁ])
2. Alveolar tap [ɾ] or trill [r]
3. Anterior approximants (e.g. [ɹ])

Figure 4.1 represents the results of the analysis for the speakers in the Holy Island corpus, whilst Figure 4.2 gives the results for the analysis of the pronunciation of /r/ in the speech of the *Diary of an Island* speakers (these are graphed separately due to the small number of tokens involved).

Table 4.1 reveals that the Northumbrian Burr was a common feature of the speech of most of the speakers recorded in Holy Island in the early 1970s, with some obvious exceptions, but that the uvular pronunciation is entirely absent in the speech of people born in the 1960s. Overall, the frequency of uvular /r/ in the corpus is 69.20% (n = 4189). Excluding the younger speakers in the sample, who have no uvular /r/ at all, the overall frequency is 74.20% (n = 3889). Looking at the difference between N and Q speech, and comparing only those speakers who produced speech of both sorts, uvular /r/ occurs at a frequency of 64.00% (n = 1225) in N speech in the corpus, and at a frequency of 87.63% (n = 1213) in Q speech. The difference between the frequencies for the two speech types is highly significant (χ^2 (1) = 185, p < 0.0001), with uvular /r/ more likely to occur in questionnaire speech than in everyday

---

[6] Berger (1980) contains a substantial number of phonetic transcriptions of words as pronounced in the Holy Island dialect, drawn from the same corpus of recordings as is analysed in this chapter. These transcriptions are not analysed here, since they indicate that /r/ was pronounced as [ʁ] 100% of the time in the corpus, which is clearly not the case (see Figure 4.1). It seems that Berger was presenting a selection of the data in the Holy Island corpus only in order to illustrate certain local characteristics of it.

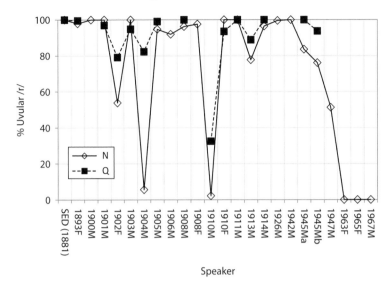

Figure 4.1: The frequency of uvular /r/ in the Holy Island corpus.

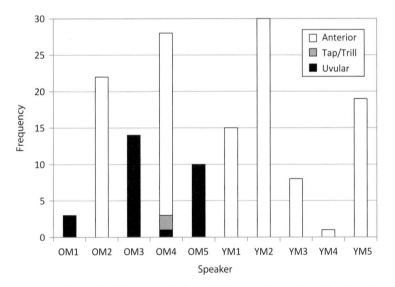

Figure 4.2: The pronunciation of /r/ by the *Diary of an Island* speakers.

conversation. This indicates that the methodologies of traditional dialect surveys, such as the SED, were having the desired effect of eliciting more localised forms of speech (though it would be necessary to check a wider range of features and types of features to see whether this holds across the board), and it is noteworthy that some speakers in particular (1902F, 1904M, 1910M and 1945M) increase their levels of uvular /r/ in Q speech quite significantly (χ^2). As a result, it is likely that traditional methodologies do not give a completely accurate picture of the *actual* (rather than *potential*) levels of traditional features in the dialects under investigation. On the other hand, levels of uvular /r/ in everyday speech are also rather high, and some speakers have up to 100% frequency of the traditional pronunciation regardless of speech type. Thus, for example, 1893F, 1901M, 1903M, 1905M, 1908M, 1910F and 1914M have no significant difference between the two different speech types and have nearly 100% uvular in their speech, whilst 1900M, 1906M, 1908F, 1926M and 1942M, for whom we have no Q data, all have almost 100% (in some cases exactly 100%) uvular /r/ in their everyday speech.

Amongst the older speakers in the sample, 1904M and 1910M (and, to an extent, 1902F) stand out rather sharply – these speakers have much lower rates of uvular /r/ in their speech in everyday conversation (the two males have almost none, in fact), but when asked to give Holy Island pronunciations in the questionnaire they produce much higher levels of the feature (especially 1904M, who is almost 'bidialectal' in this respect – see Smith and Durham [2012] for a discussion of this phenomenon). In effect, they don't use the Northumbrian Burr, but they know that it is a feature of the dialect and can use it when required.[7] And, of course, the three younger speakers in the sample have no instances of uvular /r/ in their speech whatsoever. Although they only provided N speech in the interviews, my impression from speaking and listening to them, and to other residents from the same generation, is that they are about as likely to produce a uvular /r/ as a younger speaker from some-where like Tyneside (that is, not at all), their speech being almost entirely devoid of traditional Holy Island features. The analysis of the pronunciation of /r/ in the speech of the *Diary of an Island* speakers is given in Figure 4.2. As the number of tokens is small for each speaker, the raw frequency of each variant is given. The overall frequency of the three variants in *Diary of an Island* is as follows: 18.67% uvular; 1.33% alveolar trill/tap; 80.00% anterior approximant. There is a clear difference between the behaviour of the older males (36.36% uvular) and the younger males (no uvular pronunciations at all), even though one of the older males has no uvular pronunciations at all and

---

[7] 1910M is the only speaker in the corpus to produce a significant number of pronunciations with [ɾ] or [r] (14.84%). Other than him, 1947M is the only speaker to produce more than one or two such tokens (and most speakers produce none), at 3.65%.

another has only one. The results in Figure 4.2 match the results in Figure 4.1 quite well (especially the complete lack of uvular /r/ in the speech of younger natives of the Island), but they give an added insight into the variable linguistic behaviour of speakers born in the middle of the twentieth century.

4.   Discussion

This chapter examines the rather striking disparity between traditional accounts of dialects in the north-east of England, which almost exclusively record uvular pronunciation of /r/, and modern accounts of dialects from this area, which find that uvular /r/ is essentially absent from them. To reiterate, the questions asked earlier in this chapter were as follows: (1) Did people really speak this way in the mid-twentieth century, using the Northumbrian Burr all the time, as the traditional dialect surveys suggest? (2) Do traditional dialect surveys give a misleading impression of how common this feature was as result of their methodological practices? (3) Have people been abandoning the Burr in Northumberland, and is it true that this quintessential feature of the north-east of England has disappeared?

The answer to the first of these questions is clearly yes. For many of the older people in the Holy Island corpus, born at the end of the nineteenth and the start of the twentieth centuries, uvular /r/ was normal in everyday speech. Quite a few of them have levels of it at or near 100%, whether they are speaking normally or answering SED-style questions. For them, then, the Northumbrian Burr is quite possibly a sociolinguistic indicator, not subject to stylistic variation, which is not surprising if it is the sole realisation of /r/ in their speech. This is true even for some speakers born as late as the 1940s. 1942M, in both Berger's recordings and in *Diary of an Island*, has 100% uvular /r/ in everyday speech, whilst 1945M has levels which are not far below this (and, since there is much more data for him than for 1942M, this is probably a truer reflection of the kind of variation that can be found amongst some fishermen of his generation). However, this is not the whole story. Even amongst Berger's sample of older natives from this isolated location, three show much lower levels of uvular /r/. In fact, 1904M and 1910M have almost none of it at all in their everyday speech, even though they produce it at higher levels when under questioning. Although these two speakers have somewhat different life histories than some of the other speakers in the corpus (1904M trained and worked in a specialist job away from the Island in his youth, whilst 1910M was a local expert on the history and wildlife of the Island), the same is true of several other speakers in the sample. 1893F was a 'herring girl' who followed the herring fleets around the coasts of Britain from Lewis to Great Yarmouth for many years, 1914M worked in the navy and appears to have been stationed in and around Italy for a substantial period, and 1926M spent

30 years of his life as a painter and decorator in London before retiring back to Holy Island. Nevertheless, these speakers have retained very high levels of uvular /r/. But the fact remains that, even for speakers from deepest rural Northumberland born at the start of the twentieth century, uvular /r/ could be absent.

This is one way that traditional dialect surveys such as the SED misrepresent the linguistic situation in rural Britain in the mid-twentieth century. Through a careful selection of their informants, they exclude precisely those speakers, however locally-based they might be, whose speech was not characterised by traditional features such as the one under investigation here (see Orton 1962 for a description of the SED's informant selection criteria, and Chambers and Trudgill 1980, and Petyt 1980 for a critical analysis of these methods). Traditional studies do not allow us to gauge how common speakers of the sort they record were in the community (the Holy Island corpus suggests that, for this feature at least, they were not uncommon, but that this is only part of the story). And that is even before we consider the other kinds of speakers that lived in these rural communities – in particular, children and non-natives. Berger's Holy Island recordings do not really help us with finding out how children on the Island spoke, but the evidence from the younger speakers in the corpus and in *Diary of an Island* suggests that some of these speakers were more likely to have lower levels of uvular /r/, even in the mid-twentieth century. Berger's recordings do, however, give us some insight into the linguistic behaviour of non-native residents and visitors on Holy Island at the time. In addition to the native speakers in Table 4.1, the recordings contain brief stretches of conversation by non-natives, such as a publican from south-east England, a bar-worker from Yorkshire, a partner of one of the natives from Tyneside, a woman with a near-RP accent, a tourist from the United States, and a visitor from somewhere else in north Northumberland. Apart from this last individual, none of these non-natives uses uvular /r/ (or other traditional Northumberland features) at all.

But traditional dialect surveys mislead us in another way. As the analysis in Figure 4.1 reveals, and as socio-dialectologists such as Chambers and Trudgill (1980) and Petyt (1980) argue, traditional dialectology surveys may over-emphasise the extent to which traditional features were current in the speech of the informants being recorded. This was intentional. The aim of traditional dialect surveys was to record the most old-fashioned forms of speech still current in rural Britain (see Ellis 1889 and Orton 1962) in order to determine endogenous patterns of change (see also Milroy and Gordon 2003: 12). The elicitation methods they used were developed to encourage speakers to produce their most localised forms of speech, even if this was not how these people spoke all of the time (see, e.g., Orton 1962: 15–16, where he discusses using 'bilingual' speakers for the SED). This is quite apparent for some of the speakers in the Holy Island corpus, who understood that the purpose of the

SED-style questionnaire sessions was the elicitation of their most local pro-nunciations; the result was that they produced higher levels of uvular /r/ (see Figure 4.1). The upshot of this and the very careful selection of informants is that we cannot assume that everyone spoke in the way that traditional dialect surveys imply in the mid-twentieth century. It is clear that this is one reason why there is a striking difference between the frequency of the Northumbrian Burr in mid-twentieth century accounts and later reports.

Nonetheless, this is only part of the story. It is clear from the analyses of the Holy Island data in this chapter that there has also been a dramatic change in the pronunciation of /r/ there in the course of the twentieth century. The younger speakers in the corpus and in *Diary of an Island* have no uvular /r/ in their speech whatsoever (in the same way that their speech is essentially devoid of traditional Holy Island dialect features more generally). Although the number of speakers so far analysed is small and work remains to be done (though it is worth pointing out that there are not in fact many young natives left on Holy Island), this is indicative of a whole-scale change in the pronunciation of /r/ in this part of north-east England, as has been indicated to be the case elsewhere (Påhlsson 1972, Beal *et al*. 2012, Llamas 2010, Llamas *et al*. 2009). Amongst these younger speakers, [ɹ] is the norm, though [ʋ] can also be heard (see Foulkes and Docherty 2000). This appears to be a case of 'dialect levelling' (see Beal 2010: 74–82 for a discussion). As Williams and Kerswill (1999: 149) put it, this is 'a process whereby differences between regional varieties are reduced, features which make varieties distinctive disappear, and new features emerge and are adopted by speakers over a wide geographical area'. In particular, loss of uvular /r/ is a case of what Kerswill (2003) calls 'levelling', the loss of a highly localised variant as a result of contact and accommodation between speakers of different dialects. It is not difficult to see how this has happened for these younger speakers, who were schooled in Berwick (including boarding there through the week) and have often had to leave the Island for periods of training and work. In fact, the extent to which the younger speakers from Holy Island have abandoned local traditional dialect forms suggests that this is not just a case of dialect levelling, but one of 'dialect death' (Schilling-Estes and Wolfram 1999, Britain 2009).[8] These young speakers do not speak the Holy Island dialect

---

[8] It is tempting to relate the variability in rates of uvular /r/ production amongst the Holy Island speakers to the idea that there are high rates of inter-speaker linguistic variability during the process of language death (see Cook 1989 for discussion and Schilling-Estes and Wolfram 1999 for the connection to dialect death). But it is not clear that such a claim can be made based on these data, which in fact show high levels of uvular /r/ production for most speakers, then a complete disappearance of it in the speech of speakers born in more recent decades. The three older speakers who have atypically low levels of the Burr (1902F, 1904M, 1910M) have somewhat different life histories and social characteristics compared to the other older speakers in the sample, so their divergent linguistic behaviour need not necessarily be interpreted as an example of increased variability as a result of dialect death.

at all, which is now really only typical of a small and dwindling number of older (mostly retired) farmers and fishermen on the Island (for instance 1942M, 1945M and 1947M). In a couple of decades, uvular /r/ will have disappeared from use on Holy Island, as it has elsewhere in north-east England.

Although the loss of the Northumbrian Burr in Holy Island has accelerated in recent times, it is apparent in the analysis of the Holy Island corpus that this loss has been on-going on a smaller scale for some time. Speakers such as 1904M and 1910M did not really use it either (nor do some of the older males, born in the 1940s, in the *Diary of an Island* sample), whilst speakers such as 1902F, 1913M, 1945M and 1947M show evidence of its loss to one degree or another. For these speakers, uvular /r/ is likely to be a sociolinguistic marker, subject to stylistic variation, as Figure 4.1 indicates. But uvular /r/ has likely ceased having this sociolinguistic status for the younger members of the sample who, if they recognise the pronunciation at all, are likely to view it as a feature of old-fashioned farmer and fisherman speech (that is, it has almost certainly become a stereotype, assuming it has any linguistic salience for them at all).

There appears to be something else going on with the Burr on Holy Island as well, however. Two speakers in the older sample who otherwise are not particularly dialectal in their speech (1914M and 1926M) nevertheless have uvular /r/ at extremely high levels in their everyday speech (96.43% and 100% respectively). These are two speakers that we might actually expect to have much lower levels of the feature. 1914M appears to have spent a period of his youth in the navy, stationed in and around Italy, and gives the impression that he has educated himself to a fair degree. Other dialect features, such as the traditional monophthong /u/ in the MOUTH lexical set are uncommon in his everyday speech (he has 12.50% monophthongal MOUTH). The same is true for 1926M, who spent at least thirty years of his life away from the Island, first in the Merchant Navy and then as a painter and decorator in London (where his wife comes from), before retiring to Holy Island (he has 15.48% monoph-thongal MOUTH). Is it likely to be the case that these two speakers (especially 1926M) retained their exotic uvular pronunciations of /r/, at least at such high levels, when they lived away from the Island, surrounded by people who never used this feature? It is possible that they did so, as a way of enregistering their Northumberland and Holy Island identity. However, it is also possible that they did not, and that they picked up the feature again when they returned to the Island and used it at levels which we would not expect someone with their life history to do. In this case, the Northumbrian Burr had become for them not just a stylistic marker but an essential marker of local identity, not quite a stereotype, but at least a way of showing that their absence from the Island and the absence of other, more stigmatised, traditional dialect features in their speech did not mean that they are not Islanders. This reminds us of Defoe's comment that 'the Natives value themselves upon that Imperfection, because, forsooth, it shews the Antiquity of their Blood' (1724–7, vol. iii: 23–33); the Northumbrian Burr was something to be proud of as a Northumbrian, not something to be supressed in the same way as other non-standard dialect features. That this social meaning of the Northumberland Burr has come to an end is suggested by the complete absence of a similar phenomenon in the younger speakers of the Island.

5.   Conclusion

The Northumbrian Burr was still a common feature of at least some dialects in Northumberland in the mid-twentieth century, constituting, as Påhlsson (1972: 222) says, 'a vigorous feature'. With a history of over 300 years, it had become a unique shibboleth of the speech of natives of the north-easternmost reaches of England, and one which acted as a marker of local identity in a way that other non-standard features of their dialect did not. It seems likely that it was afforded a special status as a result, making it resistant to loss and a feature which could be maintained by those who otherwise did not have particularly local forms in their speech. But in the face of wide-ranging social changes, especially the transformation of the local economy, populations, and educational practices the Northumbrian Burr began to lose its privileged status. This effect is evident even in the speech of people born in the early twentieth century in isolated places such as Holy Island, where, by the middle of the century, there is evidence that the Burr was in decline. But it was in the second half of the last century that the inexorable forces of dialect levelling and dialect death really had an effect on the way people spoke on the Island, leading to a complete loss of the Burr and other traditional features of speech from the community. Unlike larger places, such as Newcastle or even Berwick, which have large enough populations for some traditional features to survive amongst certain social groups, the effects of these exogenous changes on this small community have been far-reaching. Nonetheless, although the Northumbrian Burr is absent in the speech of the younger generations in places like Holy Island, it still survives in the speech of older local males in such out of the way places as a normal feature of their speech. However, it will not be long before this unique feature of the dialects of north-east England disappears as a genuine feature of the speech of the people of that region, and it will indeed become, as Beal (2008: 140) suggests, no more than a 'party trick'.

REFERENCES

Aitken, A. J. 1984. 'Scottish accents and dialects', in Trudgill, Peter (ed.) *Language in the British Isles*. Cambridge: Cambridge University Press. pp. 94–118.
Beal, Joan C. 2000. 'From Geordie Ridley to Viz: popular literature in Tyneside English'. *Language and Literature* 9: 343–59.

2008. 'English dialects in the north of England: morphology and syntax', in Kortmann, Bernd and Clive Upton (eds.) *Varieties of English I: The British Isles.* Berlin: Mouton de Gruyter. pp. 373–403.

2009. 'Enregisterment, commodification and historical context: "Geordie" versus "Sheffieldish"'. *American Speech* 84: 138–56.

2010. *An Introduction to Regional Englishes.* Edinburgh: Edinburgh University Press.

Beal, Joan C., Lourdes Burbano-Elizondo and Carmen Llamas 2012. *Urban North-Eastern English: Tyneside to Teeside.* Edinburgh: Edinburgh University Press.

Berger, Jörg 1980. *The Dialect of Holy Island: A Phonological Analysis.* Bern: Peter Lang.

Britain, David 2009. 'One foot in the grave? Dialect death, dialect contact, and dialect birth in England'. *International Journal of the Society of Language* 196: 121–55.

Chambers, J. K. and Peter Trudgill 1980. *Dialectology.* Cambridge: Cambridge University Press.

Cook, Eung-Do 1989. 'Is phonology going haywire in dying languages? Phonological variations in Chipewyan and Sarcee'. *Language in Society* 18: 235–55.

Defoe, Daniel 1724–7. *A Tour Through the Whole Island of Great Britain.* London: Dent.

Ellis, Alexander 1889. *The Existing Phonology of English Dialects, Compared with That of West Saxon Speech.* New York: Greenwood Press.

Elmer, Willy 1973. *The Terminology of Fishing.* Bern: Francke Verlag.

Foulkes, Paul and Gerard Docherty 2000. 'Another chapter in the story of /r/: "labiodental" variants in British English'. *Journal of Sociolinguistics* 4: 30–59.

Heslop, Oliver 1892–4. *Northumberland Words: A Glossary of Words Used in the County of Northumberland and on the Tyneside.* London: Kegan Paul, Trench, Trübner & Co.

Kerswill, Paul 2003. 'Dialect levelling and geographical diffusion in British English', in Britain, David and Jenny Cheshire (eds.) *Social Dialectology: In Honour of Peter Trudgill.* Amsterdam: John Benjamins Publishing Company. pp. 223–43.

Labov, William 1994. *Principles of Linguistic Change*, Vol. 1: Internal Factors. Malden, Oxford and Carlton: Blackwell Publishing.

Llamas, Carmen 2010. 'Convergence and divergence across a national border', in Llamas, Carmen and Dominic Watt (eds.) *Language and Identities.* Edinburgh: Edinburgh University Press., pp. 227–36.

Llamas, Carmen, Dominic Watt and Daniel E. Johnson 2009. 'Linguistic accommodation and the salience of national identity markers in a border town'. *Journal of Language and Social Psychology* 28: 381–407.

Maguire, Warren, April McMahon, Paul Heggarty and Dan Dediu 2010. 'The past, present and future of English dialects: quantifying convergence, divergence and dynamic equilibrium'. *Language Variation and Change* 22: 1–36.

Milroy, Lesley and Matthew Gordon 2003. *Sociolinguistics: Methods and Interpretation.* Malden: Blackwell Publishing Ltd.

Orton, Harold 1962. *Survey of English Dialects (A): Introduction.* Leeds: E.J. Arnold and Son Ltd.

Orton, Harold and Eugen Dieth (eds.) 1962–71. *Survey of English Dialects (B): The Basic Materials.* Leeds: Arnold & Son.

Påhlsson, Christer 1972. *The Northumbrian Burr*. Lund: Gleerup.

Petyt, Keith 1980. *The Study of Dialect: An Introduction to Dialectology*. London: Deutsch.

Rydland, Kurt 1998. *The Orton Corpus: A Dictionary of Northumbrian Pronunciation*. Oslo: Novus Press.

Schilling-Estes, Natalie and Walt Wolfram 1999. 'Alternative models of dialect death: dissipation vs. concentration'. *Language* 75: 486–521.

Smith, Jennifer and Mercedes Durham 2012. 'Bidialectalism or dialect death? Explaining generational change in the Shetland Islands, Scotland'. *American Speech* 87: 57–88.

Trudgill, Peter 1999. 'New dialect formation and dedialectalization: embryonic and vestigial variants'. *Journal of English Linguistics* 27: 319–27.

Viereck, Wolfgang 1966. *Phonematische Analyse des Dialekts von Gateshead-upon-Tyne, Co. Durham*. Hamburg: Cram, de Gruyter & Co.

Wales, Katie 2006. *Northern English: A Social and Cultural History*. Cambridge: Cambridge University Press.

Wells, John C. 1982. *Accents of English*. Cambridge: Cambridge University Press.

Williams, Ann and Paul Kerswill 1999. 'Dialect levelling: change and continuity in Milton Keynes, Reading and Hull', in Foulkes, Paul and Gerard Docherty (eds.) *Urban Voices: Accent Studies in the British Isles*. London: Arnold. pp. 141–62.

Wright, Peter 1964. 'Proposal for a short questionnaire for use in fishing communities'. *Transactions of the Yorkshire Dialect Society* 11: 27–32.

Websites and Media

DHIL: *The Dialect of the Holy Island of Lindisfarne* corpus: http://research.ncl.ac.uk/decte/dhil.htm.

Diary of an Island. Tyne Tees Television, 2007.

Millennium Memory Bank: http://sounds.bl.uk/accents-and-dialects/millenium-memory-bank/.

Part II

Describing Places

5   Corpora for Regional and Social Analysis

Karen P. Corrigan

1.   Introduction

As Corrigan (2011: 183) notes, Widdowson (1999: 81) first raised the possibility of exploiting archival corpus resources as 'primary evidence for the study of linguistic variation and change'. He concluded that: 'the data remains hidden and inaccessible' (1999: 84) and advocated initiatives for the identification and enhancement of these archives for future exploitation. Subsequent publications documenting and analysing digital resources like this demonstrate the extent to which Widdowson's vision has had an impact (see Sections 3.1 and 3.3.1).

However, as Kretzschmar *et al.* (2006) note, the enhancement of legacy corpora for re-use in analysing regional and social differences is not without its challenges, nor indeed is the direct comparison of even synchronic corpora when they have been collected using distinctive protocols and for the purpose of fulfilling divergent research objectives (D'Arcy 2011).[1]

This chapter highlights the advantages and disadvantages that arise with respect to fulfilling Widdowson's (1999) aim by examining two corpora I have created and digitised: the *National Folklore Collection's South Armagh Corpus* (NFCSAC) and the *Diachronic Electronic Corpus of Tyneside English* (DECTE). Although I will demonstrate that both are invaluable resources, there are aspects of the content and digitisation of each which are reminiscent of Labov's (2001: 11) description of working with historical data more widely, namely, that it is: 'The art of making the best use of bad data'.

This chapter developed from a Sense of Place colloquium plenary honouring Joan Beal. We worked closely developing the corpus described in Section 3 and I am indebted to her for encouragement over the decades it took to resurrect surveys for regional and social analyses. These surveys would have languished at Newcastle University to this day had it not been for our efforts, which began in 1994 with Catherine Cookson Foundation funding. I am also grateful to the AHRB/C, which funded later phases of this corpus, as well as to the Department of Education for Northern Ireland, which provided a doctoral award to create the corpus in Section 2. Thanks also go to the colloquium audience for comments and to the editors and an anonymous reviewer for invaluable suggestions as to how to improve upon a previous draft.

[1] Kretzschmar *et al.* (2006) define 'enhancement' as both the preparation of legacy materials and their compilation into a sustainable corpus, compliant with world standards.

This chapter explores the considerable 'artistry' involved in order to make the 'best use' of the data to answer sociolinguistic questions. It also reflects on decisions made during the process. Not only do these choices have important consequences for the re-use and long-term preservation of the resources themselves, but they also give insights into best practices in corpus construction.

2.   The National Folklore Collection's South Armagh Corpus

The original data for the NFCSAC were collected by Michael J. Murphy, a folklorist working in the South Armagh (SA) area of Northern Ireland (1942–74).[2] In addition to personal narratives of experience on folkloric themes, the materials also contain images as well as correspondence between Murphy and his employers. Given the fact that the narratives, in particular, were collected for more than thirty years of Murphy's career, the archive has the potential to further our understanding of South Armagh English as it developed. The region is especially interesting from a linguistic contact perspective, since its isolation helped maintain South Armagh Irish into the 1940s, but improved transport links and other socio-economic changes in the area after World War II opened up this dialect to contact with different varieties of English, which had important linguistic consequences (Corrigan 1997; 2011).

The NFCSAC dataset used to construct the corpus exploited in Corrigan (1997) *inter alia* covers topics considered to be relevant to understanding the folkloric customs local to the region, for example agriculture and trade. NFCSAC comprises 59,583 words and contains more than 200 narratives, as defined by Labov and Waletzky (1967) and Labov (1997). Murphy recorded participants in his own backyard of SA, all of whom can be considered homogeneous not only from the perspective of place (they were all born and reared there), but also because they share socio-economic traits and social networks.

Although Murphy originally made his recordings using a wax-cylinder Ediphone device and, from the 1950s onwards, a magnetic tape recorder,[3] it was his transcripts of this audio material that became the source of the NFCSAC. The fact that the corpus consists of only the written transcripts, naturally, raises questions of their accuracy regarding the original speech events. As Tagliamonte (2007: 209–10) notes, the linear nature of writing is poorly designed for capturing conversation. Transcribers require protocols that accurately retain enough of the original speech signal to allow for linguistic and other forms of analysis, but should not be so complex as to render the resulting transcriptions unreadable and excessively time-consuming to complete. Despite the fact that this data was not originally collected for linguistic

---

[2] See: www.ucd.ie/folklore/en/.   [3] For details see www.ucd.ie/irishfolklore/en/audio/.

purposes, Murphy did generally strike the right balance since his transcripts do contain many features associated with natural speech, such as the reformulations highlighted in (1):

(1)   So then **she went to ... took patients to** a priest in England, who was
         supposed to have great power, and he told her that she had the same power

The punctuation here also indicates that Murphy has followed contemporary typographical conventions by indicating the fact that the relative clause is non-restrictive by placing it inside commas. However, Murphy's use of this and other typographical practices is not always consistent, as can be seen in (2), which is similarly non-restrictive, but is missing the conventional punctuation:

(2)   They belonged to his uncle who was Dr McDonald who was the parish
         priest . . .

Given the fact that research questions relating to the types of relative clause preferred by males versus females and the extent to which both groups have adopted Standard English norms in their lifetimes were amongst those that this project was to address, issues such as these are problematic. However, the costs of 'trade-offs' like this are worth bearing when it is clear that, in so many other respects, Murphy's transcriptions are indeed 'consistent' with the 'real language' he was aiming to 'represent' (Tagliamonte 2007).

There are elements of the Murphy corpus, then, that in Labov's (2001: 11) sense are 'bad data' and cannot be overcome. However, there are very strong arguments that the data remain 'good' enough for certain types of linguistic analysis, as demonstrated in the diachronic analyses of relativisation in the corpus published as Corrigan (2009), and in the analysis of vernacular verb forms sketched in Section 2.3.1. Indeed, Murphy (1973: 65) himself likens his task to that of the 'linguistic quest' of dialectologists, in that both enterprises are what he describes as 'coldly scientific'. We can assume that what he is referring to here is his claim that his recordings always 'aimed at the highest possible fidelity towards the speech' (Murphy 1975: vii). Hence, the use of swear words like *frig* and blasphemous lexemes, which would have been considered very strong language for the time and place, are instances of such authenticity (see Andersson and Trudgill 1990; Farr and Murphy 2009).

Moreover, Glassie (1982: 734, fn.4) confirms Murphy's objectives stating that the discipline of folklore relied on collecting 'accurate texts'. Indeed, Murphy's particular insistence on the careful preservation of his narratives has been much commented on since his death (see Smyth 1997).

In addition to the mimetic commitment demonstrated in the previous paragraphs, it is also important to consider the intrinsic value of Murphy's status as a native speaker in the SA community, in which he acted as a participant observer. His family was indigenous to the area and he is known to be the third generation to have lived there. His lack of geographical mobility increases the likelihood that the dialect used by his informants will have matched his own. Hence, he is unlikely to have misunderstood the speakers or to have felt the need to normalise their output. Indeed, Murphy (1975: ix) makes it clear that he will not standardise the material even for a more general readership. Furthermore, as a folklorist, Murphy's fundamental interest was in the content of his informants' stories. He was insistent, therefore, that the narrative be conveyed intact and believed this could be achieved only by faithful transcription.

Murphy has insider-status in this community and while one would not expect his personal relationship with each informant to be identical, his role of collector remains constant and he shares his informants' personal communication networks. Moreover, unlike the sociolinguistic interview techniques practised within the Labovian tradition (see Labov 1981; Milroy and Gordon 2003; Tagliamonte 2006), Murphy does not have absolute control over the exchange in which he participates. His technique seems to have been to initiate the narrative turn with what he terms a 'topical tag' and defines as 'any event or calamity' (1973: 38), which is somewhat comparable to 'danger of death' questions articulated in Labov (1981). By contrast to the usual folklorist practice, which Glassie (1982: 743) describes as: 'isolating tales out of conversations', Murphy appears to have given his interlocutors a relatively loose rein thereafter, so that the ordering of topics is left to them. However, topic choice is constrained by Murphy's role (see 1973: 38). Hence, while there are exchanges relating to the immediate situation of the conversation, the narratives are autonomous and cover a narrow range of themes. From a sociolinguistic perspective, the constancy of the speech event in all these respects is extremely helpful since it has been shown that changes in topic, setting, and audience can induce code-switching, which would not be desirable for subsequent social and regional analyses where style was not an independent variable.

2.1   Corpus Dimensions and Representativeness

From the perspective of quantifying the distribution of features, an important concern raised by the corpus dimensions is the fact that the potential occurrence of linguistic variables is skewed by gaps in the dataset. These are partly due to the speech event and partly to the fact that Murphy's output was more prolific in some years.

Although the Gaelic custom associated with keening was largely the preserve of women, *seanchaí* were predominantly men (Glassie 1982: 742, fn.17). Murphy (1975: vii) notes this for SA and so his participants are not evenly divided between males and females, which is problematic for ascertaining gender differences. There are fourteen female versus forty-eight male narrators, resulting in the corpus containing a negative ratio of male to female

Table 5.1: *Number of words and percentage occurrence of words in the Murphy corpus by gender (1942–1974).*

YEAR	N Male Words	% of Total Male Words in Corpus per Year	N Female Words	% of Total Female Words in Corpus per Year	N Total Words	% of Total Words in Corpus
1942	1257	3.37			1257	2.41
1945	14331	38.45	10206	68.41	24537	47.02
1946	947	2.54	312	2.09	1259	2.41
1947	310	0.83			310	0.59
1948	408	1.09	1665	11.16	2073	3.97
1949			428	2.87	428	0.82
1951	1135	3.05	991	6.64	2126	4.07
1956	718	1.93			718	1.38
1958	345	0.93			345	0.66
1959	121	0.32			121	0.23
1961	540	1.45	544	3.65	1084	2.08
1963			167	1.12	167	0.32
1964	584	1.57			584	1.12
1965	3971	10.66			3971	7.61
1968	1743	4.68			1743	3.34
1969	1716	4.60			1716	3.29
1970	1957	5.25			1957	3.75
1971	1122	3.01			1122	2.15
1972	2231	5.99			2231	4.28
1973	2877	7.72	343	2.30	3220	6.17
1974	954	2.56	262	1.76	1216	2.33
TOTAL	37267		14918		52185	

words. This imbalance means that the kind of statistical analysis possible is limited to demonstrating tendencies and, even then, it requires some means of accounting for female unrepresentativeness. As such, it is doubtful that the usual quantitative techniques associated with the sociolinguistic paradigm could be applied successfully (particularly GoldVarb X/Rbrul, as detailed in Johnson 2009; Sankoff *et al.* 2005; and Tagliamonte 2006 *inter alia*).

Table 5.1, which summarises the corpus dimensions, illustrates the nature of the problem. There are a number of years for which Murphy, by chance, did not collect any data from females (shaded grey). Moreover, male speakers in 1949 and 1963 are excluded entirely (in black) since in these years only females were recorded. Additionally, Murphy's collection phase was most prolific in the 1940s with over 47 per cent of the entire corpus being collected in a single year (1945) during which almost 70 per cent of the female data was gathered.

These difficulties are exactly what one might expect of a corpus like this which is available for linguistic analysis by chance rather than design. Since NFCSAC's fundamental advantage lies in the degree of objectivity with which it was collected – combined with the possibility that it can, nevertheless, track real-time constraints on certain variables – it is analogous in many ways to the type of imperfect data available in historical linguistics (see Nevalainen and Raumolin-Brunberg 1996: 62).

However, the NFCSAC is superior, in that there is consistency in its method of collection and there is considerably more metadata available to describe its content and its speakers' demographic characteristics than we could ever hope for regarding historical corpus materials (see Beal *et al.* 2007).

2.2   *Digitisation, Annotation, and Metadata*

The original data that NFCSAC is derived from is held in bound manuscripts at University College, Dublin (UCD). Their regulations/workspace during corpus creation meant the process had to be manual, leading to short cuts of various kinds with important consequences for the re-purposing of the data longer-term. The conventions used in the manuscripts suggest that Murphy transcribed his recordings using a 'discourse-oriented approach' (Slembrouck 1992: 103), in that the quoted insets also contain transcriber comments on accents, etymologies, and idioms. Moreover, narratives are arranged by topic and the identities of the speaker–hearer and their social role relationship with the collector are marked. Thus, the extract in Figure 5.1 contains important metadata, noting that the topic is 'Woman with a Cure', that the informant, Brigid O'Hare, has kinship ties to Murphy and that the narrative's physical setting is 'Dromintee, Dromintee Parish (Newry) South Armagh'.

During the transfer to computer-readable text, doggerel verse, extraneous exchanges and notes made by Murphy that appeared not to have any linguistic relevance at the time (though they did contain relevant metatadata that would have been useful to preserve for subsequent potential uses of the corpus) were edited out. Hence, NFCSAC consists exclusively of the personal narratives. Thus, in Figure 5.1, neither the introductory exchange between Murphy and his niece, establishing who exactly Mary Reed (the subject of the narrative) was, nor the bracketed section four lines into the start of the conversation denoting Crobane's location, appears in the digitised version (Figure 5.2). This begins with the narrative proper only, though it does preserve certain metadata, such as the date of recording and the fact that the participant was female since knowing these facts was pertinent to the research hypotheses. No attempt was made to provide pseudonyms since this was not the practice in the folkloric tradition, and it was envisioned as a corpus designed only for personal use.

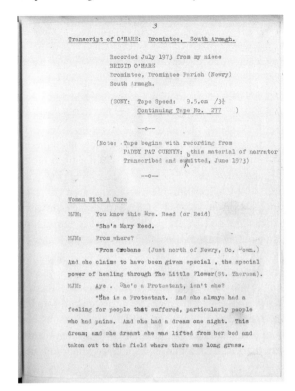

Figure 5.1: Transcript from the original NFCSAC archive.

Otherwise, the original was kept as intact as possible including punctuation and glosses that were linguistically relevant. This entailed preserving Murphy's misspellings and his attempts at rendering the pronunciation of Irish and South Armagh dialect lexical items. Hence, I retain spellings like *jasus* for *Jesus* representing typical MEAT-MATE mergered pronunciations (Corrigan 2010: 34; Harris 1985; Milroy and Harris 1980) as well as spellings influenced by eye dialect/folk etymology like *sirosis* for *sclerosis*.

In keeping with the recommendations of Kretzschmar *et al.* (2006) and Sinclair (2005), the NFCSAC version retains metadata relevant to the speakers' demographic characteristics, as well as certain linguistic issues. New annotations to represent features potentially relevant for subsequent analyses (like the relative clause marker coding <REL-WH> indicated in Figure 5.2) were also added to the computer-readable copy as well as other annotations like <§> designating new paragraphs, since spacing of this type needs to be more clearly represented in digital formats. Moreover, there are other aspects of the corpus design which comply broadly with the

MANUSCRIPT: *1810*   **DATE:** *July 1973*
INFORMANT: *Mrs. Brigid O'Hare*   **LOCATION:** *Dromintee*
TOPIC: *Woman with a Cure*
She is a Protestant. And she always had a feeling for people that <REL-TH>
suffered, particularly people who <REL-WH> had pains etc.

Figure 5.2: Truncated transcript from the digitised NFCSAC.

Open Language Archives Community (OLAC) (www.language-archives
.org/OLAC/metadata.html) and Dublin Core (DC) (http://dublincore.org/
documents/dces/) guidelines on corpus metadata, such as providing a
detailed description of the electronic resource and how it relates to the
original manuscript version at UCD. NFCSAC does not, however, adhere
to all fifteen elements defined in DC. This is hardly surprising, though,
since the digitisation process ended in 1993 and thus pre-dates these 1995
standards.

The NFCSAC corpus was always intended to be private so issues of rights
and the kinds of human subject documentation advocated in Kretzschmar *et al.*
(2006) and DC/OLAC played a marginal role in its design (cf. Bauer 2002:
98–9). In addition, NFCSAC remains as a plain text version with manual
additions of diamond bracketed mark-up to highlight pertinent features and has
never been converted to XML format,[4] despite its important benefits (see
Section 3.2).

2.3   *The Value of NFCSAC as a Corpus for Regional and Social Analysis*

2.3.1   Analyses of NFCSAC   A significant advantage of this corpus is its
potential to contribute to our understanding of the extent to which South
Armagh English has been subject to change across real-time, and indeed which
linguistic features do or do not index variation. To demonstrate this, I outline
below a quantitative analysis of vernacular verbs. This is a well-documented
feature of non-standard Englishes (see Cheshire 1982) and is illustrated by
NFCSAC in examples such as *bruck, catched* and *step* for *broke, caught* and
steeped, respectively.

Figure 5.3 displays all occurrences of this variable in NFCSAC and, whilst
there are some obvious peaks and troughs, the average number of tokens
overall remains steady and the figures for 1942 and 1974 are almost identical.
This suggests that vernacular verbs in South Armagh English are particularly
well integrated in the grammars of Murphy's participants. As such, they seem

---

[4] 'Extensible Markup Language' (XML), as defined by the Text Encoding Initiative (TEI) at:
www.tei-c.org/release/doc/tei-p5-doc/en/html/SG.html.

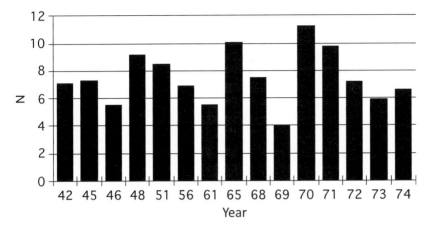

Figure 5.3: Occurrence of vernacular verbs for all informants (N = Frequency of occurrence per 1,000 words per year).

to be one of the few morpho-syntactic features examined in Corrigan (1997) that do not index societal change in SA.

2.3.2   Summary   As outlined in the analysis sketched in Section 2.3.1 and in Corrigan (1997), despite the issues already described, NFCSAC has proved to be an invaluable resource for the analysis of constraints operating on the development of South Armagh English from the 1940s to the 1970s. Moreover, the data has also been successfully used to test theoretical models of language acquisition, contact and (parametric) variation so that the considerable 'labour and expense' in Sinclair's (2005) terms associated with NFCSAC's creation (which Sinclair warns against for this reason) have indeed been worthwhile.

3.   The Diachronic Electronic Corpus of Tyneside English

The second corpus discussed in this paper, DECTE (Corrigan *et al.* 2012), was formed by amalgamating datasets dating back to the late 1960s. Unlike NFCSAC, DECTE is a public corpus and is not sample but monitor in nature. It currently consists of audio recordings, transcriptions, and associated material related to three different research projects: (i) the *Tyneside Linguistic Survey* (TLS) (1971–2), (ii) the *Phonological Variation and Change in Contemporary Spoken British English* (PVC) project (1994–7) and (iii) the *Newcastle Electronic Corpus of Tyneside English 2* (NECTE2). The last of these three began in 2007 and has a broader geographical reach than either the TLS or PVC (see Figure 5.4). From 2001 to 2005, the TLS and PVC datasets were updated

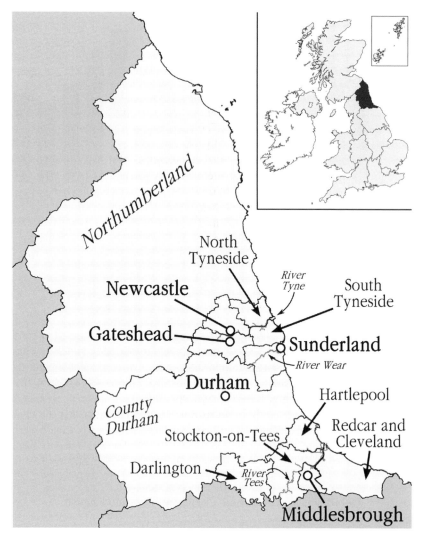

Figure 5.4: North East Map indicating the locations of DECTE interviews.

to form the *Newcastle Electronic Corpus of Tyneside English* (NECTE), a single enhanced XML-encoded and aligned corpus that conformed to the standards established by the TEI for the digital representation of documents. DECTE is also an XML, TEI-compliant corpus and was formed by amalgamating NECTE and NECTE2. This enhances DECTE's sustainability as well as its interoperability in ways that will be discussed in Section 3.2.

3.1 Corpus Dimensions and Representativeness

Table 5.2 and the accompanying notes outline the dimensions of DECTE and summarise the dates of interviews, genders of the interviewees, and number of words in the transcriptions/hours in the audio recordings. Although DECTE's current size is small by comparison to mega-corpora like the CNN corpus (Hoffman 2007), it is considerably larger than the NFCSAC, for instance, which acted as a starting point for DECTE's design. Thus, it shares NFCSAC's key characteristics of being a regionally delimited corpus, comprising speech data from males and females recorded in real-time. However, it surpasses NFCSAC not only in terms of their relative dimensions to one another, but also because the speech data that DECTE contains was sampled using strict sociolinguistic criteria to ensure representativeness. Murphy, described as the last of the 'uneducated intellectuals' in the South Ulster area, will have been entirely unaware of such criteria (Murphy 2012). While the original data sample for the TLS is not replicated in DECTE for reasons that relate to its legacy status, the surviving material, in terms of its dimensions and its balance between genders, is comparable to that of the PVC dataset. This similarity has allowed certain kinds of longitudinal comparisons of sociolinguistic variants to be successfully undertaken (see Barnfield and Buchstaller 2010; Beal and Corrigan 2007; Moisl and Maguire 2008; Fehringer and Corrigan 2015). As Table 5.2 summarises, DECTE comprises three separate sub-corpora (TLS/PVC/NECTE2) containing ninety-nine interviews with a grand total of 160 informants. We also have access to additional data from the TLS and NECTE2 sub-corpora, which are in the process of being XML-encoded, but are not yet complete. For the former, this is because new materials have only recently come to light and for the latter, this is because up to ninety new interviews are conducted to augment NECTE2 each year since the monitor phase of the corpus began in 2007, and only those between then and 2013 had been XML-encoded at the time of writing.[5]

3.2 Digitisation, Annotation, and Metadata

The digitisation and annotation processes surrounding DECTE's construction have already received considerable attention (see Allen *et al.* 2007;

---

[5] The TLS deficits also arise on account of inheriting poor quality audio-recordings and our inability to locate tapes – particularly for the Newcastle sample. In December 2013, an additional twenty-three previously unknown tapes were discovered. These appear to contain a further thirteen Gateshead interviews and recordings with perhaps as many as sixty Newcastle informants. It is not yet clear how many of these interviews will be recoverable but, if they can be digitised, there is every reason to believe that we will eventually be able to access and XML-encode a sample that is a much better reflection of the original sampling frame.

Table 5.2: *DECTE's composition.*

	DECTE	TLS	PVC	NECTE2
		Components		
Recording Dates	1971–2013	1971–1972	1994	2007–2013
		XML-encoded Corpus		
Interviews	99	37*	18	44
Words	804,266	229,909	208,295	366,062
Audio (hrs:min:sec)	71:45:43	22:53:55	17:34:25	31:17:23
Informants†	160	37	35	88
Female	87	20	18	49
Male	73	17	17	39
		Full Collections		
Interviews	588	88*		482
Words	c. 4.7 million	c. 584,000	*as above*	c. 3.9 million
Audio	c. 408 hours	c. 60 hours		c. 330 hours

* The TLS corpus also contains seven phonetic transcriptions of Newcastle informants. There are no orthographic transcriptions or audio recordings for these interviews, so they are not included here.

† The PVC and NECTE2 interviews have two informants per interview, while the TLS has one. There are thirty-five (rather than thirty-six) informants recorded for the eighteen PVC interviews because one participant was recorded twice.

D'Arcy 2011; McEnery and Hardie 2012; and Mearns (2015); as well as: http://research.ncl.ac.uk/necte/documentation.htm and http://research .ncl.ac.uk/decte/documentation.htm). As far as digitisation is concerned, a key issue was how to handle the analogue reel-to-reel recordings associated with the TLS. The state in which the materials were found is an excellent example of what Widdowson (1999) describes as neglected archival data. All the TLS recordings included in NECTE were digitised in WAV format at 12000 Hz 16-bit mono and were enhanced to counter the 'meltdown' (Widdowson 1999: 84) of the originals by amplitude adjustment, graphic equalisation, clip/hiss elimination, as well as speed regularisation. This strategy improved the audio files considerably to the point where it has become possible to analyse the materials using tools like CLAN, PRAAT and WinPitch (see Amand 2014; Martin 2013; and Parisse 2013).

As far as annotation is concerned, an important objective of the NECTE initiative was to provide a fully searchable, grammatically tagged corpus, in which the audio files and orthographic transcriptions were linked. Given the fact that this sociolinguistically sampled corpus, by comparison to NFCSAC, was to be a public corpus, and costly to produce, it was crucial to ensure that the end result was sustainable on the one hand and interoperable on the other,

```
KWIC list:                                                                  NEWCAST
y i got eh i get a hundred and <eh> <pause/>    fifty like or somewhat or like
undred and eh <pause/>    fifty <like> or somewhat or like lee got a hundred ar
/>    fifty like or somewhat or <like> lee got a hundred and eighty because he
cause he done two years in one <well> if i <pause/>    i 'm doing two years <ur
r/> <pause/>    like two years <you know> what i mean mm hm in one <pause/>
two years you know what i mean <mm> hm in one <pause/>    because i 'm jumping
years you know what i mean mm <hm> in one <pause/>    because i 'm jumping str
ng straight into third year so <i mean> well i had this hundred pound and i wa
ight into third year so i mean <well> i had this hundred pound and i was going
>    and i was going to keep it <like> for a deposit on a flat or something anc
d just buying clothes and that <aye> <pause/>    just spending it well i mean i
ye <pause/>    just spending it <well> i mean if i get money like that you knov
ause/>    just spending it well <i mean> if i get money like that you know <pau
 mean if i get money like that <you know> <pause/>    and in the end <pause/>
 not doing i 'm dumping a year <aye> aye i know <unclear/>    so i mean eh <p
 doing i 'm dumping a year aye <aye> i know <unclear/>    so i mean eh <pause
e aye i know <unclear/>    so <i mean> eh <pause/>    i i think i 'll go for a
 know <unclear/>    so i mean <eh> <pause/>    i i think i 'll go for a car yc
 i i think i 'll go for a car <you know> <pause/>    get my father to insuranc
/>    christmas more likely but <i mean> eh <pause/>    it 'd be nice to have yc
ristmas more likely but i mean <eh> <pause/>    it 'd be nice to have your own
```

Figure 5.5: Concordance list identifying discourse markers in NECTE.

so that it could be searched alongside other datasets like the *Scottish Corpus of Texts and Speech* (see www.gla.ac.uk/schools/critical/research/fundedresearch projects/enroller/). As such, it was decided to encode the data for 'distribution following standards established by corpus linguistics' (McEnery and Hardie 2012: 117). Thus, we chose TEI-compliant XML as the basis for the mark-up and subjected the orthographic transcripts to part-of-speech (POS) tagging. Having reviewed the full range of software available, the Constituent Likelihood Automatic Word-Tagging System (CLAWS), was selected. This is a grammatical tagger developed for annotating speech in the British National Corpus (BNC) (see Beal *et al.* 2007 and http://ucrel.lancs.ac.uk/claws/). It fulfilled our requirements as a mature system, consistently achieving an accuracy rate of over 96 per cent.

In the first instance, the CLAWS lexicon was expanded to accommodate items not in the BNC, such as the verb *gan* (equivalent to the standard verb 'go'). Given the fact that CLAWS was originally designed to be used on standardised (written) texts, the tag 'FU' also had to be created for coping with speech phenomena that cannot be lemmatised like that which Murphy annotated as <…..> in (1). The CLAWS (C8) tagset, prior to its application to NECTE, did not have a specific tag to represent discourse pragmatic markers (DPMs) either, for exactly the same reason, since they do not constitute a discrete grammatical category that was easily recognisable by such software. The solution was to expand the application of an already existing tag, namely 'UH', which was originally applied to interjections in the BNC, so that it could also identify the DPMs illustrated in Figure 5.5 from Beal *et al.* (2007).

The entire corpus was then POS tagged by the CLAWS4/Template taggers using the UCREL C8 tagset, and output samples were proof-read. Because the corpus was much smaller and more dialectally homogeneous than the BNC, it offered greater opportunities for identifying issues created by automatic tagging. Naturally, the process also entailed arriving at solutions to accommodate the anomalies with the bonus that they could then be subsequently applied to the annotation of other corpora.

The public nature of DECTE presented a significant challenge with respect to the legal/ethical issues already discussed in relation to NFCSAC's metadata. It was clear that consent for even the earliest interviews in the NECTE sub-corpus had been given for the use of the data to further research. However, only the interviewees in the NECTE2 sub-corpus gave explicit permission for their data to be downloadable. The technology was only invented in 1989, decades after the TLS project finished and a mere five years before the PVC interviews.[6] The interviewees, and any personal information by which they could be identified, can be anonymised, of course, but the fact that DECTE contains audio as well as transcribed data means that it is impossible to guarantee privacy. Moreover, as McEnery and Hardie (2012: 62–3) have argued, even corpora that have been systematically anonymised may contain text that nevertheless betrays the identity of a participant or discussant. A case in point is the conversation in (3) between <PVC16a> and <PVC16b> who both went to Newcastle's Canning Street School. Although the teacher's surname has been anonymised (*Mr (NAME)*), the surrounding context plus the personal description could well lead to his being identified:

(3)   <PVC16b> ... head teacher hasn't changed at Canning Street he's still there what's he called Mr <pause> oh God <pause> ... <interruption> Mr (NAME) <Line 0862><Informant PVC16a> mm <Line 0863><Informant PVC16b> pitch black hair <pause>

It was for these reasons that the decision was made to restrict DECTE's availability with potential end users being asked to prove their credentials.

3.3   *The Value of DECTE as a Corpus for Regional and Social Analysis*

3.3.1   Analyses of DECTE   Since NECTE's launch in 2005, datasets relating to what eventually became DECTE have been used for teaching and research at Newcastle University, as well as further afield (see Amand 2014).

---

[6] Moreover, the PVC interviews were conducted just one year after CERN agreed that World Wide Web technology would be available for anyone to use on a royalty-free basis (http://tenyears-www.web.cern.ch/tenyears-www/Welcome.html), so it is likely that very few of the thirty-five participants might have envisaged publication of this kind.

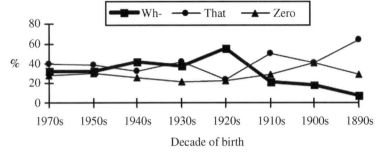

Figure 5.6: Relative marking in NECTE by birth decade.

The corpus has provided new insights into the relationship between language and society in north-eastern England. Moisl and Maguire (2008), for instance, used the TLS sub-corpus to identify the main phonetic determinants in the region that group speakers socially. In a similar vein, Beal and Corrigan (2007) examined the trajectories of socio-syntactic change across real-time in NECTE, like those involved in relative clause marking illustrated in Figure 5.6, which they found to be both internally and externally constrained. It was clear from their longitudinal investigation that the 1890s-born informants very rarely use *wh-* (preferring *that* or zero forms) and that, whilst *wh-* usage increases gradually in the 1900s and 1910s-born cohorts, the most dramatic rise occurs in the speech of those born in the 1920s. Thereafter, *wh-* usage levels off, until the proportions for the 1950s and 1970s-born cohorts are very similar. Indeed, from the 1950s period onwards, the distribution of all three relative markers in NECTE is more or less equivalent.

Real-time changes like these can, of course, be even more revealing when they are viewed across the entire time depth of DECTE (namely, to include NECTE2) and this has been very nicely demonstrated in Barnfield and Buchstaller's (2010) investigation of longitudinal change in the intensification system (Figure 5.7). It shows that both *really* and *dead* increased in frequency between the 1960s and 1990s and, while usage of the latter drops off dramatically in the twenty-first century, the former continues to compete with *very* as a popular intensifier.

Even more recently, DECTE has been used by researchers from a comparative sociolinguistic perspective (Tagliamonte 2004) to examine language variation and change cross-dialectally, permitting a view on north-eastern English that accounts not only for local trends but also examines the extent to which speakers there follow global changes (Childs *et al.* (2015), Fehringer and Corrigan [in press]).

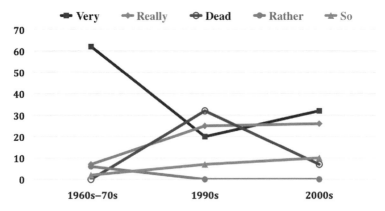

Figure 5.7: Rates of intensifier usage in DECTE (1960s–2000s).

3.3.2   Summary   Since impact is increasingly viewed as a measure of success with respect to research output, the fact that requests to use DECTE by scholars have come from all corners of the globe demonstrates its reach.[7] This access has led to other important research contributions, in addition to those already outlined, that have brought insights in the fields of regional and social analyses as well as beyond these (see, e.g., Martin 2013; and Parisse 2013). The scholarship that has been built on DECTE is a testament to its utility and is also a pay-off for the considerable investment that the corpus has required. There is always room for improvement, of course, and the team have their sights fixed on revisions like upgrading the interface so as to make it more suitable for users of iPhones (see Mehl et al. 2016).

4.   Conclusion

Although NFCSAC and DECTE are very divergent corpus building enterprises in terms of their aims, this chapter has demonstrated that there are points of congruence with respect to their design. In addition, while there have been challenges associated with their creation, each of them can be regarded as having achieved some measure of success, however that might be defined. Key issues that have arisen in the discussion are the importance of documenting, digitising and enhancing archival data so that it can be re-purposed and used longer-term. There is also the need to make the most of automated tools for annotation and, of course, to bear in mind that these

---

[7] Applications for access are recorded from as far afield as the National University of Mongolia and the Pontifical Catholic University of Peru.

techniques will in the end require some level of manual checking. Sociolinguists interested in the analysis of variation must also engage with computational linguists and software developers so that the valuable annotations they require for marking up 'real language' in Tagliamonte's (2007) terms are allowed for in the available technology, as advocated by Smith *et al.* (2008). The abundant, though idiosyncratic, annotation applied to NFCSAC has been retained so that, to the present day, I can locate every relative clause marker (even those which are zero). However, the annotation information on relative clause marking developed for Beal and Corrigan's (2007) analysis of relativisation in the north-eastern data that eventually became DECTE could not be retained. This was because the kind of eclectic mark-up invented during earlier transcription phases denoting such additional grammatical information (affectionately known as 'cockroaches' and 'pesky critters' – see Beal *et al.* 2007) was sacrificed for the greater good of a TEI-compliant XML corpus, because there simply was no mechanism for preserving such unconventional interpretive information.

This chapter also serves as a timely reminder to researchers who are increasingly striving towards 'big data' that developing good practices with respect to the ethical treatment of linguistic materials, whether or not they are subject to legislative protection already, is ever more crucial. Corpus creators require protocols for the ethical treatment of human subjects, such as that advocated in Kretzschmar *et al.* (2006), and more research is needed to better understand the ethical issues surrounding corpus construction and use, particularly with respect to the increasingly large collections of legacy data which are being re-purposed for linguistic applications (see Hasund 1998; McEnery and Hardie 2012: 57–70; and Rock 2001).

As Bender and Good (2010: 1) are keen to point out, scaling up the kinds of datasets normally used is crucial if we are to meet what they describe as its 'grand challenge' of integrating theoretical frameworks and analytical approaches from various sub-fields of linguistics, including 'language in social interaction', an important sub-theme of this chapter and indeed of this volume as a whole. In the same way that I have already noted the importance of accounting for the legal/ethical implications of legacy datasets like those described here, 'big data' initiatives that target corpora for regional and social analyses also need to remain respectful of the different social dynamics which pertain across communities. These factors must not be lost sight of when striving to collect and share datasets on a significantly grander scale than those described here (see also Kendall 2011). A balance needs to be struck between being in a position to mine megacorpora, and fully understanding the very unique social and regional contexts from which the constituent corpora derive.

REFERENCES

Allen, William, Joan. C. Beal, Karen P. Corrigan, Warren Maguire, and Hermann Moisl 2007. 'A linguistic "time-capsule": The Newcastle Electronic Corpus of Tyneside English', in Beal, Joan C., Karen P. Corrigan, and Hermann Moisl (eds.), *Creating and Digitizing Language Corpora, volume 2: Diachronic Databases*. Houndmills, Basingstoke: Palgrave-Macmillan. pp. 16–48.

Amand, Maelle 2014. 'Revisiting the TLS sociophonetic analysis of Tyneside English'. Paper presented at the ALOES Workshop, Paris-Diderot.

Andersson, Lars and Peter Trudgill 1990. *Bad Language*. Oxford: Basil Blackwell.

Barnfield, Kate and Isabelle Buchstaller 2010. 'Intensifiers on Tyneside: Longitudinal developments and new trends'. *English World-Wide* 31: 252–87.

Bauer, Laurie 2002. 'Inferring variation and change from public corpora', in Chambers, Jack K., Peter Trudgill and Natalie Schilling-Estes (eds.) *The Handbook of Language Variation and Change*. Oxford: Blackwell. pp. 97–114.

Beal, Joan C. and Karen P. Corrigan 2007. '"Time and Tyne": A corpus-based study of variation and change in relativisation strategies in Tyneside English', in Elspass, Stephan, Nils Langer, Joachim Scharloth and Wim Vandenbussche (eds.) *Germanic Language Histories 'from Below' (1700–2000)*. Berlin: Walter de Gruyter. pp. 99–114.

Beal, Joan C., Karen P. Corrigan, Paul Rayson and Nicholas Smith 2007. 'Writing the Vernacular: Transcribing and tagging the Newcastle Electronic Corpus of Tyneside English (NECTE)', in Meurman-Solin, Anneli and Arja Nurmi (eds.) *Annotating Variation and Change, volume 1*. Available online from www.helsinki.fi/varieng/journal/volumes/01/beal_et_al/.

Bender, Emily M. and Jeff Good 2010. 'A grand challenge for linguistics: Scaling up and integrating models'. Paper contributed to the NSF's SBE 2020 initiative. Available online from www.nsf.gov/sbe/sbe_2020/submission_detail.cfm?upld_id=81.

Cheshire, Jenny 1982. *Variation in an English Dialect: A Sociolinguistic Study*. Cambridge: Cambridge University Press.

Corrigan, Karen P. 1997. *The Syntax of South Armagh English in Its Socio-Historical Perspective,* unpublished, PhD thesis, University College Dublin.

    2009. 'Irish daughters of Northern British relatives: Internal and external constraints on the system of relativization in South Armagh English', in Filppula, Markku, Juhani Klemola, and Heli Paulasto (eds.) *Vernacular Universals and Language Contacts: Evidence from Varieties of English and Beyond*. London: Taylor and Francis/Routledge. pp. 133–62.

    2010. *Irish English, Volume 1: Northern Ireland*. Edinburgh: Edinburgh University Press.

    2011. 'The "art of making the best use of bad data": Mining the Irish National Folklore Collection for evidence of linguistic contact, variation and change', in Hickey, Raymond (ed.) *Researching the Languages of Ireland*. Uppsala: Uppsala Universitet. pp. 183–205.

Corrigan, Karen P., Adam Mearns, and Hermann Moisl 2014. 'Feature-based versus aggregate analyses of the DECTE corpus: Phonological and morphological variability in Tyneside English', in Szmrecsanyi, Benedikt and Bernhard, Wälchli (eds.) *Aggregating Dialectology, Typology and Register Analysis*. Berlin: Walter De Gruyter. pp. 113–49.

Corrigan, Karen P. and Adam Mearns (eds.) 2016. *Creating and Digitizing Language Corpora, Volume 3: Databases for Public Engagement*. Basingstoke: Palgrave Macmillan.

D'Arcy, Alexandra 2011. 'Corpora: Capturing language in use', in Maguire, Warren and April McMahon (eds.) *Analysing Variation in English*. Cambridge: Cambridge University Press. pp. 49–71.

Farr, Fiona and Bróna Murphy 2009. 'Religious references in contemporary Irish English: "For the love of God almighty . . . I'm the holy terror for turf"'. *Journal of Intercultural Pragmatics* 6: 535–59.

Fehringer, Carol and Karen P. Corrigan 2015. 'The rise of the going to future in Tyneside English: Evidence for further grammaticalisation'. *English World-Wide* 36: 198-227.

Glassie, Henry 1982. *Passing the Time in Ballymenone: Folklore and History of an Ulster Community*. Dublin: The O'Brien Press.

Harris, John 1985. *Phonological Variation and Change: Studies in Hiberno-English*. Cambridge: Cambridge University Press.

Hasund, K. 1998. 'Protecting the innocent: the issue of informants anonymity in the CLOT corpus', in Renouf, Antoinette (ed.). *Explorations in Corpus Linguistics*. Amsterdam: Rodopi. pp. 13–28.

Hoffman, Sebastian 2007. 'From web-page to mega-corpus: The CNN transcripts', in Hundt, Marianne, Nadja, Nesselhauf and Carolin Biewer (eds.), *Corpus Linguistics and the Web. Amsterdam: Rodopi*. pp. 69–86.

Johnson, Dan E. 2009. 'Getting off the GoldVarb standard: Introducing Rbrul for mixed effects variable rule analysis'. *Language and Linguistics Compass* 3: 359–83.

Kendall, Tyler 2011. 'Corpora from a sociolinguistic perspective', in Gries, Stefan (ed.). *'Corpus Studies: Future Directions'*, Special Issue of *Revista Brasiliera de Linguistíca Aplicada* 11. pp. 361–89.

Kretzschmar, William. A., Jean. Anderson, Joan C. Beal, Karen P. Corrigan, Lisa Lena Opas-Hänninen and Bartek Plichta 2006. 'Collaboration on corpora for regional and social analysis'. *Journal of English Linguistics* 34: 172–205.

Labov, William 1981. *Field Methods Used by the Project on Linguistic Change and Variation*. Texas: South Western Educational Developmental Laboratory.

1997. 'Some further steps in narrative analysis'. *Journal of Narrative and Life History: Special Issue - Oral Versions of Personal Experience* 7: 395–415.

2001. *Principles of Linguistic Change: Volume I Internal Factors*. Oxford: Blackwell.

Labov, William and Joshua Waletzky 1967. 'Narrative analysis: oral versions of personal experience', in Helm, June (ed.) *Essays on the Verbal and Visual Arts*. Seattle: University of Washington Press. pp. 12–44.

Martin, Philippe 2013. 'Using WinPitch as a multifile concordancer for the NECTE corpus'. Paper presented at Corpus Interoperability and Diachrony: The NECTE-DECTE Corpora, Paris-Diderot.

McEnery, Tony and Andrew Hardie 2012. *Corpus Linguistics*. Cambridge: Cambridge University Press.

Mearns, Adam, 2015. 'Tyneside', in Hickey, Raymond (ed.) *Researching Northern English*. Amsterdam: John Benjamins. pp. 161–182.

Mehl, Seth, Sean Wallis, and Bas Aarts, 2016. 'Language learning at your fingertips: Deploying corpora in mobile teaching apps', in Corrigan, Karen P. and Adam Mearns (eds.) *Creating and Digitizing Language Corpora, Volume 3: Databases for Public Engagement*. Basingstoke: Palgrave Macmillan. pp. 211–240.

Meurman-Solin, Anneli and Arja Nurmi (eds.) 2007. *Annotating Variation and Change, Volume 1*. Available online from www.helsinki.fi/varieng/journal/volumes/01/beal_et_al/.

Milroy, James and John Harris 1980. 'When is a merger not a merger?: the MEAT/MATE problem in present-day vernacular English'. *English World-Wide* 1: 199–210.

Milroy, Lesley and Matthew Gordon 2003. *Sociolinguistics: Method and Interpretation*. Oxford: Blackwell.

Moisl Hermann and Warren Maguire 2008. 'Identifying the main determinants of phonetic variation in the Newcastle Electronic Corpus of Tyneside English'. *Journal of Quantitative Linguistics* 15: 46–69.

Murphy, K. 2012. 'The Folklore of South Armagh'. Lecture presented on 18th March 2012, Newry and Mourne Museum.

Murphy, Michael J. 1973. *Tyrone Folk Quest*. Belfast: Blackstaff.
    1975. *Now You're Talking*. Belfast: Blackstaff.

Nevalainen, Terttu and Helena Raumolin-Brunberg 1996. 'The corpus of early English correspondence', in Nevalainen, Terttu and Helena Raumolin-Brunberg (eds.) *Sociolinguistics and Language History*. Amsterdam: Rodopi. pp. 39–54.

Parisse, Christophe 2013. 'Converting the NECTE files into CLAN readable format'. Paper at Corpus Interoperability and Diachrony: The NECTE-DECTE Corpora, Paris-Diderot.

Rock, Frances 2001. 'Policy and practice in the anonymisation of linguistic data'. *International Journal of Corpus Linguistics* 6: 1–26.

Sankoff, David, Sali A. Tagliamonte and Eric Smith 2005. '*GoldVarb X*', Department of Linguistics, University of Toronto, Toronto, Canada. http://individual.utoronto.ca/tagliamonte/GoldVarb/GV_index.htm.

Sinclair, John 2005. 'Corpus and Text - Basic Principles' in Wynne, Martin (ed.) *Developing Linguistic Corpora: A Guide to Good Practice*, Oxford: Oxbow Books. pp. 1–16.

Slembrouck, Stef 1992. 'The parliamentary Hansard "verbatim" report: the written construction of spoken discourse'. *Language and Literature* 1: 101–19.

Smith, Nick, Sebastian Hoffman and Paul Rayson 2008. 'Corpus tools and methods, today and tomorrow: Incorporating linguists' manual annotations'. *Literary and Linguistic Computing* 23: 163–80.

Smyth, Daragh 1997. 'Murphy's Lore', *Special issue of Artslink*. Belfast: Northern Ireland Arts Council.

Tagliamonte, Sali A. 2004. 'Comparative sociolinguistics', in Chambers, J. K., Peter Trudgill and Natalie Schilling-Estes (eds.) *The Handbook of Language Variation and Change*. pp. 729–63.

Tagliamonte, Sali A. 2006. *Analyzing Sociolinguistic Variation*. Cambridge: Cambridge University Press.

2007. 'Representing real language: Consistency, trade offs and thinking ahead!', in Beal, Joan C., Karen P. Corrigan, and Hermann Moisl (eds.) *Creating and Digitizing Language Corpora, Volume 2: Diachronic Databases*. Houndmills, Basingstoke: Palgrave-Macmillan. pp. 205–40.

Widdowson, John D. A. 1999. 'Hidden depths: Exploring archival resources of spoken English'. *Lore and Language* 17: 81–92.

6   Using Archives to Conduct Collaborative Research on Language and Region

Fiona Douglas

1.   Introduction

This chapter describes the innovative approach to dialect study that underpins the *Language, History, Place* project: a research, teaching, and public engagement initiative that brings together materials from an existing language and cultural heritage archive, the *Leeds Archive of Vernacular Culture* (*LAVC*), with real-life objects in the museum setting. The chapter explores the substantial research opportunities and benefits offered by reuniting tangible with intangible heritage; it discusses the intellectual and methodological challenges associated with trying to reuse archive data for purposes not originally envisaged, and investigates the possibility of augmenting the archive by inviting visitors to contribute their own linguistic heritage through various enactive engagement activities. The paper seeks to address a number of questions: what is and is not possible, defensible, or allowable within the parameters of publicly engaged sociolinguistic research? Is it possible to collect useful research data using such methods, whilst at the same time significantly enriching museum collections and providing an enhanced, enjoyable, and stimulating visitor experience? Must historical archives such as the *LAVC* remain closed, completed repositories or can they be open, dynamic resources that we reuse, reframe, and repurpose, and to which new materials are added?

2.   The LAVC: An Historic Archive

The *Leeds Archive of Vernacular Culture* is a unique multimedia archive collection relating to the study of dialect and folk life in England. It is derived from two main sources: materials from the *Survey of English Dialects* (*SED*) developed by Harold Orton and Eugen Dieth during the 1950s and 1960s (see Orton and Dieth 1971; Sanderson and Widdowson 1987; Upton *et al.*1994; Upton and Widdowson 2013) and materials from the former Institute of Dialect and Folk Life Studies (*IDFLS*). Following the closure of the *IDFLS* in 1983, the *SED* and *IDFLS* archives were rather neglected, before being relocated to the University of Leeds Brotherton Library's Special Collections in the early 1990s. A successful bid to the AHRB's Resource Enhancement scheme in 2002, designed to make the collections 'accessible to researchers and ensure their long term preservation' (University of Leeds 2014), facilitated the development of a detailed catalogue for the renamed *Leeds Archive of Vernacular Culture* collection (Wiltshire and Jenner 2005), and the digitisation of an extensive range of sound recordings. A tantalising sample of twenty-three digitised photographs and sixteen audio files was made available on the project website in order to indicate the types of material held in the archive.

The *LAVC* contains all the materials associated with the *SED*, both published and unpublished, including nine subject-specific books containing the responses to the Survey's 1,300 questions (administered in 313 locations). This material also comprises all the fieldworkers' notebooks (a fascinating record of sociolinguistic research from a previous era before audio recordings in the field were routine), word maps showing dialect isoglosses, the Basic and Incidental Materials, and a series of photographs commissioned as part of the Survey (taken by renowned ethnographical photographer Werner Kissling). With advances in audio technology, it became increasingly possible to capture recordings in the field, hence some of the original locations and contributors were later revisited, and a series of informal conversations on home, farm, and working life were recorded as a complement to the original Survey materials, between the original survey and the early 1970s. The *LAVC* also contains the outputs from the *IDFLS*, also based at the University of Leeds, which, originally under the direction of Stewart Sanderson, operated from 1964 until the early 1980s. In total, the archive comprises some 2,000 photographs, over 900 audio recordings, more than 220 student theses and dissertations, myriad research papers, newspaper cuttings, administrative records, and Survey and Institute correspondence. All were collected over a period of thirty years and provide exceptional insights into language, culture and everyday life in twentieth-century England.

Unquestionably, the *LAVC* is a marvellous and exciting collection; but despite the 2002–5 project's cataloguing of the archive, and its digitisation of the sound recordings (some of which are available via the British Library's sound archive website (see http://sounds.bl.uk/Accents-and-dialects/Survey-of-English-dialects), the collection remains locked away in Special Collections – safely preserved but largely inaccessible to, and unused by, the communities from which its rich dialect and cultural materials were collected. Visitors can, of course, make appointments to consult it (and the *LAVC* catalogue has made it possible to map the scope of the archive, and to locate specific resources), but, realistically, only bona-fide academic researchers, or determined and motivated individual members of the public, are ever likely to access it. Consequently, the archive is underused and underpublicised, a fate that befalls all too many of our important collections. Its status has thus diminished over time and, like many other such resources, although carefully preserved, it is in danger of becoming a historical artefact and linguistic reliquary.[1]

3.   The *Language, History, Place* Project: An Archive Reborn

The *Language, History, Place* project seeks to breathe new life into the *LAVC* by using the archive as a catalyst for new research and teaching activities, coupled with public engagement initiatives within the communities from which the archive materials originally came. The project embraces the UK's National Coordinating Centre for Public Engagement (NCCPE)'s (2014) definition of public engagement as: 'the myriad of ways in which the activity and benefits of higher education and research can be shared with the public. Engagement is by definition a two-way process, involving interaction and listening, with the goal of generating mutual benefit'. The project is based on a partnership, established in 2009, between the School of English at the University of Leeds, the Brotherton Library's Special Collections, and three Yorkshire museums: the Dales Countryside Museum in Hawes, the Ryedale Folk Museum in Hutton-le-Hole, and the Shibden Hall Folk Museum outside Halifax. To date, project activities have been a six-month Museum Library and Archive (MLA) Council-funded pilot (2010), and various undergraduate student research opportunities at the University of Leeds, such as a research scholarship (2010), the *Language, Identity and Community* option module (2011 onwards), and final year dissertations (2014).

The museums are located in different parts of Yorkshire, and each seeks to reflect the area's local culture and heritage. Though different in character, governance, and funding structures, all have vernacular culture or folk life[2] collections centring on traditional ways of life and everyday objects that might once have been found in the home, on the farm, or in a craftsman's workshop. Whereas the museum collections and displays focus on 'tangible heritage', as manifested by historical artefacts, the *LAVC* contains complementary and contemporaneous 'intangible heritage'[3] materials, with especial strengths in 'oral traditions and expressions, including language as a vehicle of the

---

[1] See Kendall (2013) for a useful overview on managing data preservation and access to linguistic data after projects have expired, and Corti and Thompson (2006) for discussion of how best to reuse, rework, and reanalyse different types of archived qualitative data.

[2] Both terms seem patronising to modern ears, but see Wilks and Kelly (2008). Essentially, the focus in both is on traditional ways of life, and the associated tangible and intangible heritage. (See note 3.)

[3] UNESCO (2003) defines intangible heritage as 'the practices, representations, expressions, knowledge, skills – as well as the instruments, objects, artefacts and cultural spaces associated therewith – that communities, groups and, in some cases, individuals recognize as part of their cultural heritage'.

intangible cultural heritage' (UNESCO 2003). Many folk museums, including the three Yorkshire partners, have their origins in the post-war period, especially during the 1950s and early 1960s,[4] when vernacular culture collections were often assembled in response to the perceived threats of increased industrialisation (Smith 2012). Thus, as the *SED* and *IDFLS* were busy collecting 'genuine' dialect from older, 'ordinary' people in mainly rural locations, with a view to preserving it for future generations before it was irrevocably changed by increasing social and geographical mobility, the folk life museums were simultaneously gathering the everyday objects that were rapidly becoming, or were already, obsolete and in danger of being lost forever.

The *Language, History, Place* project aims to open up the very substantial archives of the *LAVC* to much wider audiences by marrying digitised copies of archive materials with the physical artefacts to which they relate within these museums, hence returning them to the local community context. Not only does this enrich the museums' displays and enhance the visitor experience, it also puts these resources back into the communities from whence they came, upholding Wolfram's (1993) *principle of linguistic gratuity* (see also Wolfram *et al.* 2008; Wolfram 2010, 2012). To date, use of the *LAVC* has been largely restricted to the academic community. But given its cultural, historic, and linguistic importance, it is not only desirable, but ethically responsible, to ensure that its resources are made accessible to a wider and non-specialist audience. After all, these materials were collected from local communities. It is their voices that speak on the audio recordings, their pronunciations, and their words for everyday objects that were collected and analysed, their customs, beliefs and ways of life that are documented by the extensive photographic and folk life collections. By locking these resources up in academic repositories, treating them as artefacts of a bygone age, and separating them from the way of life they describe as well as their communities of origin, we lose much of their vital energy and significance.

By uniting the *LAVC*'s language and other resources with the museums' physical artefacts, we have the opportunity to unlock meaning and reawaken connections. Language has the power to connect us with places and history, and with remote or unfamiliar cultural heritage. There is something powerfully evocative about hearing voices from the past, or learning about the unfamiliar words people used for everyday objects of a bygone age, that connects us to the original community. As Anderson (1991: 145) says: 'nothing connects us affectively to the dead more than language'. Voices from the past may be in the form of dialect recordings, such as those from the *LAVC*, or oral history recordings held in museums, libraries, or oral history archives; both can

---

[4] The same period heralded the launch of the Society for Folk Life Studies, in 1961, and the launch of the *Folk Life* journal, in 1963 (Mastoris 2012).

provide valuable data for the sociolinguist (e.g. Maguire's (2014) *Dialect of the Holy Island of Lindisfarne* (*DHIL*) corpus, Moore's (2010) *Scilly Voices* project (see Sections 1 and 3 of this volume respectively), and Leach's (2014) work with Stoke-on-Trent museums on *Voices of the Potteries*. Miller (2008) argues for everyday objects as important means by which people connect with both the past and human relationships; 'the "past" is embodied and commodified in the things that people buy and use' (Shove *et al.* 2009: 7). By reuniting tangible and intangible heritage, bringing together the language, stories, voices, and visual representations of the past with the physical objects they describe, and doing so within the communities from which they originated, both the *LAVC* and museum collections gain new meaning and salience. To quote one of the museum directors: 'your language resources will make our objects sing'.

4.   Enactive Engagement in the Museum Contact Zone

Museums have much in common with academic archives: both are safe places for the long-term storage, curation, and preservation of historical collections, and both are loci of trusted knowledge and institutional authority; but unless carefully managed and reinvigorated, each runs the risk of having collections that become static and moribund. In the case of the partner folk life museums, their fascinating collections of everyday objects from the past represent earlier ways of life that grow increasingly remote from visitors' experience with each passing year. Smith (2012: 56) argues that such museums face significant problems as the passage of time results in artefacts becoming 'divorced from the intangible cultural heritage that gave them significance'.

As is often the case in folk life museums, objects are displayed as they might have been found in situ, not locked away in glass cases and given scholarly labels, but located in reconstructed rooms and workshops and presented as though the person had just stepped out for a moment, leaving their tools or everyday objects behind them. Despite these naturalised settings, folk life museums have to work hard to make their collections relevant and meaningful to present-day audiences. Because there is little traditional written interpretation in the form of labels, visitors are required to have 'cultural competence' (McIntosh and Prentice 1999: 591) – which entails having a cultural, historical, cognitive, and sensory competence that enables them to experience the display in a way that is understandable, stimulating, and satisfying. In short, without detailed interpretative labels attached to each object, people need to be able to draw on their own 'funds of knowledge' (González et al. 2005) to help them make sense of the artefacts. 'Funds of knowledge' are acquired on the basis of lived experience, and may be particular to family or local life. An important cultural resource, they are often passed down the generations, but can be damaged or lost by cultural or temporal dislocation (Vélez-Ibáñez and Greenberg 2005).

When originally established in the 1950s and 60s, folk life museums could rely on some of their visitors being able to recognise objects from their childhood, bringing their own life experiences to bear on interpreting the displays. With time, however, fewer and fewer visitors can be expected to make sense of objects that represent a culture of which they have little or no direct experience; in short, their 'funds of knowledge' have been lost, and they are disconnected from the past and its associated cultural heritage. Craftsmen's tools used by blacksmiths, coopers, saddlers, and wheelwrights, commonplace objects associated with domestic routines such as dairying and laundry, implements from rural life, farming, and agriculture – all of this tangible heritage can mean little to the present-day museum visitor. The objects themselves, though interesting, are seldom especially beautiful or valuable; these are the bits and pieces of everyday life from a bygone era, not aesthetically prized, and it would be easy to dismiss them as dull and uninteresting, 'a pile of rusty old stuff'. This situation presents significant challenges to the museums: how can they best engage with visitors who do not have the requisite cultural competence, and for whom the objects displayed and ways of life represented are remote, unfamiliar, and difficult to relate to?

One powerful means of doing so is via 'enactive engagement' (Hooper-Greenhill 1994), which some would argue is essential in folk life and living museums. Enactive engagement is 'the opportunity ... for visitors to participate themselves, and become part of the exhibition experience, rather than act as passive bystanders'. This harnesses the potential of the 'nostalgic memories that visitors share and may transmit to one another' and to staff, demonstrating the evocative power of stories that have been passed down the generations (Wilks and Kelly 2008: 132–5). In so doing, visitors are helping to generate meaning, and the whole experience becomes a 'collective activity' with both personal and interpersonal significance. Whereas individuals can transmit their memories simply by talking about them first-hand, Halbwachs (1925) argued that a community's 'social' or 'collective' memory is more disconnected from original events. Importantly for the *Language, History, Place* project, storytelling, objects, and a sense of place can help to remake these connections (Halbwachs 1925; Connerton 1989; Fentress and Wickham 1992; Feld and Basso 1996; Winter 2009; Crane 2011). Crucially, social memory is 'an active and ongoing process' (Van Dyke and Alcock 2003: 3), so by offering visitors these opportunities, it is possible to maintain a dynamic dialogue between past and present.

Clifford (1997) conceptualises museums as 'contact zones',[5] places of 'encounter', with permeable walls, where communities, cultures, and the museum itself interact, intersect, and influence each other. Though the theory has since been challenged (most especially by the work of Bennett 1998, see also Dibley 2005), reworked and revisited (Macdonald 2002; Boast 2011; Onciul 2013; Schorch 2013), it remains an influential, pervasive, and productive concept (Peers and Brown 2003; Crooke 2007). The 2011 conference, *Revisiting the Contact Zone: Museums, Theory, Practice*, established the theory as significant for ongoing debates. The contact zone's emphases on dialogic encounter and the role of the visitor (Witcomb 2003; Mason 2011) have particular importance for the *Language, History, Place* project. The Leeds project's partner museums are places where meanings and significations can be negotiated and co-created by encounters between visitors, staff, space, objects, and ideas (Hennes 2010). Peers and Brown (2003: 4) argue that artefacts function as 'contact zones', both as 'sources of knowledge' and 'catalysts for new relationships – both within and between ... communities'. This dialogic dynamism is also characteristic of intangible cultural heritage, which UNESCO (2003) characterises as being 'transmitted from generation to generation', 'constantly recreated by communities' and providing them with 'a sense of identity and continuity'. It represents both past 'inherited traditions' and 'contemporary urban and rural practices in which diverse cultural groups take part' (UNESCO 2014).

Visitors bring to the contact zone their own ideas, funds of knowledge, narratives, memories, and cultural heritage; in so doing, they create new meanings, new ideas, and new intersections. Crucially for the *Language, History, Place* project, they also bring their own linguistic heritage, identities, and practices; this gives them a way in to interpreting unfamiliar cultural heritage (e.g. by hearing voices from the past which bring the museum objects to life), and also means they have something valuable to contribute within the contact zone.

So, the project goes beyond reuniting tangible and intangible heritage, important though that is. The purpose is not just to make the *LAVC*'s existing academic research data and cultural resources available to museum communities, and to the wider public, through the enrichment of museum displays (both physical and virtual/online exhibitions) by combination with museum artefacts; it also aims to use these resources as a stimulus, creating a range of public engagement opportunities that both enhance the visitor

---

[5] Clifford adapts the term from Mary Louise Pratt's (1992) work on literacy and writing within the multilingual classroom. For Pratt (1992: 7), the contact zone is 'an attempt to invoke the spatial and temporal co-presence of subjects previously separate by geographic and historical disjunctures, and whose trajectories now intersect'.

experience and enable us to collect new present-day language data from visitors. By harnessing the potential of enactive engagement within the museum context, we can help visitors to (re)connect with a sense of themselves, their heritage, their history, their language, and their sense of place and identity. The experience is participatory in the fullest sense, given that the visitors are invited to share their present-day language with us, for the benefit of other visitors, the museums and their displays, and the ongoing research project.

With time, as the gap widens between the objects displayed in these museums and the cultural competence of visitors, and as funds of knowledge are lost (Vélez-Ibáñez and Greenberg 2005), this type of activity is likely to increase in importance. In many cases, they are what we might term 'privileged encounters' – privileged because they occur within that specific space owing to the convergence of particular circumstances, social actors, and stimuli. In other words, without the co-presence in the museum space of people and objects, we are unlikely to glean many of these stories, and the associated language practice. Without the museum context to reunite tangible and intangible heritage, many of these conversations would never happen, and the discovery of a shared cultural inheritance and distinctive linguistic practice would be lost to researchers and visitors forever.

5.   Transformative Encounters for All

Hennes (2010) emphasises the potentially transformative importance of these encounters in the museum context. By focusing attention on the objects in front of them, by spending time engaging with and thinking about the ideas and stories presented, visitors may discover things they have repressed or not yet realised. By making sense of the exhibition, it may also transpire that they are able to make sense of themselves in relation to it. By giving to the process, they gain from it. There are clear benefits such as a more enjoyable and memorable museum visit, because one has taken part in something meaningful rather than simply consuming the thoughts or narratives of others. There may also be educational benefits, given that activities can be designed to inform as well as to engage. If other visitors are simultaneously engaged in the same activity, then as a group they may begin to uncover shared ideas, narratives, and cultural or linguistic heritage. Even where visitors have no immediate connection to the objects and ideas presented, they are still likely to be discussing and reacting to what they see, hear, and experience within the museum space. If invited to consider thematic topics, such as *home life* or domestic objects as well as history and place, everyone has an opportunity to contribute and to have their contribution valued (see Pahl and Pollard 2010; Pahl and Roswell 2010; Pahl 2012). In this way, even visitors with no geographical or cultural links to the museum's artefacts can become involved with what is on offer. Properly managed, enactive engagement is an inclusive rather than exclusive experience.

6.   Language Research in the Museum

The *Language, History, Place* project's emphasis on language gives all visitors a point of entry, regardless of background or education, because it is something that most of us use daily, to which we can easily relate, and to which we can all contribute. Language is an important part of our identities: it says much about who we are, where we come from, what we value. As the chapters in this volume show, it gives us a sense of place and history. Language also connects us to others within the community in the present-day, so it has a horizontal as well as vertical reach: 'there is a special kind of contemporaneous community which language alone suggests' (Anderson 1991: 145). It is simultaneously inclusive and exclusive: inclusive because it gives us a sense of belonging; exclusive because it underlines difference. Both sides of the coin offer enactive engagement opportunities: familiarity stimulates discussion around similarities to visitors' own varieties; difference often prompts them to supply their own words, sayings and pronunciations. Most people are very willing to discuss their language use and that of others, their linguistic likes and dislikes, favourite words and accents, and generally they enjoy doing so. Thoughtfully harnessed, all of this can provide valuable data for language research, as well as enhancing the visitor experience and museum displays. All we have to do is collect it – but how best to do so? What are the opportunities and challenges of gathering language data in this context, and how do we address issues of comparability with earlier datasets such as those of the *LAVC*?

7.   Challenges, Opportunities and Comparability

In most types of research involving the collection or analysis of sociolinguistic material, data integrity and robustness are usually deemed essential, and researchers will go to considerable lengths to preselect data samples, control variables, and ensure consistency. What does this mean for the reuse of legacy archive data in sociolinguistic research alongside the collection of new, present-day language data from museum visitors?

Firstly, there is the question of how best to reconcile the existing and new datasets so as to ensure comparability. What were the data collection protocols for the original studies, and which parameters should inform the new data collection strategies? How can comparability across two different datasets, collected for different purposes over different time periods, and according to different conventions, be achieved? Other sociolinguistic research projects which reuse and augment legacy data have faced similar issues, for example the *Diachronic Electronic Corpus of Tyneside English* (DECTE)[6] (Beal 2009; Corrigan *et al.* 2012; Beal and Corrigan 2013, and Corrigan, Chapter 5, this volume). Secondly, there is the question of the extent to which it is possible to add to the archive by using self-selecting contributors whilst still maintaining representativeness. Thirdly, there is the matter of the logistical and methodological mechanics of collecting language data from museum visitors.

Traditional dialectology, of which the *SED* is a good example, was largely concerned with tracing connections between dialect and older forms of the language, so it had a strong historical dimension. Although such work is valuable, and provides useful historical comparisons for present-day language researchers, it has been criticised for being unrepresentative, most especially because it offers only limited information about variability within individual speech communities, as in most cases only a few and the 'best' dialect speakers were selected for inclusion (Chambers and Trudgill 1998; Foulkes and Docherty 2007). Representativeness was never the aim of the *SED*, and the data collection methods favoured older, predominantly male, speakers from rural communities in the belief that they would best represent the 'pure' dialect forms of the past. The *Language, History, Place* project does not seek to be a present-day *SED*. Influential and significant as it was and still is, the *SED* is not without its flaws. The questionnaire format is both expensive and time-consuming to administer, and it yields data with its own idiosyncrasies and problems. *SED* participants were selected, not on the basis of being a representative sample of the overall population, but according to the rather dubious criterion of the state of their dentition:

The informants themselves were *predominantly natives from rural communities*, with preference being given to those who had spent *little or no time away from their home village, to males* (who were less inclined to correct their speech) and to those who were intelligent and *had a good set of teeth (!)* (University of Leeds 2014 [my emphases])

Unless the present-day data collection activities were to reproduce the *SED* methodologies and sampling regime, absolute data comparability cannot be guaranteed. But, as already discussed, working within the museum context via interactive public engagement activities, it is not desirable to exclude swathes of visitors on the basis of their social/cultural background, geographical origins, age, or indeed on the state of their teeth! To what extent, then, is it

---

[6] DECTE is comprised of the existing *Newcastle Corpus of Tyneside English* (NECTE1) dating from c. 1979, and NECTE2 'an ongoing collection of interviews conducted in the North East of England since 2007' (Varieng 2011); see also NECTE (2007) and Allen *et al.* (2007).

possible to undertake useful sociolinguistic analysis if you are not in a position to select and control the sample?

Many sociolinguistic studies aim to have fixed proportions of specific age-groups, genders, socio-economic profiles and so on (see chapters on methodology in Mallinson *et al.* 2013; Schilling 2013). Whilst such controls seem to promise more reliable data, they may unwittingly skew the final results. There are many advantages in collecting language from a self-selecting volunteer sample, rather than from a preselected and conservative group like the NORMs favoured by the *SED* and other traditional dialect surveys. By inviting everyone to participate, we can gain insight into the range of visitor profiles. Self-selection offers its own brand of representativeness, though like all museum work, we need to be aware of potential lacunae in socio-economic profiles. If we operated with predetermined categories based on regional and social demographic criteria, we might find they do not readily suit visitor profiles. By not excluding visitors from beyond the museum's geographical area, and by not setting predetermined sociolinguistic criteria, we not only ensure a more inclusive visitor experience, but are likely to gain a richer and less restricted dataset. By asking visitors to submit non-intrusive accompanying metadata information (e.g. their and their parents' place of origin and residence, an indication of age range, and other social and demographic data) whilst contributing their own language to the project, we can build the collection from the bottom up rather than by the top-down approach usually favoured in sociolinguistic studies. The dataset can be augmented as necessary by running event days, putting out special appeals, and experimenting with online crowdsourcing collection methods. We therefore have the potential to explore both synchronic and diachronic comparisons with existing and new archive data. And because the project welcomes linguistic contributions from all visitors, not just those who recognise or share the dialect varieties exhibited, or who fit predetermined sociolinguistic categories, everyone can share in the experience.

The museums likewise are keen that we research actual language use in all its rich variety as evidenced across the range of their visitors. They are not looking to preserve a community or its language in aspic, or to build exhibitions and experiences that focus only on times past. The Dales Countryside Museum, for example, is interested in current life in the Dales, which is not only about rural farming communities, but also includes the rich variety of individuals who currently live, work, and visit there. It encompasses both those with long-standing family connections to the area, and those with no family links to the Dales who may have moved there more recently, some of whom may fully or partially work from home in non-traditional Dales occupations such as finance, PR, web design, and also day-trippers and holidaymakers. In short, they are interested in both locals and incomers, or *off-cumdens* as the latter are known in Yorkshire. Ultimately, museums want to relate to their audiences, whoever they may be.

It is well known that elicitation techniques can have a major impact on the type and quality of data collected. The Observer's Paradox remains a bugbear for all who try to collect language data, and eliciting casual or naturalistic language often seems to be the holy grail of sociolinguistic studies, especially for those investigating 'non-standard' or 'dialect' usage. Both individual and group data collection approaches have been used by others harnessing the opportunities offered by public engagement. The British Museum's 2010 *Evolving English* exhibition used a mock telephone booth to collect language data from respondents reading aloud from *Mr Tickle* or a short word list (British Library b). In 2005, *BBC Voices* took a variety of approaches in its attempt to obtain a snapshot of language use at the start of the twenty-first century, and combined audio-recorded group interactions with individual voluntary website-elicited responses to the project's thematically structured spidergrams[7] (Elmes 2013; Robinson *et al.* 2013).

Where does all of this leave us? There is clearly no one ideal method of collecting dialect data, and so the *Language, History, Place* project tests different methods of enactive engagement and data elicitation, using both individual and group data collection strategies to see which are the most effective in the museum context. It is hoped that collecting language data as part of a museum visit that is both enabling and enjoyable for participants makes much more feasible the eliciting of good and perhaps even naturalistic data. Visitors are likely to be relaxed and enjoying themselves. The context is fairly informal, and sharing one's words or pronunciations for things may seem much less threatening or odd in that context than it would within a traditional academic research environment where people may feel they need to be on their best linguistic behaviour. Researcher observation suggests that, when presented with even basic *LAVC* stimuli in the museum, such as photographs, audio recordings, and word maps among other things, visitors often spontaneously begin to discuss and reminisce with each other, and that process of interaction yields much richer and less self-conscious linguistic data than responses to targeted questions within a controlled environment.

Activities tested by the *Language, History, Place* project to date, within the context of the pilot study and the undergraduate research opportunities (which enable students to carry out primary research and public engagement activities within the museum context) have been multifarious, have yielded rich research data, and have been warmly welcomed by the partner museums and their visitors. We have used a variety of stimulus materials from the *LAVC* to elicit

---

[7] This methodology was borrowed from earlier work on the *Survey of Regional English (SURE)* (Kerswill *et al.* 1999; Llamas 1999).

present-day language from museum visitors, and set up recording stations on site, inviting people to come along and share their memories and language with us. The community links offered by the museums, both via their physical location and their extensive networks of museum friends and volunteers, present exciting and unique opportunities. By collaborating with visitors and volunteers, we have seen that encounters with artefacts and voices from the past within the museum contact zone yield new experiences and insights, and we have been able to make links between past and present. For example, we interviewed someone who remembers the original visits made to her father by Kissling and the *SED* researchers; some fifty years on, she was able to shed new light on *SED* fieldwork and photographs. Students have made an educational film about dialect for one of the museums, drawing on the first-hand experience of one of the volunteers who remembers World War II evacuees arriving in the village and their bewilderment on first encountering the local dialect variety. We have also carried out mini surveys where visitors have been invited to 'post' their words in the dialect letter-box. Visitors have responded enthusiastically to all of these invitations, and valuable and diverse language data has been collected in a relatively brief period. The results have been analysed and compared with existing research data (past and present), and students have written up as their work as academic essays and as accounts for lay audiences, with the latter being displayed both in the museum and online via museum blogs. In this way, students learned to work between the academic and museum environments, 'translating' their research for different audiences. Even activities that superficially may have seemed like 'just a bit of fun', such as the dialect-informed *Call my Bluff* [8] game run at a museum open day, have revealed the public's appetite and enthusiasm for all things language-related. (Although primarily aimed at children, we soon found that adult visitors were keen to take part in guessing which dialect words were real and which were bluffs.) All of these activities can yield rich language data, and in ways that have benefits for all concerned.

8.   The Legacy of Privileged Linguistic Encounters

The *Language, History, Place* project invites visitors to make a lasting contribution to both the museums and research partners, and, by extension, to the communities within which the museums are situated. By taking part in these activities, visitors contribute their language, stories, and cultural heritage to the project for the benefit of other visitors, themselves, the museums and

---

[8]   *Call my Bluff* was a British television panel show, in which multiple definitions of unusual words were described by one team of panellists. The other team had to guess the true definition of the word.

academic researchers. Nowadays, many museums have interactive displays which encourage visitors to tell their own stories, or contribute their thoughts to a visual display; but all too often such activities, whilst fulfilling for visitors during their actual visit, lack legacy value. After a brief period on display, such contributions are all too often discarded or, if retained, put into storage or the museum archive. Simon (2010: 15) talks about the problem of 'broken feedback loops' where individuals who have contributed to participatory museum activities do not 'see their work integrated in a timely, attractive, respectful way', and she stresses the need for museums to think carefully about the scaffolding, parameters, flexibility, and 'rewards' for visitor participation. In short – contributing should count.

Further to the benefits of enactive engagement already cited, this project offers additional advantages that are linked to the focus on language and its often overlooked capacity for ensuring social inclusion. One consequence of these transformative encounters is powerful validation of the importance of the language varieties that people bring with them. All too familiar are situations where individuals have been told and believe that the language they use is 'slang', or somehow inferior to more prestigious standard forms. Even by labelling a variety as 'non-standard' or 'dialect', we immediately invoke, intentionally or otherwise, ideological presuppositions about value, desirability, and appropriateness. The *Language, History, Place* project makes no value judgements about linguistic varieties. It is not looking only for *correct*, *proper* or *standard* varieties. Nor, unlike the *SED*, is it looking only for *conservative*, *good*, *broad* or *traditional* dialect, or carefully choosing a preselected group of 'dialect informants'. All contributions are valued equally, and for those visitors who may have previously felt or been told that their variety is non-standard, or somehow 'substandard', there is a validating effect in having that language seen as worthy of collection, public display, and further study. Helping visitors to discover and celebrate their individual linguistic practice and recognise its place within a larger linguistic heritage has long-lasting benefits that extend well beyond the life of any project.

By harnessing the potential of enactive engagement for dialect research within the museum, we stand to gain new knowledge as researchers, and perhaps to uncover novel, unforeseen research avenues. By enabling serendipitous, as well as planned, encounters within the museum contact zone, we open up the archive, and ourselves, to fresh insights. By encouraging the public to engage with, contribute to, and have a sense of ownership in the archive, we democratise access to these rich cultural resources. But crowdsourcing and self-selecting data collection methodologies mean we also have to relinquish some control. We may even have to go as far as modifying our traditional scholarly notions of *authority* and *the expert*. By allowing so-called *non-experts* or *laypersons* to help us reframe the archive through their encounters with it, things may get messy, or beyond our control, but this is not necessarily a negative outcome. There are undoubtedly significant implications attached to throwing open the archive doors to all, but to continue concentrating our efforts on simply preserving it and keeping most people out will bring more serious consequences, including potentially the death of the archive. Rebirthing the archive is tricky, but ultimately it can mean fresh beginnings for our carefully garnered and conserved, precious resources. Our existing archives and repositories have the potential to be reanimated and reframed – to become living, culturally significant resources that bring forth new and perhaps unforeseen research and public engagement benefits. Each encounter with the archive has the potential to change it. As researchers and custodians, it is our responsibility to enable these transformative archival interventions, to breathe new vitality into our archives, and so secure their future.

By inviting visitors to share their language with us, and by respecting them as co-creators and co-curators of knowledge, we can make this an empowering encounter for all concerned. Visitors' contributions are a valuable and rich resource, and will help to shape our understanding of language use (and indeed museum visitor patterns and behaviour) in the twenty-first century. By asking visitors to share their linguistic heritage, we can ensure that their contributions will feed into the research, archive, and museum collections of the future. By contributing their language to the project, visitors have the opportunity to discover more about themselves, more about their cultural heritage, and to have their linguistic heritage valued, studied, and preserved. There are several ways we can keep the doors to the *Language, History, Place* archive open and its walls permeable:

1. By collaborating with local museums, communities, and members of the public;
2. By engaging in proper dialogue with them;
3. Via embedding our ongoing research in their collections, collective memories, and individual funds of knowledge;
4. Through ensuring they share ownership in the data we collect.

To attain these goals would be to achieve enactive engagement and linguistic research at their very best: empowering, inclusive, meaningful and with lasting legacies.

REFERENCES

Allen, William, Joan C. Beal, Karen Corrigan, Warren Maguire and Hermann Moisl 2007. 'A linguistic time-capsule: The Newcastle Electronic Corpus of Tyneside English', in Beal, Joan, C., Karen Corrigan, and Hermann Moisl (eds.) *Creating and Digitising Language Corpora, Vol. 2: Diachronic Databases*. Houndmills: Palgrave Macmillan. pp. 16–48.

Anderson, Benedict 1991. *Imagined Communities: Reflections on the Origins and Spread of Nationalism*, Second edition. London: Verso.

BBC. 2011. *BBC Voices*. www.bbc.co.uk/voices/.

Beal, Joan C. 2009. 'Creating corpora from spoken legacy materials: variation and change meet corpus linguistics'. *Language and Computers* 69: 33–47.

Beal, Joan C. and Karen Corrigan 2013. 'Working with "unconventional" existing data sources', in Mallinson, Christine, Becky Childs, and Gerard Van Herk (eds.) *Data Collection in Sociolinguistics: Methods and Applications*. London: Routledge. pp. 213–16.

Bennett, Tony 1998. *Culture: A Reformer's Science*. London: Sage.

Boast, Robin 2011. 'Neocolonial collaboration: Museum as contact zone revisited'. *Museum Anthropology* 34: 56–70.

British Library. n.d. a. Sounds Archive: Survey of English Dialects. http://sounds.bl.uk/Accents-and-dialects/Survey-of-English-dialects.

British Library. n.d. b. *Evolving English: One language, many voices*. www.bl.uk/evolvingenglish/maplisten.html.

Chambers, J. K. and Peter Trudgill 1998. *Dialectology*, Second edition. Cambridge: Cambridge University Press.

Clifford, James 1997. 'Museums as contact zones', in Clifford, James (ed.) *Routes: Travel and Translation in the Late Twentieth Century*. Cambridge, Massachusetts: Harvard University Press. pp. 188–219.

Connerton, Paul 1989. *How Societies Remember*. Cambridge: Cambridge University Press.

Corrigan, Karen, Isabelle Buchstaller, Adam Mearns, and Hermann Moisl 2012. *The Diachronic Electronic Corpus of Tyneside English*. Newcastle University. http://research.ncl.ac.uk/decte/index.htm.

Corti, Louise and Paul Thompson 2006. 'Secondary analysis of archived data', in Seale, Clive, David Silverman, Jaber F. Gubrium, and Giampietro, Gobo (eds.) *Qualitative Research Practice*. SAGE: London. pp. 297–313.

Crane, Susan A. 2011. 'The conundrum of ephemerality: Time, memory, and museums', in Macdonald, Sharon (ed.) *A Companion to Museum Studies*. Oxford: Wiley-Blackwell. pp. 98–109.

Crooke, Elizabeth M. 2007. *Museums and Communities*. Oxford: Routledge.

Dibley, Ben 2005. 'The museum's redemption: Contact zones, government and the limits of reform'. *International Journal of Cultural Studies* 8: 5–27.

Elmes, Simon 2013. 'Voices: A unique BBC adventure', in Upton, Clive and Bethan Davies (eds.) *Analysing 21st-Century British English: Conceptual and Methodological Aspects of the BBC 'Voices' Project*. Oxon: Routledge. pp. 1–11.

Feld, Steven and Keith H. Basso (eds.) 1996. *Senses of Place*. Santa Fe: School of American Research Press.

Fentress, James and Chris, Wickham 1992. *Social Memory*. Blackwell: Oxford.

Foulkes, Paul and Gerard Docherty 2007. 'Phonological variation in England', in Britain, David (ed.) *Language in the British Isles*. Cambridge: Cambridge University Press. pp. 52–74.

Halbwachs, Maurice 1925. *Les cadres sociaux de la mémoire*. Alcan: Paris.

Hennes, Tom 2010. 'Exhibitions: From a perspective of encounter'. *Curator* 53: 21–33.

Hooper-Greenhill, Eilean 1994. *Museums and Their Visitors*. London: Routledge.

Kendall, Tyler 2013. 'Data preservation and access', in Mallinson, Christine, Becky Childs, and Gerard Van Herk (eds.) *Data Collection in Sociolinguistics: Methods and Applications*. London: Routledge. pp. 195–205.

Kerswill, Paul, Carmen Llamas, and Clive Upton 1999. 'The First SuRE Moves: Early steps towards a large dialect project', in Upton, Clive and Katie Wales (eds.) *Dialectical Variation in English: Proceedings of the Harold Orton centenary conference 1998*, Leed Studies in English 30. Leeds: University of Leeds. pp. 257–70.

Leach, Hannah 2014. *Voices of the Potteries: Accent, identity, and social history in Stoke-on-Trent.* http://hannahleach.co.uk/?page_id=86.

Llamas, Carmen 1999. 'A new methodology: Data elicitation for social and regional language variation studies'. *Leeds Working Papers in Linguistics* 7: 95–119.

Maguire, Warren 2014. *DHIL: The Dialect of the Holy Island of Lindisfarne.* http://research.ncl.ac.uk/decte/dhil.htm.

Mason, Rhiannon 2011. 'Cultural theory and museum studies', in Macdonald, Sharon (ed.) *Behind the Scenes in the Science Museum*. Oxford: Berg. pp. 17–32.

Mastoris, Steph 2012. 'Folk life at fifty: People, places, and publications during the society's first half-century'. *Folk Life-Journal of Ethnological Studies* 50: 95–121.

McIntosh, Alison and Richard Prentice 1999. 'Affirming authenticity: Consuming cultural heritage'. *Annals of Tourism Research* 26: 589–612.

Miller, Daniel 2008. *The Comfort of Things*. Cambridge: Polity.

Moore, Emma 2010. *Scilly Voices: Language and Oral History on the Isles of Scilly.* www.hrionline.ac.uk/scillyvoices/.

NCCPE. 2014. *What is Public Engagement?* www.publicengagement.ac.uk/explore-it/what-public-engagement.

NECTE. 2007. *The Newcastle Electronic Corpus of Tyneside English.* http://research.ncl.ac.uk/necte/.

Onciul, Bryony 2013. 'Community engagement, curatorial practice, and museum ethos in Alberta, Canada', in Golding, Viv and Wayne Modest (eds.) *Museums and Communities: Curators, Collections and Collaboration*. London: Bloomsbury. pp. 79–97.

Orton, Harold and Eugen Dieth (eds.) 1971. *Survey of English Dialects* (Vols. 1–6). Leeds: University of Leeds.

Pahl, Kate and Andy Pollard 2010. 'The case of the disappearing object: Narratives and artefacts in homes and a museum exhibition from Pakistani heritage families in South Yorkshire'. *Museum and Society* 8: 1–17.

Pahl, Kate and Jennifer Rowsell 2010. *Artifactual Literacies: Every Object Tells a Story*. New York: Teachers College Press.

Pahl. Kate 2012. 'Every object tells a story: Intergenerational Stories and Objects in the Homes of Pakistani Heritage Families in South Yorkshire, UK'. *Home Cultures* 9: 303–28.

Peers, Laura and Alison, K. Brown 2003. 'Introduction', in Peers, Laura and Alison K. Brown (eds.) *Museums and Source Communities*. London: Routledge. pp. 3–16.

Pratt, Mary L. 1992. *Imperial Eyes: Travel Writing and Transculturation*. London: Routledge.

Robinson, Jonathan, Jon Herring and Holly Gilbert 2013. 'Voices of the UK: The British Library description of the BBC Voices Recordings Collection', in Upton, Clive and Bethan Davies (eds.) *Analysing 21st-Century British English: Conceptual and Methodological Aspects of the BBC 'Voices' Project*. Oxon: Routledge. pp. 136–61.

Sanderson, Stewart and John D. A. Widdowson 1987. *Word Maps: A Dialect Atlas of England*. London: Routledge.

Schilling, Natalie 2013. *Sociolinguistic Fieldwork*. Cambridge: Cambridge University Press.

Schorch, Philipp 2013. 'Contact zones, third spaced, and the act of interpretation'. *Museum and Society* 11: 68–81.

Shove, Elizabeth, Frank Trentman, and Richard Wilk 2009. *Time, Consumption and Everyday Life: Practice, Materiality and Culture*. Oxford: Berg.

Simon, Nina 2010. *The participatory museum.* www.participatorymuseum.org.

Smith, Rhianedd 2012. 'Searching for community: Making English rural history collections relevant today'. *Curator* 55: 51–63.

UNESCO 2003. *Intangible Heritage: Text of the Convention.* www.unesco.org/culture/ich/index.php?lg=en&pg=00006.

    2014. *What Is Intangible Cultural Heritage?* www.unesco.org/culture/ich/index.php?lg=en&pg=00002.

University of Leeds. 2014. 'The Leeds Archive of Vernacular Culture?' http://library.leeds.ac.uk/special-collections/collection/61/the_leeds_archive_of_vernacular_culture.

Upton, Clive, David Parry and John D. A. Widdowson 1994. *Survey of English Dialects: The Dictionary and Grammar*. London: Routledge.

Upton, Clive and John D. A. Widdowson 2013. *An Atlas of English Dialects: Region and Dialect*. London: Routledge.

Van Dyke, Ruth M. and Susan E. Alcock 2003. 'Archaeologies of memory: An introduction', in Van Dyke, Ruth M. and Susan E. Alcock (eds.) *Archaeologies of Memory*. Oxford: Blackwell. pp. 1–13.

Varieng. 2011. *Diachronic Corpus of Tyneside English.* www.helsinki.fi/varieng/CoRD/corpora/DECTE/index.html.

Vélez-Ibáñez, Carlos and James Greenberg 2005. 'Formation and transformation of funds of knowledge', in González, Norma, Luis C. Moll and Cathy, Amanti (eds.) *Funds of Knowledge: Theorizing Practices in Households, Communities, and Classrooms*. Mahwah, NJ: Lawrence Erlbaum. pp. 47–69.

Wilks, Carol and Catherine Kelly 2008. 'Fact, fiction and nostalgia: An assessment of heritage interpretation at living museums'. *International Journal of Intangible Heritage* 3: 128–40.

Wiltshire, Robin and Kathryn, Jenner 2005. 'Enhancing a Valuable Resource: Approaches to the Creation of an Online Finding Aid for the Leeds Archive of Vernacular Culture', conference proceedings, Dialect and Folk Life Studies in Britain: The Leeds Archive of Vernacular Culture in its Context. http://library.leeds.ac.uk/special-collections/collection/61/the_leeds_archive_of_vernacular_culture/75/lavc_conference_proceedings.

Winter, Caroline 2009. 'Tourism, social memory and the Great War'. *Annals of Tourism Research* 36: 607–26.

Witcomb, Andrea 2003. *Re-Imagining the Museum: Beyond the Mausoleum*. London: Routledge.

Wolfram, Walt 1993. 'Ethical considerations in language awareness programmes'. *Issues in Applied Linguistics* 4: 225–55.

　　2010. 'Collaborative issues in language variation documentaries'. *Language and Linguistics Compass* 4: 793–803.

　　2012. 'In the profession: Connecting with the public'. *Journal of English Linguistics* 40: 111–17.

Wolfram, Walt, Jeffrey Reaser, and Charlotte Vaughn 2008. 'Operationalizing linguistic gratuity from principle to practice'. *Language and Linguistics Compass* 3: 1109–34.

7   Maps and Mapping in (Perceptual) Dialect Geography

Chris Montgomery

1.   Introduction

In this chapter, I will discuss the role of maps and mapping techniques in the field of dialectology, exploring methods and data from Great Britain. Maps are 'something to which very many people seem instinctively to be drawn, of which they feel they have some immediate understanding' (Upton 2010: 144), and they have a long tradition in the field of dialectology. I conceive the field to include data which not only reveal what people do (data relating to production), but also data that expose what they think about what they and others do (data relating to perception). By taking this approach, I adopt an integrated folk linguistic approach to the study of language and place, following Preston (1999). This type of approach allows researchers to treat space as relative, acknowledging that 'human beings *live space*, rather than *live in space* [italics in original]' (Auer *et al.* 2013: 3), and recognising that 'our perceptions of the physical and socialised spaces around us can lead us to act and behave in differing ways' (Britain 2010: 71).

Treating space as dynamic, shaped both by our interactions and perceptions, means that scholars working in the field of dialectology must avoid treating space as a 'blank canvas' (Britain 2010: 87) onto which we paint our results in the form of static maps. As noted by Tufte (1990: 12), despite our living in a three-dimensional world, 'the world portrayed on our information displays is caught up in the two-dimensionality of the endless flatlands of paper and video screen'. When visualising information, 'escaping this flatland is an essential task' (Tufte 1990: 12) in order that we better understand the world around us. Just as Nichols (2013) has demonstrated 'that areal linguistics has paid insufficient attention to the variable of altitude' (Auer *et al.* 2013: 11), researchers working in the field of language and place need to understand the role of language users' ideologies and perceptions. Following Szmrecsanyi (2013: 239), I argue that these factors matter, perhaps even more so than 'objective' maps created by geographers.

This more nuanced understanding will not come from research that treats space, the people who live (in) that space, and the language that they use as static, according to fixed coordinate points. Instead it will be brought about from research that integrates what we know about language and place, and how they represent and signal their local belonging (e.g. Beal 1999; 2009), with the huge wealth of data available relating to how people live their lives (e.g. census data and other large-scale datasets). One way to more fully understand the relationship between language and place is to make use of technology from other fields, such as Geographical Information Systems (GIS), to bring together linguistic and other datasets. In this chapter, I will discuss data types in dialectology, before examining the ways in which technology might be used to process these types of data, and concluding the chapter with a case study that uses perceptual dialectology data and GIS.

2.   Dialect Survey Data Types

Szmrecsanyi (2012) has commented the science of traditional dialectology began as a result of three factors: (1) the need to test the Neogrammarian principle of exceptionless sound change (also discussed by Chambers and Trudgill 1998: 14), (2) a desire to study 'authentic' non-standard dialects and (3) the related will to discover the boundaries of dialect areas. In order to do this, dialectologists surveyed individuals in particular locations, either indirectly (as in the case of Ellis [1889]) or directly via the use of fieldworkers (as in the Survey of English Dialects [Orton 1962: 15–16]). In this section, I focus on data produced by traditional dialect surveys, using the Survey of English Dialects (SED) as an exemplar. In SED-type dialect surveys, the respondents were usually older males who had lived in the same (usually rural) location all of their lives.

The introduction to the SED demonstrates a clear awareness of wider socio-linguistic issues, as shown in the following observations from Orton (1962: 14): 'it is amongst the rural populations that the traditional types of vernacular English are best preserved today', and 'in this country men speak vernacular more frequently, more consistently, and more genuinely than women' (1962: 15). Nonetheless, such statements demonstrate that it was expressly not the focus of traditional dialect surveys to investigate sociolinguistic variation. Instead, dia-lectologists such as Orton sought to document the state of traditional dialects using a questionnaire, which resulted in a particular type and amount of data.

The SED used a network of 313 locations, chosen according to various factors, such as relative isolation of the community, the stability of the population, and the presence of natural boundaries (Orton 1962: 15). In each location, (typically) single item responses to 1,322 questions aimed at eliciting different data types were gathered. This approach generated 'more than 404,000 items of information' (Upton *et al.* 1994: v). In the case of the SED, the data have been published in various forms, from tables of data in the four volumes of the 'Basic Materials' (e.g. Orton and Barry 1969), to a synthesis of these volumes in dictionary form (Upton *et al.* 1994). Dialect atlases, discussed in the following sections, were also published.

Data gathered by the methods outlined above tie question responses to specific co-ordinate points on the basis of one respondent's answer. This approach assumes that the respondent is representative of the location (and is as representative of the location as other respondents in the 'panel' of people recruited to complete the questionnaire, if one was used). Data is then catalogued for each location and used as a basis of comparison with other locations. Although representativeness is an issue here, traditional dialectological approaches produced extremely valuable resources. As a guide to the traditional dialects of English, the systematically collected data of the SED is invaluable, and has 'provided data for linguistic enquiries of kinds undreamt of when [the SED team] began their work' (Upton and Widdowson 1996: x).

Despite the benefits of dialect survey data of this type, I argue below that its nature has led to interpretative approaches that have abandoned ideas of 'relative space' (Auer *et al.* 2013: 3–4). Such approaches have considered only how to represent dialect forms using lines or symbols on maps, and along the way have abandoned the idea that the data we use are concerned primarily with people. In order to fully understand dialect data, methods that abandon 'spatially sensitive' (Britain 2009: 144) approaches are insufficient. In the following sections, I will consider how both dialectologists and dialectometrists have mapped survey data, and how these approaches have neglected to consider more nuanced senses of space in their analyses.

3.   Dialectology and Mapping

The point-based data generated by dialect surveys is beneficial for the creation of maps that examine the distribution of variants. In the case of the SED, a linguistic atlas of England was the project's 'ultimate aim' (Orton 1962: 14), and the questionnaire was developed with this in mind (Dieth and Orton 1952). Such an approach would allow the geographical distribution of large numbers of systematically gathered dialect forms in England to be visualised for the first time.

The first attempt to display data from the SED was Kolb's (1966) phonological atlas of the six northern counties of England, an example of which is shown in Figure 7.1. It sought to display the phonological variation present in all of the data, and chose data from one specific region (as opposed to the whole country), as this would permit 'the fine differentiation necessary to bring out all the local differences in pronunciation' (Kolb 1966: 11). This logic dictates that maps of the whole country would not be able to deal with the number of forms they had to plot without over-simplification. Whether simplification is necessarily a bad thing when trying to create a useful map that avoids 'hiding critical information in a fog of detail' (Monmonier 1991: 1) is

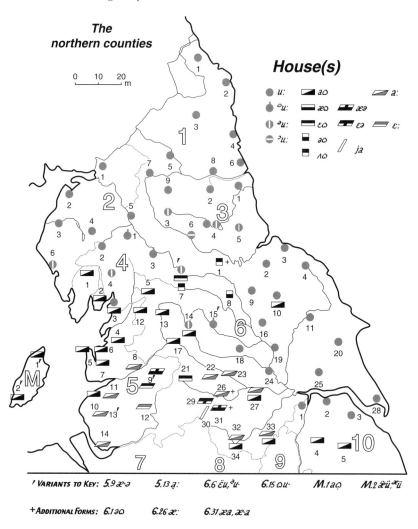

Figure 7.1: Realisation of vowel in House(s) in SED data, from Kolb (1966: 257). Reproduced with permission from Narr Franke Attempto Verlag GmbH + Co. KG.

not considered by Kolb. The resulting collection of display maps (Chambers and Trudgill 1998: 25) presents data using numerous symbols and three colours (black, white, and red [in the original version of the map]), for 165 questions from the SED. For each individual question, unique symbols were generated for each variant, showing the range of variation present in the northern counties. The use of symbols has an 'undoubted immediacy' (Upton 2010: 148), although McDavid (1983) dismissed representation of the totality of variation in such a way as 'treat[ing] too many variants with too many symbols' (McDavid 1983: 49).

Some selection, generalisation, and interpretation would address McDavid's concerns. This type of hybrid approach can be seen in Orton, Sanderson, and Widdowson's linguistic atlas, which uses both symbols and interpretative lines (see, for example, 1978: Ph149). By contrast, Orton and Wright's (1974) lexical atlas chose a wholly interpretative route (for example, 1974: 63). Interpretative maps do not attempt to display all variation present, and instead use isoglosses ('the obvious, problematic approach' according to Upton [2010: 150]) to suggest patterns in the data to readers of the map. Such approaches are widely used (e.g. Upton and Widdowson 1996) but, as Upton notes, are not without their problems; the act of drawing lines immediately suggests an intended reading, as well as the impression of sharp boundaries which have little in common with the situation on the ground. In any event, Orton and Wright's (1974) atlas did little to placate McDavid (1983: 49), who described it as 'not a word geography; for it nowhere summarizes, in statement or maps, the characteristic vocabulary of any region in England'.

McDavid's statement suggests unease examining individual responses to questions and displaying them on a map either in display or interpretative form. Critics such as McDavid claimed that these approaches risk missing the bigger picture of variation according to regions (or dialects, as we might otherwise call them). By examining items in isolation, map by map, researchers are less able to make inferences about the wider state of variation. Even examination of isoglosses for coincidence is problematic as they may not overlap, as noted by Upton (2006: 386) (and are not always drawn consistently [see Macaulay 1985: 175]). Upton (2006: 384–6) discusses whether examining variation in terms of dialect areas is desirable; Although in addition to noting the fictional notion of 'dialect areas' (Upton 2006: 386), he also observes that researchers are unable account for particular forms being more salient than others (e.g. the STRUT-FOOT split in England) when forms are treated in isolation. However, despite the criticism expressed in Upton (2006), dialectometrists have developed their own methods of working with large-scale survey data to investigate dialect areas using large numbers of features, as discussed in the following section.

4.   Dialectometry and Mapping

Dialectometry is an approach that 'proceeds from the scientific conviction that dialectal data are too complex to be studied one at a time' (Nerbonne and Kretzschmar 2013: 2). Whilst clearly addressing the concerns expressed by McDavid, this conflicts with traditional dialectological practice, which has tended to display or interpret patterns on a feature-by-feature basis. Examining features in isolation in this way is flawed, according to Nerbonne and Kretzschmar (2006: 388), who state that:

individual features . . . are associated only weakly with geography. For every promising candidate of a feature which might 'define' a dialect area, it always turns out that there are exceptional sites within and without the area which run counter to the candidate definition.

If one's aim is to define dialect areas on a map, focusing on single features is clearly an issue. Data aggregation was found to be the solution to the problem, and was first proposed by Séguy (1973) in the form of 'counting the number of items on which the neighbours [in different survey locations] disagreed' (Chambers and Trudgill 1998: 138). This quantitative approach permitted the calculation of dialect areas in an objective fashion, avoiding the serious biases (Nerbonne 2010: 477) of the selective approach characterised by interpretative maps or analyses that attempted to present dialect areas on the basis of only a few features (e.g. Trudgill 1999).

Goebl (1993) continued Séguy's work on the quantification of dialect areas, although his focus was on the calculation and mapping of similarities rather than differences (Heeringa and Nerbonne 2013). Working with colleagues in the Salzburg school of dialectometry (Goebl 2011: 435), Goebl sought to refine both theoretical and methodological aspects of dialectological mapping, most notably introducing Thiessen tiling. This method converts point data in polygons by drawing lines around each point as evenly as possible (Heeringa and Nerbonne 2013). Thiessen tiling permits the creation of choropleth maps that allow similarity or difference to be displayed over a continuous surface (Heywood *et al.* 2006: 258). This technique produces the honeycomb maps that are characteristic of dialectometry, in which patterns are shown for single and grouped items, generally using colour to show the relatedness (or lack of it) between data tiles (see Goebl 2011). Other 'schools' of dialectometry have worked in a similar fashion to Goebl; most notably in recent years, the Groningen school has championed the exploration of various clustering techniques in order to understand variation further (Wieling *et al.* 2013).

A good deal of effort in dialectometry has focussed not only on mapping variation, but also the methods of mapping this variation. As objectivity is a central aim for all scholars, early methods that relied on researchers setting thresholds, cut-offs, and the interpretation of statistical results, meant that for Chambers and Trudgill (1998: 138) no 'method can ever completely remove the dialectologist from the analysis'. Relatively recent developments in computer technology have permitted the automation of much of the process of working with data in dialectometry (Nerbonne and Kretzschmar 2003). More recent still is the proliferation of the free online tools that enable researchers to conduct their own dialectometric analyses on their data. Tools such as Visual Dialectometry (VDM) (see Goebl 2011: 436), and its successor GabMap (Nerbonne *et al.* 2011), along with DiaTech (Aurrekoetxea *et al.* 2013) allow the easy input of data and produce an output of maps and statistical representations of the data.

The contribution of dialectometry to the study of dialect variation is clear, although reservations do remain about the central focus of the discipline on aggregate data. As Wieling *et al.* (2013: 31–2) comment:

> the professional reception of dialectometry has been polite but less than enthusiastic, as some scholars express concern that its focus on aggregate levels of variation ignores the kind of linguistic detail that may help uncover the linguistic structure in variation.

Wieling *et al.* (2013) address this central problem by presenting exciting advances in clustering techniques, which enable assessments of the role of specific variants in dialect area clusters. Such advances are, of course, welcome, although there is clearly some way to travel before agreement is reached over the best way to cluster and display dialectometric results.

Perceptual dialectology is another subfield in which there have been multiple methods of processing data, and I consider some of these in the following section.

5.   Perceptual Dialectology and Mapping

The aim of perceptual dialectology (Preston 1989) is to gather data relating to non-linguists' perception of the dialect landscape. The most frequently used technique in perceptual dialectology is the 'draw-a-map' task (Preston 1982), in which respondents are asked to draw lines on a map in order to indicate where they believe dialect areas to exist. Data from 'draw-a-map' tasks is quite difficult to use and has therefore required employment of novel techniques for its analysis. The primary factor that makes data from 'draw-a-map' tasks hard to work with is the use of a map itself. The range of data that can be gathered is wide and varied, with data relating to perceptions of dialect area placement and extent, dialect area names, as well as qualitative data, all finding their way onto respondents' maps, as shown in Figure 7.2.

Dialect area names and qualitative data are relatively easily dealt with, but it is the data relating to the placement and extent of dialect areas that is much more difficult for the researcher to use. Some perceptual dialectology studies that have used the draw-a-map approach have chosen to disregard this geographical data in their analyses (e.g. Bucholtz *et al.* 2007; Bucholtz *et al.* 2008). This permits more swift examination of survey responses, but it ignores the geographical elements of the data. Not paying attention to this means that it is not possible to assess respondents' mental maps of dialect areas, which is one of the key aims of perceptual dialectology (Preston 2002: 51). In addition,

Figure 7.2: 17-year-old female respondent's completed draw-a-map task.
Respondent from Presteigne, Wales (marked on the map with a star).

this approach neglects to consider a further aim of perceptual dialectology, which has always been to arrive at an aggregation of geographical perception data (Preston and Howe 1987: 363).

Arriving at this aggregation technique has proved a long road. An obvious 'low-tech' solution to aggregating dialect area placement and extent data is the use of overhead transparencies or tracing paper. I used this technique in early perceptual dialectology research in England and Wales (Montgomery 2007: 59–61) and would recommend that it only be used for preliminary investigation of patterns, and not with more than thirty respondents' maps.

Computerised techniques are far more robust than their non-electronic counterparts, and this is the direction perceptual dialectology data processing has taken. Preston and Howe's (1987) article discusses a method that permits the capture of respondent lines and the calculation of perceptual dialect areas at various levels of agreement. This approach was built upon by Onishi and Long (1997), who developed Perceptual Dialectology Quantifier for Windows (PDQ). PDQ was able to sophisticate additional functions to Preston and Howe's approach, displaying data on a single map with levels of percentage agreement relating to dialect areas' placement and extent. Such an advance allowed immediate analysis of perceptions of core and peripheral dialect areas without overlaying various percentages, the only recourse in Preston and Howe's approach. Long (1999) and Long and Yim (2002), along with Montgomery (2007) demonstrate the use of PDQ.

These early computer-based solutions were valuable, but they were also flawed. Both Preston and Howe's technique and PDQ relied on technology in place only in the location in which they were developed and, in the case of PDQ, it was usable only in conjunction with other programmes and computers. This type of bespoke and static technology was not suitable for use amongst the worldwide research community of perceptual dialectologists.

Most recently, researchers have alighted on Geographical Information Systems (GIS) to help process data, and have developed numerous protocols in order to cultivate a standardised method of processing perceptual dialectology data worldwide. A GIS is defined as a system which integrates the three basic elements of hardware, software, and data 'for capturing, managing, analysing, and displaying all forms of geographically referenced information' (ESRI 2011). Given the map-based approach taken in perceptual dialectology, the use of a GIS is an obvious choice, as demonstrated by its use in numerous recent studies (Evans 2011, 2013; Cukor-Avila et al. 2012; Montgomery 2012; Stoeckle 2012; Montgomery and Stoeckle 2013).

Montgomery and Stoeckle (2013) discuss the GIS method for processing perceptual dialectology data fully, but a brief explanation is provided here. Draw-a-map data, such as that shown above in Figure 7.2, is difficult to process because it involves respondents drawing lines on maps that seek to delimit the boundaries of areas. Lines and areas are considered separate types of data by geographers. Vector data refers to line data, and raster data is that relating to areas. Vector data can be thought of as a list of values which give the points through which a line is drawn. Raster data is stored as a matrix, the cells of which are given a value indicating whether or not they are part of the area in question.

Of course, when respondents draw lines on maps, they do not have any awareness of such technical details, and they are tasked with trying to outline the boundaries of dialect areas (or 'areas in which people speak differently', e.g. see Cukor-Avila *et al.* [2012]; Evans [2013]). This means that, in order to aggregate draw-a-map data, there has to be a conversion process whereby the vector data are converted to raster data. Once each area drawn by a respondent has been converted to a raster, multiple responses can be added together, and calculations performed which produce outputs showing the extent of agreement and overlap between respondents' perceptions of the placement, and the extent of individual dialect areas. These agreement calculations are typically displayed using shading (either in black and white, as in this chapter, or in colour, as in Montgomery and Stoeckle [2013]). Shading techniques tend to use darker shades to represent greatest agreement over the placement and extent of an area, and lighter shades to show lesser agreement. Multiple areas can then be added to a single map, permitting the relative distribution of the perceptions of different areas. Figures 7.4 and 7.5 show these shading techniques, and comparisons between the placement and extent of different areas. All of this can be done in a GIS, as discussed in Montgomery and Stoeckle (2013), and resulting outputs can be used in the spatially sensitive fashion discussed earlier. This is due to the fact that a GIS uses georeferencing to assign real-world coordinate points to data, in order to 'anchor' layers of data to a point on the earth's surface. This means that multiple layers of data can be added together in order to look for patterns and explain the spatial distribution of data.

The use of GIS for perceptual dialectology has four main benefits. Firstly, and most importantly, it permits conversion and processing of the type of data generated by the draw-a-map task. The second benefit, which is only slightly less important than the first, is that, throughout the processing stages and at the point of data output, a GIS works with spatially meaningful data. This means that the data have a relationship to the earth's surface and are not simply graphical. There are clear advantages to this, as perceptual dialectologists are now able to compare their data with other similarly georeferenced datasets in order to find patterns and explore and understand their data further. The final two benefits are that GIS software is widely available (with open-source software also available), and that it has the ability to produce professional quality outputs.

In the remainder of this chapter, I will present a case study demonstrating the benefits of using GIS and georeferenced data to interpret and understand linguistic data.

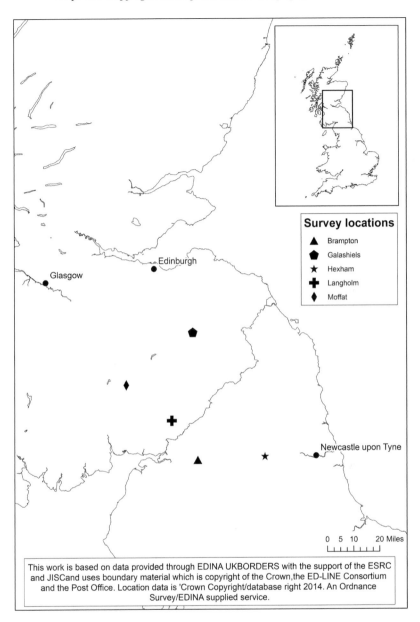

Figure 7.3: Survey locations.

6.   Perceptual Dialectology and GIS

The case study presented here uses GIS to work with the multifaceted responses to draw-a-map tasks, and to map additional data in order to aid explanation of these responses. It shows that mapping data in perceptual dialectology is important in order to understand the perceptions of respondents that could not be accessed using numerical data alone.

The data are taken from a perceptual dialectology study of the Scottish-English border region. Respondents in five locations completed a draw-a-map task which asked for their large-scale perceptions of dialect regions in Great Britain. Figure 7.3 shows the location of each of the survey points.

School-aged respondents from each of the survey locations were given a minimally detailed map and were asked to draw lines on the map indicating where they believed dialect areas to exist. The task lasted for 10 minutes and, in order to assist respondents, a location map which contained a number of cities and towns in England, Scotland and Wales was shown to respondents for the first 5 minutes of the task. In total, 151 respondents completed hand-drawn maps. Seventy-six were from the three locations on the Scottish side of the border, and seventy-five from the two on the English side. Their mean age was 16 years and 6 months. After the draw-a-map task had been completed, the data were processed in ArcGIS using the method discussed earlier.

In total, respondents drew 970 lines delimiting seventy-nine separate areas (a mean of 6.4 areas drawn per map). Overall numerical data are presented in Table 7.1, which I will address according to the differential levels of dialect area recognition by respondents either side of the Scottish-English border. Table 7.1 shows the twenty most recognised dialect areas for Scottish and English respondents in rank order. Recognition levels for each area are given in the 'Recognition' column, which expresses a bare number referring to the number of lines drawn indicating the area. The bracketed figures relate to the percentage of respondents who drew the area. In order to aid interpretation, non-Scottish areas are shaded.

Table 7.1 shows both similarities and differences in Scottish and English respondents' recognition levels. The clearest difference is that of the perception of non-Scottish dialect areas amongst the two groups of respondents. The expected effect of proximity (Montgomery 2012) sees Scottish respondents drawing 118 lines in recognition of Scottish dialect areas (29 per cent of all lines drawn for 'top twenty' dialect areas). In contrast, English respondents drew only fifty-nine lines (14 per cent of all 'top twenty' lines).

The English respondents' ten most frequently drawn dialect areas are predominantly English, with the only Scottish areas occupying the ninth and tenth slots. For English areas, the recognition rates for these areas are very similar to those found in previous research undertaken in different locations in England (Montgomery and Beal 2011), and reflect the impact of both

Table 7.1: *Recognition of dialect areas by respondents' country, non-Scottish dialect areas shaded.*

Scottish respondents (n=76)			English respondents (n=75)		
Rank	Dialect area[1]	Recognition (%)	Rank	Dialect area	Recognition (%)
1	Geordie [Newcastle]	53 (69.9)	1	Geordie [Newcastle]	55 (73.3)
2	Weeji [Glasgow]	53 (69.9)	2	Scouse [Liverpool]	53 (70.7)
3	Scouse [Liverpool]	52 (68.4)	3	Brummie [Birmingham]	41 (54.7)
4	Welsh	46 (60.5)	4	Cockney	40 (53.3)
5	Brummie [Birmingham]	38 (50.0)	5	Manc [Manchester]	40 (53.3)
6	Cockney	27 (35.5)	6	Welsh	36 (48.0)
7	Manc [Manchester]	27 (35.5)	7	Cumbrian/ Carlisle	31 (41.3)
8	Aberdeen	13 (17.1)	8	Yorkshire	23 (30.7)
9	Borders	12 (15.8)	9	Scottish	17 (22.7)
10	Strong/broad Scottish	11 (14.5)	10	Weeji [Glasgow]	15 (20.0)
11	West Country	11 (14.5)	11	Strong/broad Scottish	11 (14.7)
12	Highlands	11 (14.5)	12	London	11 (14.7)
13	Gaelic	11 (14.5)	13	Aberdeen	10 (13.3)
14	London	10 (13.2)	14	West Country	9 (12.0)
15	Cumbrian/ Carlisle	9 (11.8)	15	Bristol	8 (10.7)
16	Yorkshire	7 (9.2)	16	Cornwall	7 (9.3)
17	Scottish	7 (9.2)	17	Southern	7 (9.3)
18	Bristol	6 (7.9)	18	Highlands	6 (8.0)
19	Cardiff	6 (7.9)	19	West Cumbria	6 (8.0)
20	Lancashire	3 (3.9)	20	Midlands	5 (6.7)

proximity and 'cultural prominence' (Montgomery 2012: 658–60). By contrast, the 'top ten' dialect areas for Scottish respondents contain four Scottish areas and six in England, with the English areas recognised by Scottish respondents similar to those recognised by English respondents.

Despite the similarity in the perception of English areas, further consideration of the frequently recognised dialect areas by country reveals the different way in which the border impacts on perception according to respondents' country of residence. For Scottish respondents, the most frequently drawn dialect areas are

---

[1] The names in this column are the ones given by the majority of respondents, and are glossed in square brackets for those unfamiliar with the folk-linguistic names for these areas.

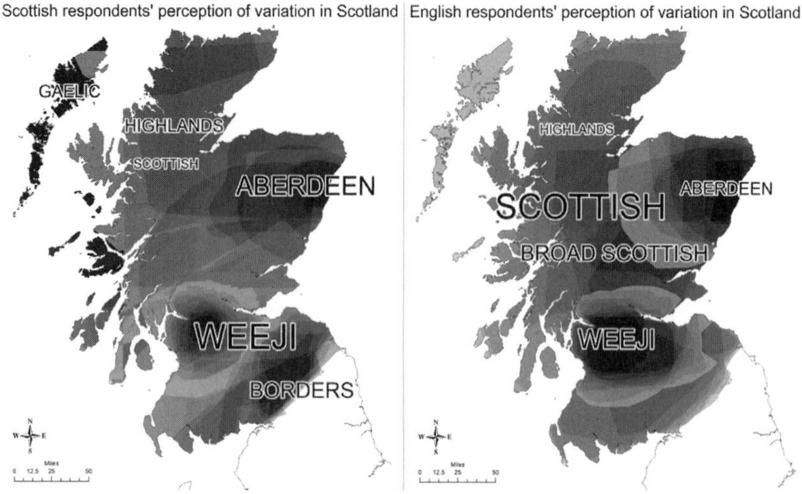

Figure 7.4: Perception of Scottish dialect areas.[2] Permisson granted by John
Wiley and Sons.

'Geordie' and 'Weeji', both identified by 69.9 per cent of respondents. For
English respondents, the 'Weeji' area is the most frequently recognised city-
based area in Scotland, but its recognition rate of 20 per cent is nowhere near
the rates for other city-based dialect areas. This suggests that the Scottish-
English border is working to inhibit the perception of dialect areas in the United
Kingdom, but that this effect is felt most by respondents living in England.

Moving on to the map-based data, Figure 7.4 shows composite map data
relating to the perception of dialect variation in Scotland, with corresponding
data shown for England in Figure 7.5. In both figures, dialect areas are labelled
according to their recognition level (with larger labels indicating greater levels
of recognition) and shaded according to agreement levels (darker areas indicate
greater agreement over the placement of an area).

The composite maps shown in Figure 7.4 demonstrate that the mental maps of
the 'Scottish' dialect area differ considerably for respondents from Scotland and
England. There is a greater acknowledgement of variation in Scotland amongst
Scottish respondents, and less awareness on the part of English respondents.

---

[2] This work is based on data provided EDINA UKBORDERS with support of the ESRC and JISC
and uses material which is derived from the National Imagery and Mapping Agency VMAP
geospatial data along with boundary material that is copyright of the Crown. Further data is
provided with the support of the ESRC and JISC and uses boundary material which is copyright
of the Crown the ED-Line Consortium. Location information is Crown Copyright/Database right
2011. An Ordnance Survey/EDINA supplied service.

Figure 7.4 displays a focussed 'Weeji' dialect area, an Aberdeen dialect area, and a Borders area, as well as a Gaelic area, and a Highlands area (a similar space to the 'Scottish' area on the English respondents' map). For Scottish respondents the 'Strong/broad Scottish' area is not included as it did not appear to relate to one specific geographical area. Figure 7.5 shows fewer areas for English respondents. These are, in turn, less focussed than those drawn by their Scottish counterparts. The 'Weeji' area is included on the map, as is Aberdeen, Broad Scottish, and Highlands. However, the most frequently drawn area was the 'Scottish' area. Respondents choosing to add this area simply drew a circle around Scotland, and generally did not indicate any further subdivisions. The large 'Scottish' label on the map indicates this general area, which serves as a backdrop for the other composite areas shown in Figure 7.4.

The generalised perception of variation in Scotland amongst English respondents, versus the more specific perceptions of Scottish respondents, is perhaps unsurprising. It is not controversial to assume that respondents would have more knowledge of their own country, as well as an increased motivation for detailing it. One might therefore expect the situation to be similar for English dialect areas. As I have already discussed in relation to Table 7.1, this is not the case, and the maps in Figure 7.5 show that the areas drawn by English and Scottish respondents are remarkably similar. Both composite maps reveal the perception of a greater amount of variation in the north of England. Here, five distinct areas are

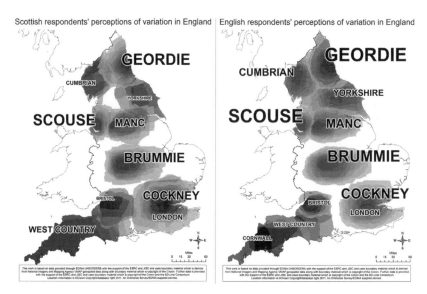

Figure 7.5: Perception of English dialect areas. Permisson granted by John Wiley and Sons.

recognised ('Geordie', 'Cumbrian', 'Yorkshire', 'Scouse' and 'Manc'), and there is very little difference between their placement and extent for Scottish and English respondents. The same is true of the remaining areas on the maps.

It is important to take both the numerical and map data together, but without the composite map data it would be particularly difficult to assess the extent to which respondents had similar (or dissimilar) mental maps of the dialect areas they were drawing. The map is central to the study of perceptual dialectology and, without it, we are simply left with a list of prominent dialect area concepts. This highlights the central importance of mapping to the perceptual dialectologist, and illustrates how the GIS approach adds to our analytical toolkit.

Whilst attitudinal factors clearly impact on the way in which dialect areas in Scotland might be perceived amongst English respondents (see Montgomery 2014), other factors such as contact are also important. Here, the use of GIS, which ensures data are spatially relevant, opens up the possibility of working with large-scale datasets in order to investigate how people interact with the spaces and places in which they live.

One such large-scale dataset is based on data gathered in the UK census. The UK census takes place every ten years and includes questions relating to commuting and migration. The question relating to migration is relatively limited, as noted by Buchstaller and Alvanides (2010). However, data relating to commuting is perhaps more useful for the dialectologist's purpose, and I consider these as 'routinised social practices' (Britain 2009: 151) important in the creation of regions (see Britain 2009: 151–4). Commuting data make it possible to measure the possibility for contact amongst people living in different areas. Of course, not all people in an area have equal access to resources in their communities, with the result that different people will experience different levels of interaction from others (highlighting the importance of micro-level sociolinguistic study, see Moore and Carter, and Snell, this volume). However, as a proxy for likeliness of contact between populations, the commuting data are useful.

Commuting data for 2011 (Office for National Statistics 2011) were extracted in an origin-destination matrix on the basis of Local Area District (LAD) geography. For 2011, there were considered to be 404 LAD areas in the United Kingdom, and data were extracted from the twenty-two districts that lay within 50 miles of the Scottish-English border. Commuting data were then mapped with ArcGIS using the centre points of each of the districts, and line thickness to indicate population flow. Figure 7.6 displays commuting flows from the LADs north and south of the Scottish-English border, shaded so that the LADs containing survey locations are darker than other areas. The survey locations used in this study are sited in 'Dumfries and Galloway' (Langholm and Moffat), 'Scottish Borders' (Galashiels), 'Carlisle' (Brampton), and 'Northumberland' (Hexham).

Figure 7.6 shows clusters of interaction centred on Edinburgh in Scotland, and Carlisle and Newcastle upon Tyne in England, and demonstrates more

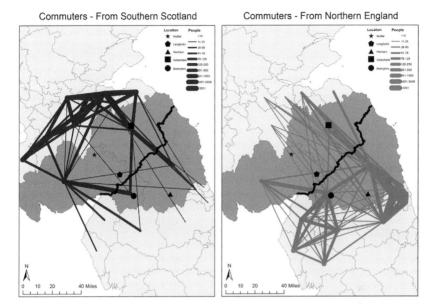

Figure 7.6: Commuting flows along the Scottish-English border.[3]

commuting across the Scottish-English border from the English side than from the Scottish side. On the west side of the maps, a sizeable amount of reciprocal commuting is revealed. There is commuting to and from the Carlisle District (in England) and the Dumfries and Galloway District (in Scotland). There is a smaller amount of reciprocity on the east side of the map.

The maps reveal that, based on these commuting data, there is likely to be a greater amount of contact with English dialect speakers in the south of Scotland than there is contact with Scottish dialect speakers in the north of England. Table 7.2 subjects the commuting data to further interrogation for the purpose of understanding the commuting patterns and possible links between these and the recognition of dialect areas. The table summarises the commuting data, dividing commuters from outside specific Interaction Districts on the basis of their country of origin (Scotland or England). Also included in the table are the mean percentage dialect area recognition levels for respondents in each survey location.

Table 7.2 shows that outside-area commuting is more likely in English LADs than Scottish ones. When the data for these outside district commuters is examined more closely, a stark contrast between districts in Scotland and England is

---

[3] Crown copyright material is reproduced with the permission of the Controller of HMSO and the Queen's Printer for Scotland. Source: 2011 Special Workplace Statistics – LAD Level – Open Government License.

Table 7.2: *'Out-of-area' commuting data, with recognition levels for Scottish and English dialect areas.*

Local Authority District (2011)	Carlisle	Northumberland	Scottish Borders	Dumfries and Galloway	
Containing survey location	Brampton	Hexham	Galashiels	Langholm	Moffat
Economically active population[4]	79531	233224	58659	75727	75727
'Outside District' commuters (%)	10055 (12.6)	21789 (9.3)	2517 (4.3)	1957 (2.6)	1957 (2.6)
Of these, total from England (%)	7671 (76.3)	20584 (94.5)	937 (37.2)	955 (48.8)	955 (48.8)
Of these, total from Scotland (%)	2384 (23.7)	1205 (5.5)	1580 (62.8)	1002 (51.2)	1002 (51.2)
% recognition of English areas	31.6	26.0	27.4	22.0	18.8
% recognition of Scottish areas	13.9	10.8	27.8	22.5	21.5

revealed. In Scotland, there is a much higher percentage of commuters from England in Scotland than when the situation is reversed. In the Dumfries and Galloway LAD, for example, the ratio of English to Scottish commuters is nearly 50:50 whereas in the English LADs commuters are generally from England. In the Carlisle district, 76.3 per cent of commuters are from England, and in the Northumberland district 94.5 per cent commute from other English LADs.

These data mean that the opportunities for contact with speakers of English varieties are similar in all of the Scottish survey locations. In English locations, this opportunity is generally diminished. Such disparities in contact opportunities could explain differences in the perception of dialect variation. Scottish survey locations have a similar mean percentage recognition level for English and Scottish dialect areas, and a high percentage of English commuters working in their LADs. In contrast, the decreased opportunities for contact in the English areas, particularly in the Northumberland district, could be one of the reasons for the lower level of Scottish dialect area recognition in England, and the lowest recognition level in Hexham specifically.

---

[4] Economic activity relates to whether or not a person who was aged 16 to 74 was working or looking for work in the week before census. Rather than a simple indicator of whether or not someone was currently in employment, it provides a measure of whether or not a person was an active participant in the labour market.

Ensuring that data processing in perceptual dialectology is spatially accurate brings with it is own advantages in terms of guaranteeing that data can be manipulated and analysed in a meaningful fashion. The ability to visualise large numbers of respondents' perceptions of dialect areas means that we are able to understand the similarities and differences of respondents' views of the world, and the use of large-scale spatial datasets, such as the census commuting data, means that we can account for respondents differing views of the world around them.

7.   Conclusion

In this chapter, I have argued that in order to understand dialectological data researchers must pay attention not only to the distribution of linguistic phenomena, but also what the use of these phenomena mean to the people on the ground. I have argued that maps, although generally useful for the display of data, do have their drawbacks associated with overlaying data onto a 'blank canvas' (Britain 2010: 87). These approaches do not pay attention to how people live space, and how this might impact on our understanding of the data. As noted above, this is not a new argument (Britain 2009; Britain 2010; Auer *et al.* 2013). Nonetheless, my contribution proposes a possible solution to the problem in the form of using GIS to tie together many layers of geographically meaningful data.

Although the case study presented here is based on perceptual data, there is no reason why GIS, and the geospatial techniques it relies upon, could not be used to analyse production data. As with the perceptual data example, the use of these techniques may more effectively incorporate data from outside dialectology. Additionally, an understanding of the benefits of this type of method may allow more visually appealing incorporation of sociolinguistic factors into our dialectological analyses, long recognised as essential to the field (Chambers and Trudgill 1998).

GIS is of course not a magic bullet. As historians such as da Silviera have noted, the use of GIS 'did not bring about a revolution in knowledge production in history' (da Silviera 2014: 29). Nor is GIS synonymous with the production of maps, as 'maps can be produced more easily with many standard drawing applications' (Jessop 2007: 43). Instead, dialectologists should embrace the possibilities of GIS not only to visualise our data, but also to 'analyse and display data in a variety of maps, graphics, networks or hierarchy trees *as well as extending database functionality to the investigation of spatial relationships*' (Jessop 2007: 39 [my italics]). The investigation of spatial relationships will permit dialectologists to use data relating to how people use space as a tool for better understanding linguistic data and the patterns presented within it. I contend that dialectologists and dialectometrists should have fewer debates about the correct clustering techniques for analysing variation, and spend more time considering how valuable linguistic data can be used alongside other datasets in order to produce spatially meaningful accounts of language use.

GIS technology allows us to do this, as do geo-browsers like Google Earth (de Vriend *et al.* 2011), but both rely on georeferenced data that has a real-world reference point. Researchers working in the field are, of course, not ignorant of the concept of georeferenced data, GIS, or geo-browsers, as numerous articles demonstrate (Kirk and Kretzschmar 1992; Light and Kretzschmar 1996; Labov *et al.* 2006; Nerbonne *et al.* 2011; de Vriend *et al.* 2011; Gregory and Hardie 2011). However it seems that the full opportunities of such technology have not yet been seized. For example, the dialectometry interface GabMap works with Google Earth in order to import real-world coordinate data for survey points into the mapping interface, but does not permit output of data into either a GIS or geo-browser, leaving data in the form of a graphical output that cannot be interrogated further using spatial analyses.

More recent work has demonstrated the possibilities of working with georeferenced data in R (R Core Team 2014); in particular, Grieve has produced spatial statistical analyses of large datasets (e.g. Grieve 2014), marrying linguistic data with census data in order to suggest reasons for innovation diffusion (Grieve *et al.* 2014). Although R is not at present useable for perceptual dialectology data, the underlying georeferenced data means that datasets can be combined and examined together.

Working with multimodal data in this way means that researchers interested in language and place can work with data, not just as points or polygons on a blank surface, but as something spatially meaningful. This enables us to further understand the relationship between language and place, rather than simply ascribing forms to locations. Put simply, combining linguistic and other datasets will enable researchers to understand much more about 'lived space' and how this affects the language that research subjects use.

REFERENCES

Auer, Peter, Martin Hilpert, Anja Stukenbrock and Benedikt Szmrecsanyi 2013. 'Integrating the perspectives on language and space', in Auer, Peter, Martin Hilpert, Anja Stukenbrock and Benedikt Szmrecsanyi (eds.) *Space in Language and Linguistics: Geographical, Interactional, and Cognitive Perspectives*. Berlin: de Gruyter. pp. 1–18.

Aurrekoetxea, Gotzon, Karmele Fernandez-Aguirre, Jesus Rubio, Borja Ruiz and Jon Sanchez 2013. '"DiaTech": A new tool for dialectology'. *Literary and Linguistic Computing* 28: 23–30.

Beal, Joan C. 1999. '"Geordie nation": Language and regional identity in the northeast of England. *Lore and Language* 17(1). 33–48.

2009. 'Enregisterment, commodification, and historical context: "Geordie" versus "Sheffieldish"'. *American Speech* 84(2). 138–56. doi:10.1215/00031283-2009-012.

Britain, David 2009. 'Language and space: The variationist approach', in Auer, Peter and Jürgen E. Schmidt (eds.) Language and Space: An International Handbook of Linguistic Variation. Berlin: Mouton de Gruyter. pp. 142–62.

2010. 'Conceptualisations of geographic space in linguistics', in Lameli, Alfred, Roland Kehrein, and Stefan Rabanus (eds.) *Language and Space: An International Handbook of Linguistic Variation*. Volume 2: Language Mapping. Berlin: Mouton de Gruyter. pp. 69–97.

Bucholtz, Mary, Nancy Bermudez, Victor Fung, Lisa Edwards and Rosalva Vargas 2007. '*Hella nor Cal or Totally so Cal?* The perceptual dialectology of California'. *Journal of English Linguistics* 35: 325–52.

Bucholtz, Mary, Nancy Bermudez, Victor Fung, Rosalva Vargas and Lisa Edwards 2008. 'The normative north and the stigmatized south: Ideology and methodology in the perceptual dialectology of California'. *Journal of English Linguistics* 36: 62–87.

Buchstaller, Isabelle and Seraphim Alvanides 2010. 'Applying Geographical Sampling Methods to Regional Dialectology in North East England'. Paper presented at the 4th Northern Englishes workshop, University of Sheffield.

Chambers, J. K. and Peter Trudgill 1998. *Dialectology*, Second edition. Cambridge: Cambridge University Press.

Cukor-Avila, Patricia, Lisa Jeon, Patricia C. Rector, Chetan Tiwari and Zak Shelton 2012. *"Texas–It's Like a Whole Nuther Country": Mapping Texans' Perceptions of Dialect Variation in the Lone Star State*. Proceedings of the Twentieth Annual Symposium about Language and Society, Austin.

da Silveira, Luís Espinha 2014. 'Geographic Information Systems and historical research: An appraisal'. *International Journal of Humanities and Arts Computing* 8: 28–45.

de Vriend, Folkert, Lou Boves, Roeland van Hout, and Jos Swanenberg 2011. 'Visualization as a research tool for dialect geography using a geo-browser'. *Literary and Linguistic Computing* 26: 17–34.

Dieth, Eugen and Harold Orton. 1952. A questionnaire for a linguistic atlas of England. *Proceedings of the Leeds Philosophical and Literary Society, Literary and Historical Section*, Volume VI, Part IX, 605–700. Leeds.

Ellis, Alexander J. 1889. *On Early English Pronunciation, Part V: Existing Dialectal as Compared with West Saxon Pronunciation*. London: Trübner and Co.

ESRI. 2011. What is GIS? www.gis.com/content/what-gis.

Evans, Betsy E. 2011. '"Seattletonian" to "Faux Hick": Perceptions of English in Washington State'. *American Speech* 86: 383–414.

2013. 'Seattle to Spokane: Mapping perceptions of English in Washington State'. *Journal of English Linguistics* 41: 268–91.

Goebl, Hans 1993. 'Probleme und Methoden der Dialektometrie: Geolinguistik in globaler Perspektive', in Viereck, Wolfgang (ed.) *Proceedings of the International Congress of Dialectologists 1*. Stuttgart: Franz Steiner Verlag. pp. 37–81.

2011. 'Dialectometry and quantitative mapping', in Lameli, Alfred, Roland Kehrein, and Stefan Rabanus (eds.) *Language and Space: An International Handbook of Linguistic Variation*. Volume 2: Language Mapping. Berlin: Mouton de Gruyter. pp. 433–57.

Gregory, Ian N and Andrew Hardie 2011. 'Visual GISting: Bringing together corpus linguistics and Geographical Information Systems'. *Literary and Linguistic Computing* 26: 297–314.

Grieve, Jack 2014. 'A comparison of statistical methods for the aggregation of regional linguistic variation', in Szmrecsanyi, Benedikt and Bernhard Wälchli (eds.) *Aggregating Dialectology, Typology, and Register Analysis: Linguistic Variation in Text and Speech*. Berlin: Walter de Gruyter. pp. 53–88.

Grieve, Jack, Diansheng Guo, Alice Kasakoff, and Andrea Nini 2014. 'Big-data Dialectology: Analyzing Lexical Spread in a Multi-billion Word Corpus of American English'. Paper presented at the AACL 2014, Flagstaff, Arizona.

Heeringa, Wilbert and John Nerbonne 2013. 'Dialectometry', in Hiskens, Frans and Johan Taelderman (eds.) *Language and Space. An International Handbook of Linguistic Variation, Volume III: Dutch*. Berlin: Walter de Gruyter. pp. 624–46.

Heywood, Ian, Sarah Cornelius, and Steve Carver 2006. *An Introduction to Geographical Information Systems*, 3rd edn. Harlow: Pearson Prentice Hall.

Jessop, Martyn 2007. 'The inhibition of geographical information in digital humanities scholarship'. *Literary and Linguistic Computing* 23: 39–50.

Kirk, John M. and William A. Kretzschmar 1992. 'Interactive linguistic mapping of dialect features'. *Literary and Linguistic Computing* 7: 168 –75.

Kolb, Eduard 1966. *Phonological Atlas of the Northern Region: The Six Northern Counties, North Lincolnshire and the Isle of Man*. Bern: Francke Verlag.

Labov, William, Sharon Ash, and Charles Boberg 2006. *The Atlas of North American English: Phonetics, Phonology, and Sound Change: A Multimedia Reference Tool*. Berlin: Walter de Gruyter.

Light, Deanna and William A. Kretzschmar 1996. 'Mapping with numbers'. *Journal of English Linguistics* 24: 343–57.

Long, Daniel 1999. 'Geographical perception of Japanese dialect regions', in Preston, Dennis R. (ed.) *Handbook of Perceptual Dialectology*. Amsterdam: John Benjamins. pp. 177–98.

Long, Daniel and Young-Cheol Yim 2002. 'Regional differences in the perception of Korean dialects', in Preston, Dennis R. (ed.) *Handbook of Perceptual Dialectology*. Amsterdam: John Benjamins. pp. 249–75.

Macaulay, Ronald 1985. 'Linguistic maps: Visual aid or abstract art?', in Kirk, John M., Stewart Sanderson, and John D. A. Widdowson (eds.) *Studies in Linguistic Geography*. London: Croom Helm. pp. 172–86.

McDavid, Raven I. 1983. 'Retrospect'. *Journal of English Linguistics* 16: 47–54.

Monmonier, Mark 1991. *How to Lie with Maps*. Chicago: University Of Chicago Press.

Montgomery, Chris 2007. 'Northern English dialects: A Perceptual Approach'. Unpublished PhD thesis, University of Sheffield.

    2012. 'The effect of proximity in perceptual dialectology'. *Journal of Sociolinguistics* 16: 638–68.

    2014. 'Perceptual ideology across the Scottish-English border', in Watt, Dominic and Carmen, Llamas (eds.) *Language, Borders and Identities*. Edinburgh: Edinburgh University Press. pp. 118–36.

Montgomery, Chris and Joan C. Beal 2011. 'Perceptual dialectology', in Maguire, Warren and April McMahon (eds.) *Analysing Variation in English*. Cambridge: Cambridge University Press. pp. 121–48.

Montgomery, Chris and Philipp Stoeckle 2013. 'Geographic information systems and perceptual dialectology: A method for processing draw-a-map data'. *Journal of Linguistic Geography* 1: 52–85.

Nerbonne, John 2010. 'Mapping aggregate variation', in Lameli, Alfred, Roland Kehrein, and Stefan Rabanus (eds.) *Language and Space: An International Handbook of Linguistic Variation*. Volume 2: Language Mapping. Berlin: Mouton de Gruyter. pp. 476–95.

Nerbonne, John and William Kretzschmar 2003. 'Introducing computation techniques in dialectometry'. *Computers and the Humanities* 37: 245–55.

    2006. 'Progress in dialectometry: Toward explanation'. *Literary and Linguistic Computing* 21: 387–97.

    2013. 'Dialectometry++'. *Literary and Linguistic Computing* 28: 2–12.

Nerbonne, John, Rinke Colen, Charlotte Gooskens, Peter Kleiweg and Therese Leinone 2011. 'GabMap: A web application for dialectometry'. *Dialectología Special Issue* 2: 65–89.

Nichols, Johanna 2013. 'The vertical archipelago: Adding the third dimension to linguistic geography', in Auer, Peter and Jürgen E. Schmidt (eds.). *Language and Space: An International Handbook of Linguistic Variation*. Berlin: Mouton de Gruyter. pp. 38–60.

Office for National Statistics. 2011. Special Workplace Statistics - LAD Level. ESRC/JISC Census Programme, Census Interaction Data Service, University of Leeds and University of St. Andrews. https://wicid.ukdataservice.ac.uk/ (1 July, 2015).

Onishi, Isao and Daniel Long 1997. *Perceptual Dialectology Quantifier (PDQ) for Windows*. http://nihongo.hum.tmu.ac.jp/~long/maps/perceptmaps.htm. (15 February, 2017).

Orton, Harold 1962. *Survey of English Dialects: Introduction*. Leeds: Edward Arnold and Sons Limited.

Orton, Harold and Michael V. Barry 1969. *Survey of English Dialects: Volume II, The West Midland Counties*, Part 1. Leeds: Edward Arnold and Sons Limited.

Orton, Harold and Nathalia Wright 1974. *A Word Geography of England*. London: Seminar Press.

Orton, Harold, Stewart Sanderson and John D. A. Widdowson (eds.) 1978. *The Linguistic Atlas of England*. London: Croom Helm.

Preston, Dennis R. 1982. 'Perceptual dialectology: Mental maps of United States dialects from a Hawaiian perspective'. *Hawaii Working Papers in Linguistics* 14: 5–49.

    1989. *Perceptual Dialectology: Non-Linguists' View of Aerial Linguistics*. Dordrecht: Foris.

    1999. 'Introduction'. Preston, Dennis R. (ed.) *Handbook of Perceptual Dialectology*. Amsterdam: John Benjamins. pp. xxiii–xxxix.

    2002. 'Language with an attitude', in Chambers, J. K., Peter Trudgill, and Natalie Schilling-Estes (eds.) *The Handbook of Language Variation and Change*. Oxford: Blackwell. pp. 40–66.

Preston, Dennis R. and George M. Howe. 1987. 'Computerized studies of mental dialect maps', in Denning, Keith M., Sharon Inkelas, Faye McNair-Knox, and John Rickford (eds.) 1987. *Variation in Language: NWAV-XV at Stanford*. Stanford: Department of Linguistics, Stanford University. pp. 361–78.

R Core Team. 2014. *R: A Language and Environment for Statistical Computing.* Vienna: R Foundation for Statistical Computing.

Séguy, Jean 1973. 'La Dialectométrie dans l'Atlas linguistique de la Gascogne'. *Société de linguistique romane* 73: 1–24.

Stoeckle, Philipp 2012. 'The folk linguistic construction of local dialect areas: Linguistic and extra-linguistic factors', in Hansen, Sandra, Christian Schwarz, Philipp Stoeckle, and Tobias Streck, (eds.) Dialectological and Folk Dialectological Concepts of Space: Current Methods and Perspectives in Sociolinguistic Research on Dialect Change. Berlin: De Gruyter Mouton.

Szmrecsanyi, Benedikt. 2012. 'Methods and objectives in contemporary dialectology', in Seržant, Ilja A. and Björn Wiemar (eds.) *Contemporary Approaches to Dialectology: The Area of North, Northwest Russian and Belarusian Vernaculars.* Bergen: Slavica Bergensia 13. pp. 81–92.

2013. 'Lost in space? The many geographies and methodologies in research on variation within languages', in Auer, Peter, Martin Hilpert, Anja Stukenbrock and Benedikt Szmrecsanyi (eds.) *Space in Language and Linguistics: Geographical, Interactional, and Cognitive Perspectives.* Berlin: de Gruyter. pp. 238–41.

Trudgill, Peter 1999. *The Dialects of England*, Second edition. Oxford: Blackwell.

Tufte, Edward R. 1990. *Envisioning Information.* Cheshire, Connecticut: Graphics Press USA.

Upton, Clive 2006. 'Modern regional English in the British Isles', in Mugglestone, Lynda (ed.) 2006. *The Oxford History of English.* Oxford: Oxford University Press. pp. 379–414.

2010. 'Designing maps for non-linguists', in Lameli, Alfred, Roland Kehrein, and Stefan Rabanus (eds.) *Language and Space: An International Handbook of Linguistic Variation.* Volume 2: Language Mapping. Berlin: Mouton de Gruyter. pp. 142–57.

Upton, Clive, David Parry, and John D. A. Widdowson 1994. *Survey of English Dialects: The Dictionary and Grammar.* London: Routledge.

Upton, Clive and John D. A. Widdowson 1996. *An Atlas of English Dialects.* Oxford: Oxford University Press.

Wieling, Martijn, Robert G. Shackleton, and John Nerbonne 2013. 'Analyzing phonetic variation in the traditional English dialects: Simultaneously clustering dialects and phonetic features'. *Literary and Linguistic Computing* 28; 31–41.

8   Which Way to Look?
Perspectives on 'Urban' and 'Rural' in Dialectology

David Britain

1.   Introduction

The ways we conceptualise 'urban' and 'rural' are strongly conditioned by a range of discourses (institutional, public, media) – discourses which are dynamic yet which often have roots reaching well back into earlier times, discourses which are interactive and which shape how we see, read, and interpret the landscape. These discourses themselves are also often deployed to deliberately *manipulate* how we interpret these landscapes: they are used to commodify certain landscapes (e.g. in tourist promotional materials) or to package and sell particular partial and politicised representations of landscape (witness, e.g. how the Countryside Alliance in the United Kingdom portrayed the countryside in its attempt to prevent a ban on fox hunting). The way in which we see the city and the countryside, then, is shaped by these discourses and is deeply ideological.

In this chapter, I argue that these circulating ideological discourses have also shaped the way dialectologists – traditional and variationist – have gone about their business of understanding the nature of language change, and shaped the way dialectologists have seen, understood, and 'exploited' 'rural' and 'urban' in their research. Drawing upon applications of Foucault's work by urban and rural geographers, I will apply the concept of the rural and urban 'gaze' (e.g. Abram 2003) to help understand the contrasting ways in which 'rural' and 'urban' have been theorised in different forms of dialectology. *Gaze* is defined by Woods (2011: 103) as 'an act of power in which collective social norms define not only how we interpret the things we see, but also what we actually see (and do not see) and where we look'. As this definition makes clear, our gaze not only leads us to see things in certain ways, but also leads us

The work presented in this chapter has been conducted with the help of funding from the Swiss National Science Foundation ("Contact, mobility and authenticity: language ideologies in koinei-sation and creolisation": 100015_146240). I am grateful to two anonymous reviewers for their comments on an earlier draft of this chapter.

not to see certain things too. Woods (2011: 103), for example, points to Foucault's original concern with the 'medical gaze', which showed that, until the eighteenth century, 'mental illness' was not seen as such, because the symptoms of such illness were interpreted as evidence that the sufferer was 'possessed' and not as a symptom related to general health. I will also show how the rural and urban gazes in dialectology have often meant that scholars have not 'seen' and therefore not investigated contexts of change which tend to fall outside of our usual associations and expectations of those landscapes.

I begin from an assumption that, despite society's very different conceptual-isations of rural and urban, *typologically* language changes in the same way in both (Britain 2009, 2012). Remarkably, this assumption seems to surprise many people. Some dialectologists have gone as far as to argue that there are certain linguistic changes which are *unique* to cities (Calvet 1994; Bulot and Tsekos 1999; Messaoudi 2001; Bulot 2002). Calvet, for example, asked:

Why the city? One needs only to look at rates of urbanisation in different countries around the world to realise that the city represents an inevitable outcome of our recent history. People from rural areas everywhere are lured by the false promises of urban life, by its bright lights and the hope of better paid work. And this coming together of migrants to the city has linguistic consequences ... the city also produces specific linguistic forms, urban dialects ... Urban sociolinguistics cannot be content to study urban contexts, it must tease out what is specific about these contexts and build a specific approach to these contexts. (Calvet 1994: 15, my translation)

Calvet proposes semantic transparency and the levelling of grammatical and morphological redundancy as examples of these specific linguistic forms. Such types of change are indeed often found in cities, but not rarely found also in rural areas. In Britain (2009, 2012), I argued that contact, not urban location, is typologically most responsible for many of the changes that Calvet lists, and proposed that there are large-scale sociolinguistic processes which are perhaps most obviously and vividly expressed in cities, but are not confined politically, sociologically, or epistemologically to an urban context.[1]

Hubbard (2006: 9) argues that geographers, too, once identified cities as distinctive spaces and consequently sought specific ways to describe and explain them. By the late 1960s, however, geographers were beginning to question the explanatory fruitfulness of the opposition, and there is now a general consensus that the distinction between the two cannot be explanatory. Pahl (1968: 263, 302) was an early especially critical supporter of this view, arguing that 'in a sociological context, the terms rural and urban are more

---

[1] In a similar vein to Calvet, Marshall (2004), in examining linguistic variation in rural Scotland, correlated linguistic variables with a speaker's apparent 'mental urbanisation', measured on the basis that international food tastes, attentiveness to fashion, IT, media, and electronic consump-tion, as well as a dislike of rural themes on TV were 'urban' traits, and the reverse 'rural.'

remarkable for their ability to confuse than for their power to illuminate ... any attempt to tie particular patterns of social relationships to specific geographical milieu is a singularly fruitless exercise'. Additionally, Harris (1983: 104) argued that defending the distinction between urban and rural 'encourages us to believe that the term urban might explain something. To the contrary ... in its spatial sense 'urban' adds nothing to our understanding of proximity and its effects, as they vary in intensity over space. This conclusion offers new support to the emerging consensus that, when applied to the present, 'urban' explains nothing. If the ghost has not yet been laid, there is now another nail in the coffin' (see Britain 2009, 2012 for further confirmation of the non-explanatory nature of 'urban' and 'rural').

I proceed now to expand on the idea of the rural and urban gaze, considering how this gaze is rooted in ideologies about the countryside and the city, and how it has shaped dialectological practice. As we will see, 'rural' and 'urban' are often represented as opposites, and it is often 'negative' ideologies of the city which help shape 'positive' ones of the countryside, and vice versa. As Kroskrity (1999: 12) reminds us, ideologies are multiple, divergent, often seemingly contradictory and created by a diverse range of actors. Nevertheless, ideologies of the rural and urban are powerful and, as we shall see later, can trigger significant language change-inducing consequences.

2.   Thatched Cottages, Chocolate Boxes, Rhoticity and NORMs

In an excellent overview of rural geography, Woods (2011), countering essentialist notions of urban and rural, argues that 'rurality is understood as a social construct ... an imagined entity that is brought into being by particular discourses of rurality that are produced, reproduced and contested by academics, the media, policy-makers, rural lobby groups and ordinary individuals. The rural is therefore a 'category of thought'' (Woods 2011: 9). Consequently, 'the importance of the rural lies in the fascinating world of social, cultural and moral values that have become associated with rurality, rural spaces and rural life' (Cloke 2006: 21). One of the more dominant ideologies of the rural is that of the *rural idyll*, an ideology that is 'an enduring, far-reaching, deeply ingrained contemporary imagining of rurality'' (Horton 2008b: 389).[2] Space precludes the possibility of an extensive summary of the large literature on the rural idyll (see Woods 2011: 21–2), but the notion bundles together bucolic discourses of the countryside: the rural as peaceful, tranquil, stable, simple, virtuous, moral, unspoilt yet fragile, and vulnerable to 'contamination' from

---

[2] I focus here on the circulating ideologies of urban and rural life in England. We cannot assume that similar 'categories of thought' function or function in the same way in other societies. Ideologies of the rural in England understandably differ from those in Canada, for example.

the urban, supportive and community-driven and, importantly, as traditional –
a site of heritage and preservation. Woods (2011: 17) shows that many of these
ideas of the rural date back at least to Classical Roman times and Bunce (1994)
has argued that many of them, furthermore, are generated and reproduced from
outside, from urban and suburban sitting rooms, from the 'armchair countryside'. As Woods (2011: 30) makes clear, there are a multitude of discourses of
rurality, and the rural idyll competes with other representations of the countryside, for example the rural as backward, conservative, boring, dangerous,
threatening, uncultured and uneducated. Horton (2008b: 389) points to a
number of authors who have suggested that 'this "rural idyll" has too often
borne particular (typically white, Anglocentric, conservative, heterosexist,
elitist) cultural/ideological "baggage"'. Others have added 'male' to the list.

The rural idyll has (of course) been commodified – in promotional literature
for rural tourism, for example, and, of course, in the stereotypical images of
thatched cottages on confectionary boxes that have generated the adjective
'chocolate-box' which now rarely has anything to do with chocolate.[3] Crucially, this concept has been circulated and reproduced through the mass
communication media. Phillips *et al.* (2001) point to the fact that dramas set
in rural areas are amongst the most popular (and enduring) programmes on
television – consider the popularity of British comedy and drama series such as
Last of the Summer Wine, Heartbeat, Midsomer Murders, Peak Practice, but
also non-fictional series such as *Escape to the Country*, and, even, *One Man
and His Dog.*[4] They, and others, argue that such programmes present a very
partial, middle-class view of the countryside, and 'a stylised and exaggerated
version of the rural that is detached from the everyday material experience of
rural life' (Woods 2011: 36). Woods (2011: 36) has argued that through these
programmes, many urban viewers come to know the rural. The role the media
play in the intergenerational entrenchment of such vistas of the rural can be
seen in the popularity of series for young children in which idyllic pastoral
representations of the countryside are presented: most notably *Postman Pat* (a
British programme about a mail delivery driver, working in a small village, see
Horton [2008a, 2008b] for discussions of the reproduction of the rural idyll in
Postman Pat).

The concept of the rural gaze suggests that when we 'look at' or 'interpret'
the countryside, our view is 'directed' and steered by circulating social

---

[3] For example: 'The Cotswolds are brimming with chocolate box holiday cottages that are perfect
for discovering the local attractions, farm parks and fine dining restaurants'
www.holidaycottages.co.uk/cotswolds, accessed 23 February 2015).

[4] These series are, respectively: a gentle comedy about old people in a rural village; a police drama
set in 1960s rural England; a police drama set in contemporary rural England; a drama set in a
rural doctor's surgery; a programme supporting people trying to move home from the city to the
countryside; and a sheepdog trial competition.

ideologies about the rural, and our perceptions of rural authenticity are often measured by the extent to which 'reality' matches the hegemonic picture. In the case of the rural, dominant ideologies mask many of the less serene realities of social life in the countryside, so the rural gaze also shapes what we do *not* see or understand too. It also guides how we see the countryside *linguistically*. The rural dialectological gaze tends to draw especially on the countryside as site of tradition and of the archaic. In the south of England, for example, rhoticity – a now declining characteristic of the Englishes of south-western England (Piercy 2006) – is routinely recruited to phonologically perform rurality, and is regularly used and commodified in characterisations of the English south-west, both dramatic and comedic. Examples include Exeter City football fans' chant of 'Oooh arrrr, we are Exeter', the Scrumpy and Western band *The Wurzels'* hyperrhoticised cover version of Gina G's 1996 non-rhotic rendition of Eurovision song 'Ooh ahh just a little bit', and mocking references to the Cornish National Liberation Army as being the 'Ooh-Arr-A'.[5] As is often the case with iconicised ideological representations, a particular characteristic of some members of a group is deemed to hold for all members of that group. Rhoticity has, in some discourses, been assumed to be characteristic of *all* of the rural south of England, even in those parts where rhoticity has long disappeared, such as East Anglia. Consequently, the speech of some older and less educated characters, especially, in drama series set in East Anglia such as Stephen Fry's *Kingdom*[6] is rhotic, even though this area was already reported as being absent of rhoticity back in the late nineteenth century (Ellis 1889). And rhoticity is regularly used in comedic representations of East Anglia too (e.g. see comedian Russell Howard's use of rhoticity to represent the English of Norwich in *Right Here, Right Now* (Howard 2011)). For many, iconic representations of East Anglia are performed through yod-dropping,[7] a traditional, but also declining feature of the local variety that became enregistered as a result of a series of frozen turkey advertisements from the 1980s onwards. Almost invariably, it is traditional, often obsolescent characteristics of rural dialects which are iconised and, to reword Woods, these present stylised and exaggerated versions of the rural soundscape that are similarly detached from everyday dialect use in the countryside.

Many of these ideologies that steer the rural gaze have shaped dialectological practice from the earliest days right through to the present. For the

---

[5] www.thesun.co.uk/sol/homepage/news/245741/Ooh-arr-on-Cornish-terror.html, accessed 23 February 2015.
[6] A British comedy series about a rural lawyer.
[7] Yod-dropping refers to the deletion of the glide /j/ in words such as 'view' [vu:] and 'tune' [tu:n]. See, for instance, Trudgill (1974).

traditional dialectologist, the conservative, traditional, nostalgic, simple, peaceful, unadulterated qualities of the gaze made rural areas especially appealing for work aiming to, in the words of Ellis (1889: 92 [his emphasis]), 'determine with considerable accuracy the different forms *now* or *within the last hundred years* ... in passing through the mouths of uneducated people, speaking an inherited language, in all parts of Great Britain where English is the ordinary medium of communication between peasant and peasant'. Unlike many working in the traditional approach, Ellis did collect some data from towns and cities, though most data collection localities were rural. Most data came via local contacts, often clergy, who were asked to 'translate' texts into the local accent using conventional spelling. He recognised, furthermore, the problem of getting clergy to do his translations, but asked:

But why not go to the peasantry at once? Why not learn from word of mouth, so that the errors would be limited to the writer's own appreciation? ... there are many difficulties in the way. First the peasantry throughout the country have usually two different pronunciations, one which they use to one another, and this is that which is required; the other which they use to the educated ... is absolutely worthless for the present purpose. If I, having no kind of dialectal speech, were to go among the peasantry, they would of course use their 'refined' speech to me. I have therefore not attempted it. (Ellis 1889: 3–4)

Later dialectological work was much more explicitly anti-urban in its approach. For the Survey of English Dialects (SED), preference was given in informant selection to 'agricultural communities that had had a fairly stable population of about five hundred inhabitants for a century or so ... newly built up locations were always avoided' (Orton and Dieth 1962–71: 15). As well as avoiding urban locations, the SED sought a very specific sort of informant:

The kind of dialect chosen for study was that normally spoken by elderly speakers of sixty years of age or over belonging to the same social class in rural communities, and in particular by those who were, or had formerly been, employed in farming, for it is amongst the rural populations that the traditional types of vernacular English are best preserved to-day ... Great care was taken in choosing the informants. Very rarely were they below the age of sixty. They were mostly men: in this country men speak vernacular more frequently, more consistently and more genuinely than women ... dialect speakers whose residence in the locality had been interrupted by significant absences were constantly regarded with suspicion. (Orton and Dieth 1962–71: 14–16)

Note the association of data they deem 'authentic' with many of the component ideologies shaping the rural gaze – associations with agriculture, stability, fragility in the face of urban incursion, the traditional. While the types of informants that the SED fieldworkers sought are clearly defined, the extent to which they were able to realise their goal is another matter. Although many agricultural workers were exempt from military service after

World War II – agriculture was deemed an 'essential service' – the SED Basic Materials reveal that many of the SED informants had military experience during World War I, a significant 'leveller' in many respects, including linguistic.[8]

Whilst, as we will see, developments in dialectology from the 1960s largely turned the focus away from the countryside, the rural gaze persists in some forms of variationist sociohistorical linguistics which seek to trace sources of pre-migratory dialect patterns. Tagliamonte's (2013) work on the British roots of North American dialects deliberately and specifically sought localities that were apparently rural, remote and stable, as well as informants who were old.

The rural dialectological gaze goes further, however. The focus on NORMs (Chambers and Trudgill 1998: 29) – non-mobile old rural men – as suitable informants for dialect investigations generally and the ensuing portraits of rural dialect variation as socially homogeneous but regionally differentiated helped feed not only ideologies (including academic ideologies) of rural dialects as highly localised – of the 'you go to the next village and you can't understand a word they say' kind – but also of rural locations as *socio*linguistically barren, as hyperconservative, and as static.

The problematic view of the dialectological landscape through the rural gaze was one of the triggers for the variationist, sociolinguistically oriented dialectology of the 1960s. At this time, academic dialectology acquired an urban gaze that has largely persisted to this day. I turn now to consider the urban gaze and its implications for variationist approaches, before considering the ways in which both gazes have tended to make invisible forms of social change that have profound linguistic outcomes.

3.   Where It's All Happening: The Urban Gaze

The way we see and interpret cities is *constructed* in the same ways as the rural gaze, through cycles of the emergence, circulation, and reproduction of official, lay, academic, mediated, and other ideological discourses. The discourses themselves are again multiple and deep-seated, but often contradictory and, understandably, quite different in content. Hubbard (2006: 61) argues that, unlike for the countryside, where the 'rural idyll' mythology is dominant, there are two oppositional ideologies that compete to shape our understanding of the city. One is an anti-urban view that sees the city as

---

[8] A number of older informants from my Fenland research (Britain 1991) had army experience from World War II and/or subsequent military peacekeeping roles in, for example, Palestine. Many reflected on how aware they became of their local dialects at that point and recounted their efforts to not 'stand out' linguistically.

'a nadir of human civility' and 'associated with sin and immorality, with a movement away from "traditional" order and mutual values' (Hubbard 2006: 60), with ugliness, decay, alienation, criminality, disorder and a lack of belonging. It is an ideology that is propped up by that of the rural idyll that presents the countryside as promising everything positive that the urban cannot, and Hubbard suggests both helped inform the garden city movement of the early twentieth century in Britain, which tried to create cities injected with many elements of rural living.

The other more liberal ideology is that of the city as vibrant, exciting, cultured, creative, diverse, tolerant, entrepreneurial, connected, cosmopolitan and 'edgy', innovative, at the forefront of new ideas – where it's all happening. To these characteristics, Hubbard adds the ideology of the city as cultural melting pot. This, he says, 'valorises the very size of the city as providing opportunities for variety, social mixing and vibrant encounters between very different social groups. Because of this, the city may be seen as having a radical potential, where it is possible to challenge entrenched order' (Hubbard 2006: 66). And just as the rural idyll reinforces anti-urbanist perspectives, so the view of the vibrant city of culture, social heterogeneity, education, and creativity is given strength by comparisons with the 'ignorant and brutish yokel', and with 'isolationist and technophobic' ruralites (Hubbard 2006: 64).

Mediated portrayals of the city help reproduce these ideologies. On the one hand, it is not hard to find representations of anti-urbanism. Futuristic dystopian worlds in literature and cinema are overwhelmingly urban; one of the largest selling computer game series, *Grand Theft Auto*, is set amongst scenes of urban disorder, and, Hubbard (2006: 62) reminds us, the chaos and lawlessness of some cities can only be contained by cinematic superheroes such as Batman, Spiderman, or, more recently, the Incredibles. On the other hand, there are many media portrayals that show the city as a buzzing, frenetic but ultimately sociable and supportive locale, such as *Sex in the City* and the aptly named *Friends*.

The urban gaze, then, is more contested, and not dominated by one particular way of seeing. How does it shape the way we see the city linguistically? Certainly city dialects appear to be more well recognised (Montgomery 2007) and are more likely to have been enregistered, at least in Britain. Many more cities have specific labels for their dialects than rural areas – Geordie, Scouse and Cockney, for instance, though language attitudes research tends to show that urban dialects are evaluated poorly in terms of prestige and social attractiveness (see Bishop *et al.* 2005, who show that it is the dialects of Birmingham, Liverpool, and London that are evaluated most negatively in attitudinal studies conducted 35 years apart). London's repertoire of commodified language features includes both elements of Cockney, such as rhyming slang and TH-fronting on the usual array of T-shirts[9], mugs and tea towels, as well as Multicultural London English (see, e.g., Cheshire *et al.* 2011), in the form of comedic characterisations, such as the Sacha Baron Cohen character Ali G.

We can now examine how the urban gaze has shaped dialectological practice. As we saw earlier, variationist sociolinguistics emerged partly in reaction to traditional approaches to dialectology that were strongly steered by the rural gaze. In addition, though, this and other emergent forms of sociolinguistics coincided with a growing politicisation of social problems centred around ethnicity, gender, and disadvantage, which were at their most visible and pressing in large multicultural urban centres. All of the main founders of the broader discipline were engaged (and continue to be so) in attempts to address these concerns as they applied to language, for example, Labov in his (ongoing) educational and advocacy work on behalf of speakers of AAVE (see, for instance, Labov 1982), and Fishman in his work counteracting misunderstandings about multilingualism and on language revitalisation (see, for instance, Fishman 1991).

Perhaps somewhat ironically, the first major fully variationist study (and the one that appears to have best survived the test of time) in what became widely known as 'urban sociolinguistics' was Labov's study of rural Martha's Vineyard. When contrasting his work there with the later study of the Lower East Side of New York, Labov made it clear that the latter represented 'a much more complex society' (Labov [1966] 2006: 3). Certainly 'urban as complex' is one routine element of the urban gaze, though few of the early urban variationist studies matched the Martha's Vineyard research in terms of the number of social variables actually analysed empirically. Labov's ([1966] 2006) New York study was ultimately distilled down to the variables of age, class, ethnicity, and gender – some, but not all, of the factors relevant to explaining sociolinguistic diversity in Martha's Vineyard. As the results of Labov's analysis demonstrated, Martha's Vineyard showed considerable sociolinguistic diversity with respect to age, location, occupation, ethnicity, orientation towards the island, and desire to stay or leave (1972: 22, 25, 26, 30, 32, 39). In terms of social and linguistic structure, Martha's Vineyard hardly fits the rural stereotype of quiet and sleepy pastoralism, or of traditional dialectological NORMs. But dialectology had now moved to the city and it has largely stayed there since.

In some senses, the urban gaze provided a number of motivations for shifting dialectology to the city. If, as Weinreich *et al.* (1968) make clear, the main goal of variationism is to understand the orderly heterogeneity of the

---

[9] TH-fronting refers to the pronunciation of $/\theta/$ and non-initial $/\eth/$ as $/f/$ and $/v/$, respectively. See, for example, www.zazzle.ch/norf_london_shirts-235451363698774736.

speech community undergoing change, where better to examine it than in communities which appear to be the most vibrant, diverse, fluid, socially heterogeneous, and innovative. The motivations are clear, though the practice has not usually been able to live up to the full diverse spectacle – few studies examined variation within different parts of the city (though Trudgill 1974 did so in Norwich), a good number focussed on one small part of a city (e.g. Labov [1966] 2006), and rarely do early studies stretch beyond a rather limited set of social variables. In most early work, non-natives and late arrivals to the community were excluded, so despite the attraction of finding order in the messiness of the city, a lot of that messiness was ignored (see Britain 2009, 2012).

Nevertheless, the literature demonstrates that dialectologists tend to travel to the city in their search for socially diverse communities to probe. We can point to a number of other consequences of the urban gaze on variationist dialectology:

1. The view of urban as innovative (and rural as conservative) has strongly shaped models of geolinguistic innovation diffusion, and assumptions are made that cities are the sources, generators, and projectors of change.
2. The view of urban as a diverse and vibrant melting pot has certainly very strongly shaped variationist examinations of multiethnolects, though again diversity is often (and understandably) somewhat simplified for the purposes of empirical analysis.
3. Very recent research, often linked to work on multiethnolects, under the label 'superdiversity' (see Blommaert 2013) (note the use of the mostly positive prefix super-) is, too, confined to urban locales.
4. Cities are often seen as "*par excellence*' places of contact and heterogeneity' (Miller 2007: 1), associated with weak social network ties (yet many analyses that have demonstrated the local norm enforcement power of strong social networks have been carried out in cities, for example, in Reading [Cheshire 1982], Belfast [Milroy 1987], and Brazlandia [Bortoni-Ricardo 1985]).

4.   Looking Beyond the Gaze

It is appropriate at this point to make it absolutely clear that I have no dispute with conducting variationist research in cities. I certainly do not deny that many linguistic innovations are generated in cities, that dialect contact can be especially intense in cities, or that the potential for the emergence of multiethnolects is particularly great. It is fully understandable why such research is usually carried out there, and equally understandable, as mentioned earlier, that in investigating complex communities, the full apparent diversity of the sociolinguistic setting cannot be readily captured methodologically, analytically, or theoretically. I have no complaints either with traditional dialectology's focus on NORMs, or Tagliamonte's (2013) comparative variationist sampling of only older speakers, given their research agendas, and, in the case of the traditional dialectologists, given their resources and technology (see Britain 2009, 2012). What I do want to highlight, however – and this is where we especially see the power of the gaze construct – is that both the urban and rural gazes, while directing our dialectological attentions in certain directions, *hide from view other sites of sociolinguistic variation and change.*

The rural gaze, directing us to see the dialectological countryside as isolated, conservative, and a preserve of linguistic heritage, diverts us from examining and interpreting urban areas in terms of conservatism and isolation. The patterns of linguistic variation and change that we encounter in the traditional dialectological enterprise are, we must not forget, the product of a distinct period. The informants of both Ellis and the SED were born in the nineteenth century, which saw massive population increases (a tripling of the population over the century), urbanisation, and a rural exodus. Millions left the countryside to seek their fortune in the city. In the twentieth century, however, it was the turn of a number of urban areas to experience demographic decline. Liverpool's population has declined by almost 400,000 since 1931 (over 45 per cent), that of Manchester by 250,000. What are the dialectological implications of such extensive population decline? While sociologists and geographers are beginning to examine more closely the similarities among shrinking cities across the Western World – Detroit, Leipzig, Halle, as well as Liverpool and Manchester (see, e.g., Oswalt and Rieniets 2006), there is the potential to begin to examine dialectological developments too in light of this demographic change. I have argued elsewhere that the types of changes currently underway in Liverpool (e.g. Watson 2006) are not atypical of those usually associated with variation and change in isolated communities – both resistance to and divergence from outside supralocal changes (Britain 2012).

Furthermore, the rural gaze, in presenting the countryside as an isolated, remote agricultural preserve, obscures the dramatic economic shift in some rural areas away from agriculture and towards consumption, especially tourism. In Britain (2013), I argue that we cannot underestimate the dialectological importance of fleeting and mundane but mass-scale mobilities (and changes in those mobilities) triggered by, for example, tourism and consumption. But the anonymous and the fleeting are associated with an urban not a rural gaze.

The urban gaze, meanwhile, has tended to obscure examination of a number of demographic changes, some substantial, that have affected the countryside. While, as far as the impacts of migration are concerned, the dialectological gaze has been firmly fixed on international arrivals and the creation of new multi-ethnic dialects in cities, rural areas, on the other hand, have been experiencing a demographically more substantial impact from internal migration, especially, but not solely, triggered by *counterurbanisation*, an overall demographic shift from city to country. Allinson (2005: 171), for example, shows not only that year on year there were around 300,000–400,000 moves from metropolitan areas to non-metropolitan areas, there were, in addition, again year on year, between 600,000 and 800,000 moves from one non-metropolitan area to another. These figures are considerably more significant than moves to or within metropolitan areas. Champion's (2001, 2005a, 2005b) analyses showed that it was the most rural areas of England that have been the most significantly affected by counterurbanisation (see also Champion *et al.* 2009).

Interestingly, the rural idyll is held responsible for a good proportion of this counterurbanisation movement, with urban residents influenced by the rural gaze (and the anti-urbanist one) departing for the 'good life' in the country. But counterurbanisation is not the only form of mobility that has caused massive demographic churn in rural areas over the past half century (see further Britain 2010, 2011, 2013). Despite this, however, there are few empirical dialectological studies examining change in the light of the very socially differentiated nature of counterurbanisation and other similar forms of internal mobility (for examples, see Piercy 2010, Britain 2011, 2013, in preparation).

It is also important to note that rural demographic churn is not restricted to the twentieth century. Pooley and Turnbull (1998: 93–146), in a detailed account of mobility in Britain since the 1700s, demonstrate that, whilst there is, throughout the eighteenth and nineteenth centuries, an overall migratory shift from rural to urban, movement up the urban hierarchy only narrowly outstrips movement down. There was considerable mobility within rural areas, and overall shifts were predominantly of a relatively local, relatively short-distance nature. The eighteenth- and nineteenth-century English countryside was neither static nor straightforwardly or wholeheartedly depopulating. And whilst agricultural workers have been the least likely to move long distances, the proportion of the population actually employed in agriculture has declined from 22 per cent in 1841 (Phillips and Williams 1984: 38) to less than 1 per cent today. Even in the nineteenth century, but especially in the twentieth, a sample consisting of non-mobile farm labourers fails to representatively capture the typical demographic of rural England.

A related consequence is that we have almost entirely failed to examine the dialectological ramifications of international migration to the countryside. One extremely widely held view is that international migrants always

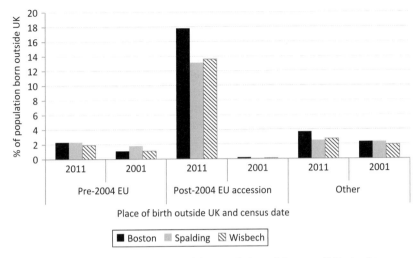

Figure 8.1: The percentage of the population of three small Fenland towns born outside of the United Kingdom (in pre-2004 member states, in the new post-2004 accession states, and elsewhere) from the 2001 and 2011 census.

head for the city. While there has been a *tendency* for immigration to be city-bound in the past century, rural areas too have also experienced periods of significant arrivals from abroad. The Commission for Rural Communities (2007: 11) examined migration to rural areas in light of the addition of eight Eastern European countries to the EU in 2004. They showed that the district with the highest number of new work registrations in the country, one way in which institutions have measured EU-internal migration in the absence of border counts, was rural Herefordshire; a number of other rural areas also saw significant numbers, especially relative to the size of the local population, including south Lincolnshire,[10] Cambridgeshire, West Norfolk (essentially the Fens), and parts of rural Somerset and north Devon. The 2011 census also shows how some small rural towns have seen dramatic demographic change since 2004.

Figure 8.1 shows the non-UK born population of three small Fenland towns between 2001 and 2011, and highlights the impact of the post-2004 EU accession states of (mostly) Eastern Europe. Similarly, a number of rural areas have significant and relatively stable migrant populations – for example, the

---

[10] *The Guardian* newspaper reports, for example, that in one school in the rural south Lincolnshire town of Boston, over 60 per cent of the children have migration backgrounds www.theguardian.com/uk/2012/dec/11/census-boston-eastern-european-immigration, accessed 23 February 2015).

significant Portuguese community in the small Norfolk towns of Thetford, Dereham, and Swaffham (Pina *et al.* 2010: 36).[11]

Recent research has also highlighted that historically, too, rural areas have been the destination of immigrants. The *England's Immigrants* project at the University of York's Centre for Medieval Studies has revealed that a significant number of international arrivals in medieval times settled and worked in rural areas.[12] Our urban gaze expects multiethnolects in the city, but not in the countryside, so as yet there appear to be no studies of Multicultural Rural Englishes in the literature, not because they do not or cannot exist, but again because we have not looked.

Our expectations that linguistic innovations have urban sources have largely led us not to seek innovation in the countryside, but, if studies have been conducted at all, examine the impact of urban innovations on the countryside. I am to some extent guilty of that myself (Britain 2005), but not entirely. In Britain (1997), I examine contact-based innovations that had a rural source. Our view of the countryside, then, is one of conservatism, not entirely because we have regularly empirically examined rural sites and found it to be that way, but also because we largely have not looked or, at least, not looked for the right things.

5.   Conclusion

I certainly do not want to claim that we would find *typologically* different manifestations of linguistic change if we were to investigate the 'super-diverse' countryside, or conservatism in cities, or the consequences of commuting in remote villages. We may well, however, locate innovations, witness the emergence of new ethnolects, or discover the consequences of unresearched contact situations if we are aware of the limitations circulating ideologies place on not only how we look, but how and where we investigate, and also how we interpret the dialectological landscape. Our job as dialectologists is to unpick and deconstruct those forces which are causing language variation and change to operate with different outcomes in different places. Ultimately, the very same cultural, economic, social, and political processes and conflicts can affect rural areas as affect urban – perhaps less routinely, less visibly, less intensively (or of course more routinely, visibly,

---

[11] Somewhat ironically, a good number of the Portuguese community in these towns work in the frozen turkey factory whose TV advertisements had contributed to the enregisterment of yod-dropping as iconic of traditional East Anglian dialects of English www.thetimes.co.uk/tto/career/graduate/article1796141.ece, accessed 23 February 2015).

[12] See 'Living and working together: England's immigrants in the Middle Ages': www.york.ac.uk/news-and-events/news/2015/research/immigrants-middle-ages/, accessed 23 February 2015.

intensively), but affect them, nevertheless. In examining the rural and urban gaze, I hope to have demonstrated not only the role that ideological forces play in propelling us to dialectologically examine rural and urban areas in certain and distinctive ways, but also how those forces can prevent us from looking at these landscapes in ways that would be innovative, productive, and significantly add to our understanding of what is possible as language varies and changes.

REFERENCES

Abram, Simone 2003. 'The rural gaze', in Cloke, Paul (ed.) *Country Visions*. Harlow: Pearson. pp. 31–48.

Allinson, John 2005. 'Exodus or renaissance? Metropolitan migration in the late 1990s'. *The Town Planning Review* 76: 167–89.

Bishop, Hywel, Nicholas Coupland, and Peter Garrett 2005. 'Conceptual accent evaluation: Thirty years of accent prejudice in the UK'. *Acta Linguistica Hafniensia* 37: 131–54.

Blommaert, Jan 2013. *Ethnography, Superdiversity and Linguistic Landscapes: Chronicles of Complexity*. Bristol: Multilingual Matters.

Bortoni-Ricardo, Stella M. 1985. *The Urbanization of Rural Dialect Speakers*. Cambridge: Cambridge University Press.

Britain, David 1991. *Dialect and Space: A Geolinguistic Study of Speech Variables in the Fens*. Unpublished PhD dissertation, University of Essex.

1997. 'Dialect contact and phonological reallocation: "Canadian Raising" in the English Fens'. *Language in Society* 26: 15–46.

2005. 'Innovation diffusion, "Estuary English" and local dialect differentiation: the survival of Fenland Englishes'. *Linguistics* 43: 995–1022.

2009. '"Big bright lights" versus "green and pleasant land"? The unhelpful dichotomy of "urban" v 'rural" in dialectology', in Al-Wer, Enam and Rudolph de Jong (eds.) *Arabic Dialectology: In Honour of Clive Holes on the Occasion of His Sixtieth Birthday*. Leiden: Brill. pp. 223–48.

2010. 'Supralocal regional dialect levelling', in Llamas, Carmen and Dominic Watt (eds.) *Language and Identities*. Edinburgh: Edinburgh University Press. pp. 193–204.

2011. 'The heterogenous homogenisation of dialects in England'. *Taal en Tongval* 63: 43–60.

2012. 'Countering the urbanist agenda in variationist sociolinguistics: Dialect contact, demographic change and the rural-urban dichotomy', in Hansen, Sandra, Christian Schwarz, Phillip Stoeckle and Tobias Streck (eds.) *Dialectological and Folk Dialectological Concepts of Space*. Berlin: de Gruyter. pp. 12–30.

2013. 'The role of mundane mobility and contact in dialect death and dialect birth', in Schreier, David and Marianne Hundt (eds.) *English as a Contact Language*. Cambridge: Cambridge University Press. pp. 165–81.

in preparation. *The Linguistic Consequences of Counterurbanisation*. Manuscript.

Bulot, Thierry 2002. 'La double articulation de la spatialité urbaine: 'espaces urbanisés' et 'lieux de ville' en sociolinguistique'. *Marges linguistiques* 3: 91–105.

Bulot, Thierry and Nicolas Tsekos 1999. 'L'Urbanisation linguistique et la mise en mots des identités urbaines', in Bulot, Thierry (ed.) 1999. *Langue urbaine et identité*. Paris: L'Harmattan. pp. 21–34.

Bunce, Michael 1994. *The Countryside Ideal: Anglo-American Images of Landscape*. London: Routledge.

Calvet, Louis-Jean 1994. *Les voix de la ville: introduction à la sociolinguistique urbaine*. Paris: Éditions Payot et Rivales.

Chambers, J. K. and Peter Trudgill 1998. *Dialectology*, Second edition. Cambridge: Cambridge University Press.

Champion, Tony 2001. 'The continuing urban-rural population movement in Britain: Trends, patterns, significance'. *Espace, Populations, Sociétés* 1–2: 37–51.

2005a. 'Population movement within the UK', in Chappell, Roma (ed.) *Focus on People and Migration*. Basingstoke: Palgrave Macmillan. pp. 92–114.

2005b. 'The counterurbanisation cascade in England and Wales since 1991: The evidence of a new migration dataset'. *Belgeo: Revue Belge de Géographie*: 85–101.

Champion, Tony, Mike Coombes and David L. Brown 2009. 'Migration and longer-distance commuting in rural England'. *Regional Studies* 43: 1245–59.

Cheshire, Jenny 1982. *Variation in an English Dialect: A Sociolinguistic Study*. Cambridge: Cambridge University Press.

Cheshire, Jenny, Paul Kerswill, Sue Fox, and Eivind Torgersen (2011) 'Contact, the feature pool and the speech community: The emergence of Multicultural London English'. *Journal of Sociolinguistics* 15: 151–96.

Cloke. Paul 2006. 'Conceptualising rurality', in Cloke, Paul, Terry Marsden and Patrick Mooney (eds.) *Handbook of Rural Studies*. London: Sage. pp. 18–28.

Commission for Rural Communities 2007. *A8 migrant workers in rural areas*. Cheltenham: CRC.

Ellis, Alexander 1889. *On Early English Pronunciation: Part V*. London: Truebner and Co.

Fishman, Joshua A. 1991 *Reversing Language Shift: Theory and Practice of Assistance to Threatened Languages*. Clevedon: Multilingual Matters.

Harris, R. 1983. 'The spatial approach to the urban question'. *Environment and Planning D* 1: 101–5.

Horton, John 2008a. 'Postman Pat and me: Everyday encounters with an icon of idyllic rurality'. *Journal of Rural Studies* 24: 399–408.

2008b. 'Producing Postman Pat: The popular cultural construction of idyllic rurality'. *Journal of Rural Studies* 24: 389–98.

Howard, Russell 2011. *Right here, right now* (DVD). London: Channel 4.

Hubbard, Phil 2006. *City*. London: Routledge.

Kroskrity, Paul 1999. 'Regimenting languages: language ideological perspectives', in Kroskrity, Paul (ed.) *Regimes of language: ideologies, polities and identities*. Santa Fe: School of American Research Press. pp. 1–34.

Labov, William 1972. *Sociolinguistic patterns*. Oxford: Blackwell.

1982. 'Objectivity and commitment in Linguistic Science: The case of the Black English trial in Ann Arbor'. *Language in Society* 11: 165–202.

2006. *The Social Stratification of English in New York City*, Second edition. Cambridge: Cambridge University Press.

Llamas, Carmen and Dominic Watt (eds.) 2010. *Language and Identities*. Edinburgh: Edinburgh University Press.

Marshall, Jonathan 2004. *Language Change and Sociolinguistics: Rethinking Social Networks*. London: Palgrave Macmillan.

Messaoudi, Leila 2001. 'Urbanisation linguistique et dynamique langagière dans la ville de Rabat', in Bulot, Thierry, Cécile Bauvois and Philippe Blanchet (eds.) *Sociolinguistique urbaine Rennes: Presses Universitaires de Rennes* 2. pp. 87–98.

Miller, Catherine 2007. 'Arabic urban vernaculars: development and change', in Miller, Catherine, Enam Al-Wer, Dominique Caubet and Janet Watson (eds.) *Arabic in the City: Issues in Dialect Contact and Language Variation*. Abingdon: Routledge. pp. 1–32.

Milroy, Lesley 1987. *Language and Social Networks*, Second edition. Oxford: Blackwell.

Montgomery, Chris 2007. *Northern English dialects: A perceptual approach*. Unpublished PhD dissertation, University of Sheffield.

Orton, Harold and Eugen Dieth (eds.) 1962–71 *Survey of English Dialects: Basic Materials: Introduction and 4 Volumes (each in 3 parts)*. Leeds: E. J. Arnold & Son.

Oswalt, Philipp and Tim Rieniets (eds.) 2006. *Atlas of Shrinking Cities/Atlas der Schrumpfenden Städte*. Berlin: Kulturstiftung des Bundes.

Pahl, Ray 1968. 'The Rural-Urban Continuum', in Pahl, Ray (ed.) *Readings in Urban Sociology*. Toronto: Pergamon pp. 263–94.

Phillips, David and Allan Williams 1984. *Rural Britain: A Social Geography*. Oxford: Blackwell.

Phillips, Martin, Rob Fish and Jennifer Agg 2001. 'Putting together ruralities: towards a symbolic analysis of rurality in the British mass media'. *Journal of Rural Studies* 17: 1–27.

Piercy, Caroline 2006. ''Mixed with others it sounds different, doesn't it?': A quantitative analysis of rhoticity from four locations in Dorset.' Unpublished MA thesis, University of Essex.

　　2010. 'One /a/ or two?: the phonetics, phonology and sociolinguistics of change in the TRAP and BATH vowels in the southwest of England'. Unpublished PhD thesis, University of Essex.

Pina Almeida, José C. and David Corkill 2010. 'Portuguese migrant workers in the UK: a case study of Thetford, Norfolk'. *Portuguese Studies* 26: 27–40.

Pooley, Colin and Jean Turnbull 1998. *Migration and Mobility in Britain since the 18th Century*. London: UCL Press.

Tagliamonte, Sali A. 2013. *Roots of English*. Cambridge: Cambridge University Press.

Trudgill, Peter 1974. *The Social differentiation of English in Norwich*. Cambridge: Cambridge University Press.

Watson, Kevin 2006. 'Phonological resistance and innovation in the North-West of England'. *English Today* 22: 55–61.

Weinreich, Uriel, William Labov and Marvin Herzog 1968. 'Empirical foundations for a theory of language change', in Lehmann, Winfred and Yakov Malkiel (eds.) *Directions for Historical Linguistics*. Austin: University of Texas Press. pp. 97–195.

Woods, Michael (2011). *Rural*. London: Routledge.

Part III

Identifying Places

9   Identifying Places
The Role of Borders

Dominic Watt and Carmen Llamas

1.   Introduction

Human beings take territoriality to an extreme level. As a species, we seem very strongly predisposed towards partitioning and demarcating our spatial surroundings for the purposes of controlling access to natural resources and maintaining oversight of the activities of other individuals and groups. This apparent imperative is not enacted in an arbitrary or unconstrained way, of course: the earth's surface is already divided into zones according to geographical terrain, habitat type, and climatic factors, and the boundaries between these zones are sometimes abrupt rather than gradual. Deserts, rivers, lakes, and mountain ranges can be significant obstacles to movement, and the oceans present barriers that have been insuperable for the great majority of human history. Within these limits, though, we have sought to carve up the earth's land surface into larger and smaller units in ways that, in time, come to seem natural or inevitable. The processes by which borders between territories are rationalised and justified are complex and fascinating ones, combining as they do the collective histories and mythologies of tribal groups, religious and ethnic ideologies and, latterly, the political states that co-exist at the global level. Rather soon after a new state is founded, its inhabitants may come to believe that the status quo is effectively how things have always been, and that it could not tolerably be any other way (see Breuilly 2013).

It seems almost self-evident that language plays a crucial part in how territories bounded by borders with their neighbours are defined. In the early nineteenth century – this side of the watershed in European political history that has been dubbed 'The Great Divide' (Burke 2013: 21) – the emergent nation states of Europe sought to codify national languages that would be spoken everywhere that fell under the state's control, right up to the territory's outermost edges. A common language would, it was thought, help to unite citizens of the same state who might previously have felt more affinity with their neighbours just across the border than they did with the inhabitants of a distant capital city or remote provinces hundreds or even thousands of miles away. However, two centuries of language standardisation, linguistic prescriptivism, and the suppression of minority languages and dialects did not wipe the European map clean of state-internal linguistic variation as many of the founders of the nation states might have wished. Although a lamentably large number of European languages and dialects have been lost in recent centuries, some minority varieties have been remarkably tenacious. Others have flourished as, following the quite sudden *volte face* in late twentieth century national language planning policies across Europe, relegitimated ethnic identities and linguistic traditions have been given governmental endorsement and financial support, and celebration of cultural diversity is now strongly encouraged (Baldauf and Kaplan 2006). In a significant number of cases, the areas in which minority languages and dialects are spoken straddle international borders, producing especially fruitful contexts in which to explore the dynamics of the interaction between language and identity.

It must not be supposed, having said this, that only minority languages and dialects are worth considering in such borderland contexts. It is equally interesting to consider how speakers of powerful majority languages like English make use of linguistic resources to mark their national and regional affiliations at state boundaries. The border between the Republic of Ireland and Northern Ireland, for instance, has been the focus of a number of studies (Zwickl 2002; Kallen 2014), as has that between the United States and Canada (Chambers 1995; Dollinger 2012; Boberg 2014). In each of these contexts, and others like them, the complex connections between linguistic behaviour, identity, and place are particularly intriguing to social scientists, not least sociolinguists. In this chapter we consider further the last of these concepts as it relates to the language and identity issues in the Scottish-English border area.

2.   Place

Later in this chapter we will look more closely at aspects of how the distributions of linguistic forms in the Scottish-English borderland correlate with identity factors, and how these forms are used to encode information about place. First, though, it is worth posing the following question. What, in fact, do we mean by 'place'? The *Oxford English Dictionary* defines the term in two different ways. The first set of definitions, which relate to space or location, are what we might call the 'literal' ones:

5.   a. A particular part or region of space; a physical locality, a locale; a spot, a
        location. Also: a region or part of the earth's surface; 10. A particular spot
        or area inhabited or frequented by people; a city, a town, a village.

These are, in other words, positions which do not necessarily bear any direct relation to entities found within them, but which might merit identification as a discrete position in space by virtue of their significance to human habitation or activities.

Secondly, there are somewhat more figurative definitions, which pertain to position or situation with reference to its occupation or its occupant, for example:

12.   a. A proper, appropriate, or natural position or spot (for a person or thing).

When we talk of people 'being in place', 'finding their place', 'having their proper place', 'being well placed to do something', or 'having a firm place to stand', we are not necessarily talking about their physical location. Place is about geographical positions that can be pointed to on maps or identified using GPS coordinates, to be sure, but it is also about states of mind, stances and attitudes, and the status that individuals hold within their social networks and society at large. We will focus in this chapter chiefly on place in its more concrete senses, but will not neglect the other ways in which the concept of place can inform how we interpret our linguistic data.

The notion of place has been subjected to a number of stringent theoretical treatments since classical times, and has come to preoccupy scholars across a spectrum of research disciplines including linguistics (see Auer and Schmidt 2010; Auer *et al.* 2013) and also encompassing cognitive and social psychology, geography, history, anthropology, town and transport planning, communications and informatics, archaeology, and numerous others (see Scheider and Janowicz 2010, 2014; Winter and Freksa 2012; Raubal *et al.* 2013; Richter and Winter 2014). Scheider and Janowicz's (2010: 1) 'requirements for non-reductionist accounts of place', which build on the work of human geographers concerned with the 'phenomenological aspect' of place, are comprised of the following axioms:

1) Places are located, but are not locations.
2) Places are primary categories of human experience and social constructs.
3) Places have stabilizing functions that afford insideness.
4) Places have material settings (surface layouts).

In (1), we can talk of places which are not locations as such, in that they are potentially mobile (e.g. the deck of a ship, or a market which might appear only once a week and perhaps in different locations). Places must also be distinguished from locations, according to (2), in that locations can feasibly be anywhere and hence are isomorphic and arbitrary, whereas places are 'meaningful aspects of human experience [that] involve emotional attachment and social identification' (Scheider and Janowicz 2010: 1–2). Naming, or the association of linguistic forms with places, is a crucial component of their construction *as* places. Thirdly, the functions of places to 'stabilise' or arrest motion, as in (3), give them sets of properties that 'fix mutual expectations among people, allowing them to meet and communicate' (Scheider and Janowicz 2010: 2). Finally, (4) proposes that places 'always have a concrete identifiable material form' (Scheider and Janowicz 2010: 2). This might seem too narrow a requirement when one considers that places need not exist in any objective sense (where, e.g., are 'the developed world', 'suburbia', or 'the street'?). However, Scheider and Janowicz extend the scope of Gibson's (1979) term *surface layout* to imagined places, which can be argued to share properties, if only on the conceptual level, with physically observable places.

It is worth stressing the point that even in work on place that derives from research in fields quite far removed from linguistics, matters of language are often ascribed an important, even crucial, role. Places become part of the social environment through being thought significant enough to be given names, and language is of course the principal medium by which these names and other information about places are transmitted across space and time. Language is also used as a proxy for place, in the sense that pronunciations, grammatical structures, words, and writing systems come to be associated with particular localities or regions, meaning that we can deploy linguistic resources to index non-linguistic information about our geographical provenance. Moreover, the choices that speakers make among alternative forms in their linguistic repertoires act as signals that help listeners to align speakers with relevant ingroups and outgroups. Discovering how this kind of knowledge is acquired and activated in interactions is of course one of the key objectives of sociolinguistic inquiry.

The theorisation of place and space in sociolinguistic research has progressed significantly in recent decades, thanks to the work of scholars such as Peter Auer, Joan Beal, David Britain, and Barbara Johnstone (e.g. Beal 2006; Auer and Schmidt 2010; Britain 2010, 2014, this volume; Johnstone 2010, this volume; Auer *et al.* 2013). Britain proposes a taxonomy of space which depends on its conceptualisation as simultaneously *physical*, *social*, and *perceptual*. Physical space, he argues, is objective and geometric. In this view, space is scaled linearly, such that if measured in miles or kilometres, places X and Y could be said to be the same distance apart as Y and Z. However, with respect to social distance, the gap between X and Y may be much larger than that between Y and Z. An international border may divide X and Y, for example. But even within contiguous territories, social space may present bigger divides than geography alone would predict. There are many cities around the world in which adjacent neighbourhoods may be so socioeconomically segregated (e.g. an exclusive gated community abutting a shanty town) that the inhabitants of the respective communities may never come into contact with one another. The residents of the affluent neighbourhood may have much higher levels of interaction with people from a similar suburb miles across the city. The mapping of social space onto physical space may thus be complex and distorted.

Perceptual space, finally, is a useful notion when attempting to understand how people construct their perceptions of the world around them, and how they orient to their 'home patch' and to places that are physically or socially removed from it. Inhabitants of a community which is well connected by transport links to a large faraway city may think of it as closer in some sense than a nearby town which is poorly connected to their own. Issues such as journey time may be a major factor in how the space is perceived, but other relevant psychological factors might include whether a state or provincial boundary intervenes, or whether there is a significant geographical barrier (for instance, a large river or mountain range) between two places. Britain (2002, 2010, 2013) argues that perceptual space is constructed by people's everyday practices, and that 'place' and 'region' emerge through the routinisation of these practices. That is, through the mundane day-to-day routines that people perform – such as travelling to work, shops, or leisure facilities – locations and areas acquire coherence in psychological space that need not map in any direct way to physical geography. Viewed in this way, place can be seen as a 'process' that is shaped by practice, operating within the constraints of institutional and infrastructural factors. Factors of the latter sort may force the inhabitants of a place to revise their notions of social and perceptual space: a stark example from recent British history would be the radical reconfigurations of social networks caused by the relocation of city-centre slum dwellers to peripheral housing estates during the post-war period. Perceptions of distance and proximity were also influenced by the closure of large sections of the UK's railway network during the 1960s, and then changed again by a growth in car ownership (Vannini 2010).

On a subtler level, the reassignation of some towns and cities to new higher-order political units (such as counties, states) may affect how people see themselves. As Beal (2010: 225) puts it, 'the stroke of a bureaucrat's pen can have as much effect on a speaker's sense of place and identity as ... innovations in transport infrastructure and communication'. The potential knock-on effects of this kind of restructuring of social and perceptual space on speakers' linguistic behaviour has been investigated by Llamas (2007) in the north-eastern English town of Middlesbrough. Middlesbrough was originally in the North Riding of Yorkshire but was subsequently reallocated to the County Borough of Teesside (1968), then to a new county (Cleveland, in 1974), and finally to its own unitary authority (1996). Llamas found correlations between the distribution in informants' speech of a range of consonants and vowel variants, the political unit to which Middlesbrough belonged during individual speakers' formative years, and the identity labels that speakers assigned to themselves, to indicate that they thought of themselves as natives of Yorkshire, Teesside or Middlesbrough.

Beal (2010) reports something similar for Warrington, in north-west England, which became part of Cheshire after a redrawing of local county boundaries divided it from its original county of Lancashire. That decision met resistance among some older Warringtonians, many of whom cleave to Warrington's historical links with the working-class 'northern' culture of Lancashire and resent the association of the town with the north-midland county of Cheshire, a relatively affluent part of England widely perceived to be 'middle-class'. These perceptions may mean little to young Warringtonians, however, whose view of their hometown appears to be influenced less – perhaps not at all – by its erstwhile Lancastrian affiliation. As Beal points out, place 'is not a given, to be taken for granted in our research designs: what appears to be a town or city delimited by boundaries on the map may actually be several different places to different groups of speakers, whose allegiance to these "places" may be indexed by linguistic variables' (Beal 2010: 226).

As test sites for the investigation of how linguistic behaviour is connected to identities and perceptions of place, boundary zones of this kind could scarcely be bettered. Long-standing political divides, such as those between Britain's historic counties, or indeed between the constituent countries of the United Kingdom, are ideal. It was for this reason that the Scottish-English border area was identified as a zone of particular sociolinguistic interest. It must also be acknowledged that the presence of the Scots language in the region weaves additional threads into the local linguistic fabric, but because English was the language spoken by all our informants as well as by our interviewer, we will not concern ourselves here with questions of the degree to which local people have competence in Scots *per se*.

3.   The AISEB Project

The *Accent and Identity on the Scottish/English Border* (AISEB) project [1] sought to address a number of problematic questions concerning the degree to which impedance of the progress of sound changes can be attributed to identity factors and attitudes among speakers, and the part that speaker agency may play in the synchronic and diachronic distribution of phonological forms (Llamas 2010; Watt et al. 2014a, 2014b; 2014c). Rather than attempt to survey every community along the border's length, we opted to collect sociolinguistic data in four towns: Gretna (Scotland) and Carlisle

[1] We are grateful for the generous financial support of the UK Economic and Social Research Council (RES-062-23-0525). See www.york.ac.uk/language/research/projects/completed/aiseb

Figure 9.1: Map of Scottish-English border region, showing the four fieldwork sites (labels in bold type).

(England) at the border's western end, and Eyemouth (Scotland) and Berwick upon Tweed (England) at its eastern end (Figure 9.1).

Our initial hypotheses led us to expect that the speech patterns of people on the Scottish side of the border would differ markedly from those of people living just a few miles away on the English side, not least because the existing dialectological literature seemed unequivocally to suggest that the political border coincides with an entrenched linguistic divide (e.g. Ellis 1889; Zai 1942; Kolb 1966; Kolb *et al.* 1979; Aitken 1992; Glauser 2000). There were also good grounds for thinking that towns at either end of the border would be sociolinguistically divergent from one another, even if they were in the same country (e.g. Gretna versus Eyemouth), owing to their geographical separation and a lack of significant contact between their inhabitants.

We also thought it important to take account of the presence of the border from the socio-psychological point of view, through probing people's attitudes towards it. Political borders are objective boundaries insofar as they may be physically visible (fences, walls, signage, customs posts, clear-cut felling lines through forests) and/or can be pointed to on maps, and to that extent we may suppose there to be an absence of variation in how they are perceived. However, for those living in close proximity to a border, and assuming that their movement across it is not restricted, borders may acquire more subjective, symbolic qualities (Diener and Hagen 2010; Donnan and Wilson 2010). The border may be perceived and evaluated differently by inhabitants living on either side of it, and even by people living in the same locality. In the case of the four towns investigated in the AISEB study, it seemed plausible that being close to the border might be a common factor that lent a sense of common identity to people in the four towns. Though physically at the margins of their respective nations, the towns may alternatively be seen as being at the centre of a borderland region that straddles the political divide. The border, in other words, might not be defined principally by its demarcative properties that emphasise difference, but could be seen as something that gives people in towns on either side of it a sense of affinity as 'borderlanders'. Indeed, the region is sometimes termed 'The Borders', though the tendency is now to use this name just for the Scottish part of the area ('Scottish Borders' is the official name for the unitary authority that now subsumes the old counties of Berwickshire, Peeblesshire, Roxburghshire, and Selkirkshire). But even in a region where the border may be crossed freely, it does not necessarily follow that sharp inter-group categorisations will not emerge and persist, as theorists of borderlands such as David Newman (2006) have demonstrated. Linguistic behaviour is arguably the foremost member of the suite of cues that borderlanders can draw upon to flag their allegiances and stances. In the following section we examine one facet of the AISEB informants' speech production, by way of illustrating this principle.

3.1   AISEB Project Design

AISEB took a tripartite approach to the analysis of sociophonetic variation in the Scottish/English border region, by gathering data on speech production, social/political/linguistic attitudes and identity factors, and speech perception. Focussing solely upon production patterns would reveal little about informants' motivations for adopting or resisting phonological changes, and it could tell us only indirectly about their subjective evaluations of the pronunciations used by speakers in and beyond the fieldwork sites. We therefore attempt to integrate the three types of evidence, such that, as well as seeing *how* speech forms are distributed in the region, we may also come closer to understanding *why* the observed patterns of linguistic variation and change come about.

A total of 160 speakers (40 per town), balanced according to gender and age group (Young = 16–25; Older = 57+), were recruited via the 'snowball' method (Milroy and Gordon 2003) and interviewed for the most part in self-selected pairs in their own homes or another familiar setting. They were assigned to two social class groups (working and middle-class) according to educational criteria. Samples of read speech (word lists, text passages) were collected, but the majority of the interview was based on a questionnaire designed to elicit responses on topics relating to attitudes towards the border and the linguistic habits of people living near it, national identities (Scottish, English, British), social and political orientations, relevant ingroups and outgroups, and other issues of local concern. Interviewees were recorded using Marantz and Zoom solid-state digital recorders with professional-quality external microphones.

The variable we examine in the sections that follow is the voice onset time (VOT) of the stop consonants /p t k b d g/, which was hypothesised to vary in line with the location and age groups of our speakers. We then assess the patterns in the production data in the light of responses that our informants gave to the questionnaire. We opted to focus on VOT as a phonetic feature that is relatively subtle compared to other features examined in the AISEB material, in order to look closely at comparatively non-salient speech parameters (that may vary systematically in line with non-linguistic factors), alongside features that speakers are more likely to be consciously aware of. Finding consistent patterns correlating with locality, speaker age, gender, and so forth, would lend weight to our claims that the speech of people in this region is influenced by the proximity of the border in ways that are unlikely to be under their conscious control.

3.2   Voice Onset Time

VOT is a measure of the lag between the release of the stop closure ('occlusion') and the onset of voicing for the following vowel. English is usually said to feature short-lag VOT for /b d g/ and long-lag VOT for /p t k/, with substantial post-aspiration accompanying the latter set where they occur in initial pre-vocalic positions (Lisker and Abramson 1964; Docherty 1992), but there are varieties for which typical values are lower across the board, notably in southern Scotland (Johnston 1997; Scobbie 2006; Watt and Yurkova 2007). Given the heavy functional load of the stop consonants in English, there is likely to be considerable pressure to maintain audible phonetic distinctions between the pairs /p b/, /t d/ and /k g/, such that if aspiration on /p t k/ is minimal there is a greater likelihood of finding negative VOT values ('prevoicing') among tokens of /b d g/, as per the contrasts found in languages like French and Spanish (Lisker and Abramson 1964; Cho and Ladefoged 1999). It has also been claimed that the stop consonants in some accents of northern England are characterised by somewhat shorter VOT values than those reported for British Received Pronunciation (Lodge 1966; Wells 1982; Catford 1988). We have reasons to expect, then, that in the four borderland varieties investigated here we will observe relatively short VOT values for /p t k b d g/, with the difference being more pronounced on the Scottish side of the border.

The data discussed in Section 3.4, which were originally described in Docherty *et al.* (2011), are drawn exclusively from the read material, so as to reduce the effects of interspeaker variation in speech rate and stress placement, and to maximise lexical comparability from speaker to speaker.

3.3   Method

VOT values were measured using *Praat* (Boersma and Weenink 2014) for a total of approximately 4,600 tokens of word- or syllable-initial pre-vocalic /p t k b d g/, drawn from the AISEB wordlist and text passage recordings. The VOT interval was defined by the portion of the pressure waveform lying between the abrupt transient signalling the stop release, and the start of the first complete phonation cycle corresponding to the periodic vibration of the vocal folds, i.e. voicing (Foulkes *et al.* 2010; Thomas 2011).

The data were then subjected to multiple regression analysis using the *lme4* library in R to investigate the magnitude of the effects on VOT distribution of the following non-linguistic variables: *Nation* (England vs. Scotland), *Coast* (west vs. east), and *Speaker*, the last of which subsumed the variables *Age* (older vs. young), *Sex* (male vs. female) and *Class* (working vs. middle). All of these were treated as fixed effects; additional models in which *Speaker* was included as a random effect made a negligible difference to the results, so we report below on the fixed-effects models only. Two separate analyses were run: one for the voiced stops (/b d g/ together), the other for the voiceless stops (/p t k/ together).

3.4   Results

Figure 9.2 shows, in the form of probability density function curves, the VOT results for the /p t k/ and /b d g/ sets pooled across place of articulation within each set, for each of the four fieldwork sites. Speaker age is also represented, where the solid lines represent the data for older speakers and the dashed lines those for young speakers.

It is immediately clear that there are differences in each town with respect to age group, particularly for /b d g/ (main effect for speaker age: $t_{1,1337} = 20.02$, $r^2 = 0.2589, p < 0.001$).[2] In the upper panel of each pair, the curve for the young group is a sharp peak centred on approximately 20 milliseconds (ms), while the corresponding curves for the older speakers in each town are bimodal, and consequently considerably flatter. The bimodality – which is not unexpected for English (see Lisker and Abramson's [1964] results for American English) – indicates significant levels of pre-voicing, with VOT values tending to cluster between -50 and -100ms. In all four cases the other peak falls within the same positive VOT range as that found for the young speakers. The older speakers, in other words, use a combination of long-lead and short-lag VOT for /b d g/,

---

[2] The statistical analysis was carried out by Jennifer Nycz, whose valuable input we would like to acknowledge.

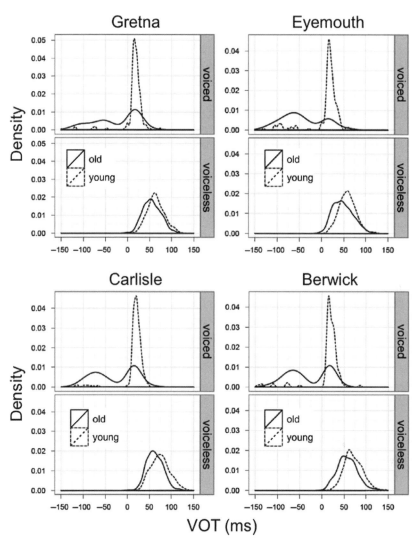

Figure 9.2: VOT values (represented by probability density functions) across the four AISEB fieldwork sites, split by speaker age group (solid lines = older speakers; dashed lines = young speakers). The pooled results for /b d g/ are shown in the upper panel in each pair ('voiced'), those for /p t k/ in the lower panel ('voiceless').

while the young speakers favour short-lag VOT almost exclusively (see the very similar results for Aberdeen English reported by Watt and Yurkova 2007). It is also noticeable that for Eyemouth, unlike the other three localities, the peak corresponding to pre-voiced tokens is more prominent than that for the short-lag VOT tokens, skewing the density curve markedly leftwards.

Looking next at the pooled data for the voiceless set /p t k/, it appears that there are small but consistent differences between the age groups in each town. Again, the VOT values for the young speakers are higher overall, as we might predict if contrast between the voiced and voiceless sets is to be maintained (/p t k/ main effect for age: $t_{1,3313} = 16.15$, $r^2 = 0.1693$, $p < 0.001$). As we saw for /b d ɡ/, the VOT values for older Eyemouth speakers are on average the lowest of the four communities. This finding is in line with Johnson's (1997) account of VOT in Scots-influenced varieties of English spoken in the Scottish Borders, whereby a lack of aspiration on /p t k/ correlates with a greater incidence of zero or negative VOT in the /b d ɡ/ set.

Overall, for /p t k/, the average VOT for the two Scottish varieties is lower by approximately 10ms than it is for the two English ones. Although the difference is a slight one, and there is a substantial overlap in the distributions, it nonetheless yields a significant effect for the *Nation* variable ($t_{1,3313} = 14.19$, $r^2 = 0.1693$, $p < 0.001$). There is also an east/west split, with Eyemouth and Berwick having shorter /p t k/ VOT values than Gretna and Carlisle (effect for *Coast*: $t_{1,3313} = 7.40$, $r^2 = 0.1693$, $p < 0.001$). Durational differences on this scale are not imperceptibly small: experimental studies have shown listeners to be sensitive to discrepancies in VOT values of as little as 10ms (Cole *et al.* 1978; Blumstein *et al.* 2005).

Before proceeding any further, it is important to consider the results of studies that have shown a link between speaker age and VOT (Benjamin 1982; Liss *et al.* 1990; Ryalls *et al.* 1997; Torre and Barlow 2009). Their findings reveal that, as a result of physiological changes, older speakers tend to use shorter VOT durations than younger speakers. The age effect found in the present study supports that generalisation. It does not explain, however, why the disparities in VOT values between the age groups are different across the four towns, nor why the *Nation* and *Coast* variables also appear to have an influence on VOT durations. We would suggest instead that the use of longer and shorter VOT among the AISEB speakers is related to attitudes and identity in the area, about which we say more in the following section.

4.   Identity Factors

In view of its long history as a zone of conflict and contestation, and lately as a focal point for questions pertaining to issues of political autonomy – questions that culminated in the 2014 independence referendum (see, for instance,

Daniel 2014)[3] – the Scottish-English border region is fertile ground for the investigation of social and political attitudes. The AISEB interviews were completed in 2011, prior to the announcement of the referendum but well after the establishment of the Scottish Parliament in 1999, so questions relating to the benefits or otherwise of recent and potential future constitutional changes were a reliable way of garnering opinions from interviewees.

Accompanying these relatively weighty questions were ones which sought information about participants' attitudes towards the local area (including questions concerning the border in particular), their day-to-day routines, and how language is used in the region. Examples of the set of twenty-one identity questions are shown below.

- If you were watching a regional news programme, what places would you expect to hear news from?
- If you wanted a day out shopping, where would you go?
- How often do you cross the border?
- Do you see the border as a divide of some sort?
- Where, geographically, would you say people stop talking the same as you and start sounding different?
- Are there any pronunciations or ways of saying things that you would hear and think, that sounds really Scottish or really English?

Participants were also asked to complete tasks based upon Visual Analogue Scales (VAS; Redinger and Llamas 2014; Llamas and Watt 2015). In one task a VAS was used as a means of quantifying a participants' strength of agreement with authentic statements made by people from one of the four AISEB localities – for example, 'I've been abroad and everybody thinks about Britain as England so when they're talking about Britain, they're really talking about England'– by drawing a vertical stroke somewhere along a horizontal line representing a continuum between 'agree' and 'disagree'. In another task, the one we focus on in the present chapter, participants drew multiple vertical lines

---

[3] It should be noted that the areas of Scotland abutting the border with England were in fact among the regions that were least in favour of Scottish independence at the 2014 referendum. Scottish Borders and Dumfries and Galloway (the local authorities in which Eyemouth and Gretna are respectively located) returned 'No' votes that were, after that of the Orkney Islands, the two highest in the country (Scottish Borders 66.5%; Dumfries and Galloway 65.6%). See www.scotlandreferendum.info. Voting behaviour in the 2014 European election also reflected a tendency towards favouring the Union in this part of Scotland, whereby the largest share of the vote in both Dumfries and Galloway and the Scottish Borders went to the Conservative and Unionist Party www.scottish.parliament.uk/ResearchBriefingsAndFactsheets/S4/SB_14-38.pdf. Gretna lies in Dumfriesshire, Clydesdale, and Tweeddale, which is Scotland's only UK parliamentary constituency represented by a member of the Conservative Party (Eyemouth is in Berwickshire, Roxburgh and Selkirk, which typically returns Liberal Democrat candidates). Finally, both Gretna and Eyemouth are in constituencies represented by Conservative MSPs (Members of the Scottish Parliament). www.scottish.parliament.uk.

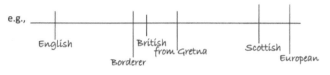

Figure 9.3: Example of a Relational Analogue Scale (RAS) completed by an 18-year-old woman from Gretna. The positions and spacing of the labels she has chosen are quantified relative to British, the identity label available to all AISEB informants.

across a 'most important' to 'least important' cline (the 'Relational Analogue Scale', RAS) to represent identity labels they felt applied to them. A list of suggested labels was shown above the RAS, tailored to the locality in question. In Gretna, for instance, the suggested labels were *Borderer, British, English, European, from Gretna* and *Scottish* (Figure 9.3).

Informants could opt to place all, any, or none of these along the RAS cline, and were free to add labels of their own choosing. The completed RAS thus shows not just the ranking of labels along a gradient of importance, it also allows the fine-grained measurement of distances between each vertical stroke and (a) the ends of the RAS cline and (b) the other vertical strokes. The latter was achieved by scanning the hard copies of the RAS and using an on-screen measuring tool in the software package *ImageJ*.[4] Because all of the AISEB informants can be described as British (even if they choose not to attribute this label to themselves), we used the *British* label as the anchor point, expressing its position as a percentage based on its distance from the 'least important' end of the cline, and the positions of other labels relative to it (also as percentages;

---

[4] Freely downloadable at http://imagej.nih.gov/ij/.

for the speaker shown in Figure 9.3, *British* was placed at 97.4%, exceeding *Scottish* on the importance scale by 5.7%, *from Gretna* by 20.6%, and *Borderer* by 71.2%). Where participants placed British at the 'least important' pole of the RAS we assigned a nominal score of 0.1% so as to distinguish these cases from those in which *British* was not used at all (0%).

Figure 9.4 is a summary of the RAS data relating to the relative rankings of *British* and *Scottish* (for informants in Gretna and Eyemouth) and *British* and *English* (for those in Carlisle and Berwick) among the 132 participants who used both *British* and one of the national labels on their RAS. The scores for individual participants are split according to age group, and the age group means are superimposed on each plot. These have been linked by a connecting line to highlight the magnitude and direction of the difference between the age groups in each of the four towns.

Points falling above the zero line indicate that the individual participant preferred either *Scottish* or *English* over *British*. In each locality there is a spread of positive and negative values, but the greatest concentration of high positive values among the Eyemouth speakers indicates that they tended to rank *Scottish* considerably higher than *British*, and the very few points with negative values in the Eyemouth plot show that ranking *British* over *Scottish* was quite strongly disfavoured there. This is true for both the older and young groups: of the older group members, only 16.1% placed *British* higher than *Scottish*, and among the young group the figure was still lower (15.4%). The means for the older and young groups are consequently relatively high, even if the trend appears to be a downward one overall, such that *Scottish* is not ranked so highly above *British* among the young Eyemouthers as it is among their older counterparts.

Similar patterns can also be seen for the Gretna and Carlisle participants, though the average distances between *British* and *Scottish/English* are lower overall. In Carlisle, a clear age distinction is apparent, whereby the general preference for *English* over *British* among the older informants is not shared by the young group, who are evidently more likely to feel more strongly *British* than they do *English* (26.7% of the older group members ranked *British* higher than *English*, as opposed to 68% of the young group). An age-related trend is not apparent in Berwick, where speakers in both the older and young groups seem overall to be fairly equivocal about the *British* and *English* labels. Only around a third (34.8%) of the older speakers in Berwick said that *English* was a more important label than *British* to them, while the young Berwickers were split evenly (50%).

Looked at another way, it seems that on both sides of the border young people are more ready to describe themselves as *British* than are older ones (if older ones expressed a preference for their relevant national label), but that resistance to this trend is stronger in the two Scottish towns – and particularly

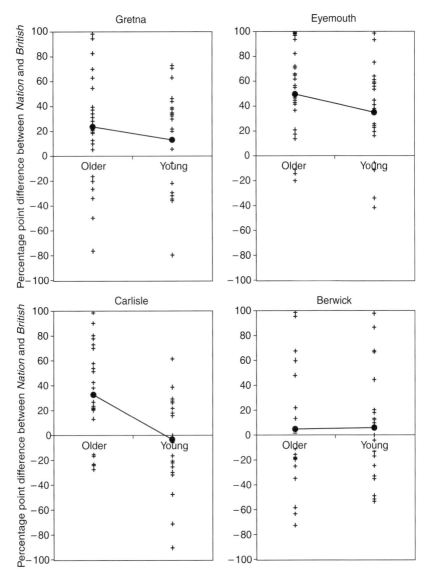

Figure 9.4: Relational Analogue Scale (RAS) data for the four fieldwork sites, showing individual and mean group distances (%) between the British and national (Scottish or English) labels, split by speaker age group. Individual speakers are represented by crosses, while the age group means are shown by filled circles linked by a solid line, the slope of which is an indication of size of the difference between group means. Points falling above the zero line denote a preference for ranking *Scottish* or *English* higher in importance than *British*.

Eyemouth – than it is south of the border. The proportion of informants who did not choose *British* at all during the RAS task was overall considerably higher in Eyemouth (17.5%) than in the other localities (Gretna = 7.5%; Carlisle = 3.6%). In Berwick it was 10.2%, but an equal proportion there chose not to use *English* at all either; see the sociological research of Kiely *et al.* (2000), who found that Berwickers tended to reject the identity labels that Kiely and his colleagues had expected them to embrace; see Section 5).

On the basis of earlier findings that have emerged from the AISEB project, we have ascertained that national identity preferences and production patterns in certain key phonological variables – notably (r) (Llamas *et al.* 2009; Llamas 2010; Watt et al. 2014a) – correlate closely in the Scottish-English border region. In the final section of this chapter, we consider how the RAS responses might relate to the VOT data from these informants' wordlist readings.

5.   Linking VOT Production to the Attitudinal Data

As mentioned in Section 4, the regression analysis carried out on the data revealed that the *Nation, Coast,* and *Speaker Age* variables all had significant effects on the distribution of VOT values. That is, VOT was shorter among older speakers than among their young counterparts in all four towns but, in line with the claims made by Johnston (1997) and others, it was found to be significantly shorter overall in the Scottish localities (Gretna and Eyemouth) than in the English ones (Carlisle and Berwick). It was also shorter on the east coast (Eyemouth and Berwick) than on the west (Gretna and Carlisle). As anticipated, then, VOT in /p t k b d g/ was shortest in Eyemouth and longest in Carlisle. This observation tallies with our expectations, given that in respect of several other phonological variables we have investigated – (r) and the NURSE vowel, amongst others – Eyemouth speech is the most conservatively Scottish of the four AISEB varieties, while the Carlisle dialect is the most congruent with those of northern England, and indeed England generally. The Gretna and Berwick varieties each occupy an intermediate 'hybrid' space between these two extremes. Consequently, it is unsurprising that our Gretna speakers often say that they are thought to be English when they talk to other Scots. Similarly, it is unsurprising that Berwickers are reported by fellow Northumbrians to sound Scottish, but are described as Northumbrian or 'Geordie' (Newcastle) (and indisputably English), by their near-neighbours living just across the border in Eyemouth (Kiely *et al.* 2000).

The fact that the VOT figures seem to correspond rather well with the attitudinal data reported in Section 4 confirms that there appear to be parallels between the speech patterns of the informants in our sample and the ways in which they choose to attribute identity labels to themselves. The changes we see in VOT values, which are undergoing a wholesale upward shift across the region, are reflected in the changing preferences for the *British* and *Scottish/ English* identity labels, whereby young Scottish informants tend to place *Scottish* closer to *British* than older ones do, on both the west (Gretna) and east (Eyemouth) coasts. In the latter town, the tendency to rank *Scottish* higher than *British* is considerably stronger. On the English side of the border, we see in Carlisle an increase in VOT values and a sharp decrease in the preference for *English* over *British* as an identity label. In Berwick no such correlation seems to hold, however. In both age groups there seems to be a lack of any consistent tendency to rank *English* over *British*, recalling Kiely et al.'s (2000: 1.6–1.7) conclusion that, by not readily claiming English identity and by rejecting the label *British* altogether, their Berwick interviewees were declining to 'play by the prevailing identity rules' and 'claiming, attributing, rejecting, accepting and side-stepping national identity, in ways that we had seldom or never previously encountered'. VOT values in Berwick speech are nonetheless evidently on the rise overall, to that extent Berwick speakers appear to be participating in a sound change that is in train both north and south of the border.

It would be hard to argue that there is any direct link between the trend to increase VOT in /p t k b d g/ and a closing of the gap between the use of the national labels *Scottish/English* and *British* in the results of an identity questionnaire. It does seem likely, though, that this and other phonetic changes that appear to be taking place in the speech of the four AISEB localities do coincide with a reappraisal among younger people of what it means to be Scottish, English, and British. It would not be especially controversial to suggest that changes in the relative importance of identity choices might, over the course of a generation or two, have knock-on effects on pronunciation preferences, even at a level as comparatively subtle as that seen in the VOT data.

However, in spite of the similarity between the patterns found in the two Scottish towns and Carlisle, we must not lose sight of the significance of the border as a robust and persistent linguistic divide. Eyemouth and Berwick lie a mere 9 miles (15km) apart by road, and yet there remain a host of significant phonological differences between the varieties spoken there, in spite of regular and plentiful contact between the two localities. Gretna and Carlisle are about the same distance apart as Eyemouth and Berwick, and though the distinctiveness of Gretna English and Carlisle English is less marked than that between the eastern varieties, we have still been able to catalogue a series of systematic differences between them (e.g. with respect to rhoticity and the NURSE vowel; see Llamas 2010; Watt et al. 2014c). Corroboration of our observations about accent similarity across the four sites has recently been provided via automated analysis of AISEB recordings, using metrics imported from the domain of speech and speaker recognition technology (Brown 2014; Brown and Watt 2014), on which we will report more fully in future publications.

6.   Conclusions: The Border as a Place

As we have explored the AISEB corpus, we have found increasingly compelling evidence that the Scottish-English border has a multiplicity of meanings to people living in the region, and that its effects on their linguistic behaviour take many forms. The VOT data reported in this chapter are just a fragment of the complex mosaic of interconnections between language, attitudes, and identities that characterises the sociolinguistic landscape of this part of the English-speaking world. Nonetheless, they illustrate how, even at the level of slight durational differences in the pronunciation of stop consonants, we can find correspondences between speakers' locations and how speakers orient them-selves socio-psychologically towards these places, the larger geopolitical units within which they fall, and towards neighbouring communities. Though the border satisfies Scheider and Janowicz's fourth criterion in that it has a 'concrete identifiable material form' (2010: 2) manifested by the signage, flagpoles, boundary stones, and monuments that mark its presence, it is also highly porous, offering no obstacle to free movement from one side to the other. To this extent, it is more relevant in the present context to think of its significance in more abstract terms, as per those laid out in Scheider and Janowicz's (2010) axiom (2): the border can be thought of as a place by virtue of its effects on how people behave linguistically and non-linguistically, and how their linguistic behaviour influences and is influenced by the notion of the border as an historical, political, cultural and ideological divide. We should also take account of the third criter-ion – 'places have stabilizing functions that afford insideness' (Scheider and Janowicz 2010: 1) – in our evaluation of the extent to which the border serves on the one hand to compartmentalise people into their respective national territories and, on the other, to bring them together as 'borderers', even if this particular label is not one that appears to resonate very strongly among the AISEB participants. The border is thus simultaneously a place that can be conceptual-ised as an edge, a sharp interface between places, and as a zone or region. In some senses it is also an interstice, a narrow space between Scotland and England proper, where, as Kiely *et al.* (2000) found in Berwick, some of the normal rules of national identity have been suspended.

Britain's (2010) taxonomy also provides a cogent framework for the interpretation of our results. The border is fundamentally a demarcation of physical space, but on top of this basic property it also represents a bundle of divisions in social space: the boundary between two jurisdictions, between two distinct religious traditions, between two education systems (Kearney 2006; Torrance 2013), and between two linguistic continua, that of English and that of Scots (e.g. Britain 2007). The physical and social aspects of the border respectively underpin its various meanings to local people in the domain of perceptual space, according to which the border may be seen as almost inconsequential to some borderers, but as a highly valued symbol of national distinctiveness to others.

A key lesson to be learned from AISEB and studies like it (see Watt & Llamas 2014) is that when it comes to drawing conclusions about the relationships between language and identity along national or regional borders it can at times be exceedingly difficult to make generalisations. At less than 100 miles in length, the border between Scotland and England is by most standards a short one. Yet we find that changes in the English spoken in towns at either end of it are proceeding in different ways, and that the lack of east/west symmetry appears to correlate with the ways in which the inhabitants of these towns choose to describe themselves. We believe that future research projects which attempt to treat borders all of a piece, as AISEB set out to do, are likely to yield results that are equally rich and multi-layered with respect to the evidence they provide in support of our theoretical models of the relationships between language, identity, and place.

REFERENCES

Aitken, A. J. 1992. 'Scots', in McArthur, Tom (ed.) *The Oxford Companion to the English Language*. Oxford: Oxford University Press. pp. 893–9.

Auer, Peter, Martin Hilpert, Anja Stukenbrock and Benedikt Szmrecsanyi (eds.) 2013. *Space in Language and Linguistics: Geographical, Interactional, and Cognitive Perspectives*. Berlin: de Gruyter.

Auer, Peter, and Jürgen E. Schmidt (eds.) 2010 *Language and Space: An International Handbook of Linguistic Variation – Theories and Methods*. Berlin: Walter de Gruyter.

Baldauf, Richard B. and Robert B. Kaplan (eds.) 2006. *Language Planning and Policy in Europe, vol. 2: The Czech Republic, the European Union and Northern Ireland*. Bristol: Multilingual Matters.

Beal, Joan C. 2006. *Language and Region*. London: Routledge.
    2010. 'Shifting borders and shifting regional identities', in Llamas, Carmen and Dominic Watt (eds.) *Language and Identities*. Edinburgh: Edinburgh University Press. pp. 217–26.

Benjamin, B. J. 1982. 'Phonological performance in gerontological speech'. *Journal of Psycholinguistic Research* 11: 159–67.

Blumstein, Sheila E., Emily B. Myers and Jesse Rissmann 2005. 'The perception of Voice Onset Time: An fMRI investigation of phonetic category structure'. *Journal of Cognitive Neuroscience* 17: 1353–66.

Boberg, Charles 2014. 'Borders in North American English', in Llamas, Carmen and Dominic Watt (eds.) *Language and Identities*. Edinburgh: Edinburgh University Press. pp. 44–54.

Boersma, Paul and David Weenink 2014. *Praat: Doing Phonetics by Computer*. [Computer program]. Version 5.4, retrieved 9th February 2017 from www.praat.org.

Breuilly, John 2013. 'Nationalism and national unification in 19th century Europe', in Breuilly, John (ed.) *The Oxford Handbook of the History of Nationalism*. Oxford: Oxford University Press pp.49–175.

Britain, David 2002. 'Space and spatial diffusion', in Chambers, J. K., Peter Trudgill and Natalie Schilling-Estes (eds.) *The Handbook of Language Variation and Change*. Oxford: Blackwell. pp. 603–37.

(ed.) 2007. *Language in the British Isles*. Cambridge: Cambridge University Press.

2010. 'Supralocal regional dialect levelling', in Llamas, Carmen and Dominic Watt (eds.) *Language and Identities*. Edinburgh: Edinburgh University Press. pp. 193–204.

2013. 'Space, diffusion and mobility', in Chambers, J. K. and Natalie Schilling (eds.) *Handbook of Language Variation and Change*, Second edition. Oxford: Wiley-Blackwell. pp. 471–500.

Brown, Georgina 2014. *Y-ACCDIST: An Automatic Accent Recognition System for Forensic Applications*. Unpublished MA thesis, University of York.

Brown, Georgina and Dominic Watt 2014. 'Performance of a novel automatic accent classifier using geographically-proximate accents'. Poster presented at the 2014 Colloquium of the British Association of Academic Phoneticians, University of Oxford, April 2014.

Burke, Peter 2013. 'Nationalisms and vernaculars, 1500–1800', in Breuilly, John (ed.) *The Oxford Handbook of the History of Nationalism*. Oxford: Oxford University Press. pp. 21–35.

Catford, John C. 1988. *A Practical Introduction to Phonetics*. Oxford: Oxford University Press.

Chambers, J. K. 1995. 'The Canada–US border as a vanishing isogloss: The evidence of *chesterfield*'. *Journal of English Linguistics* 23: 155–66.

Cho, Taehong and Peter Ladefoged 1999. 'Variation and universals in VOT: Evidence from 18 languages'. *Journal of Phonetics* 27: 207–29.

Cole, R. A., J. Jakimik and W. E. Cooper 1978. 'Perceptibility of phonetic features in fluent speech'. *Journal of the Acoustical Society of America* 64: 44–56.

Daniel, Brian 2014. '"We're not English or Scottish": How Scottish independence could transform life in the Borders', *The Journal*, 14 September 2014. www.thejournal.co.uk/north-east-analysis/analysis-news/were-not-english-scottish-how-7769407.

Diener, Alexander C. and Joe Hagen (eds.) 2010. *Borderlines and Borderlands: Political Oddities at the Edge of the Nation-State*. Lanham, Maryland: Rowman and Littlefield.

Docherty, Gerard J. 1992. *The Timing of Voicing in British English Obstruents*. Berlin: Foris Publications.

Docherty, Gerard J., Dominic Watt, Carmen Llamas, Damien Hall and Jennifer Nycz 2011. '*Variation in Voice Onset Time along the Scottish/English border'*, *Proceedings of the 17th International Congress of Phonetic Sciences*, Hong Kong.

Dollinger, Stefan 2012. 'The western Canada-US border as a linguistic boundary: The roles L1 and L2 speakers'. *World Englishes* 31: 519–33.

Donnan, Hastings and Thomas M. Wilson (eds.) 2010. *Borderlands: Ethnographic Approaches to Security, Power, and Identity*. Lanham, Maryland: University Press of America.

Ellis, Alexander 1889. *On Early English Pronunciation, Part V: The Existing Phonology of English Dialects Compared with that of West Saxon*. London: Truebner and Co.

Foulkes, Paul, Gerard J. Docherty and Mark J. Jones 2010. 'Analysing stops', in Di Paolo, Marianna and Malcah Yaeger-Dror (eds.) *Sociophonetics: A Student's Guide*. London: Routledge. pp. 58–71.

Gibson, James J. 1979. *The Ecological Approach to Visual Perception*. Boston: Houghton Mifflin.

Glauser, Beat 2000. 'The Scottish/English border in hindsight'. *International Journal of the Sociology of Language* 145: 65–78.

Johnston, Paul 1997. 'Regional variation', in Jones, Charles (ed.) *The Edinburgh History of the Scots Language*. Edinburgh: Edinburgh University Press. pp. 433–513.

Johnstone, Barbara 2010. 'Language and geographical space', in Auer, Peter and Jürgen E. Schmidt (eds.). *Language and Space: An International Handbook of Linguistic Variation – Theories and Methods*. Berlin: Walter de Gruyter. pp. 1–17.

Kallen, Jeffrey 2014. 'The political border and linguistic identities in Ireland: What can the linguistic landscape tell us?', in Watt, Dominic and Carmen Llamas (eds.) *Language, Borders and Identity*. Edinburgh: Edinburgh University Press. pp. 154–68.

Kearney, Hugh 2006. *The British Isles: A History of Four Nations*, Second edition. Cambridge: Cambridge University Press.

Kiely, Richard, David McCrone, Frank Bechhofer and Robert Stewart 2000. 'Debatable land: national and local identity in a border town', *Sociological Research Online* 5.2. www.socresonline.org.uk/5/2/kiely.html.

Kolb, Eduard 1966. *Phonological Atlas of the Northern Region*. Bern: Franck.

Kolb, Eduard, Beat Glauser, Willy Eimer and Renate Stamm 1979. *Atlas of English Sounds*. Bern: Franck.

Lisker, Leigh and Arthur. S. Abramson 1964. 'A cross-language study of voicing in initial stops: Acoustical measurements'. *Word* 20: 527–65.

Liss, Julie M., Gary Weismer and John C. Rosenbek 1990. 'Selected acoustic characteristics of speech production in very old males'. *Journal of Gerontology* 45: 35–45.

Llamas, Carmen 2007. '"A place between places": Language and identities in a border town'. *Language in Society* 36: 579–604.

  2010. 'Convergence and divergence across a national border', in Llamas, Carmen and Dominic Watt (eds.) *Language and Identities*. Edinburgh: Edinburgh University Press, pp. 227–36.

Llamas, Carmen and Dominic Watt 2015. 'Scottish, English, British? Innovations in attitude measurement'. *Language and Linguistics Compass* 9: 610–17.

Llamas, Carmen, Dominic Watt, and Daniel E. Johnson 2009. 'Linguistic accommodation and the salience of national identity markers in a border town'. *Journal of Language and Social Psychology* 28: 381–407.

Lodge, Ken 1966. 'The Stockport dialect'. *Le Maître Phonétique* 126: 26–30.

Milroy, Lesley and Matthew Gordon. 2003. *Sociolinguistics: Method and Interpretation*. Oxford: Blackwell.

Newman, David 2006. 'Borders and bordering: Towards an interdisciplinary dialogue'. *European Journal of Social Theory* 9: 171–206.

Oxford English Dictionary 2015. www.oed.com.

Raubal, Martin, David M. Mark and Andrew U. Frank (eds.) 2013. *Cognitive and Linguistic Aspects of Geographic Space: New Perspectives on Geographic Information Research*. Heidelberg: Springer Verlag.

Redinger, Daniel and Carmen Llamas 2014. 'Multilingual Luxembourg: Language and identity at the Romance/Germanic language border', in Watt, Dominic and Carmen Llamas (eds.) *Language, Borders and Identity*. Edinburgh: Edinburgh University Press. pp. 169–85.

Richter, Kai-Florian and Stephan Winter 2014. *Landmarks: GIScience for Intelligent Services*. Cham: Springer Verlag.

Ryalls, John, Allison Zipprer and Penelope Baldauff 1997. 'A preliminary investigation of the effects of gender and race on voice onset time'. *Journal of Speech, Language, and Hearing Research* 40: 642–45.

Scheider, Simon and Krzysztof Janowicz 2010. 'Places as media of containment', in GIScience Extended Abstracts, University of Zürich. www.geovista.psu.edu/publications/2010/Scheider_GIScience_10.pdf, retrieved 9th February 2017.

     2014. 'Place reference systems: A constructive activity model of reference to places'. *Applied Ontology* 9: 97–127.

Scobbie, James M. 2006. 'Flexibility in the face of incompatible English VOT systems', in Goldstein, Louis M., Douglas H. Whalen and Catherine T. Best (eds.) *Laboratory Phonology 8: Varieties of Phonological Competence*. Berlin: Mouton de Gruyter. pp. 367–92.

Thomas, Erik R. 2011. *Sociophonetics: An Introduction*. Basingstoke: Palgrave Macmillan.

Torrance, David 2013. *The Battle for Britain: Scotland and the Independence Referendum*. London: Biteback Publishing.

Torre, Peter and Jessica A. Barlow 2009. 'Age-related changes in acoustic characteristics of adult speech'. *Journal of Communication Disorders* 42: 324–33.

Vannini, Phillip 2010. 'Mobile cultures: From the sociology of transportation to the study of mobilities'. *Sociology Compass* 4: 111–21.

Watt, Dominic, Carmen Llamas and Daniel E. Johnson 2014a. 'Sociolinguistic variation on the Scottish-English border', in Lawson, Robert (ed.) *Sociolinguistics in Scotland*. Basingstoke: Palgrave Macmillan. pp. 79–102.

Watt, Dominic, Carmen Llamas, Gerard J. Docherty, Damien Hall and Jennifer Nycz 2014b. 'Language and identity on the Scottish/English border', in Watt, Dominic and Carmen Llamas (eds.) *Language, Borders and Identity*. Edinburgh: Edinburgh University Press. pp. 8–26.

Watt, Dominic, Carmen Llamas, Tyler Kendall and Anne H. Fabricius 2014c. 'Interaction of derhoticisation and NURSE merger from synchronic and diachronic perspectives'. Paper presented at the *Symposium on Historical Phonology*, Edinburgh, January 2014.

Watt, Dominic and Jillian Yurkova 2007. 'Voice Onset Time and the Scottish Vowel Length Rule in Aberdeen English'. *Proceedings of the 16th International Congress of Phonetic Sciences*, Saarbrücken, August 2007.

Wells, John C. 1982. *Accents of English* (3 vols). Cambridge: Cambridge University Press.

Winter, Stefan and Christian Freksa 2012. 'Approaching the notion of place by contrast'. *Journal of Spatial Information Science* 5: 31–50.

Zai, R. 1942. *The Phonology of the Morebattle Dialect (East Roxburghshire)*. Luzern: Räber.

Zwickl, Simone 2002. *Language Attitudes, Ethnic Identity and Dialect Use across the Northern Ireland Border: Armagh and Monaghan*. Belfast: Cló Ollscoil na Banríona.

10   'I Stole It from a Letter, off Your Tongue It Rolled.'[1] The Performance of Dialect in Glasgow's Indie Music Scene

Miriam Krause and Jennifer Smith

1.   Introduction

With the advent of pop and rock in the 1950s, a noted characteristic of British acts was to sing with an 'American' or 'mid-Atlantic' accent (Trudgill 1983: 253). However, successive waves of bands – starting with The Beatles in the 1960s (who gradually decreased the frequency of mid-Atlantic features in their singing throughout their career (Trudgill 1983: 258), the arrival of punk and new wave in the 1970s (Trudgill 1983: 261–4), and the phenomenon of Britpop, post-punk and indie music in the late 1980s and 1990s – have used an increasing number of local vernacular forms in song in the United Kingdom (Simpson 1999: 361–4). One recent example of a band moving towards the use of local dialect in song is the northern English indie group, Arctic Monkeys. Beal's (2009) illuminating qualitative analysis of morphological, lexical and phonetic dialect forms across both speech and song lead her to conclude that the 'Arctic Monkeys are singing in their "own" accents' (Beal 2009: 236). She suggests that, by doing so, the band indexes place through 'localness' and 'northern-ness' while at the same time rejecting the mainstream music industry standard of 'mid-Atlantic' norms (Beal 2009: 238).

In this paper, we contribute to research on dialect in song and how it might represent 'place' through a variationist analysis of the indie music scene in Scotland. It has been claimed that, in the 1980s and early 1990s, Scottish indie bands showed little to no markedly Scottish features in singing.[2] If they did step away from the 'mid-Atlantic' accent of previous decades, their linguistic variation seemed to be a nod towards the indie scene of the south of England, with a rather generic Standard British English accent. In more recent years, however, it has been suggested that, along with the changing political context of Scotland, a rise in the use of Scots in contemporary music can be observed.[3]

---

[1] The Twilight Sad, 'Reflections Of The Television', *Forget The Night Ahead*, FatCat Records 2009.

[2] See www.theguardian.com/music/2012/mar/08/scottish-music-rock-north.

[3] The naming practice for varieties of languages is complicated – here we use 'Scots' in its most generic definition: the language used by people of Scottish birth.

Specifically, 'talk of independence is giving Scottish culture a boost – especially in the thriving music scene. The new bands are inspired by the country's traditional music, and they sing in their own accents too'.[4] To date, however, no empirical analysis of the use of Scots in song has been undertaken, thus the linguistic outcomes of this changing political context remain unknown. In the current analysis, we address this gap by targeting the speech and song of two frontmen from contemporary indie bands in Glasgow: James from *The Twilight Sad*, and Craig from *The Unwinding Hours*. Both singers come from Scotland and both speak with an identifiably Scots accent. However, one of them, James, is noted to also sing in a broad Scottish accent, as demonstrated in the quotes from reviews and interviews:

(1)   a. '... *James Graham's shaggy Glaswegian accent* ... '.[5]
        b. '... *James Graham, whose broad Scots brogue is instantly recognisable in a musical landscape of bogus Yankee twangs.*'[6]
        c. '... *wryly sardonic lyrics muttered in Scots-burr* ... '.[7]

James himself is well aware of using Scots in song: '[My accent is] too thick for them, ... if you don't like the Scottish accent you won't like it ... if someone's writing about me, it's just always the Scottish brogue, which I am fed up of reading about. (laughter) Or Groundskeeper Willie, from The Simpsons.'[8] No such descriptions are found for Craig, and he himself says: 'I don't think I sing in a Scottish accent. ... I feel completely separate from that. I don't feel any pressure to sing ... in a Scottish accent. ... it's just a natural thing. It's just the voice that came out.'

Thus we have two very different overt stances on the use of Scots by these two performers, but how does this correlate with their actual use? Is it really the case that James has a 'thick brogue' in song? And is Craig's singing accent 'just a natural thing?' To answer these questions, we target an iconic stereotype of Scots, postvocalic /r/. Through quantitative and qualitative analysis, we investigate how the singers' use of the different variants across speech and song may index their attitudes and concepts of place and social identity (Beal 2009: 236–8).

We first begin by reviewing the literature on use of dialect in song and the current situation in Scotland. We then provide a brief overview of

---

[4] See www.theguardian.com/music/2012/mar/08/scottish-music-rock-north.
[5] See www.stylusmagazine.com/reviews/the-twilight-sad/fourteen-autumns-and-fifteen-winters .htm.
[6] See http://ravechild.co.uk/2012/02/23/interview-the-twilight-sads-james-graham/.
[7] See www.dustedmagazine.com/reviews/3615.
[8] All of James's and Craig's speech quotes are extracted from the sociolinguistic interviews carried out for this research by the first author. All quotes from songs are from the two bands in the current analysis.

postvocalic /r/ followed by the data and methodology for the present study. Finally, we turn to the quantitative analysis and discuss the results in the context of the qualitative findings regarding the singers' attitudes.

2.   Sociolinguistic Variation in Song

Whilst no research on the sociolinguistics of singing in the Scottish context has been conducted, a number of studies look at accents in song with regard to place (e.g. New Zealand - see Gibson 2008) or enregisterment with a specific music genre (e.g. Hip-hop – see Clarke and Hiscock 2009). We consider the following four studies of paramount importance for this research.

One of the earliest and most influential sociolinguistic studies on language variation in song is by Trudgill (1983). He notes the adoption of General American (GA) variants by British bands, and explains this in the context of 'Acts of Identity' (Le Page and Tabouret-Keller 1985), where speakers' linguistic behaviour is motivated by the wish to resemble as closely as possible that of the group or groups with which they wish to identify. As Trudgill (1983: 254) states 'Americans have dominated the field, and cultural domin-ation leads to imitation: it is appropriate to sound like an American when performing what is predominantly an American activity; and one attempts to model one's singing style on that of those who do it best and who one admires most.'

His quantitative analysis of /t/ and /r/ reveals a more nuanced view of the British/American split: the use of these features by The Beatles and the Rolling Stones shows that they move from a predominantly 'mid-Atlantic' to a more British use over a six-year period from 1963 to 1969. Trudgill (1983: 253) claims that this is further evidence of British singers modifying and manipu-lating their singing accent towards a culturally dominant linguistic model: at first towards the American features of the globally successful US artists of the early 1960s, but later towards a British-based use as a result of the growing popularity and power of the UK music scene. In his words, 'British pop music acquired a validity of its own, and this has been reflected in linguistic behav-iour' (Trudgill 1983: 261). Moreover, Trudgill (1983: 262) goes on to show that the advent of punk in the mid-1970s brought an increase in markedly British, and particularly working-class Cockney, features, with the singers adapting to the linguistic model of their targeted audience – the urban working-class youth.

In a follow up to Trudgill's study, Simpson (1999: 343) notes that 'pop and rock singers, when singing, often use accents which are noticeably different from those used in their ordinary speech styles'. He suggests that the perceived homogeneity resulting from globalisation in the music industry has led to a breakdown into different styles, with artists trying 'to carve out their identity

by searching for some generic label that marks them out as different or unique'
(Simpson 1999: 362). Crucially, he argues that in examining the use of accent
and dialect in song 'such a study also needs to take into account those aspects
of the wider sociopolitical and cultural context which act as determinants on
particular singing styles' (Simpson 1999: 364).

In his study on British singing styles, Morrissey (2008) extends the linguistic discussion to include phonological considerations, deliberating factors such
as 'musical genre, song topics and cultural considerations, as well as ...
performance' (Morrissey 2008: 194) and 'singability' – the variants' ability
to carry sound (Morrissey 2008: 213) in sung performance. He points out that
singing is largely unidirectional, lacking an interpersonal interaction between
singer and audience (Morrissey 2008: 195). Nonetheless, he draws upon Bell's
(1984) 'Audience Design' framework to distinguish between *Outgroup Referee Design* (the singers' wish to identify with a linguistic group they do not
belong to, but consider prestigious) and *Ingroup Referee Design* (their interaction with an outgroup by referencing their own – possibly absent – ingroup's
style features) (Bell 1984: 197–8).

The latest analysis of dialect use in song comes from Beal (2009), who takes
a language-ideological approach by examining the linguistic behaviour of the
lead singer of Yorkshire indie band Arctic Monkeys. She compares his
linguistic behaviour in song with his speech in a radio interview. Beal comes
to the conclusion that the original 'mid-Atlantic' features adopted in the past
have become enregistered as appropriate for the performance of mainstream
pop. In other words: they have become socially recognised as indexical (Agha
2005: 38) of a pop singing accent. Singers who diverge from this model
express their rejection of it (Beal 2009: 238). Moreover, Beal argues that the
Artic Monkeys' Sheffield singing accent is not 'merely a default' accent
resulting from said rejection of the American model (Beal 2009: 237). It is,
in fact, a consciously made 'positive choice' in favour of specific traditional
and modern local features indexing 'localness', independence and authenticity,
and thus a case of enregisterment not only of their hometown variety, but also
with attributes of British indie music (Beal 2009: 238). Singing is a highly
performed act – a fact which complicates 'the links between sociolinguistic
practice and social meaning, [but] can also expose those links quite strikingly
and make them available for critical reassessment' (Coupland 2007: 171).
Hence song is not merely a simple analogue of speech, but a metalinguistically
constructed act, which constitutes a most interesting medium for the study of
enregisterment.

These studies demonstrate that the accent a singer or band chooses to
portray in song is highly context-dependent, and includes both convergence
with and divergence from outgroups and ingroups (Morrissey 2008: 197–8)
in the pull between mainstream and local musical identities. In order to

contextualise the present study, we next describe the indie music scene in the United Kingdom and Scotland in particular, and consider how it is situated within the current social, political and linguistic environment.

2.1   Dialect Use in British and Scottish Indie Music

The term 'indie' music, deriving from 'independent', comprises a number of musical genres characterised by 'real or perceived independence'[9] from the commercial music industry. The UK Indie Charts were first published in 1980, and independent labels have kept growing and improving their organisation through the decades since (Harris 2003: 386–99), signing artists out of an 'ideological commitment to experiment and difference', without the commercial drive of the major labels (Hesmondhalgh 1998: 263). Indie music in the United Kingdom reached the height of its popularity with Britpop and indie rock from the 1990s onwards (Morrissey 2008: 196), with artists like Blur, Oasis, and Pulp singing in local accents, using regional dialect features (Morrissey 2008: 210) in an attempt to embrace and embody British identity in music with a uniting Anglo-centric cause (Harris 2003: 98). In spite of indie becoming more 'mainstream' itself during this period, and many indie artists and labels collaborating with major record companies (Hesmondhalgh 1999), most 'indie disciples' (Harris 2003: xv) distance themselves from this type of music capitalism. According to Grossberg, indie 'apparently exists outside of its relation to the dominant culture; it does not want the world' (Mitchell 1996: 231). Thus indie does not describe a specific sound in music, but rather the ideology and the artists' strong personal attitudes that stand behind the production of said sound.[10] This includes a critical stance towards mainstream music and mass-market success at the cost of 'artistic purity' (Harris 2003: xv) and authenticity.

Turning now to Glasgow, the city was awarded the title of 'UNESCO City of Music' in 2008[11] and is home to a number of indie record labels including Chemikal Underground, Postcard Records, Rock Action Records and Shoeshine Records. These labels have signed and produced Scottish musical talent for decades, and seen many of their artists grow to become internationally successful.

As indicated in the Introduction, the early days of Scottish indie music in the 1980s and early 1990s saw artists singing in either a 'mid-Atlantic' or a generic Standard British accent. To sing in a fully Scottish 'brogue' was largely restricted to folk music or folk rock, as most aptly demonstrated by The

---

[9] See http://charlottepepperg324.blogspot.co.uk/2011/09/conventions-of-indie-music.html.
[10] See http://charlottepepperg324.blogspot.co.uk/2011/09/conventions-of-indie-music.html.
[11] See www.unesco.org.uk/glasgow,_unesco_city_of_music.

Proclaimers.[12] This attitude changed with the breakthrough of Scottish band Arab Strap in 1996. Members Aidan Moffat and Malcolm Middleton, both now successful solo artists, have always made use of Scottish dialect features and local references in their singing, 'providing an instant focus for the press and the public'.[13] Many peers followed their lead, and while Arab Strap were perhaps the catalyst for the increasing use of Scots in indie music, it may also have been further bolstered by the changing political situation; Scottish Devolution in 1999 and, more recently, the vote on Independence in September 2014, have led to an increased debate on 'Scottishness'[14] including discussion of Scottish language. The pro-independence Yes-Campaign made use of Scottish linguistic features in slogans, such as frequently replacing 'Yes' with 'Aye' or coining the phrase 'Bairns not Bombs' to protest against the UK's war politics and Trident programme[15]. Scottish artists could be found on either side of the campaign, with the National Collective formed by Yes-supporters, discussing the Referendum's political impacts on culture and awareness for Scottish arts UK-wide and globally. The debate also raised questions about the independence of the Scottish music scene (Cloonan 2007: 20–9), paving the way for creative funding and new music industry institutions (such as the Scottish Music Industry Association) and events (such as the Scottish Album of the Year Award), and giving singers a confidence boost regarding their Scottish identity and use of local language features in song. Due to this increasing use of Scottish singing accents in indie music, as well as the nature of song as a medium that travels across geographical borders, and 'Scottishness' becoming a talking point, the awareness of Scots features in song is growing nationally and internationally. This has the consequence that more salient linguistic forms are becoming enregistered as Scottish. It is within this changing linguistic and political context that the current study is set.

3.   Data and Methodology

3.1   The Participants

James, 27 years old at the time of this study, was born in Glasgow to Scottish parents and has been living in North Lanarkshire all his life. He is the singer, lyricist, and founding member of The Twilight Sad (TTS), a Scottish indie

---

[12] See www.heraldscotland.com/arts-ents/music-features/the-sensational-history-of-scottish-rock-1.933852.

[13] See www.encyclopedia.com/doc/1G2-3495100011.html.

[14] See http://bbc.co.uk/news/magazine-20048521; http://theconversation.com/young-fathers-must-we-label-themercury-winners-as-scottish-33662. and http://theconversation.com/young-fathers-must-we-label-the-mercury-winners-as-scottish-33662.

[15] See www.banthebomb.org/index.php/102-uncategorised/1502-bairns-not-bombs.

rock band formed in 2003. TTS were signed by Brighton-based indie label FatCat Records, who sent them to America to record their debut EP, a US-only release in late 2006.[16] Their complete debut album 'Fourteen Autumns & Fifteen Winters' (2007) received great critical acclaim. Three more studio albums (2009, 2012, and 2014), several EPs and live albums followed. Due to performing in the United States long before in their hometown and country, the band has a big audience in America, but is also an important member of the Scottish indie music scene.

Craig, 36 years old at the time of this study, was born in Glasgow to Scottish parents and grew up in Dunblane, near Glasgow. He moved to Glasgow in the 1990s and has resided there ever since. He is the vocalist, lyricist, and one of the music-writers and guitarists in The Unwinding Hours (TUH), a two-piece Scottish indie rock band formed in 2008. Their debut, eponymous album was released in 2010, and their second album 'Afterlives' followed in 2012. TUH are signed to Glasgow-based indie label Chemikal Underground and have toured the United Kingdom and Europe. Craig was formerly with the critically acclaimed post-rock band Aereogramme, which also had an international following and toured worldwide.

The two singers share an upbringing in Central Scotland and subsequent immersion in the Glasgow indie music scene. Moreover, both bands have a local and international following, their audiences being both local and global. At the same time, perceptions of how these frontmen sound in song differ, as indicated in the Introduction. In addition, the singers themselves have very different perceptions of how they sound. The question we want to ask is: How are these perceptions translated into actual language use? To answer this, we provide an empirical analysis of postvocalic /r/ across speech and song. In order to situate the current study, we first provide an overview of this variable in Scots.

3.2   Postvocalic /r/ in Scots

Scots is stereotypically described as a rhotic accent (Wells 1982: 10–1) and the historical record indicates that /r/ was once an apical tap [ɾ] and often a trill [r] (Grant 1914, Johnston 1997). However since the nineteenth century, derhoticisation in working-class speech has been noted, with the increasing use of approximant forms of / r / as in (2a–c) and the traditional stereotypical trill (2d) increasingly circumscribed to the speech of adult broad Scots speakers, particularly in rural areas (Johnston 1997: 511; Macafee 1983: 32; Scobbie *et al.* 2006: 4). The following examples demonstrate these features:

---

[16] One reviewer comments that this may have an impact on James's accent. We note that his time in the States was limited to a number of weeks.

(2)   a. '*And then sometimes, it's just- it's* **wei[ɹ]d**, *it just clicks like that.*' (James: speech)

       b. '*I'd move from the drums to pick up the* **guita[ɻ]**.' (Craig: speech)

       c. '*It's the dance that I will* **neve[ɚ]** *share.*' (James: song)[17]

       d. '*The* **cu[r]tains** *closed again.*' (James: song)[18]

This change has led to a sociophonetic continuum in the realisation of postvocalic /r/ from weakly to strongly rhotic as demonstrated in Table 10.1 (adapted from Lawson *et al.* 2014: 61).

For urban Scots, /r/-vocalisation is becoming increasingly common in working-class speech (Johnston 1997: 511; Romaine 1978; Macafee 1983: 32; Stuart-Smith *et al.* 2007: 241). However, in Glasgow, a complex class split has emerged in use of /r/: working-class speech is characterised by increasing derhoticisation, with speakers using barely audible pharyngealised or plain vowel-sounds, while middle-class speakers, on the other hand, appear to be becoming more and more /r/-ful, using strongly rhotic postvocalic realisations such as [ɹ] (Lawson *et al.* 2011: 257; Lennon 2011; Stuart-Smith *et al.* 2014).

Furthermore, speakers may have the ability to 'style-drift' from one end of the continuum to the other (Stuart-Smith 2003), thus this particular variable may be available to do sociolinguistic work. To answer the question of how James and Craig make use of this continuum, we now turn to the analysis of the data at hand.

3.3   Analysis

For the song data, we analysed six songs of TTS's Acoustic EP, and eight of TUH's debut album, amounting to 53.76 minutes of data for analysis. For the speech data, the first author recorded the speakers using classic sociolinguistic interview techniques in order to elicit the most unmonitored speech (Labov 1984: 32–4) with each interview lasting approximately 60 minutes. A Marantz Model PMD660 portable recorder and Audio-Technica/Sony lapel microphones were used for the recordings. The data were orthographically transcribed in Praat in the first instance.

Table 10.1: *Continuum of use for postvocalic /r/.*

Weakly Rhotic						Strongly Rhotic
no /r/	derhotic	alveolar	retroflex	schwar[19]	tap	trill

[17] The Twilight Sad, 'Seven Years of Letters', *Acoustic EP,* FatCat Records 2011.
[18] The Twilight Sad, 'That Birthday Present', *Acoustic EP,* FatCat Records 2011.
[19] 'Schwar' refers to the central rhotic vowel, a highly rhoticised variant (Lawson *et al.* 2014: 60).

Using the Principle of Accountability (Labov 1972: 72), every instance where postvocalic /r/ could appear was extracted from the data, with approximately 150 tokens per speaker across speech and singing. We excluded syllable onset tokens as in (3a–b) and medial tokens as in (3c–d), as these are not fully variable. Following standard sociolinguistic methodology (Tagliamonte 2006: 51–63) a number of other contexts were excluded: neutralisation contexts where it is impossible to decipher whether the /r/ is word-final, word-initial or both (3e–f); proper names (3g–h); false starts (3i–j). Tokens which were inaudible were also excluded.

(3)   a. '*Although your **f**riend went wrong.*' (James: song)[20]
        b. '***R**aise a glass to me sometime.*' (Craig: song)[21]
        c. '*It's a **sorry** affair.*' (James: song)[22]
        d. '*I'm **surrou**nded by the pale and the lonely.*' (Craig: song)[23]
        e. '*. . . and don't fight 'cause you**'re** right.*' (James: song)[24]
        f. '*If you**'re** running from me now.*' (Craig: song)[25]
        g. '*I got Andy and **Mark** over at the house . . .* ' (James: speech)
        h. '*Because this Olympic **Swimmers** song is . . .* ' (Craig: speech)
        i. '*. . . the one thing I like about writing music is that kinda wee **exper**—the wee things that . . .* ' (James: speech)
        j. '*It should be the ex – you know, **for** – well, sorry, for me what's interesting about music is the extremes.*' (Craig: speech)

Narrow auditory transcription was carried out by the first author using Praat and a subsample checked by the second author.

A number of variants were identified in the data reflecting the continuum from rhotic to non-rhotic in Table 10.1: no /r/ (4a), derhotic (4b), alveolar (4c), retroflex (4d), schwar (4e), tap (4f), trill (4g).[26]

(4)   a. '*Here's a **lette**∅ to you now . . .* ' (Craig: song)[27]
        b. '*. . . maybe even when **we'[V̞]e** playing*[28].' (James: speech)
        c. '*. . . you can hear the work, and you can **hea[ɹ]** the . . .* ' (Craig: speech)
        d. '*. . . comparing a beautiful piece of **a[ɻ]twork** to painting by **numbe[ɻ]s**.*' (Craig: speech)
        e. '*I don't think he **eve[ɚ]** went . . .* ' (Craig: speech)

---

[20] The Twilight Sad, 'The Neighbours Can't Breathe', *Acoustic EP, *FatCat Records 2011.
[21] The Unwinding Hours, 'Peaceful Liquid Shell', *The Unwinding Hours,* Chemikal Underground 2010.
[22] The Twilight Sad, 'Seven Years of Letters', *Acoustic EP,* FatCat Records 2011.
[23] The Unwinding Hours, 'Tightrope', *The Unwinding Hours,* Chemikal Underground 2010.
[24] The Twilight Sad, 'The Neighbours Can't Breathe', *Acoustic EP,* FatCat Records 2011.
[25] The Unwinding Hours, 'Tightrope', *The Unwinding Hours,* Chemikal Underground 2010.
[26] Here we use the convention where the target variant only appears in IPA script.
[27] The Unwinding Hours, 'Tightrope', *The Unwinding Hours,* Chemikal Underground 2010.
[28] We follow Lawson et al. (2011) in the representation of the derhoticised form with [V̞].

Table 10.2: *Overall distribution of variants.*

	no /r/	derhotic	alveolar	retroflex	schwar	tap	trill
	Weakly rhotic				Strongly rhotic		
Ns	144	225	61	19	22	125	2
%	24.1	37.6	10.2	3.2	3.7	20.9	0.3

    f. '**You**[ɾ] *head next to my head.*' (James: song)[29]
    g. '*And you'll go* **nowhe**[r]*e, if you tiptoe so slowly.*' (James: song)[30]

In assigning a category to each token, we followed Lawson et al.'s (2014: 62) criteria, namely: 'no /r/ referred to no auditory percept of /r/, so the word sounded as if it ended in a (non-rhoticised) vowel; derhotic referred to variants where there was a hint of /r/, or some other feature which could be associated with rhoticity such as pharyngealisation or velarisation of the vowel, but no segmental rhotic ... Alveolar referred to an alveolar approximant with a less strong rhotic quality than the retroflex approximant (which referred to a variant which sounded strongly rhotic), and finally schwar was a central rhotic vowel [ɚ].'

To these carefully described categories we add a tap and the most traditional, strongly rhotic trill. Tokens which were difficult to categorise auditorily were excluded from the analysis. After these exclusions, the total number of tokens for analysis was 598, with 239 in speech and 359 in song.

4.   Results

Table 10.2 shows the overall distribution of the seven variants in the dataset. It reveals that the non-rhotic and derhoticised variants together make up the majority of forms at over 60% of the data, with the alveolar and retroflex accounting for 10% and 3% respectively. The most interesting result from Table 10.2 is the lack of strongly rhotic variants in this Scottish context: schwar is used only 3% of the time and, perhaps not surprisingly for an urban dialect, there is an almost total lack of the traditional Scots trill, with only two tokens. However, the outlier in this continuum from weakly to strongly rhotic is the use of the tap, at a full 21%.

Closer investigation of the individual speakers may shed further light on this use. Table 10.3 shows the results for James and Craig separately.

---

[29] The Twilight Sad, 'Suck', *Acoustic EP*, FatCat Records 2011.
[30] The Twilight Sad, 'That Birthday Present', *Acoustic EP*, FatCat Records 2011.

Table 10.3: *Postvocalic /r/ by speaker.*

		no /r/	derhotic	alveolar	retroflex	schwar	tap	trill
James	*N*	63	137	6	5	16	122	2
	%	17.9	39.0	1.7	1.4	4.6	34.8	0.6
Craig	*N*	81	88	55	14	6	3	0
	%	32.8	35.6	22.3	5.7	2.4	1.2	0

Table 10.4: *Postvocalic /r/ by speaker across speech and song.*

		Song		Speech	
		N	%	N	%
James	no /r/	31	14	32	28
	derhotic	85	40	52	46
	alveolar	1	0	5	4
	tap	97	45	25	22
Craig	no /r/	43	34	38	38
	derhotic	55	44	33	33
	alveolar	26	21	29	29
	tap	2	2	1	1

Table 10.3 reveals a key difference across these individuals: James shows a polar use between the weakly and strongly rhotic variants of the continuum (compare 57% no /r/ and derhotics to 35% taps), whereas Craig is situated at the weakly rhotic end of the spectrum (with a full 90% no /r/, derhotics and alveolar approximants). In other words, James and Craig have very different patterns of variant use.

Due to the marginal use of the retroflex, schwar and trill variants, these are removed from subsequent analysis. We further reconfigure the data to look at the crucial effect of speech versus singing in the deployment of these variants. Table 10.4 shows the results, repeated graphically in Figure 10.1.

Table 10.4 and Figure 10.1 illustrate noteworthy differences between the speakers and styles. Craig shows a similar distribution for variants in song and speech, with a high level of alveolar approximants and derhoticised variants across both. James on the other hand, shows a different pattern; in song he uses much higher rates of the tap compared to his speech.

Closer examination of James's use of the tap can be gleaned from the phonetic context in which it occurs, specifically the following phonetic environment. Previous research on Scottish English has shown that phonetic

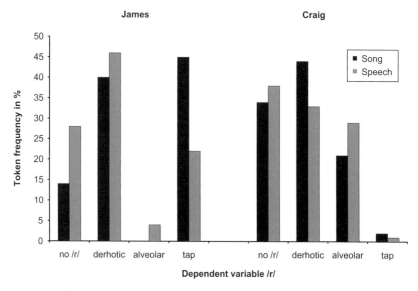

Figure 10.1: Postvocalic /r/ by speaker across song and speech.

environment influences which variants are used and when (Romaine 1978; Macafee 1983; Stuart-Smith *et al.* 2007; Schützler 2010). For example, Romaine (1978) finds that the loss of postvocalic /r/ is most likely to appear in prepausal contexts, and [ɹ] is most frequent when followed by a consonant-initial word. Linking contexts, namely a following vowel, are most likely with [ɾ]. The least likely context for the tap is prepausal. In contrast, Schützler (2010) also finds that word-final prevocalic and prepausal contexts are most likely to appear with rhotic variants.[31]

In this analysis, we divide the data into 4 different categories: coda cluster (5a–b), coda vowel (5c–d), coda consonant (5e–f), and prepausal contexts, represented by coda # (5g–h).

(5)   a. *'There's a girl in the crowd …'* (James: song)[32]
        b. *'Sin and holy words, I know.'* (Craig: song)[33]
        c. *'Put it in your eye.'* (James: song)[34]

---

[31] We also checked for individual lexical item to ensure that no individual word skewed the data. Where enough data existed, the more frequent lexical items (for example, *your*) were shown to pattern with the data more generally. In addition, individual lexical items were generally balanced across each speaker.

[32] The Twilight Sad, 'I Became A Prostitute', *Acoustic EP,* FatCat Records 2011.

[33] The Unwinding Hours, 'Peaceful Liquid Shell', *The Unwinding Hours,* Chemikal Underground 2010.

[34] The Twilight Sad, 'That Birthday Present', *Acoustic EP,* FatCat Records 2011.

Table 10.5: *James's use of postvocalic /r/ across the different linguistic contexts.*

		Song		Speech	
		N	%	N	%
Coda cluster	no /r/	3	7	3	8
	derhotic	24	56	21	58
	tap	15	35	8	22
Coda vowel	no /r/	0	0	1	7
	derhotic	2	8	4	27
	tap	23	92	9	60
Coda consonant	no /r/	10	9	28	51
	derhotic	48	42	20	36
	tap	57	50	7	13
Coda #	no /r/	18	58	0	0
	derhotic	11	35	7	88
	tap	2	6	1	12

    d. '*You're insecure and bored.*' (Craig: song)[35]
    e. '*And there's your sister with her answer and she's always right.*' (James: song)[36]
    f. '*Cause your cracked dry lips* ... ' (Craig: song)[37]
    g. '*And you'll go nowhere#*' (James: song)[38]
    h. '*And I wish that I could see you there#*' (Craig: song)[39]

Table 10.5 shows the results. Alveolar variants are removed due to the small number (N = 10).

With the exception of coda #, all the linguistic contexts show a heightened use of the tap variant: coda consonant at 50% in song versus 13% in speech, coda vowel at 92% versus 60% and coda clusters at 35% versus 22%. In other words, the linguistic contexts behave much the same with respect to variant use.[40]

[35] The Unwinding Hours, 'Child', *The Unwinding Hours,* Chemikal Underground 2010.
[36] The Twilight Sad, 'The Neighbours Can't Breathe', *Acoustic EP,* FatCat Records 2011.
[37] The Unwinding Hours, 'Traces', *The Unwinding Hours,* Chemikal Underground 2010.
[38] The Twilight Sad, 'That Birthday Present', *Acoustic EP,* FatCat Records 2011.
[39] The Unwinding Hours, 'Tightrope', *The Unwinding Hours,* Chemikal Underground 2010.
[40] We note that coda # often patterns idiosyncratically across different variables with respect to postvocalic /r/ (Romaine 1978, Schützler 2010), as indeed the category 'pause' does with other variables (Guy 1980). We currently have no explanation for why coda # is different.

5.   Discussion

The examination of the social and linguistic constraints on use reveal a number of findings:

- Overall, there is a high rate of the variants at the weakly, rather than the strongly rhotic end of our continuum. This is despite postvocalic /r/ being a classic stereotype of Scots.
- James and Craig exhibit different rates of use of the variants: the majority of Craig's variants are from the weakly rhotic end of the spectrum, whereas James uses variants from both ends of the continuum.
- Craig does not differentiate song and speech in the use of postvocalic /r/: he is generally at the non-rhotic end of the continuum in both. James's results on the other hand point to a higher rate of the rhotic tap in song when compared to speech.
- James uses the higher rates of taps in particular linguistic contexts only in song: predominantly in coda vowel and coda consonant environments, and, to a lesser extent, in coda clusters.

How can these results be explained? Despite postvocalic /r/ being a stereotype of Scots, the overall distribution of forms shows that the majority of variants appear at the weakly rhotic end of the scale. Moreover, the most iconic variant – the trill – appears only twice. This initial result aligns fully with reports that postvocalic /r/ is receding in the Central Belt, at least in working-class speech (see Stuart-Smith 1999, 2003, 2006, 2007; Stuart-Smith *et al.* 2007, 2010, 2014). Given this context of change, especially where derhoticisation is 'most advanced in the more populous western conurbation' (Stuart-Smith *et al.* 2014), these initial results are not surprising.

A more nuanced picture emerges when the results are divided across the two singers, James and Craig, who show different patterns of use. Attitudes have been shown to play a defining role in linguistic behaviour (see, e.g., Garrett 2010 for an overview of research). Comments made by Craig and James during the sociolinguistic interview with the first author regarding their attitudes towards the use of Scots may provide clues to these patterns of use.

In reflecting on the use of Scots in song over the past few years, Craig thinks that 'singing in an American accent was going too far, . . . straying way too far from your roots'. At the same time, however, 'you didn't have to sing in a particular Scottish brogue, whereas now, it's become a very popular stance . . . It's become more apparent in recent years, but when I was coming up . . . the Scottish voice wasn't as strong.' Despite this observed increase in the use of Scots in song, Craig states 'I don't think I sing in a Scottish accent' and 'I don't think about an accent at all. It's what *just comes out*'. In comparing Craig's data across the two different media, a clear picture emerges: his use of postvocalic /r/ is the same across speech and song. Thus, in spite of Craig declaring that he does not sing in the Scottish accent he uses in speech, at least for this variable, Craig is not using a 'mid-Atlantic' accent or a stereotypically Scottish accent, but instead is singing in his *own* accent. A plausible explanation for him not being aware of how similar his use of /r/ is throughout song and speech is that postvocalic /r/ is actually not enregistered as Scottish for Craig – or if it is, he associates it with a type of Scottishness he does not relate to.

In contrast to Craig, James states that he sings is his 'natural way of speaking', and that 'dialect was the only way to go about it' in his music career. Moreover, he has been under no pressure to change his accent by his record label, and indeed his Scottish accent in song has 'been a kinda unique selling point about the band'. This may explain why the no /r/ and derhotics of his speech are substituted by taps in song, suggesting that this variant indexes Scottishness for James. In other words, his sense of place.

In the projection of place, however, James has an overt concern with 'authenticity' of voice, as revealed through the interview data in the use of Scots in song:

Unless they're putting it on, ... like turning the Scottish up to ten ... I don't try and sing – ... it just comes kinda naturally, 'cause if I'm singing about a certain thing, then ... I'll use the words that I would use in general everyday kinda life. But you can tell ... some people are trying a bit too hard.

It may appear from the heightened use of taps that James is 'trying too hard'. However, the linguistic constraints reveal that he increases his use of taps across all linguistic contexts,[41] rather than on a more idiosyncratic level that we might expect from, for example, hyperdialectal use (Trudgill 1986: 75). Moreover, he uses a variant extant in his speech – the tap – rather than turning to the even more stereotypical 'Groundskeeper Willie' trill of the media comment. This suggests that he *is* doing what 'comes kinda naturally' in song – using taps as in his speech – but just at slightly heightened rates. These heightened rates could relate to the level of performance; while Morrissey emphasises the likeliness of non-rhoticity in favour of 'singability' (Morrissey 2008: 211), the high level of performance and theatricality in song might lead to James increasingly using the tap to 'style' and 'stage' his Scottish identity (Coupland 2007: 25).

---

[41] The exception to this is pause contexts. Morrissey (2008: 211) notes that non-rhotic realisations are particularly likely in sustained notes at the end of song lines as their vowel-like quality does not require closure, hence does not impact on sonority.

6.   Conclusion

Beal (2009: 224) describes indexicality as the process 'whereby linguistic features become associated with social categories and can then be used to do social work'. This utilisation of language variation works particularly well in song, since verbal performance has the power 'to transform social structures' (Bauman 1975: 305). As discussed in the Introduction, it has been suggested that there has been a rise in the use of Scots in contemporary music over the last twenty years in Scotland, and this small-scale study set out to investigate the linguistic validity of this claim. The study of the speech and song of the frontmen from two Scottish indie bands demonstrates that 'indexical meaning is created and reinforced in local practices in which different people participate in different ways, if at all' (Johnstone and Kiesling 2008: 6). Hence we cannot expect indexicalities 'to have unique social meanings, even in the same socio-cultural settings', but rather to 'become amenable to being discussed, argued over and renegotiated, metalinguistically' (Coupland 2007: 23). Our analysis of the use of postvocalic /r/ in the participants' speech and singing has shown striking differences in use, especially in the highly performed context of the latter. A number of social factors might have contributed to this divergence in singing accents, such as the singers' age gap and the difference in influences from the music industry and peers when first embarking on their music career. However, it has become apparent that what is and is not enregistered for a particular community member may also play a key role in the projection of place and social identity in an evolving music industry.

REFERENCES

Agha, Asif 2005. 'Voice, footing, enregisterment'. *Journal of Linguistic Anthropology* 15: 38–59.
Bauman, Richard 1975. 'Verbal art as performance'. *American Anthropologist* 77: 290–311.
Beal, Joan C. 2009. '"You're not from New York City, you're from Rotherham." Dialect and identity in British indie music'. *Journal of English Linguistics* 37/3: 223–40.
Bell, Allan 1984. 'Language style as audience design'. *Language in Society* 13: 145–204.
Clarke, Sandra and Philip Hiscock 2009. 'Hip-hop in a post-insular community. Hybridity, local language, and authenticity in an online Newfoundland rap group'. *Journal of English Linguistics* 37: 241–61.
Cloonan, M. 2007. 'Lessons from down under? Popular music policy and decentralised government in Scotland and Australia'. *Scottish Music Review* 1: 18–42.
Coupland, Nikolas 2007. *Style: Language Variation and Identity*. Cambridge: Cambridge University Press.

Foulkes, Paul and Gerard J. Docherty (eds.) 1999. *Urban Voices: Accent Studies in the British Isles*. Leeds: Arnold.

Garrett, Peter 2010. *Attitudes to Language*. Cambridge: Cambridge University Press.

Gibson, Andy 2008. 'Perception of sung and spoken vowels in New Zealand English'. *Laboratory Phonology* 1: 49–50.

Grant, William 1914. *The Pronunciation of English in Scotland*. Cambridge: Cambridge University Press.

Guy, Gregory R. 1980. 'Variation in the group and the individual: The case of final stop deletion', in Labov, William (ed.). *Locating Language in Time and Space*. New York: Academic Press. pp. 1–36.

Harris, John 2003. *The Last Party. Britpop, Blair and the Demise of English Rock*. London: Fourth Estate.

Hesmondhalgh, David 1998. 'Post-punk's attempt to democratise the music industry: the success and failure of Rough Trade'. *Popular Music* 16: 255–73.

1999. 'Indie: The institutional politics and aesthetics of a popular music genre'. *Cultural Studies* 13: 34–61.

Johnstone, Barbara and Scott F. Kiesling 2008. 'Indexicality and experience: Variation and identity in Pittsburgh'. *Journal of Sociolinguistics* 12: 5–33.

Johnston, Paul 1985. 'The rise and fall of the Morningside/Kelvinside accent', in Görlach, Manfred (ed.). *Focus on Scotland*. Amsterdam: Benjamin. pp. 37–56.

1997. 'Regional variation', in Jones, Charles (ed.). *The Edinburgh History of the Scots Language*. Edinburgh: Edinburgh University Press. pp. 433–513.

Labov, William 1972. *Sociolinguistic Patterns*. Philadelphia: University of Pennsylvania Press.

1984. 'Field methods of the project on linguistic change and variation', in Baugh, John and Joel Sherzer (eds.). *Language in Use: Readings in Sociolinguistics*. Englewood Cliffs: Prentice-Hall. pp. 28–54.

Lawson, Eleanor, James M. Scobbie, and Jane Stuart-Smith 2014. 'A socio-articulatory study of Scottish rhoticity', in Lawson, Robert (ed.) 2014. *Sociolinguistics in Scotland*. Basingstoke: Palgrave Macmillan. pp. 53–78.

Lawson, Eleanor, Jane Stuart-Smith, and James M. Scobbie 2011. 'The social stratification of tongue shape for postvocalic /r/ in Scottish English'. *Journal of Sociolinguistics* 15: 256–68.

Lennon, Robert 2011. A real-time study of rhoticity in Glaswegian between 1997 and 2011. Unpublished undergraduate dissertation, University of Glasgow.

Le Page, Robert B., and Andrée Tabouret-Keller 1985. *Acts of Iidentity: Creole-Based Approaches to Language and Ethnicity*. Cambridge: Cambridge University Press.

Macafee, Caroline 1983. *Varieties of English around the World: Glasgow*. Amsterdam: John Benjamins.

Mitchell, Tony 1996. *Popular Music and Local Identity. Rock, Pop and Rap in Europe and Oceania*. London: Leicester University Press.

Morrissey, Franz A. 2008. 'Liverpool to Louisiana in one lyrical line: Style choice in British rock, pop and folk singing', in Locker, Miriam A., and Jürg Strässler (eds.) *Standards and Norms in the English Language*. Berlin: Mouton de Gruyter. pp. 195–218.

Romaine, Suzanne 1978. 'Postvocalic /r/ in Scottish English: Sound change in progress?', in Trudgill, Peter (ed.). *Sociolinguistic Patterns in British English*. London: Edward Arnold. pp. 144–57.

Schützler, Ole 2010. 'Variable Scottish English consonants: The cases of /ʍ/ and non-prevocalic /r/'. *Research in Language* 8: 5–21.

Scobbie, James M., Olga B. Gordeeva and Benjamin Matthews 2006. 'Acquisition of Scottish English phonology: An overview'. *A QMUC Speech Science Research Centre Working Paper WP-7*. Available from www.qmu.ac.uk/ssrc/pubs/scobbie_et_al%202006%20wp7.pdf.

Simpson, Paul 1999. 'Language, culture and identity: With (another) look at accents in pop and rock singing'. *Multilingua* 18: 343–67.

Stuart-Smith, Jane 1999. 'Glasgow: Accent and voice quality', in Foulkes, Paul and Gerard Docherty (eds.). *Urban Voices: Accent Studies in the British Isles*. London: Arnold. pp. 201–22.

　　2003. 'The phonology of modern urban Scots', in Corbett, John, John D. McClure, and Jane Stuart-Smith (eds.). *The Edinburgh Companion to Scots*. Edinburgh: Edinburgh University Press. pp. 110–37.

　　2006. 'The influence of media on language', in Llamas, Carmen, Louise Mullany and Peter Stockwell (eds.). *The Routledge Companion to Sociolinguistics*. London: Routledge. pp. 140–8.

　　2007. 'A sociophonetic investigation of postvocalic /r/ in Glaswegian adolescents', in Trouvain, J. and W. J. Barry (eds.). *Proceedings of the 16th International Congress of Phonetic Sciences*. Saarbrücken. pp. 211–14.

Stuart-Smith, Jane, Eleanor Lawson, and James M. Scobbie 2014. 'Derhoticisation in Scottish English: A sociophonetic journey', in Celata Chiara and Silvia Calamai (eds.) *Advances in Sociophonetics*. Amsterdam: John Benjamins. pp. 59–96.

Stuart-Smith, Jane and Claire Timmins 2010. 'The role of the individual in language change', in Llamas, Carmen and Dominic, Watt (eds.) 2010. *Language and Identities*. Edinburgh: Edinburgh University Press., pp. 39–54.

Stuart-Smith, Jane, Claire Timmins, and Fiona Tweedie 2007. 'Talkin' Jockney?: Variation and change in Glaswegian accent'. *Journal of Sociolinguistics* 11: 221–60.

Tagliamonte, Sali A. 2006. *Analysing Sociolinguistic Variation*. Cambridge: Cambridge University Press.

Trudgill, Peter 1983. 'Acts of conflicting identity: The sociolinguistics of British pop-song pronunciation', in Coupland, Nikolas and Adam Jaworski (eds.) *Sociolinguistics: A Reader and Coursebook*, London: Macmillan. pp. 251–65.

　　1986. *Dialects in Contact*. Oxford: Blackwell.

Wells, John C. 1982. *Accents of English*. Cambridge: Cambridge University Press.

Websites

BBC. http://bbc.co.uk/news/magazine-20048521.

Blogspot. http://charlottepepperg324.blogspot.co.uk/2011/09/conventions-of-indie-music.html.

The Conversation. http://theconversation.com/young-fathers-must-we-label-the-mercury-winners-as-scottish-33662.

Ban the bomb. www.banthebomb.org/index.php/102-uncategorised/1502-bairns-not-bombs.

Brig Newspaper. www.brignewspaper.com/2010/11/that-scottish-accent/.

Dusted magazine. www.dustedmagazine.com/reviews/3615.

Encyclopedia.com. www.encyclopedia.com/doc/1G2-3495100011.html.

Guardian. www.guardian.co.uk/music/musicblog/2008/jan/22/itwaswhilelisteningto. www.theguardian.com/music/2012/mar/08/scottish-music-rock-north.

Herald Scotland. www.heraldscotland.com/arts-ents/music-features/the-sensational-history-of-scottish-rock-1.933852.

No Rip Cord. www.noripcord.com/reviews/music/the-twilight-sad/fourteen-autumns-and-fifteen-winters.

Ravechild. http://ravechild.co.uk/2012/02/23/interview-the-twilight-sads-james-graham/.

Stylus Magazine. www.stylusmagazine.com/reviews/the-twilight-sad/fourteen-autumns-and-fifteen-winters.htm.

UNESCO. www.unesco.org.uk/glasgow,_unesco_city_of_music.

11 Where the Black Country Meets 'Black Barnsley'[1]

Dialect Variation and Identity in an Ex-Mining Community of Barnsley

Kate Burland

1. Introduction

Recent studies have demonstrated the need to place speakers' own evaluations of local and linguistic identity at the forefront of interpretations of phonological variation (Dyer 2002; Llamas 2007; Llamas and Watt, Chapter 9 in this volume). This approach provides a more nuanced understanding of the links between a speaker's orientation to place and their linguistic practice, highlighting the relationship between locally salient identities and patterns of phonological change.

This paper will focus upon phonological variation in the dialect of Royston, an ex-mining community in the Metropolitan Borough of Barnsley in South Yorkshire. The findings will question assumptions regarding the inevitability of levelling and mutual convergence in situations of dialect contact, by demonstrating how three successive generations have resisted convergence to pan-regional phonological norms. In recent studies of dialect contact, levelling is taken as 'something of a "given"' (Kerswill 2002: 187); an anticipated consequence of this process is the gradual disappearance of linguistically marked and minority variants (Britain and Trudgill 1999: 246). Kerswill makes the distinction between levelling and geographical diffusion, the former he confines to relatively compact geographical areas, and the latter he describes as a process 'by which features spread out from a populous and economically and culturally dominant centre' (2002: 187–8). Kerswill (2002: 188) also asserts that features which spread via geographical diffusion are likely to be acquired in cities and towns before infiltrating the dialects of the rural areas 'in between'. However, both levelling and geographical diffusion depend upon mutual linguistic convergence and, to date, relatively little sociolinguistic research has focused upon speech communities which diverge *from* rather than accommodate *to*

---

[1] Daniel Defoe used this term to describe Barnsley in his work A *Tour through the Whole Island of Great Britain*, first published in 1727 (see Defoe 1986: 483).

surrounding varieties. Research by Watson (2006: 55) begins to explore the phenomenon of 'phonological resistance' establishing that aspects of Liverpool English are diverging from supralocal phonological norms. However, the factors which motivate a speech community to resist the diffusion of supralocal or pan-regional phonological norms need further exploration.

This paper will examine both production and attitudinal data in order to show that greater levels of dialect contact do not necessarily lead to the rejection or suppression of minority variants and greater linguistic homogeneity. Furthermore, it will explore the ways in which attempts to assert a distinct local identity can result in the retention and deliberate exaggeration of demographically and linguistically marked forms (see Johnstone *et al*. 2006: 92). The study will focus upon speakers' metalinguistic commentary in order to make sense of locally salient identities (Dyer 2002; Llamas 2007). It will also consider how these identities of place interact with linguistic production, recognising that ideology is key to any interpretation of speakers' linguistic choices (Eckert 2008: 456).

This paper will reinforce the need to take an ethnographic approach to the collection and analysis of data. It will also demonstrate the importance of an understanding of local historical contexts, social experiences and tensions which may impact upon the use and perception of linguistic variables. Silverstein (2003) makes the connection between language and the construction of identity, emphasising the indexical link between linguistic forms and social value judgements. His concept of an indexical order illustrates that social or indexical values are not inert, and he asserts that an effective indexical analysis must acknowledge the 'duplex' nature of language use, namely that it is both 'pragmatic' and 'ideologically informed' (2003: 227). In line with Silverstein's notion of the fluidity of indexical values, work by Britain and Trudgill (1999) demonstrates that the social meaning of variables can be adapted or *reallocated*, thus revealing complex and multifaceted aspects of local and linguistic identity. Viewing identity as a 'socio-cultural phenomenon' (Bucholtz and Hall 2005: 585), the Royston study links acts of linguistic identity to the ideological perceptions which form via membership of a speech community, in order to demonstrate how phonological resistance can act as a powerful indicator of a speaker's sense of place.

2.   The Research Location

The town of Barnsley is situated in South Yorkshire , approximately 16 miles north of the city of Sheffield, and approximately 21 miles south of the city of Leeds. Figure 11.1 shows the location of Barnsley relative to the north of England. The Metropolitan Borough of Barnsley was formed as a result of the Local Government Act 1972 and is made up of twenty-one smaller regions, or

Location of Barnsley

Figure 11.1: Location of Barnsley relative to the north of England.[2]

---

[2] Contains public sector information licensed under the Open Government Licence v3.0. Contains NRS data © Crown copyright and database right 2016. Contains OS data © Crown copyright [and database right] 2016.

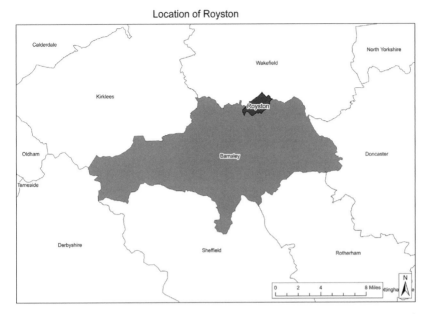

Figure 11.2: Location of Royston in relation to the Metropolitan Boroughs of Barnsley and Wakefield.[3]

wards. The borough has a total population of 231,221, which equates to approximately 4.38 per cent of the total Yorkshire region. Barnsley, once famous for its mining industry, has no working pits remaining; wholesale and retail trades now account for the majority of employment (Barnsley Council Online, Census 2011).

The urban township of Royston lies on the northernmost boundary of the Barnsley borough, a boundary which also serves to divide South from West Yorkshire. Royston has a current population of 10,728 (approximately 4.64 per cent of the borough of Barnsley as a whole) and is situated approximately 4.3 miles from the centre of Barnsley, and 7.2 miles from the centre of Wakefield in West Yorkshire. However, a journey through Royston is not the most efficient route between the two centres. The major roads linking Barnsley and Wakefield are the M1 and the A61; Royston lies well to the east of these routes, and the B6132, which links Barnsley and Wakefield via Royston, is a comparatively indirect and meandering route (see Figure 11.2).

---

[3] Contains public sector information licensed under the Open Government Licence v3.0. Contains National Statistics data © Crown copyright and database right 2016. Contains OS data © Crown copyright [and database right] 2016.

The township of Royston is relatively isolated from other settlements as recent descriptions of the area confirm: 'To the north and west are extensive areas of countryside and to the south open land separates the settlement from Athersley and Carlton in Urban Barnsley' (Unitary Development Plan, Barnsley Metropolitan Borough Council 1995: 3). This geographical isolation is, however, being eroded. Within the last decade a rapid programme of house building on the peripheries of Royston has brought the township nearer to surrounding settlements, most notably to Carlton. The potential loss of Royston's isolated status is not viewed positively by older residents, as can be seen from the comment in (1) below:

(1)   **OM5:** 'Carlton is getting nearer and nearer; it won't be long until it joins up with Royston and we'll have lost our identity altogether'

2.1   Employment and Industry

By the nineteenth century Royston had developed as an area rich in market gardens; as recently as 1893 there were at least six commercial market gardens and eight farms in the village (Elliott 2000: 4). However the nature of employment in Royston changed rapidly following the opening of Monckton Colliery in 1876. This large new colliery was situated on the edge of the township attracting large numbers of migrant workers who would initially lodge with local residents, but later settle in Royston following a period of extensive house building. As shown in Figure 11.3, census records for the first three quarters of the nineteenth century[4] reveal that the population of Royston fluctuated slightly in the decades preceding the opening of the colliery, but the total never peaked above 676. However, in the forty-year period following the opening of Monckton, Royston's population rose rapidly to over 6,000, an increase of over nine times the total prior to the establishment of the colliery.

The majority of this incoming workforce came from areas of the Black Country.[5] As Figure 11.4 shows, the Black Country lies approximately 100 miles south of Royston and is described by Asprey (2007) as: 'unusual in that it is not an area delimited by political, physical, or economic boundaries' (2007: 78). Despite the disputed boundaries of the region, the Black Country is generally thought to encompass parts of the counties of Staffordshire, Warwickshire and North Worcestershire (Asprey 2007). The

---

[4] The Royston population totals for the decades 1801-1831 are taken from the enumerator's notes from the first four English censuses. The notes have been preserved in Royston Parish Council records. (For information on census material from 1801 to 1831 see Wall *et al.* 2012).

[5] 'The Black Country' and 'Staffordshire' are used as interchangeable terms by participants in the current study, and in accounts of Royston's history to denote the area generally known as The Black Country.

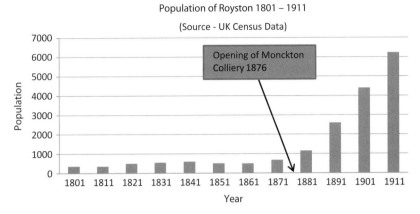

Figure 11.3: Population totals for Royston 1801 to 1911 (UK Census data).

name *Black Country* derives from the Industrial Revolution and denotes the impact of pollution on the general landscape of the region. The Black Country had embraced industrialisation rapidly and by the late nineteenth century many of the collieries in the region had been exhausted of resources leaving a workforce skilled in deep seam mining and coke production, yet in desperate need of employment (Barnsby 1971).

The 1901 census for Royston gives a sense of the proportions of incoming workers. The figures for the whole of Royston show that 31 per cent of household heads came from the Black Country compared with 12 per cent from Derbyshire and Nottinghamshire, with the latter providing the second largest portion of the influx (UK Census data 1901). In areas of Royston where most incoming workers settled, still known today as 'Little Staffordshires', the figures rise to 38 per cent from the Black Country and 13 per cent from Derbyshire and Nottinghamshire (UK Census data 1901). It is clear that the majority of long distance migration came from the Black Country, but with significant numbers from Derbyshire and Nottinghamshire. Yet Cave (2001:15) finds that only the Black Country/Staffordshire influx gains any perceived status in terms of the local character and dialect of the township:

Many people interviewed for this study referred to Royston as 'Little Staffs'. A quarter of those interviewed from Royston claimed Staffordshire or Black Country ancestry, and informants interviewed from neighbouring localities, such as Darfield, Havercroft, and Central Barnsley, confirmed that they believed Royston was full of 'Staffordshire folk' with a distinctive regional speech pattern.

Monckton Colliery reached its zenith in terms of production and employment in the early decades of the twentieth century. The colliery eventually closed

The Black Country and Royston

Figure 11.4: Location of the Black Country in relation to Barnsley and Royston.[6]

---

[6] Contains public sector information licensed under the Open Government Licence v3.0. Contains National Statistics data © Crown copyright and database right 2013 and 2016. Contains OS data © Crown copyright [and database right] 2013 and 2016.

in December 1966 and the shops and amenities that had flourished in Royston providing facilities for the community of mineworkers and their families went into rapid decline. Today the majority of Royston residents have to travel beyond the township to find work, and wholesale and retail trades now employ the greatest proportion of Royston's working population at 17.6 per cent, followed by manufacturing at 14.8 per cent (Barnsley Council Online, Census 2011).

2.2   Border Status

As previously established, Royston now lies within the borough of Barnsley, however, as Figure 11.2 clearly shows, the township is situated on the boundary between the Metropolitan Boroughs of Wakefield in West Yorkshire and Barnsley in South Yorkshire. Prior to the Local Government Act 1972, political administration of the township was undertaken by Royston Urban District Council, which operated within the West Riding County Council. The West Riding County Council headquarters (situated in Wakefield) were responsible for funding and maintenance of Royston's roads, schools, parks, street lighting and libraries. Barnsley was, at this time, a County Borough Council of sufficient size to control its own budget despite being within the geographical area of the West Riding County Council.

As a consequence of the Local Government Act 1972, the township of Royston became a local government ward of the newly formed Metropolitan Borough of Barnsley and was allotted three councillors, in line with the other wards in the borough. Following the boundary changes which were implemented in 1974, Royston remained in the Wakefield parliamentary constituency for a further decade, finally shifting to the Barnsley Central constituency in 1983. Although Royston has not encountered the kind of dramatic shifts in national status experienced in the border town of Berwick (Llamas *et al.* 2009; Llamas and Watt, Chapter 9 in this volume), or even a shift in county status as is the case with Middlesbrough (Llamas 2007) and Warrington (Beal 2010), it has experienced changes in administrative control which have impacted upon inhabitants' perceptions of local, and in turn, linguistic identity. The changes in the political and administrative parameters have helped to foster a sense of distance between Royston and the remainder of the Barnsley borough, as the following analysis demonstrates.

3.   The Data

3.1   The Variables

The two variables under scrutiny in this paper are vowels in the FACE and GOAT lexical sets (Wells 1982a). The Standard Southern British English (SSBE) FACE lexical set includes words which employ a front narrow closing diphthong, represented as /eɪ/ (Wells 1982a: 141). The SSBE GOAT lexical set includes words which employ a diphthong with a mid-central unrounded nucleus moving to a close back slightly rounded offglide, represented as /əʊ/ (Wells 1982a: 146). Wells (1982a: 146) comments that the GOAT vowel is 'variable both regionally and socially', and this variability includes both diphthongal and monophthongal forms of the vowel; the latter generally found in northern English dialects.

The two vocalic variables have particular salience for the Royston study, as previous research has established that monophthongal variants of FACE and GOAT remain the most dominant pan-northern forms (Watt and Milroy 1999; Beal 2004; Haddican *et al.* 2013) representing 'a principal shibboleth of northern English speech' in contrast to southern diphthongal forms (Haddican *et al.* 2013: 373). Metalinguistic commentary surrounding the Royston variety, however, draws attention to diphthongal realisations of both FACE and GOAT. The comment in Figure 11.5 was posted by a Barnsley resident in response to an article entitled *The Royston Accent Stands Out* featured on the website *We Are Barnsley.com*[7] in May 2013.

I noticed the Royston accent in the 1970s when I had a girlfriend from there. The comments about putting a Y into the vowel sounds are true. Other sounds differed, e.g. 'Dawn't be layte' & 'It's owver the rawrd'. I used to wonder how her and her family's accents could be so different when they only lived about 6 miles away. It wasn't until years later that I read about the Staffordshite link.

Figure 11.5: A comment from an online article about the Royston accent.

The post provides a typical example of metalinguistic commentary surrounding the Royston variety as it focuses upon the FACE and GOAT vowels. It highlights the difference between the Barnsley and Royston forms and links this variation to the influence of Staffordshire or Black Country workers, who settled in the township.

3.2   *The Participants*

In order to determine the type of FACE and GOAT forms present in the Royston variety and to examine how these variants stratify according to age, word list data was elicited from twenty-four Royston speakers, representing three generations in the township. In order to consider the impact of

---

[7] www.WeAreBarnsley.com is the companion website to Barnsley's local newspaper *The Barnsley Chronicle*.

Table 11.1: *Stratification of age and gender across the Royston, Barnsley and Wakefield samples.*

Royston Speakers			
Age Categories	Sample Age Range	Women	Men
17–29	17–19	4	4
30–60	32–57	4	4
61+	66–74	4	4
Barnsley Speakers			
Age Categories	Sample Age Range	Women	Men
17–29	18–27	4	4
30–60	35–60	4	4
61+	61–73	4	4
Wakefield Speakers			
Age Categories	Sample Age Range	Women	Men
17–29	18–29	4	4
30–60	32–59	4	4
61+	61–79	4	4

dialect contact, identical samples of Barnsley and Wakefield speakers were obtained in order to compare the Royston variants and the FACE and GOAT forms found in the dialects of these two adjacent speech communities. Table 11.1 shows the stratification of age and gender across the three samples.

3.3   Methodology

The word lists comprised 105 tokens in total; these included thirty FACE and thirty GOAT tokens. However, as previous studies have highlighted the difficulties of separating the vocalic portion from preceding or following approximants (Ferragne and Pellegrino 2010), tokens with these phonetic environments were eliminated. This reduced the total to fifteen FACE and fifteen GOAT tokens per speaker, retaining vowels with preceding/following obstruents and nasals.

Initial auditory analysis and visual inspection of the corresponding spectrogram was undertaken in Praat (Boersma and Weenink 2008) to determine the qualities of the FACE and GOAT vowels produced by speakers in the three datasets, and to code tokens as diphthongal or monophthongal realisations. This analysis was then tested via the extraction and measurement of formant data. To minimise the effects of coarticulation, measurements were extracted for F1 and F2 at the 25 per cent and 75 per cent points into the vowel segment using a script in Praat. Each speaker's tokens of FLEECE, TRAP and GOOSE were also measured and used as reference vowels for the purposes of normalisation. The data was normalised using the Watt and Fabricius modified method (see Fabricius *et al.* 2009; Flynn 2011) in NORM (Kendall and Thomas 2007).

In order to quantify the degree of movement throughout the vocalic portion of each FACE and GOAT token, the Euclidean distance between F1 and F2 at 25 per cent and 75 per cent was calculated using a script in R (R Core Team 2013) and the measurements were converted to Equivalent Rectangular Bandwidth (ERB) in a move to model human perception of frequency (see Moore and Carter, Chapter 12 in this volume). The resulting data provides a degree of diphthongisation for each speaker's FACE and GOAT tokens (see Haddican *et al.* 2013); the mean value of these totals for each participant is represented in Figures 11.6–11.8. Means lower than 1.5 ERB are classed as monophthongal as this matches most closely the auditory and visual analysis of the word list recordings. The horizontal line on each graph represents this division between monophthongal and diphthongal realisations.

The following section will examine these data in order to establish whether metalinguistic claims regarding the Royston dialect are evident in linguistic practice. It will illustrate the degree of diphthongisation of FACE and GOAT tokens produced by Royston speakers in comparison to that found in the adjacent speech communities of Barnsley and Wakefield.

4.   Results

4.1   *Degree of Diphthongisation*

Figure 11.6 clearly shows that all twenty-four Royston speakers diphthongise variants of FACE and GOAT. The degree of diphthongisation for FACE is slightly lower in the younger cohort than in the middle and older generations, but the diphthongisation of GOAT increases in the younger speakers when compared to the older generation. Overall, the distinctive diphthongisation of Royston FACE and GOAT variants shows no signs of attrition.

Figure 11.7 shows that twenty-two out of the twenty-four Barnsley speakers produce monophthongal variants of FACE and GOAT, with only two older females producing slight diphthongisation of GOAT variants. Of the three generations, the younger speakers show the greatest degree of monophthongisation indicating that the Barnsley dialect is levelling towards greater monophthongisation of FACE and GOAT forms.

The data for Wakefield in Figure 11.8 shows a slightly different trajectory; again the majority of speakers (eighteen out of twenty-four) produce

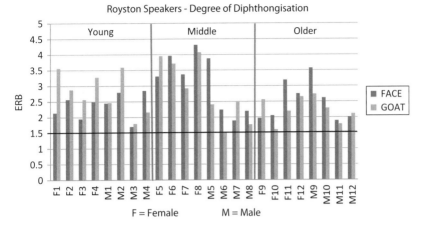

Figure 11.6: Degree of diphthongisation in ERB of FACE and GOAT tokens for Royston speakers.

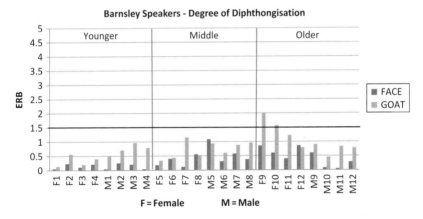

Figure 11.7: Degree of diphthongisation in ERB of FACE and GOAT tokens for Barnsley speakers.

monophthongal variants of FACE and GOAT, with four middle generation males and two older generation females producing some diphthongal variants. However, the younger generation show a stark contrast with by far the greatest degree of monophthongisation within the data set. This indicates that, as with the Barnsley dialect, the Wakefield variety is levelling towards greater mono-phthongisation of FACE and GOAT forms.

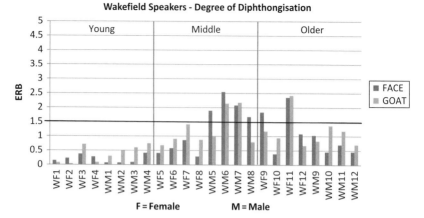

Figure 11.8: Degree of diphthongisation in ERB of FACE and GOAT for Wakefield speakers.

The following section takes a closer look at the vowel qualities produced by the Royston speakers and demonstrates how the Royston variants of FACE and GOAT contrast with forms found in other Yorkshire dialects, in particular those found in the neighbouring speech communities of Barnsley and Wakefield.

4.2   *Vowel Qualities*

Table 11.2 shows the variants produced by the Royston speakers in comparison with the adjacent speech communities of Barnsley and Wakefield. The previous section established that the majority of Barnsley and Wakefield speakers produce long monophthongal variants of both FACE and GOAT. No Barnsley participants diphthongise FACE and only two older Barnsley speakers produce *some* closing diphthongal forms of GOAT, however, these do not match the diphthongal variants found in the dialect of Royston, as shown in the table.

Six Wakefield speakers produce *some* closing diphthongal forms of FACE which resemble the Royston variants. This could indicate evidence of historic dialect contact between the two varieties. Three Wakefield participants produce *some* diphthongal forms of GOAT, but again these do not resemble the diphthongal Royston variants shown here.

Table 11.3 illustrates the standard diphthongal representations of FACE and GOAT found in RP, and the FACE and GOAT variants found across studies of Yorkshire dialects which are broadly contemporaneous with the Royston

Table 11.2: *Vowel qualities of FACE and GOAT in the Royston, Barnsley and Wakefield dialects.*

	Royston	Barnsley	Wakefield
Face	**[ɛi] ~ [ei]**	**[eː]**	**[eː]** > [ei]
Goat	**[ou]**	**[oː]** > [oʊ]	**[oː]** > [oʊ]

Table 11.3: *Vowel qualities of FACE and GOAT in RP and Yorkshire dialects. (Note that majority variants are shown in bold. > indicates difference in currency. ~ indicates equal currency.)*

	RP (Wells 1982b)	Sheffield (Stoddart et al. 1999; Finnegan 2011)	Leeds (Wells 1982b)	Bradford (Petyt 1985; Watt & Tillotson 2001; Hughes et al. 2005)	Huddersfield (Petyt 1985)	Halifax (Petyt 1985)	Hull (Williams and Kerswill 1999)
Face	**[eɪ]**	**[eː]** > [ɛɪ]	**[eː]** > [ɛɪ]	**[eː]** > [ɛɪ]	**[eː]**	**[eː]**	**[ɛː]**
Goat	**[əʊ]**	**[ɔː]** > [oʊ] > [əʊ]	**[oː]** > [əʊ]	**[ɔː]** > [oː] > [oː] > [ɔʊ] > [əʊ]	**[ɔː]** > [ɔʊ]	**[ɔː]** > [əʊ]	**[ɔ̈ː]** ~ [ɔːʂ]> [əʊ]~ [əʊ]

study. It is noticeable that the vowels produced by the Royston speakers contrast markedly with the supraregional, long monophthongal forms of FACE and GOAT found in other Yorkshire varieties. Royston speakers do produce closing diphthongal forms of FACE and GOAT; however, these do not resemble the closing diphthongal forms found in RP. The findings also show that the Royston forms do not match the diphthongal variants produced by a minority of speakers across the Yorkshire varieties, represented in Table 11.3.

In his study of the dialects of Bradford, Halifax and Huddersfield, Petyt (1985) found that some older speakers retained diphthongal forms of FACE and GOAT which were seen as relics of more traditional or 'rural' Yorkshire varieties. Petyt found that these traditional diphthongal forms had largely undergone a process of attrition making way for more modern and 'urban' supraregional norms. This is a process also observed more recently in the dialect of Tyneside (Watt 2002: 57), where speakers were found to be abandoning the more traditional or old-fashioned local centring diphthongs of FACE and GOAT in favour of more 'modern' pan-northern monophthongal forms. No younger Barnsley or Wakefield speakers produce diphthongal variants of FACE or GOAT, indicating that diphthongisation of these vocalic

Table 11.4: *Vowel qualities of FACE and GOAT in the Royston, Black Country and Derbyshire dialects.*

	Royston	Black Country (Mathisen 1999)	Black Country (Asprey 2008)	Derby (Docherty and Foulkes 1999)
FACE	[ɛi] ~ [ei]	[æi] > [ɛi]	[aɪ]	[ɛɪ]
GOAT	[ou]	[aʊ] ~ [ɔʊ]	[aʊ]	[əʉ] ~ [ou]

variables is clearly receding in the two dialects. However, Tables 11.2 and 11.3 make it clear that the dialect of Royston is resisting the geographical diffusion of pan-Yorkshire monophthongal norms of FACE and GOAT. This would suggest that, for the younger Royston speakers, the diphthongal variants of FACE and GOAT do not index 'traditional' or 'old fashioned' values as found in the studies by Petyt (1985) and Watt (2002).

There is, however, a match between the Royston FACE vowels and the minority FACE variants found in the repertoires of some older male Black Country speakers (Mathisen 1999), as shown in Table 11.4. Furthermore, there is also a match between the minority GOAT variants found in the dialect of Derby (Docherty and Foulkes 1999) and those found in the current Royston corpus. Wells (1982b: 364–5) shows that the diphthongisation of FACE and GOAT is well established in dialects of the East Midlands and the Black Country, whilst more recent studies (Docherty and Foulkes 1999; Mathisen 1999; Asprey 2008) confirm that diphthongal variants of FACE and GOAT remain the majority forms in these varieties. These findings could indicate that the influx of workers to Royston from areas of the Black Country and Derbyshire at the end of the nineteenth and early twentieth centuries may have had an impact upon the dialect of the township.

5.   Discussion

Acoustic analysis of production data reveals that diphthongisation of FACE and GOAT vowels in the Royston dialect is not receding. The younger generation of Royston speakers show greater phonological resistance to supralocal norms than the middle and older generations of speakers in the township. A small minority of the Barnsley and Wakefield corpora diph-thongise FACE or GOAT and yet there is only scant evidence of a resemblance between the vowel qualities of the Royston and Wakefield FACE diphthongs. This would indicate that FACE and GOAT variants in the Royston dialect are not influenced by dialect contact with these adjacent speech communities. There is, however, a match between current variants of FACE and GOAT in the Royston dialect and forms that *are* receding in the dialects of the Black Country and Derby. As the Black Country, Nottinghamshire and Derbyshire comprised the largest proportion of long-distance migration to Royston in the late nineteenth and early twentieth centuries, this could indicate that the regionally distinctive Royston variants have been influenced by historical dialect contact with these varieties.

Looking at the dialect of York in North Yorkshire, Haddican *et al.* (2013) found that respondents in their study were keen to retain the distinction between northern monophthongal and southern diphthongal realisations of FACE and GOAT, and that patterns of FACE and GOAT monophthongisation were 'strongly shaped by identities of place' (Haddican *et al.* 2013: 373). Prior studies have established that monophthongal forms of FACE and GOAT are emblematic of northern varieties; however, the Royston production data presented in this paper runs counter to this evidence showing that three generations of speakers in the township of Royston have resisted levelling to pan-regional norms.

The following section will examine attitudinal data in order to understand more about Royston speakers' orientation to place, and to consider why the Royston dialect has resisted the regional diffusion of long monophthongal forms of FACE and GOAT evident across other Yorkshire varieties.

5.1   Attitudinal Findings

In addition to the word list data, sociolinguistic interviews were conducted with twenty Royston participants representing younger and older generations of speakers in the township. Tables 11.5 and 11.6 show the sampling summary.

All interview participants, with the exception of OF6 and OM5, also produced word list recordings. Data was elicited via questionnaires and semi-structured interviews based upon the principles of the SuRE methodology (Kerswill *et al.* 1999). The questionnaire has two sections: section one considers the participant's attitude towards their own linguistic variety, and section two explores speakers' orientation towards Royston and Barnsley, and perceptions of local identity. The interview was based upon the format of the questionnaire, but participants were encouraged to speak freely about any topic they felt was relevant. Where possible, participants were interviewed in dyads or triads. All participants were born in Royston and have lived in the township all or most of their lives, but some have had short periods away for work or education.

Table 11.5: *A sampling summary of the younger Royston speakers.*

Speaker Code	Age	Occupation
YF1	17	A level student
YF2	19	BTEC student
YF3	18	A level student
YF4	18	NVQ2 student
YM1	18	A level student
YM2	17	A level student
YM3	19	BTEC student
YM4	17	A level student

Table 11.6: *A sampling summary of the older Royston speakers.*

Speaker Code	Age	Occupation
OF1	74	Retired factory worker
OF2	67	Retired factory worker
OF3	68	Retired telephonist
OF4	72	Retired factory worker
OF5	74	Retired midwife
OF6	78	Retired housewife
OM1	57	Ex – miner, park ranger
OM2	66	Retired librarian
OM3	69	Ex – miner/retired civil servant
OM4	69	Retired miner
OM5	73	Retired miner
OM6	74	Retired builder

The study of Pittsburghese by Johnstone *et al.* (2006) discovered that variables do not index the same meanings or categories to all speakers, nor do they necessarily index the same meanings or categories to a single speaker in all contexts and stages of their life. A focus upon the two age groups in the Royston study will illustrate the ways in which ideological values assigned to linguistic forms are strongly bound to generational perspectives regarding a sense of place.

For the older Royston speakers Black Country heritage is central to the construction of local and linguistic identity. Sixty-seven per cent of older participants claim Black Country/Staffordshire ancestry and, when asked why the dialect of Royston differs from that of Barnsley, 100 per cent of older speakers cite the Black Country connection as the major influence as the example in (2) below illustrates.

(2)   **OF5:** 'It's the As and Os, Barnsley people stretch them out but we say them differently, it's because of the Staffordshire connection'.

The quotation in (3) is from a participant whose ancestors walked from Swadlincote in Derbyshire to gain work at Monckton Colliery in the early twentieth century; however, the speaker maintains throughout the interview that Swadlincote is in Staffordshire and proudly claims Black Country heritage.

(3)   **OM6:** 'there's a place called Swadlincotes ... in Staffordshire ... they walked it most of the way from Swadlincotes up to Royston ... and most of them got set on straight away at Monckton pit'.

Older Royston speakers clearly select the indexical link with Black Country heritage from a constellation of available ideological labels demonstrating a shared orientation towards this linguistic identity. They are aware of a 'cultural schema of enregisterment of forms' (Silverstein 2003: 212), which links a particular linguistic variant with a recognisable social grouping and speakers are then able to employ these enregistered forms in the creation of identity.

The boundary changes and shift in administrative control also impact upon older Royston inhabitants' sense of place and we can see the 'socio-psychological effects' (Beal 2010: 217) of changes in local administrative boundaries in the comment in (4). The loss of Royston Urban District Council is perceived by older participants as a negative step which has seen Royston issues subordinated to the needs of the borough as a whole.

(4)   **OM2:** 'One of our councillors made a speech and talked of 'my town Barnsley', he should have said 'my town Royston', it shows where his loyalties lie'.

The shift in funding from Wakefield to Barnsley is seen by older participants as a key factor in the decline in quality of public spaces and amenities in the township. Ten out of the twelve older Royston speakers interviewed saw this event as a watershed demarcating the old Royston in which they could take pride, and an area which is now in a state of managed decline. The comment in (5) captures these sentiments showing a clear tone of bitterness and a sense that the true identity of Royston has been lost as a result of the changes. Llamas (2007: 582) found similar allegiances in her study of Middlesbrough, observing that perceptions of local identity are tightly bound to speakers' orientation to place.

(5)   **OF2:** 'We had lovely street lamps ... and lovely parks and gardens. That all changed when we became part of Barnsley'.

The older speakers have experienced a Royston pre- and post- political and administrative boundary changes; by contrast, the younger speakers have only ever known a Royston that is firmly ensconced in the borough of Barnsley, both geographically and politically. None of the younger speakers cite know-ledge of the boundary changes as significant in the historical development of the township. In such situations, Beal (2010: 217) talks of a 'generational divide', and perceptions of Royston are clearly very different for older and younger inhabitants of the township. Older speakers express an affiliation with Wakefield and Leeds rather than with Barnsley and Sheffield and gravitate towards West Yorkshire for days out, socialising and shopping. Younger speakers, however, show little or no affiliation with Wakefield; the comment in (6) shows how instead they gravitate, by necessity, towards Barnsley.

(6)   **YF2:** 'I don't really like coming to town [Barnsley] to be honest but because my friends are here and everything it's like I'm always in town but I would prefer to be in Royston'.

However, for the younger speakers, geographical gravitation towards Barnsley does not equate to linguistic affiliation, as the production data in this study has shown, and although some are aware of Royston's Black Country heritage they do not see this as a significant factor in the creation of their local and linguistic identity. There is a clear sense from younger speakers that Royston has a separate identity, that it is self-contained and detached both literally and metaphorically from the rest of Barnsley: 'it's like a community itself really Royston' (YM1). Similarly, Dyer (2002) reports that linguistic variables index distinctly different identities for the generations of speakers under scrutiny in her study of the dialect of Corby in Northamptonshire. She finds that the older Scottish speakers who settled in Corby following the closure of the large steel works in Clydeside employ typically Scottish variants in order to index their ethnicity. However, younger speakers have ideologically reconstructed the values associated with their linguistic practice to index a distinctly local Corby identity.

Younger Royston speakers also feel that the local character and dialect of the township are under threat, particularly as a result of the loss of Royston High School, which merged with the high school in the nearby settlement of Athersley in 2010. Following the merger, a brand new purpose built school, Carlton Community College, was erected on greenbelt land between the settlements of Royston and Carlton. The new building opened in early 2011 and now draws pupils from Royston, Carlton and Athersley. The siting of the new school on greenbelt land between the settlements of Royston and Carlton is seen as a further erosion of Royston's cherished isolation, and a threat to the resilience of the distinctive Royston accent, as the comment in (7) reveals:

(7)   **YF4:** 'Royston people aren't growing up with other Royston people any more, they're growing up with Athersley and other people. I've noticed lots of changes; they're different people to what they would have been if they'd gone to Royston ... I think the accent's got a bit different because they talk different to us'.

Both younger and older participants also use strategies to define Barnsley speakers as *the other* in order to establish and maintain a clear distinction between Royston and the remainder of the borough. A different dialect acts as a clear marker of separation and distance and participants are keen to emphasise the distinction between the Royston and Barnsley dialects. The comments in (8) and (9) make it clear that for both older and younger participants the Royston variety ranks more highly in a perceived hierarchy of local varieties.

(8)   **OF4:** 'I think we're posher than Barnsley people, more refined'.
(9)   **YM3:** 'I'd not want to merge with a Barnsley accent. A typical Barnsley accent is chav;[8] I don't really want to sound like a chav'.

Meyerhoff (2004: 526) comments that language is one of the ways in which speakers 'construct, maintain, or contest the boundaries of social categories and their membership in or exclusion from those categories'. Royston speakers are clearly positioning themselves with reference to the perceived *other*, exploring aspects of 'relationality' (Bucholtz and Hall 2005: 598) in order to consider their similarity to or difference from other salient speech communities.

Auditory and acoustic analysis has already shown that the Royston variants do not resemble the long monophthongal forms found most commonly in the surrounding speech communities of Barnsley and Wakefield and, furthermore, that Royston speakers are increasingly diverging *from* rather than converging *towards* pan-regional norms. It is clear from the attitudinal data that neither young nor old Royston speakers associate their local or linguistic identity with Barnsley. The unique identity of the township is evidently a factor in the retention of regionally marked forms in the Royston dialect; however, it is also the case that older and younger speakers are expressing differing interpretations of a local and linguistic Royston identity.

6.   Conclusion

This chapter provides a closer study of a place *in between*; it explores patterns of phonological divergence which suggest that speakers are actively resisting participation in the geographical diffusion of supralocal norms. A multifaceted approach has been undertaken to make sense of local and linguistic identity creation in the dialect of Royston, within broader patterns of regional dialect

---

[8] The Oxford English Dictionary (Soanes and Stevenson 2005: 293) defines the term *chav* as 'a young lower-class person typified by brash and loutish behaviour and the wearing of (real or imitation) designer clothes'. Also see Bennett (2013).

variation and change. This has shown the benefits of combining phonetic analysis with knowledge of locally significant events and a speaker's sense of place.

The Royston study demonstrates the resilience of the diphthongal Royston forms. Referring to Labov's study of Martha's Vineyard (1963), Eckert (2008: 454) observes that linguistic variables can be employed as part of a 'local ideological struggle'. In the Royston study, the nature of that ideological struggle changes according to generational perspective. Both generations of Royston speakers are using FACE and GOAT variants in order to construct social meaning. Older speakers clearly see the FACE and GOAT forms as indicative of the township's linguistic heritage employing them as part of a conscious resistance to linguistic and social change. Younger speakers, how-ever, do not associate the FACE and GOAT variants with heritage and tradition, they associate them with the unique character of the township. There is clear evidence of reallocation in terms of the ways in which the two generations assign labels to their linguistic practice. The Royston variants have, over a period of three generations, resisted levelling to supralocal norms and part of this resilience can be attributed to a process of 'socio-stylistic reallocation' (Britain and Trudgill 1999: 247), whereby new social values have been assigned to the Royston FACE and GOAT variants.

The findings from Royston clearly challenge the idea that dialect levelling is *a given* in situations of dialect contact. There is no evidence to show that Royston speakers, spanning three generations, are accommodating towards adjacent speech communities; in fact the reverse is true, and younger Royston speakers are intensifying phonological resistance to supralocal norms. The sociolinguistic situation in existence at the beginning of the twentieth century, which likely gave rise to the Royston variants of FACE and GOAT, no longer exists, and yet successive generations of speakers have maintained the distinct-ive forms as a consequence of Royston's unique demographic, political and geographical history. In order to make sense of such linguistic phenomena, it is crucial that interpretations of the history, geography and the general narrative of place come from the speakers themselves. Assumptions of place imposed from outside can distort the link between linguistic forms and the construction of local identities. The Royston study shows that patterns of dialect realloca-tion, resistance and divergence are symbiotically linked to speakers' interpret-ations of the physical and ideological landscape in which they are situated.

REFERENCES

Asprey, Esther C. 2007. Investigating residual rhoticity in a non-rhotic accent. *Leeds Working Papers in Linguistics and Phonetics* 12: 78–101.
  2008. 'Black Country English and Black Country Identity'. Unpublished PhD thesis, University of Leeds.

Barnsby, George J. 1971. 'The standard of living in the Black Country during the nineteenth century'. *The Economic History Review, New Series* 24: 220–39.

Barnsley Council Online. *Census* 2011. www.barnsley.gov.uk/services/council and democracy/statistics and census-information/the-2011-census/royston-ward-profile.

Barnsley Metropolitan Borough Council (BMBC) 1995. *Unitary Development Plan Incorporating Proposed Changes July and December*: Volume 6. Royston Community Area.

Beal, Joan C. 2004. 'English dialects in the north of England: Phonology', in Schneider, Edgar W. and Bernd Kortmann (eds.) *A Handbook of Varieties of English*. Volume 1. Berlin: De Gruyter. pp. 113–33.

   2010. 'Shifting borders and shifting regional identities', in Llamas, Carmen and Dominic Watt (eds.) *Language and Identities*. Edinburgh: Edinburgh University Press. pp. 217–26.

Bennett, Joe 2013. 'Chav-spotting in Britain: The representation of social class as private choice'. *Social Semiotics* 23: 146–62.

Boersma, Paul and David Weenink 2008. Praat: Doing Phonetics by Computer (version 5.3.66). www.praat.org.

Britain, David and Peter Trudgill 1999. 'Migration, new-dialect formation and sociolinguistic refunctionalisation: Reallocation as an outcome of dialect contact'. *Transactions of the Philological Society* 97: 245–56.

Bucholtz, Mary and Kira Hall 2005. 'Identity and interaction: A socio-cultural linguistic approach'. *Discourse Studies* 7: 585–614.

Cave, Andrew 2001. 'Language Variety and Communicative Styles as Local and Subcultural Identity in a South Yorkshire Coalmining Community'. Unpublished PhD thesis, University of Sheffield.

Defoe, Daniel [1727] 1986. A *Tour through the Whole Island of Great Britain*. London: Penguin Classics.

Docherty, Gerard J. and Paul Foulkes 1999. 'Derby and Newcastle: Instrumental phonetics and variationist studies', in Foulkes, Paul and Gerard Docherty (eds.) *Urban Voices: Accent Studies in the British Isles*. London: Arnold. pp. 47–71.

Dyer, Judy 2002. 'We all speak the same round here': Dialect levelling in a Scottish–English community'. *Journal of Sociolinguistics* 6: 99–116.

Eckert, Penelope 2008. 'Variation and the indexical field'. *Journal of Sociolinguistics* 12: 453–76.

Elliott, Brian 2000. *Britain in Old Photographs: Royston, Carlton and Monk Bretton*. Stroud: Sutton Publishing Limited.

Fabricius, Anne, Dominic Watt and Daniel E. Johnson 2009. 'A comparison of three speaker-intrinsic vowel formant frequency normalization algorithms for Sociophonetics'. *Language Variation and Change* 21: 413–35.

Ferragne, Emmanuel and François Pellegrino 2010. 'Formant frequencies of vowels in 13 accents of the British Isles'. *Journal of the International Phonetic Association* 40: 1–34.

Finnegan, Katie S. 2011. 'Linguistic Variation, Stability and Change in Middle-Class Sheffield English'. Unpublished PhD thesis, University of Sheffield.

Flynn, Nicholas 2011. 'Comparing vowel formant normalisation procedures'. *York Papers in Linguistics* 11: 1–28.

Haddican, Bill, Paul Foulkes, Vincent Hughes and Hazel Richards 2013. 'Interaction of social and linguistic constraints on two vowel changes in Northern England'. *Language Variation and Change* 25: 371–403.

Hughes, Arthur, Peter Trudgill and Dominic Watt 2005. *English Accents and Dialects*, fourth edition. London: Hodder.

Johnstone, Barbara, Jennifer Andrus and Andrew E. Danielson 2006. 'Mobility, indexicality, and the enregisterment of "Pittsburghese"'. *Journal of English Linguistics* 34: 77–104.

Kendall, Tyler and Eric R. Thomas 2007. NORM: The vowel normalization and plotting suite. http://ncslaap.lib.ncsu.edu/tools/norm/.

Kerswill, Paul 2002. 'Models of linguistic change and diffusion: New evidence From dialect levelling in British English'. *Reading Working Papers in Linguistics* 6: 187–216.

Kerswill, Paul, Carmen Llamas and Clive Upton 1999. 'The first SuRE moves: Early steps towards a large dialect project'. *Leeds Studies in English* 30: 257–69.

Llamas, Carmen 2007. '"A place between places": Language and identities in a border town'. *Language in Society* 36: 579–604.

Llamas, Carmen, Dominic Watt and Daniel E. Johnson 2009. 'Linguistic accommodation and the salience of national identity in a border town'. *Journal of Language and Social Psychology* 28: 381–407.

Mathisen, A. G. 1999. 'Sandwell, West Midlands: Ambiguous perspectives on gender patterns and models of change', in Foulkes, Paul and Gerard J. Docherty (eds.) *Urban Voices: Accent Studies in the British Isles*. London: Arnold. pp. 107–23.

Meyerhoff, Miriam 2004. 'Communities of Practice', in Chambers, Jack K., Peter Trudgill and Natalie Schilling–Estes (eds.) *The Handbook of Language Variation and Change*. Oxford: Blackwell Publishing. pp. 527–48.

Petyt, Keith M. 1985. *Dialect and Accent in Industrial West Yorkshire*. Amsterdam: John Benjamins Publishing Co.

R Core Team 2013. R: A language and environment for statistical computing. R Foundation for Statistical Computing, Vienna, Austria. www.R-project.org.

Silverstein, Michael 2003. 'Indexical order and the dialectics of sociolinguistic life'. *Language and Communication* 23: 193–229.

Soanes, Catherine and Angus Stevenson (eds.) 2005. *Oxford English Dictionary*. Second Edition (Revised). Oxford: Oxford University Press.

Stoddart, Jana, Clive Upton and John D. A. Widdowson 1999. 'Sheffield dialect in the 1990s: Revisiting the concept of NORMs', in Foulkes, Paul and Gerard Docherty (eds.) *Urban Voices: Accent Studies in the British Isles*. London: Arnold. pp. 72–89.

Wall, Richard, Matthew Woollard and Beatrice Moring 2012. *Census Schedules and Listings, 1801–1831: An Introduction and Guide*. Colchester: University of Essex.

Watson, Kevin 2006. 'Phonological resistance and innovation in the North-West of England'. *English Today* 22: 55–61.

Watt, Dominic 2002. '"I don't speak with a Geordie accent, I speak, like, the Northern accent": contact-induced levelling in the Tyneside vowel system'. *Journal of Sociolinguistics* 6: 44–63.

Watt, Dominic and Lesley Milroy 1999. 'Patterns of variation and change in three Newcastle vowels: Is this dialect levelling?', in Foulkes, Paul and Gerard Docherty (eds.) *Urban Voices: Accent Studies in the British Isles*. London: Arnold. pp. 25–46.

Watt, Dominic and Jennifer Tillotson 2001. 'A spectrographic analysis of vowel fronting in Bradford English'. *English World-Wide* 22: 269–302.

Wells, John C. 1982a. *Accents of English 1: An Introduction*. Cambridge: Cambridge University Press.

　1982b. *Accents of English 2: The British Isles*. Cambridge: Cambridge University Press.

We Are Barnsley.com. www.wearebarnsley.com/news/article/2428/royston-accent-stands-out.

Williams, Anne and Paul Kerswill 1999. 'Dialect levelling: Change and continuity in Milton Keynes, Reading and Hull', in Foulkes, Paul and Gerard Docherty (eds.) *Urban Voices: Accent Studies in the British Isles*. London: Arnold. pp. 141–62.

12   'The Land Steward Wouldn't Have a Woman Farmer'

The Interaction between Language, Life Trajectory and Gender in an Island Community

Emma Moore and Paul Carter

1.   Introduction

Discussions of language and place sometimes give the impression that the 'local' is a clearly defined and recognisable entity. This is often the case when a language feature is recognised as belonging to and defining the social characteristics of a particular place. However, as Eckert (2004: 109) has noted, 'the community is a contested entity that is differentially constructed in the practices and in the speech of different factions, as well as individuals.' This can give rise to competing and contended ideas about what it means to be 'local' (Johnstone 2004: 71).

This paper explores how life trajectory and gender interact to affect how individuals from the same small island community use language to index 'local'. In particular, we show how 'human geographies, particularly the built and social environments we inhabit, create varying opportunities for individuals and social groups' (Laws 1997: 48). These 'varying opportunities' result in the construction of alternative local identity types. In particular, we demonstrate that defining place is no straightforward endeavour when 'place' takes on specific meanings linked to alternative life trajectories, and that this is true no matter how small the community studied. As Britain (2009a: this volume) has argued, rural areas have been particularly 'fetishised' as homogeneous and uncontested entities (and this is despite the fact that the types of diversity examined in urban spaces may be considered to be relatively simplistic – see Britain 2009b: 228). By focusing on a small, rural, island community, our work will demonstrate that 'individual speakers distinguish themselves linguistically no matter what type of community they live in' (Schreier 2006: 27). We show that what matters is not the size or type of community, but the necessity for individuals to index distinct styles and identities within a particular social space.

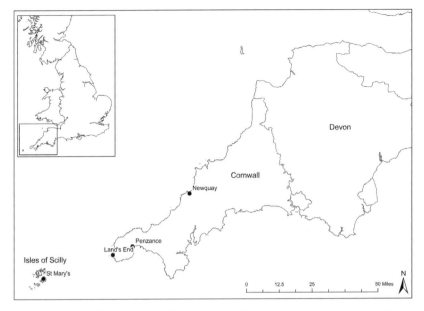

Figure 12.1: Location of the Isles of Scilly relative to the south-west of England.[1]

2.   The Research Location

The Isles of Scilly are a group of islands, situated approximately 28 miles off the south-west coast of Cornwall, England. They consist of numerous islands, but only five of these are inhabited. Of these, St. Mary's is the largest, both in terms of physical size and population. The islands as a whole had a population of 2,203 in the last census (Office for National Statistics 2011), of which 75 per cent lived on St. Mary's. All of the speakers considered in our paper come from St. Mary's.

Figure 12.1 shows the location of the islands relative to the south-west English mainland. It also indicates the mainland departure points for the islands. The islands are accessible by air and sea. Light aircrafts fly between St. Mary's and Land's End or Newquay all year round (weather-permitting), and the trip takes between 15 and 25 minutes. The islands also have a passenger ferry service, which operates between Penzance and St. Mary's from Easter to October. At all other times, the only scheduled boat is the freight service, which serves the islands three times a week year-round.

---

[1] Contains public sector information licensed under the Open Government Licence v3.0. Contains OS data © Crown copyright [and database right] 2016.

The islands' major industry is tourism, which accounts for over 85 per cent of its income (The Isles of Scilly Council 2005: 14). The tourism trade is long established, but was particularly bolstered by the arrival of the railway to Penzance in 1867, and the replacement of sailing vessels by a steamer in 1859. The islands also have a reasonably robust farming industry (which benefits from favourable weather conditions), and some small family fishing businesses.

The islands have a particularly interesting history of governance, having been leased from the Crown and managed by a series of governors between 1571 and 1920. This makes them quite distinct from the nearest Cornish mainland – a fact of which Scillonians are very proud. This can be seen in (1), a quotation from Scillonian in exile, Frank Banfield, writing in the Gentleman's Magazine in 1888.

(1) 'I think, unless my recollection of past reading is gravely at fault, that it is Mr. Wilkie Collins, who many years ago, in one of the magazines, expressed surprise that Scillonian English should be so pure, correct, and free from provincial idioms as it was … but he did not know, probably, that the Scillonians, at least the dominating element, are not Cornish. The accent of the county of which electorally they form a part is entirely wanting on their tongues … ' (Banfield 1888: 45).

Banfield (1888: 54) goes on to claim that Scilly's 'correct speech' is a consequence of the influence of the first governor, Sir Francis Godolphin, and his descendants, who 'impressed their own correcter locution and more Eastern English of inheritance and education upon the population.' The link that Banfield makes between education and 'correct speech' (by which we assume he means something akin to 'Standard English'), and the ideology that Scillonians are better educated and more well-spoken than mainlanders, can be found in metalinguistic commentary about the variety across history, as shown in (2) and (3) below.

(2) ' … the Language of Scilly refines upon what is spoken in many Parts of Cornwall; probably from the more frequent Intercourse of the Inhabitants, some more than others, with those who speak the Standard English best' (Heath 1750: 436).

(3) 'The Islanders are remarkable for speaking good English – far preferable, at least, to what is generally heard amongst the humbler classes of any county, at some distance from the metropolis … ' (Woodley 1822: 105).

It is certainly true that education has featured highly in Scillonian life. Education was made compulsory on Scilly before it was on the mainland (Mothersole 1914: 48). Also, before the islands built their own secondary school in 1966, wealthy and/or especially bright children were sent away to selective and fee-paying boarding school between the ages of 11 and 16. These education patterns undoubtedly provided ideological pressure supporting the use of Standard forms of English on Scilly. However, given that type of education also served to segregate the population, it does not necessarily follow that there was a consistent effect of ideology on language use across the population. That is to say, whilst the historical metalinguistic commentary implies a uniform orientation to standard forms on the islands, in the absence of substantial linguistic work (Scilly has been neglected in dialect surveys, although see Thomas 1979), there is no way to confirm whether these perceptions reflect actual patterns of language use across the community.

In order to explore the extent to which islanders orient to Standard English forms, we examine how a cross-section of Scillonians make use of two especially salient markers of Standard English, the vowels in the TRAP and BATH lexical sets. The next section explains the suitability of the TRAP and BATH lexical sets for this study and outlines how we undertook our analysis.

3.   The Data

The vowels in the TRAP and BATH lexical sets (Wells 1982) are particularly useful variables for our purposes because they carry a good deal of ideological baggage in English English. In particular, Mugglestone (2003: 78) refers to the pronunciation of the BATH vowel as 'a salient feature of "talking proper"'. Most historical linguists agree that, prior to the seventeenth century, words in both of these lexical sets were pronounced with the same low front vowel (Lass 1976: chapter 4; MacMahon 1998; Beal 1999: 105–11; 2004: 139; Piercy 2010: 9–24). Gradually, in Standard English English (StEE), this vowel raised for some and lengthened for all before the voiceless fricatives /f, θ, s/, and before nasal clusters. However, it is important to note that this change did not proceed to completion across every lexical item, as Piercy (2010: 17–18) has observed. Nonetheless, despite being 'a half completed sound change' (Wells 1982: 233), the outcome was a TRAP/BATH split, based on duration, with vowels in the BATH lexical set having longer duration than those in the TRAP lexical set. Then, very gradually, between the eighteenth and twentieth centuries, the BATH vowels also retracted, so TRAP and BATH eventually came to differ by vowel quality and duration.

However, this change did not proceed to completion in all varieties of English English. Most notably for our purposes, the traditional varieties of Cornish English (the mainland variety closest to the Isles of Scilly) have TRAP/BATH patterns that were fossilised at the point during which English was introduced to this area following the loss of the Cornish language (Wakelin 1975: 1986). Whilst there is some variation in this region with regard to the precise vowel quality of these vowels (reflecting the phased introduction of English westwards along the peninsula), in any given location, the vowel quality is the same for both lexical sets. In traditional varieties of Cornish English, then, the TRAP/BATH split is marked only by duration, with BATH vowels being longer than TRAP vowels.

Although the historical metalinguistic commentary emphases dialect contact with StEE speakers via the elite networks provided by the islands' governors, there has been on-going Cornish immigration into Scilly over time. For instance, in the 1901 census, almost half (48.3 per cent) of Scilly's 571 migrants were from Cornwall (data from The Isles of Scilly Museum 2007). This opens up different possibilities for our Scillonian speakers. Given that, historically, some of them had access to education in boarding schools on the mainland (and Cheshire and Trudgill 1989: 95, amongst others, consider boarding schools to be one of the main places in which Standard English is cultivated), we might expect mainland-educated Scillonians to show a more StEE-like pattern than Scilly-educated Scillonians. Furthermore, given that sociolinguistic studies have consistently shown that women lead men of the same socioeconomic group in the use of standard language features (so much so, that Holmes [1997] refers to this as a 'sociolinguistic universal'), we might expect mainland-educated women to show the most StEE-like pattern in our dataset.

To examine these patterns, we analysed a sample of data from a group of Scillonians born before the islands' own secondary school opened in 1966. This data was obtained from interviews from the Isles of Scilly Museum's Oral History Archive. This archive contains recordings made by local people interviewing other local people. The archive recordings date from the 1970s through to the present day. The purpose of the archive is to record island history, as told by the individuals who experienced it. Interviewees were selected by museum volunteers on the basis of their status as a 'Scillonian character' (a vague definition, but one which includes consideration of island heritage and community roles). Table 12.1 provides information on the participants used in our analysis.

In order to test the quality of the TRAP and BATH vowels used by these speakers, we extracted formant data, sampling formant tracks every 5ms through each vowel, with LPC order set to appropriate values for each speaker. This allowed us to obtain the median value for each formant in the vowel. We focus on F1 and F2 in our analysis, given that F1 has been found to correlate with vowel height, and F2 with how front or back a vowel is (see Ladefoged 1982, amongst others). We also measured the duration of each vowel, which we transformed into a logarithmic domain to account for the fact that hearers

Table 12.1: *Participant sample used in the analysis.*

	Birth Dates of Participants	Number of Participants
Mainland-educated males	1901–1920	3
Mainland-educated females	1905–1931	3
Scilly-educated males	1901–1924	3
Scilly-educated females	1907–1919	4

seem to perceive durations as ratios rather than as absolute amounts. This kind of transformation makes sense statistically because logarithmically transformed durations also approximate the normal distribution more closely. We also transformed our formants into the domain of the equivalent rectangular bandwidth (Glasberg and Moore 1990), as a step towards speaker normalisation. For clarity of presentation, axis notation is provided in our figures in Hertz for spectral data and milliseconds for temporal data.

We coded for a number of phonological environment factors, namely: the position of the syllable in question within each utterance (initial, final or somewhere in the middle of the utterance), the number of syllables in the word, whether the rhyme of the syllable was open or closed, the manner of articulation, the voicing of the following consonant, and whether the syllable seemed to be carrying sentence stress. We also coded for lexical versus grammatical words. In order to focus on the social patterns in our data, we do not deal with these phonological environments in this paper – only to note that the social patterns we discuss below stayed robust when linguistic factors were included in statistical models of the data (see Moore and Carter [2015] for a more comprehensive discussion of the linguistic predictors of TRAP and BATH in this dataset). In the next section we describe the outcome of our analysis.

4.   Results

Figure 12.2 shows a series of density plots of our raw formant data, according to education type and gender. Density plots are like contours on a map. Peaks show areas of greater density where formant measurements cluster. TRAP vowels are shown in grey and BATH vowels in black. Figure 12.2 reveals variation amongst our Scillonian speakers, and suggests effects of both education type and gender. As expected, the mainland-educated speakers seem to have a TRAP/BATH pattern that is more like present-day StEE. Their TRAP and BATH vowels are more distinct from one another, and they appear to have more of an F2 difference between these lexical sets; that is to say, the BATH vowels seem to be further back than the TRAP vowels. On the other hand, the Scilly-educated speakers' plots show much more similarity between TRAP and BATH, with the two vowel clusters largely overlapped. With regard to education type, these plots suggest that mainland boarding school education may indeed correlate with more StEE-like patterns of TRAP and BATH in our sample of Scillonian speakers.

The effects of gender are less easy to deduce from these plots. Whilst it seems that the Scilly-educated women have a more StEE-like pattern than the Scilly-educated men (the centre of their BATH density plot has a lower F2 value than that of their TRAP density plot, whereas the distinction is much less

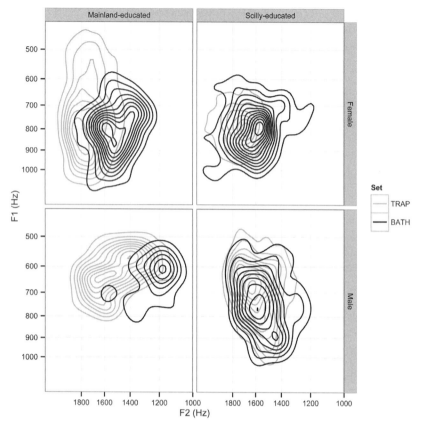

Figure 12.2: Density plot showing raw formant data for TRAP and BATH, according to education type (horizontal axis) and gender (vertical axis).

clear for the Scilly-educated men), it is not clear that the mainland-educated women are leading the mainland-educated men in having the most StEE-like pattern. The mainland-educated women's TRAP/BATH split does not appear to be any more extreme than that of the mainland-educated men – indeed, a closer look at Figure 12.2 suggests that it may be less so.[2] Furthermore, there appears to be less differentiation in the patterning of the women overall in our Scillonian sample. That is to say, Figure 12.2 suggests that it is men who

---

[2] Figure 12.2 shows a cluster of anomalous fronted BATH tokens in the data from the mainland-educated males. This data consists of four tokens from one speaker, all of which occur in a stylistically heightened interview segment. We discuss this anomalous data in depth in Moore and Carter (2015).

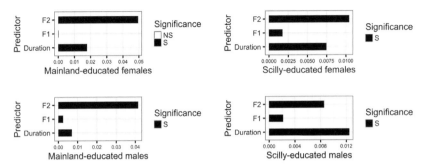

Figure 12.3: Variable importance plots predicting the relative importance of F1, F2 and duration in the TRAP/BATH split for each speaker group.

define the envelope of variation in this community: the mainland-educated men seem to have more of a distinct TRAP/BATH quality split than any other group, and the Scilly-educated men seem to have a less distinct TRAP/BATH quality split than anyone else.

In order to test the patterns suggested by the raw data in Figure 12.2, we ran random forest variable importance measures on the data. Strobl *et al.* (2008; 2009) provide an explanation of this type of modelling. Put simply, this technique models the relative importance of predictor variables in explaining the TRAP/BATH split in our data. This modelling allowed us to add duration as a predictor variable alongside F1 and F2. The results of this analysis are shown in Figure 12.3, which shows the variable importance plots predicting whether a vowel is TRAP or BATH for the data from each of the speaker groups listed in Table 12.1. Black columns indicate that a factor is a significant predictor and, the larger the bar, the more significant a factor is.

Figure 12.3 shows that F1 is not very important for predicting whether a vowel is TRAP or BATH, although it does have a small effect on the data of all of our speaker groups, with the exception of the mainland-educated females (the F1 bar here is insignificant, but the bar is so small that it is not possible to see its colour clearly in the figure). On the other hand, F2 and duration are clear predictors of whether a vowel is TRAP or BATH for all of our groups. However, these two factors do not pattern in the same ways across our speaker set. F2 is the most significant factor predicting whether a vowel is TRAP or BATH for everyone except the Scilly-educated men. For the mainland-educated males and females, and the Scilly-educated females, duration matters, but it is less important than vowel quality in differentiating TRAP and BATH, and it is *much* less important than F2 for the mainland-educated men. On the other hand, this pattern is reversed for the Scilly-educated men; duration is the most significant factor in predicting whether a vowel is TRAP or BATH for this group. F2 also matters for these speakers, but it is less important than duration.

In sum, the results shown in Figure 12.3 seem to support the patterns evident in the raw data. However, they elaborate on these results in two key ways. Firstly, Figure 12.3 suggests that the Scillonian men have oppositional patterns of language use. Their patterns of F2 and their patterns of duration work to create distinction – where one group uses more of one of these factors to mark the TRAP/BATH split, the other group use more of the other. Secondly, and in contrast to the men, the two groups of Scillonian women are much less different from one another – both groups seem to be moving towards a present-day standard-like norm, irrespective of education type, and there is much less differentiation in their linguistic patterning, as shown in Figure 12.3. We attempt to explain these patterns in the next section.

5.   Discussion: The Social Meanings of TRAP and BATH

The results in Section 4 suggest that women and mainland-educated men use more StEE-like forms and Scilly-educated men use more Cornish-like (regional vernacular) forms. Previous research has suggested that speakers use vernacular forms to index local identity. This was shown in Labov's (1963) Martha's Vineyard study, and has been demonstrated in subsequent work many times since then (see, for instance, Schilling-Estes' [1998] research in Ocracoke; Johnstone *et al.'s* [2006] work on Pittsburgh; and Wong and Hall-Lew's [2014] San Francisco study). Other research has suggested that increased use of standard language forms reflects orientation away from the local and towards less traditional or more global language norms. For instance, Holmquist's (1985: 199) study of a rural Spanish village discovered increased use of Castilian Spanish being driven by 'a general turning away from things rural'. These findings echo those in Gal's (1978) study of a rural Austrian village a decade earlier, where increased use of German (the more prestigious code in this bilingual context), was most frequent amongst those who oriented away from the community's traditional peasant roles and values. In both Holmquist's and Gal's studies, it was women who drove language change, given that, socially and economically, they suffered most in the rural economies of the locations studied. On the other hand, the men who controlled the local rural economy resisted language change the most.

It is tempting to apply these findings to the Scillonian context: we might assume that (i) the Scilly-educated men are resisting StEE-like forms to reflect and construct their stake in the local economy, whereas (ii) women and mainland-educated men are driving change towards the standard as a reflection of their orientation towards island-external prestige norms. Whilst the first part of this explanation may hold true, the second part may require further elaboration. Firstly, Scilly's unique sociocultural history suggests that it may be problematic to assume that the StEE-like patterns found on the island reflect a straightforward orientation away from the islands. Secondly, Scillonian women use StEE-like forms, but, unlike the women in Holmquist's and Gal's studies, it is not straightforwardly the case that they have the most advanced use of these forms on Scilly.

With regard to the first of these points, we refer back to the discussion in Section 2. This described a history of metalinguistic commentary linking Scillonian English and StEE. As can be seen in the quotations in (1), (2) and (3), this discourse typically juxtaposes Scilly with Cornwall, and Scillonian English with Cornish varieties of English. In this commentary, speaking in a style which more closely approximates StEE is a defining characteristic of being Scillonian according to the historical record. Consequently, one could view the use of this style as a claim regarding 'inheritance and education' (Banfield 1888: 54) and, as such, as a claim for a particular kind of Scillonian authenticity. In this sense, use of StEE-like forms may not solely indicate orientation to island-external or global language norms; it may also indicate orientation to a particular (and historically substantiated) Scillonian social type. That this is possible is further substantiated by the fact that the context of the interview itself focuses our mainland-educated speakers upon what they consider to be the important aspects of Scillonian life. That is to say, their discourse in the interview is focused on all matters Scillonian, not island-external concerns.

On the other hand, the oppositional behaviour of the Scilly-educated men suggests that they are orienting to a quite different Scillonian identity type, which is associated with different forms of status. This can be seen if we compare the roles and responsibilities undertaken by our male speakers over their lifetimes, and the dominant topics that these speakers discussed in their interviews. This information is given in Table 12.2, which suggests two distinct life trajectories for men according to education type.

Whereas the men who were educated on the mainland tended to end up being managers of their own businesses and taking on authoritative positions in the community, such as being councillors or magistrates, the men educated on Scilly tend to find employment in seafaring activities or local trades. The differences in roles and responsibilities are also highlighted in the topics the men discuss in their interviews. As noted in Section 3, the purpose of the oral history interviews was to reminisce about Scillonian life. Consequently, the topics discussed in the interviews offer a window on how our interviewees characterise Scillonian status and construct it in their talk. In line with their employment, the most frequent topic of conversation for the mainland-educated males is their management responsibilities. These might be responsibilities to do with their own businesses (Victor and Jim managed their own farm and also had various management roles in the islands transport company, and Ted managed a

Table 12.2: *The roles and responsibilities of the male participants and the topics covered in their interviews.*[3]

	Speaker	Date of Birth	Key Roles and Responsibilities	Main Interview Topics
Scilly-educated	Stan	1901	Boat transportation (during the war); Wireless operator; Bus driver/tours	Local history (WWI and II); sea employment
	Charlie	1911	Merchant navy; Boat-building and joinery; Barber; Councillor and Alderman	Local history (childhood and island places); management responsibilities (council work)
	Luke	1924	Fisherman; Farm labourer; Builder, decorator, carpenter and boatbuilder; Lifeboat (coxswain)	Sea employment; local history (childhood and family)
Mainland-educated	Victor	1905	Flower farmer from established farming family; Magistrate; Councillor; Director/ Chairman/ President of the IoS Steamship Co.	Management responsibilities (Steamship Co.)
	Ted	1914	Butcher and Hotelier; Councillor	Local history; management responsibilities (council)
	Jim	1920	Farmer from established farming family; Magistrate; Councillor; Director/ Managing Director of IoS Steamship Co.	Management responsibilities (flower farming, Steamship Co., council)

butcher's shop and a hotel), or authoritative roles such as being local councillors or magistrates. The Scilly-educated men, on the other hand, are more likely to talk about local history (that is events and occurrences on the islands) linked to their employment on the islands or at sea. For instance, Stan ran an inter-island boat service during the wars (navigating the treacherous seas around the islands in difficult conditions) and he tells stories about this time, and Luke was a fisherman and served as the lifeboat coxswain for many years, hence most of his interview is concerned with stories about lifeboat rescues.

---

[3] All names used to identify people from Scilly have been changed to pseudonyms throughout the paper.

The two different life trajectories experienced by male Scillonians prioritise different types of knowledge. Whereas the mainland-educated men achieve institutional status following their mainland schooling, there is evidence that at least some of the Scilly-educated men are strongly resistant to the idea that education gained elsewhere is more important than practical, local knowledge. In particular, the archive materials include evidence of some islanders expressing concern about too much intervention from outside the islands. This can be seen in the transcript in (4), which comes from a news report featuring a Scilly-educated Scillonian, Luke, warning against outside influences on the development of a new runway on the islands.

(4)	1	Any development company at all, or developer, I mean, he would he
	2	would turn head over heels to get his foot in here, wouldn't he? I mean
	3	look what Mr de Savaray have done over Land's End, look what they've
	4	done in Falmouth, look what they've done in all these little coastal ports
	5	around the town. I mean, they just turn them upside down in five minutes.
	6	They would have a field day in a place like this . . . You – you – see . . . You
	7	can have a hundred places like Land's End, yuppy parks sort of style, you
	8	know, I mean, those sort of centre places. But there's only one Scilly. You
	9	can't – and, and, if you change that, you won't get no more, will you? I
	10	mean, it's gone, gone forever.

In (4), Luke stresses that islanders like him have local knowledge and know what is best for the islands. This is articulated by positioning himself in opposition to mainland development companies (ll.1–2), and by opposing the ways in which mainland coastal locations have developed (1.2–5). Luke stresses Scilly's uniqueness (1.8–10), insinuating that it requires people like him to protect the islands from outside influence. Whilst Luke does not mention education in this extract, the implication is clear: knowledge about what is best for the islands comes from having a situated understanding of Scilly, and this is not necessarily achieved via formal education.

The behaviour of the men in our sample suggests that male Scillonians have adapted variants of TRAP and BATH to construct oppositional local identity types: one concerned with education and aspiration, and one concerned with local island knowledge. Britain and Trudgill (1999: 247–8) refer to this kind of adaptation as 'socio-stylistic reallocation'. It is evidenced here by the oppositional TRAP/BATH patterns in the male data and (i) the differences in the roles and responsibilities of the two groups of Scillonian men, (ii) the likely differences in social practices that such activities entail, (iii) the matters with which the men are concerned in the topics of their interviews and (iv) in other evidence available in the archive, such as the extract in (4).

Table 12.3: *The roles and responsibilities of the female participants and the topics covered in their interviews.*

	Speaker	Date of Birth	Key Roles and Responsibilities	Main Interview Topics
Scilly-educated	Tess	1907	Post woman; Taking in visitors; Flower tier	Local history (WWI and II and island stories)
	Gloria	1914	Housemaid; Shop worker; Taking in visitors; Flower tier	Local history (island folk and families)
	Sarah	1916	Housemaid; Taking in visitors	Local history (island folk and families)
	Kath	1919	Shop-worker; Taking in visitors; Working on family's farm	Local history (childhood)
Mainland-educated	Margaret	1905	Homemaker; Working on family's flower farm	Flower farming industry (local daffodil varieties)
	Elizabeth	1921	Teacher; Working on family's flower farm	Local history (education on the islands); flower farming industry
	Glenda	1931	Homemaker; Working on family's flower farm	Local history (gardening)

Turning now to our female speakers, we see that there are far fewer opportunities for women to gain explicit status within the community. Table 12.3 provides information about the roles and responsibilities undertaken by our female speakers over their lifetimes, and the topics that these speakers discussed in their interviews. Comparing the two groups of women reveals that, whilst Scilly-educated women tended to have more jobs than mainland-educated women, both groups of women undertook employment in the flower and farming industries, irrespective of their educational background or the other activities in which they were engaged. In practice, this meant that women were recruited to work in their husband's or wider family's main lines of work, by tying and packing flowers, in addition to undertaking all of the domestic responsibilities of the home, and any other form of employment they undertook. Furthermore, unlike the men, these women did not have roles and responsibilities in the community that brought them into conflict with each other. In fact, as their list of roles and responsibilities suggest, they were more often working alongside each other sustaining island industries.

This is not to say that these two groups of women are entirely homogeneous. The topics shown in Table 12.3 reveal some differences between the groups.

Like their male counterparts, Scilly-educated women talk about local history. However, they do not talk about their roles or responsibilities in relation to this history as the Scilly-educated men do. Instead they tend to talk about people, that is, island folk and their families. Sometimes this is in relation to a specific historical event; for instance, Tess was asked by her interviewer to focus on the period around the World Wars. Whilst mainland-educated women also focus on local history, their emphasis is on horticultural matters – they either talk about their own interests in gardening, or they talk about the flower farming industries managed by their husbands or fathers. For instance, Margaret talks about the varieties of flowers farmed on the farm managed by her husband, and Elizabeth talks about the way flowers were packed on the farm managed by her father. These slight differences in topic reflect that these two groups of women have different histories, concerns and priorities.

Nonetheless, Table 12.3 suggests *neither group* of women is acknowledged as having visible institutional roles in this island community. This is not to say that they do not contribute significantly to community life, but that their topics are not driven by their roles and responsibilities, because their roles are not acknowledged historically in the way that those occupied by men are. Women may sustain many of the island industries but none of these women were councillors, or chairs of local businesses; none of them served on the lifeboat crew or ran local boat services. This suggests that the type of education that women had gave them different life experiences, but it did little to affect how they are recognised within the community.

This is exemplified in the extract in (5), which provided the title of this chapter. It is taken from a story told by one of the Scilly-educated women, Tess, who is in conversation with another Scilly-educated woman, Gloria. They are talking about farmworkers' wives having to tie flowers for their husbands' employers.

(5)	1	Tess	Yes I remember when Mr Teddy Potts had that Penberthy
	2		farm before your father took over.
	3	Gloria	Yeah.
	4	Tess	And he had farm at Old Town, as well, forty acres altogether.
	5	Gloria	Was it?
	6	Tess	He used to have for- twenty steady men, and twenty part
	7		workers, flower season and potatoes.
	8	Gloria	Did you work for him, did you?
	9	Tess	Er- no my mother tied flowers for him.
	10	Gloria	Um.
	11	Tess	All the workmen's wives had to tie the flowers.
	12	Gloria	Did they?
	13	Tess	Well they were- they were asked. I suppose if they refused- which
	14		they couldn't because it meant if they refused the- their- their
	15		husbands might be out of work.

. . .

16	Tess	And my mother used to be tying til midnight... and I know my
17		Aunt Peggy, she was in bed all the time,
18	Gloria	Mmm.
19	Tess	and she used to like fried potatoes for supper. And the question
20		was mother said she wished Aunt Peggy [INAUD] because when
21		she- when she finished tying flowers at twelve o'clock she had to
22		go and fry spuds for her supper! .. But of course that was only a
23		question of her saying so. She was tired out of course.
24	Gloria	Course so, yeah.
25		. . .
26	Tess	But that was when Mr Potts had died, Mrs Corbett took over the
27		farm.
28	Gloria	Umm.
29	Tess	And then we had a Mr Howard here who was the Land Steward
30	Gloria	Um.
31	Tess	and he wouldn't have a woman farmer.
32	Gloria	He wouldn't?
33	Tess	No so the question is they had to give the farm up. But it was a
34		great pity because all the men were sacked.

The extract outlines the roles of women in the farming industry. Women are expected to work in the same industries as men, although this is often characterised as 'supporting' their menfolk, rather than perceived as work in its own right. Women may be unable to refuse to take on this work (ll.13–15), no matter what other responsibilities they have (ll.16–23). Notably, however, women are not allowed to be 'farmers' (l.31) – no matter how well educated they are, or if their deceased relative had served as a manager (ll.33–34).

The 'resilience of the Scillonian woman' is an ideological trope which has endured across time. The extract in (6) is taken from a 2014 interview with two young Scillonian women who were also discussing the role of women in the farming industry.

(6)	1	Kate	I'd say the women have always worked on the farms,
	2		[wouldn't you? You know-]
	3	Ann	[Yeah. Yeah,] cos your mum used to tie [with] my mum.
	4	Kate	[Yeah.]
	5		You know, and especially living over here. Most people did the
	6		summer jobs and then went on to the farms because of the flowers
	7		and that's where the w- work was in the winter, so I'd say,
	8		nearly everyone was, like- But, yeah, all the families I know,
	9		farmers,
	10	Ann	Umm.
	11	Kate	the wife's definitely like- your mum was a nurse,

12	Ann	Yeah.
13	Kate	and that's her main job, but she [always, yeah, worked on the
14	Ann	[Always worked on the farm.]
15	Kate	farm,] didn't she, whenever she had- Err, it was always her job as
16		well, [wasn't it?]
17	Ann	[Yeah.]
18	Kate	So she had three jobs. [House, nursing and farming.]
19	Emma	[LAUGHS] Wow.
20	Ann	[Yeah.]

. . .

21	Ann	[INAUDIBLE]
22	Kate	[And she] loved her [nursing, didn't she?]
23	Ann	[Yeah.]
24	Kate	But she did do both. Cos I think that's the thing with farming, you
25		know, I wouldn't say- I don't know there's many farmers here who
26		don't have their other half helping them.
27		[I wouldn't say, would you?]
28	Ann	[Not really, no.] I can't think of any really.
29	Kate	No.
30	Emma	Yeah.
31	Kate	So, um . . . SNIFFS No, I'd say it was kind of quite equal. But I do
32		think. . .I don't- EXHALES it's hard to say, but I think as Scillonians,
33		you do just get in with everything- you know, I think. . .

Much like the description in (5), in (6), Kate describes a situation in which women take on multiple jobs, including skilled work such as nursing. Interestingly, Kate does not perceive there to be inequity between men and women (l.31), despite defining women's roles in farming as 'helping' (l.26), rather than defining women as 'farmers', or workers in their own right. This provides further evidence to support the observation that education or training have few practical consequences on how hard or how much a woman is required to work, or how much acknowledgement she receives for this work. Whereas men get to define their Scillonian status on the basis of their education or their local knowledge, Kate characterises the true Scillonian woman as someone who 'get[s] in with everything' (l.33), despite receiving little explicit status in return for her labour.

Several sociolinguistic studies have demonstrated how women's language use may be conditioned by their access to particular 'linguistic markets' (Bourdieu 1977; Woolard 1985) and their ability to gain status within those markets (Milroy 1980; Eckert 2000). The market in which the Scilly-educated men operate is largely inaccessible to women by virtue of the sharp gender segregation in many of the activities undertaken by the Scilly-educated men. For instance, women do not engage in boating and fishing. These activities entail engagement with the tourist industry (tourists are taken on fishing trips and on pleasure trips from St. Mary's to Scilly's other islands), and they also bring Scilly-educated men in contact with other seafaring men from Cornwall, who use Scilly as a port. It is possible that contact around these shared practices may serve to reinforce, or at least support, the Scilly-educated males' Cornish English-like TRAP and BATH patterns. Dubois and Horvath (2000) observe a similar pattern of language use in the Cajun community where young men (but not young women) were found to 'recycle' traditional Cajun English features which were previously in decline. Dubois and Horvath (2000: 306) attribute this 'to the fact that the Cajun Renaissance has largely affected the sphere of traditional male activities, such as boating, fishing and hunting, and the display of Cajun culture associated with tourism'. Of course, this is not to say that the Cornish-like variants of TRAP and BATH are 'male' in any direct sense. Rather, they have acquired social meanings that are linked to characteristics that are more commonly associated with men than with women. That is to say, their social meanings are associated with styles of speakers (personae) and social stances which occur more frequently in the discourse of Scilly-educated Scillonian men.[4]

Many of the activities undertaken by the mainland-educated males are also largely inaccessible to women. In this generation, women are not councillors, managers or magistrates. However, the kinds of social meanings linked to these activities ('educated', 'discerning') index the characteristics of the historically dominant Scillonian identity type, as articulated in the metalinguistic commentary on the islands. This might explain why we find both groups of Scillonian women using relatively more standard-like variants of TRAP and BATH, irrespective of their social and educational background. StEE-like variants of TRAP and BATH index a Scillonian identity that is also in line with ideological expectations about female behaviour.

The ideologically loaded nature of TRAP and BATH may also help to explain why women are more constrained in their ability to use these particular linguistic forms to signal intra-gender differentiation. In Section 3, we discussed how the backing of the BATH vowel in StEE happened very gradually, and may not have been entirely complete until the beginning of the twentieth century – that is, at the very time that our speakers were born and acquiring their language variation. As Beal (2004: 141) has observed, when this change was in progress 'those who aspired to "correct" pronunciation in England had to steer a very narrow course, avoiding both the "broad" [ɑː] and the "mincing"

---

[4] See Wagner (2013) for an example of women adapting their language use as a consequence of accessing discourses more traditionally associated with men.

[æ]'. Tracing pronunciation guidance over this period, Mugglestone (2003: 78) notes that these pressures were particularly strong on women, for whom a less than careful enunciation may have led to their speech being perceived as '"inaccurate", "vulgar" or indeed "uneducated"'. Perhaps unsurprisingly, then, both Ellis (1869 iv: 1152) and Ripman (1906: 55), writing at the turn of the twentieth century, describe an 'intermediate' sound as more typical of female speakers.

Figures 12.2 and 12.3 suggest that our female speakers have a TRAP/BATH pattern that is situated in between that of our two groups of male speakers; that is to say, they have an intermediate pattern for these vowels. What we see for the Scillonian female speakers, then, may be sensitivity to the historical ideological pressures on TRAP/BATH usage, given the incredible salience of these particular vowels. That is to say, the female speakers' patterns reflect an orientation to a conservative and old-fashioned standard norm of pronunciation – one where TRAP has a quality distinct from BATH, but not too distinct as to risk being misinterpreted.

A counter argument to this might be that the behaviour of the mainland-educated men indicates that the uncertainty about the social meaning of backed BATH variants has passed for this generation of speakers. However, this would assume that both men and women are responding to the same linguistic norms, and that they are in the same stage of language change. It is not necessarily the case that something that is presumed 'vulgar' in female practice, necessarily carries the same evaluation when observed in male practice. As Eckert (1989) has argued, whilst sociolinguists have tended to evaluate language use in terms of oppositional gender categories, the effects of gender on language variation are not necessarily consistent across gender groups. This is likely to be particular true in communities, such as the one considered here, that demonstrate gender segregation in social and cultural roles.

It is important to stress that, although women behave more homogeneously than men with regard to their use of these variables, we do not wish to imply, as Jespersen (1922: 258) once did, that women are simply more linguistically alike than men. The nature of the variables we have analysed in this chapter is key. It is probable (and indeed likely, as our current research on other variables in this community is suggesting) that women use other, less ideologically loaded, linguistic features to mark intra-gender differentiation. With regards to their use of TRAP and BATH, female Scillonians' linguistic behaviour is constrained by the following factors: (i) the peculiar (and especially salient) status of TRAP and BATH in English, (ii) the link these variables have with 'education' and associated characteristics, (iii) the index-ical links between 'education' and the historically dominant delineation of the 'Scillonian' and, finally, (iv) the ideological constraints on women to conform to this 'educated' social type, and avoid linguistic behaviours that could be negatively evaluated.

6.   Conclusion

In this chapter, we have explored how life trajectory and gender interact in a small island community to affect how men and women use variables of the TRAP and BATH lexical sets. Our results showed that men defined the envelope of variation for these vowels. This was explained as a consequence of different educational experiences, which resulted in divergent life trajectories and the construction of two oppositional Scillonian identity types. The women in the community were found to show less differentiation in their linguistic variation for these vowels. Women's linguistic behaviour was explained as a consequence of constraints on women's sociolinguistic behaviour, irrespective of education types, limitations on the kind of Scillonian identities available to them, and ideological pressures to conform to gendered expectations about language use.

In the course of our analysis, we have questioned the assumption implicit in much sociolinguistic work that use of standard language features straightforwardly reflects orientation to norms external to the local community being studied. The complicated social history of the Isles of Scilly provides a context in which standard language forms take on local meanings linked to local identity types. This is not to say that the StEE-like variants of TRAP and BATH found on Scilly do not carry traces of social meanings available beyond the islands – indeed, our analysis has shown that the ideological baggage associated with variants of these vowels affects how they are used by different groups of speakers. Our point is that their use on Scilly expands and adapts their precise indexical values to reflect the social relations and histories of the islanders. In the context of their use on Scilly, the 'local "palimpsest"' effect (Lass 1976: 268–9) on these variants means that they are not just StEE-like forms, they are Scillonian forms.

Our study has suggested that there are multiple ways to index a Scillonian identity. These different identity types reflect different experiences of the local environment and different entitlements to local space and resources. Whilst it is tempting to find ways to 'distil' the essence of a particular location, our research suggests that place takes on a range of meanings linked to alternative life trajectories. We have found this to be true even in a very small, rural, island location. The Isles of Scilly meet many of the criteria of an isolated community (see Montgomery 2000; Schilling-Estes 2002: 65; Wolfram and Schilling-Estes 2006: 174–8); they are geographically remote, they exhibit historical continuity in their population, and they are relatively autonomous from the mainland in terms of their governance. Nonetheless, they exhibit sociolinguistic heterogeneity, linked to different claims about Scillonian identity. Geographical isolation may be less important than how open or exocentric community members are, as Andersen (1988) has observed. Schilling-Estes (2002: 77) has observed that the need to mark out very local distinctions may actually mean that some geographically isolated communities actually support heterogeneity better than less isolated communities. This seems to be the case in Smith and Durham's (2011) study, which shows divergent language use in one very tight-knit community in Shetland, and our data also suggests that this could be true. However, it may just be that research on geographically isolated communities has tended to more closely interrogate the social criteria by which speakers are identified, given that these communities less easily conform to the hierarchical social models used in sociolinguistic work. Perhaps all communities are more heterogeneous than has been assumed, and we are still in the process of findings ways to adequately conceptualise how individuals inhabit space and create meaning in relation to it.

REFERENCES

Andersen, Henning 1988. 'Center and periphery: Adoption, diffusion and spread', in Fisiak, J. (ed.). *Historical Dialectology*. Berlin: Mouton de Gruyter. pp. 39–83.

Banfield, Frank 1888. 'The Scillonians', in Urban, Sylvanus (ed.). *The Gentleman's Magazine, CCLXV*. London: Chatto & Windus. pp. 41–54.

Beal, Joan C. 1999. *English Pronunciation in the Eighteenth Century: Thomas Spence's Grand Repository of the English Language*. Oxford: Clarendon.
  2004. *English in Modern Times: 1700–1945*. London: Arnold.

Bourdieu, Pierre 1977. 'The economics of linguistic exchanges'. *Social Science Information* 16 (6): 645–68.

Britain, David 2009a. 'Language and space: The variationist approach', in Auer, Peter and Jürgen Erich Schmidt (eds.). *Language and Space: An International Handbook of Linguistic Variation*. Berlin: Mouton de Gruyter. pp. 142–62.
  2009b. '"Big bright lights" versus "green and pleasant land?": The unhelpful dichotomy of "urban" versus "rural" in dialectology', in Al-Wer, Enam and Rudolf de Jong (eds.). *Arabic Dialectology: In Honour of Clive Holes on the Occasion of His Sixtieth Birthday*. Leiden/Boston: Brill. pp. 223–47.

Britain, David and Peter Trudgill 1999. 'Migration, new dialect formation, and sociolinguistic refunctionalisation: Reallocation as an outcome of dialect contact'. *Transactions of the Philological Society* 97: 245–56.

Cheshire, Jenny and Peter Trudgill 1989. 'Dialect and education in the United Kingdom', in Cheshire, Jenny, Viv Edwards, Henk Munstermann and Bert Weltens (eds.). *Dialect and Education: Some European Perspectives*. Clevedon, England: Multilingual Matters. pp. 94–110.

Dubois, Sylvie and Barbara Horvath 2000. 'When the music changes, you change too: Gender and language change in Cajun English'. *Language Variation and Change* 11 (3): 287–313.

Eckert, Penelope 1989. 'The whole woman: Sex and gender differences in variation'. *Language Variation and Change* 1 (3): 245–67.

2000. *Linguistic Variation as Social Practice: The Linguistic Construction of Identity at Belten High*. Oxford: Blackwells.

2004. 'Variation and a sense of place', in Fought, Carmen (ed.). *Sociolinguistic Variation: Critical Reflections*. Cambridge: Cambridge University Press. pp. 107–18.

Ellis, Alexander J. 1869. *On Early English Pronunciation*. 5 vols. London: Trubner & Co.

Gal, Susan. 1978 'Peasant men can't get wives: Language change and sex roles in a bilingual community'. *Language in Society* 7: 1–16.

Glasberg, B. R. and B. C. J. Moore 1990. Derivation of auditory filter shapes from not noise data. *Hearing Research* 47: 103–38.

Heath, Robert 1750. *A Natural and Historical Account of the Islands of Scilly; Describing Their Situation, Number, Extent, Soil, Culture, Produce, Rareties, Towns, Fortifications, Trade, Manufacture, Inhabitants; Their Government, Laws, Customs, Grants, Records, and Antiquities*. London: R. Manby & H. S. Cox.

Holmes, Janet 1997. 'Women's talk: The question of sociolinguistic universals', in Coates, Jenny (ed.). *Language and Gender: A Reader*. Oxford, UK: Malden, Mass: Wiley-Blackwell. pp. 461–83.

Holmquist, Jonathan C. 1985. 'Social correlates of a linguistic variable: A study in a Spanish village'. *Language in Society* 14: 191–203.

Jespersen, Otto 1922. *Language: Its Nature, Development and Origin*. London: G. Allen & Unwin Ltd.

Johnstone, Barbara 2004. 'Place, globalization and linguistic variation', in Fought, Carmen (ed.). *Sociolinguistic Variation: Critical Reflections*. Cambridge: Cambridge University Press. pp. 65–83.

Johnstone, Barbara, Jennifer Andrus and Andrew E. Danielson 2006. 'Mobility, indexicality, and the enregisterment of "Pittsburghese"'. *Journal of English Linguistics* 34 (2): 77–104.

Labov, William 1963. 'The social motivation of a sound change'. *Word* 19: 273–309.

Ladefoged, Peter 1982. *A Course in Phonetics*. Second. New York: Harcourt Brace Jovanovich.

Lass, Roger 1976. *English Phonology and Phonological Theory*. Cambridge: Cambridge University Press.

Laws, Glenda 1997. 'Women's life courses, spatial mobility, and state policies', in Jones, John Paul, Heidi J. Nast and Susan M. Roberts (eds.) *Thresholds in Feminist Geography: Difference, Methodology, Representation*. Lanham, New York, Boulder, Oxford: Rowman & Littlefield. pp. 47–64.

MacMahon, Michael K. C. 1998. 'Phonology', in Romaine, Suzanne (ed.). *The Cambridge History of the English Language. 1776–1997, Volume IV:373–535*. Cambridge: Cambridge University Press. pp. 373–535.

Milroy, Lesley 1980. *Language and Social Networks*. Oxford: Basil Blackwell.

Montgomery, Michael 2000. 'Isolation as a linguistic construct'. *Southern Journal of Linguistics* 24: 41–53.

Moore, Emma and Paul Carter 2015. 'Dialect contact and distinctiveness: Capturing the multidimensionality of social meanings in an island community'. *Journal of Sociolinguistics* 19 (1): 3–36.

Mothersole, Jessie 1914. *The Isles of Scilly: Their Story, Their Folk and Their Flowers*. Second edition. London: The Religious Tract Society.

Mugglestone, Lynda 2003. *'Talking Proper': The Rise of Accent as Social Symbol*, Second edition, Oxford: Oxford University Press.

Piercy, Caroline 2010. 'One /a/ or Two?: The Phonetics, Phonology and Sociolinguistics of Change in the TRAP and BATH Vowels in the Southwest of England'. Unpublished PhD dissertation, University of Essex.

Ripman, Walter 1906. *The Sounds of Spoken English: A Manual of Ear Training for English Students*. London: Dent.

Schilling-Estes, Natalie 1998. 'Investigating "self-conscious" speech: The performance register in Ocracoke English'. *Language in Society* 27: 53–83.

    2002. 'On the nature of isolated and post-isolated dialects: Innovation, variation and differentiation'. *Journal of Sociolinguistics* 6 (1): 64–85.

Schreier, Daniel 2006. 'The backyard as dialect boundary: Individuation, linguistic heterogeneity and sociolinguistic eccentricity in a small speech community'. *Journal of English Linguistics* 34 (1): 25–57.

Smith, Jennifer and Mercedes Durham 2011. 'A tipping point in dialect obsolescence? Change across the generations in Lerwick, Shetland'. *Journal of Sociolinguistics* 15 (2): 197–225.

Strobl, Carolin, Anne-Laure Boulesteix, Thomas Kneib, Thomas Augustin and Achim Zeileis 2008. 'Conditional variable importance for random forests'. *BMC Bioinformatics* 9: 307.

Strobl, Carolin, Torsten Hothorn and Achim Zeileis 2009. 'Party on! A new, conditional variable-importance measure for random forests available in the party package'. *The R Journal* 1 (2): 14–17.

The Isles of Scilly Council 2005. *'The Isles of Scilly Local Plan: A 2020 Vision.'* The Isles of Scilly Council.

Thomas, Charles 1979. 'A glossary of spoken English in the Isles of Scilly'. *Journal of the Royal Institution of Cornwall*: 109–47.

Wagner, Suzanne Evans 2013. '"We act like girls and we don't act like men': Ethnicity and local language change in a Philadelphia high school'. *Language in Society* 42 (4): 361–83.

Wakelin, Martyn F. 1975. *Language and History in Cornwall*. Leicester: Leicester University Press.

    1986. *The Southwest of England*. Amsterdam: John Benjamins Publishing Company.

Wells, John Christopher 1982. *Accents of English: The British Isles*. Cambridge: Cambridge University Press.

Wolfram, Walt and Natalie Schilling-Estes 2006. *American English: Dialects and Variation*. Wiley-Blackwell.

Wong, Amy Wing-mei and Lauren Hall-Lew 2014. 'Regional variability and ethnic identity: Chinese Americans in New York City and San Francisco'. *Language & Communication* 35: 27–42.

Woodley, George 1822. *View of the Present State of the Scilly Islands: Exhibiting Their Vast Importance to the British Empire*. London: Longman and Co.

Woolard, Kathryn A. 1985. 'Language variation and cultural hegemony'. *American Ethnologist* 12: 738–48.

Part IV

Enregistering Places

13 Characterological Figures and Expressive Style in the Enregisterment of Linguistic Variety

Barbara Johnstone

1. Introduction

Linguists have traditionally thought about linguistic variation in terms of relatively stable sets of linguistic rules or conventions called 'varieties' that can be mapped onto physical or social spaces. A person who employs features of a particular variety can, in this way of thinking, be identified with the place or group the dialect maps onto. But sociolinguists' work over the past decade or two has productively complicated this picture. We now ask questions about why people use features of one variety or another rather than assuming that people inevitably speak the way they first learned to speak, and the answers we arrive at have to do with identity and agency, rather than with geography and demography. And we ask how linguistic features get linked with varieties in the first place. How do particular words, ways of pronouncing words, grammatical patterns and patterns of intonation come to point to particular identities and activities?

One way of answering this question comes from linguistic anthropologists in the semiotic tradition. Drawing on the work of Roman Jakobson and Charles S. Peirce, anthropologists Michael Silverstein (1992, 1993, 2003) and Asif Agha (2003, 2007) have developed a framework that helps us see how 'social meanings' and linguistic choices can come to be linked, and how sets of linguistic choices can come to be understood as varieties. Two of the key concepts in this framework are *indexicality* and *enregisterment*. A sign is indexical if it is related to its meaning by virtue of co-occurring with the thing it is taken to mean. When we hear thunder, we often experience lightning, rain and a darkening sky, so the sound of thunder may lead us to expect a storm. Because the sound of thunder evokes storminess in this way, thunder noise can be used to evoke a storm in a staged play. Likewise, if hearing a particular word or structure used, or a word pronounced a particular way, is experienced in connection with a particular style of dress or grooming, a particular set of social alignments, or a particular social activity, that pronunciation may evoke and/or create a social identity, eventually even in the absence of other cues.

Indexical links are created in the context of already-available models of what meanings are possible and what kinds of forms can index them. For example, people often hear the difference between two variants as meaning 'correct' in the case of one and 'incorrect' in the case of the other, or as meaning 'us' in the case of one and 'them' in the case of the other. To talk about this, it is useful to use Agha's (2003, 2007) concept of enregisterment. According to Agha (2007: 81), enregisterment refers to 'processes and practices whereby performable signs become recognized (and regrouped) as belonging to distinct, differentially valorized semiotic registers by a population.' *Registers* (which Agha also calls 'semiotic registers' or 'register formations') are 'cultural models of action that link diverse behavioral signs to enactable effects, including images of persona, interpersonal relationship and type of conduct' (Agha 2007: 145). A register emerges when a number of indexical relationships begin to be seen as related; a particular linguistic form (or nonlinguistic sign) is enregistered when it becomes included in a register. A register, in Agha's sense may be a way of speaking linked with a 'social situation.' This is, of course, how the term is traditionally used in linguistics (Biber and Finegan 1994). But registers can be associated with any sort of social meaning.

In keeping with his social constructivist, emergentist stance, however, Agha calls attention to the difficulty of using a count noun, *register*, to talk about a process. Registers appear to stabilize into nameable, describable objects only when people orient to them, and people orient to particular sets of forms in certain contexts, for certain reasons. As Agha (2007: 168) puts it, 'A register exists as a bounded object only to a degree set by sociohistorical processes of enregisterment, processes whereby its forms and values become differentiable from the rest of language ... for a given population of speakers'. Registers, as countable, bounded entities, only come into existence when there is some reason for people to reflect on them; they are, in other words, 'reflexive'.

For variationist sociolinguists, the concept of enregisterment can be of use in the exploration of linguistic variation linked with contextual variation of any kind. Much of the sociolinguistic research about enregisterment has had to do with linguistic forms or set of linguistic forms that are linked, by linguists and/ or by laypeople, with places (Johnstone *et al.* 2006; Johnstone and Kiesling 2008; Beal 2009, 2012; Remlinger 2009; Johnstone 2011a, 2011b, 2013a; Campbell-Kibler 2012; Slotta 2012; Cramer 2013), but the idea has also been fruitful in the study of 'standard' varieties (Agha 2003; Frekko 2009; Dong 2010; Managan 2011; Romero 2012; Jaspers and Van Hoof 2013), genres and situational varieties (Wilce 2008; Squires 2010; Babel 2011; Williams 2012; Donaldson 2013; Madsen 2013), social groups (Henry 2010; Eberhardt 2012) and social relations (Goebel 2007, 2008).

In this chapter, I join a number of sociolinguists who have explored how linguistic variation can be enregistered with styles, personas or identities (Newell, 2009; Gibson 2011; Marzo and Ceuleers 2011; Podesva 2011; Bennett 2012). I develop Asif Agha's (2007) idea of the 'characterological figure' as a focus of register-formation. Although he does not discuss the concept in any detail, Agha suggests that a linguistic feature or a set of features can be ideologically linked via enregisterment with a way of being and acting associated not just with a social identity in an abstract sense, but with its embodiment in a character, imagined or actually performed. Agha defines a characterological figure as an 'image of personhood that is performable through a semiotic display or enactment' (Agha 2007: 177). The chapter illustrates the utility of this notion through an analysis of two talking dolls. I show how the dolls both presuppose (point to) and entail (help to create) the characterological figure of the Yinzer, a persona with a certain kind of social identity strongly linked with the city of Pittsburgh. I focus on the appearance of the dolls and some of the visual material related to them, what the dolls say, how they talk, and how their social identities are represented in their fictional biographies. I show that artifacts like these dolls invite their consumers to re-enregister a set of forms that are already enregistered with place and known as 'Pittsburghese' with a particular communicative style and stance associated with a post-industrial stereotype of the working class.

2.   Pittsburghese

My research site is Pittsburgh, Pennsylvania, where local identity has been tightly tied since the 1960s to 'Pittsburghese' (Johnstone 2013b). Pittsburghese is Pittsburgh speech as it is locally imagined. In other words, it is a set of linguistic forms that, over the course of the twentieth century, were enregistered with the city of Pittsburgh in popular discourse. While the set of linguistic features that is represented when people talk about, perform or otherwise invoke Pittsburghese overlaps with the set of features (many traceable to the English of the earliest colonial settlers of the area) that a linguist might describe as characteristic of the area, it is not the same.[1] This is because Pittsburghese results from a different set of ideas, processes and practices than does the set of forms a linguist might describe. The set of linguistic features included in descriptions or uses of Pittsburghese is continually evolving. People continue to suggest and to use new Pittsburghese items and to argue about what should be included and why, and the visibility of particular

---

[1] For one thing, Pittsburghese is associated almost exclusively with white people. It draws very little on the speech of southwestern Pennsylvania's African Americans, except where their distinctive speech patterns overlap with those of whites.

Pittsburghese items waxes and wanes. For example, *yinz*, 'you, pl.', and various forms of the verb *jag* have long been included in glossaries of Pittsburghese, but *yinz* and *jagoff*, 'a stupid or annoying person', have become much more visible since around 2005; *grinnie*, 'chipmunk', used to show up on such lists but no longer does.

Before around 2000, representations of Pittsburghese typically arose from and reflected nostalgia for the remembered past. Dictionaries of Pittsburghese included local place names and words and phrases that the consumers of the dictionaries actually used or that they associated with things people actually remembered doing during the 1950s and 1960s. Pittsburghese was described as how Pittsburghers talk, or at least how they used to talk, and the people who talked about Pittsburghese often claimed to speak it themselves and certainly knew and regularly heard people who did.

During the first two decades of the twenty-first century, however, Pittsburghese has increasingly come to be reimagined not just as how lifelong Pittsburghers talk but as how a certain kind of Pittsburgher talks, the type known as a 'Yinzer'. The term *Yinzer* is derived from a local speech form, the pronoun *yinz*. It appears to have emerged sometime in the 1960s, possibly in high-school slang, but it was not in common use until around 2000. *Yinzer* can be used disparagingly or fondly, depending on who uses it to label whom, but it is increasingly used in the latter way, as a claim to localness. In 2003–4, in the course of sociolinguistic interviews, I asked Pittsburghers whether they were familiar with the term *Yinzer*. Older people tended not to recognize the word, while younger people did. A folk dictionary of Pittsburghese (McCool 1982) published in 1982 does not include *Yinzer*, and *Yinzer* does not appear in a corpus of print representations of Pittsburgh speech I assembled between 1997 and 2000 (Johnstone *et al.* 2002). Over the course of the 2000s, the word *Yinzer* has become more and more visible, and its appearance in the final volume of the *Dictionary of Regional American English* (Hall 2012) has given it an official seal of approval, in some people's eyes. Like the earlier processes that enregistered Pittsburghese with the remembered past, the processes that are now re-enregistering Pittsburghese with the characterological figure of the Yinzer have been driven by people who live in Pittsburgh, or are former Pittsburghers. But the development and circulation of the Yinzer persona seems to be linked to the influx in the 2000s of young, well-educated, middle- or upper-middle-class people to whom Pittsburgh appeals because of its 'gritty' industrial past together with jobs in the technology, medical and educational sectors, appealing cultural amenities, and desirable, affordable living spaces. These new residents are much less likely than older, longer-term residents to actually interact with working-class Pittsburghers on a regular basis, and their encounters with Pittsburghese are as much or more in the form of written representations of it than by talking to people who speak with local accents. It is this population, together with native Pittsburghers who likewise tend not to have local accents themselves, who constitute the primary social domain for the enregisterment of features of Pittsburghese with the characterological figure of the Yinzer.

In what follows, I explore this development by means of an analysis of two talking plush dolls called 'Yappin' Yinzers'. I ask what can be read from the way the characterological figure of the Yinzer is embodied in these plush dolls about what a Yinzer is and about the relationship between Yinzerness and Pittsburghese. I show that, as represented via artifacts like the Yappin' Yinzers, Pittsburghese is not just a set of words and phrases, but an expressive stance whose roots in the material conditions of working-class life have been for the most part erased.

3.   The Yappin' Yinzers

There are two Yappin' Yinzers, one representing an adult male and called 'Chipped Ham Sam', and the other, 'Nebby Debbie', representing an adult female. Figure 13.1 shows the home page of the website advertising them.

At 10 inches (25.4 cm) and 9 inches (23 cm), respectively, they are smaller than most dolls that are meant for children, and the battery-powered plastic sound module accessible through an opening in their backs adds to their unsuitability as toys. Each time one of the dolls is squeezed in the middle, the sound module plays a sentence uttered by someone using a Pittsburghese accent, highlighting one or more Pittsburghese words or phrases. The dolls are produced and sold by Colloquial Enterprises, LLC, which is based in a suburb of Pittsburgh. (They are manufactured in China.) The male doll, Chipped Ham Sam, went on sale in 2007, the female one, Nebby Debbie, a year or two later.

4.   How the Yappin' Yinzers Link Pittsburghese with Class

The design of the website where the dolls are for sale links the dolls with place and local practice in many ways. The primary colors on the page are black and gold, the colors of Pittsburgh's professional sports teams and the city's official seal, and the dolls are superimposed on a photograph of part of Pittsburgh's downtown skyline. A stylized version of the skyline can also be seen around the small image at the bottom center, which can be read as a cartoon representation of Chipped Ham Sam holding a cheeseburger and a mug of beer, and wearing a Pittsburgh Steelers football jersey and helmet. The dolls are also linked with Pittsburghese via their designation as 'Yappin' Yinzers', via the phrase on the homepage, 'Da yinz nowumsayin'?' (Do you know what I'm saying?), and via their names. 'Chipped ham' (a kind of sandwich meat that was invented and sold by a Pittsburgh-area dairy-store chain) is often on lists

Figure 13.1: The Yappin' Yinzers.[12]

of Pittsburghese words and phrases. Pittsburghers sometimes report not knowing that it was a regional item until they ordered it or looked for it somewhere else, an experience that often causes people to enregister words with places. 'Nebby' is an adjective of northern English and Scotch-Irish origin meaning nosy. The link between Pittsburghese and the dolls' identity is made even tighter through the rhyming of 'chipped ham' and 'Sam' and 'nebby' and 'Debbie'.

Chipped Ham Sam and Nebby Debbie represent imaginary people, and they talk. Because they have bodies, clothes, facial features, hairstyles, voices and even personal histories in the form of biographies on small cards that come with them, the dolls package Pittsburghese with particular lifestyles and biographies in ways that other artifacts do not, or do less. For one thing, the way the dolls are designed puts the connection between Pittsburghese and social class front and center, forcing us to consider what social class is, how it intersects with ethnicity, gender and other aspects of Pittsburghers' identity, and how it is linked to Pittsburgh's identity as a collective. For another thing, what Sam and Debbie's voices sound like and what they say lead us to

---

[2] http://yappinYinzers.com, accessed 10 June 2014.

consider how a particular rhetorical stance towards the world is implicated in how the people who buy them understand Pittsburghese.

It would be hard to miss the way in which Chipped Ham Sam and Nebby Debbie link Pittsburghese with the characterological figure of the Yinzer. Sam and Debbie are not just dolls that happen to speak in Pittsburghese. They are 'Yappin' Yinzers'. The Pittsburghese they speak is part and parcel of the fact that they are Yinzers. Their Pittsburgese presupposes their Yinzer identity (the Pittsburghese that emerges from the sound module when the dolls are squeezed is one of the things that identifies the dolls as Yinzers), and the Yinzerishness of their voices, their appearances, and the life stories they come with helps to identify their speech as Pittsburghese.

For one thing, the dolls' appearance links them to the characterological figure of the Yinzer and the Yinzer figure to them. Both dolls look like white people. Chipped Ham Sam has blond hair in the style popular in the 1980s known as a 'mullet'. Nebby Debbie's hair is brown, pulled back from her face except for a few bangs on her forehead. Both dolls have large, open mouths, extending almost from ear to ear. Sam's abdomen is exposed, attention drawn to it with a sewn-on plush ball representing his navel. Debbie wears gold hoop earrings and makeup: mascara, yellow eyeshadow, bright red lipstick and rust-colored finger- and toenail polish. She is wearing a black mesh top over a sleeveless gold t-shirt, tracksuit trousers with orange stripes and black mules with heels. Sam has on a Steelers jersey with the number 0 and, on the back, where a player's name usually goes, 'YINZER' is printed. He is wearing blue cut-off shorts, gold and black socks and shoes that might be taken to be construction boots. To the Pittsburghers and ex-Pittsburghers who buy them for themselves or as gifts, Sam and Debbie are likely to be taken as unsophisti-cated and somewhat backward in style.

The front of the card that comes attached to each doll's arm identifies the doll as a Pittsburgher. The top two thirds of the page have the words (in gold) 'yappin' Yinzers' superimposed on a photo of the Pittsburgh downtown skyline. Under this is 'Pittsburghers with personality' and the doll's name. The claim that the dolls have 'personality' suggests that they are to be seen as larger than life in some ways, but it also points to how they are meant to evoke personas. Inside each card on the left-hand page is a set of three bulleted 'quick facts' about each doll. On the right-hand page is the heading '9 Hilarious Pittsburgh Sayings' with three of the doll's utterances reproduced in speech balloons emanating from skyline building windows. We return to the 'sayings' shortly.

The 'quick facts' about Chipped Ham Sam are these, as they appear in the card:

1. Born of Polish and Ukrainian parents (with whom he will most likely always reside) on 12 October 1975 – exactly 9 months to the day from the Lombardi trophy's first arrival in the 'burgh'.

2. Given the nickname 'Chipped Ham' because of his insatiable desire for barbequed chipped ham sandwiches, a local delicacy.
3. A fanatical supporter of Pittsburgh sports, Sam can usually be found screaming at a television at one of his favorite South Side watering holes.

Sam is identified in ethnic terms, as having Eastern European parents. He is identified as a fan of Pittsburgh sports and implicitly as the child of sports fans, conceived right after the Steelers' first national championship. (The Lombardi trophy is held by the winners of the year's Super Bowl.) He is identified as being in younger middle age (born in 1975, which means that he would have been 32 in 2007 when he was created). He lives with his parents. He is identified by what he eats (chipped ham sandwiches) and where he drinks (South Side watering holes or bars). 'South Side' links him with an older working-class neighborhood and with its transformation into an area where people now go to drink. And he is identified as someone who 'screams at a television'.

The quick facts about Nebby Debbie are the following:

1. A life-long resident of the Pittsburgh borough of McKees Rocks and almost a graduate of the local High School, Debbie has found recent fame as the top nail stylist in the area. Her signature rhinestone-leopard nail art is most requested by her loyal customers, followed by black-and-gold zebra stripes.
2. You can find Debbie trolling for love on most Friday and Saturday nights at various Station Square, Strip District and Mt. Washington hot spots, as well as anywhere the city puts on fireworks or is giving away bobble heads.
3. Boy is Debbie nebby. She seems to know interesting little tidbits about everyone in town, and if she feels she is missing any of the scoop, believe me, she'll ask.

Debbie is not identified in ethnic terms, but instead in terms of the working-class neighborhood she is from (McKees Rocks), her education ('almost' a high-school graduate), her profession (fingernail stylist), and the tastes of her professional clients (rhinestone-leopard and black-and-gold nail designs). Like Sam, Debbie is linked with social practices and consumption, but these involve sex (trolling for love), spectacle (fireworks), and the consumption of things (bobble head dolls), rather than sports and the consumption of food. Both dolls are identified in ways that evoke a style of communication, Sam by 'screaming at [the] TV' and Debbie by being nosy ('nebby'), gossiping ('seems to know interesting little tidbits about everyone in town'), and being unafraid to dig for information ('believe me, she'll ask').

The communicative style that is both evoked and suggested by the Yappin' Yinzers is also enacted in their actual speech, in the form of the pre-recorded utterances that play when the sound module is activated with a squeeze. Although both are advertised as coming with nine 'hilarious Pittsburgh

Nebby Debbie

1. Jeat yet? 'Did you eat yet?'
2. You ain't gonna believe this, I just saw whutsername with whutsisface. 'You aren't going to believe this, I just saw what's-her-name with what's-his-name.'
3. **How 'bout yinz redd up them rooms [ruᵚmz] before comp'ny comes over [oᵚvr]?** 'How about if you (pl.) clean up those rooms before company comes over?'
4. **Yinz better settle down [da:n]!** 'You (pl.) had better settle down!'
5. **Watch out when yinz go outside, it's col' out there today.** 'Watch out when you (pl.) go outside. It's cold out there today.'
6. I hafta go da da bafroom. 'I have to go to the bathroom.'
7. **Yinz ain't 'posed to be out [a:t], yinz are grounded [gra:ndəd]!** 'You (pl.) aren't supposed to be out. You (pl.) are grounded (confined to the house).'
8. **You're 'posed to put a gumband around [əra:nd] it.** 'You're supposed to put a rubber band around it.'
9. I ain't payin' no hundert dollars [dɔwɛrz] fer 'at! 'I will not pay a hundred dollars for that.'
10. What's goin' [goᵚɪn] on? 'What's going on?'
11. **Get [gɪt] out of [a:tə] town [ta:n]!** 'Get out of town!'

Chipped Ham Sam

1. *What yinz doin' over [oᵚvr] dere?* 'What are you (pl.) doing over there?'
2. *Come off it, fer cryin' out [a:t] loud [la:d]!* 'Come off it, for crying out loud!'
3. *Hows come yinz ain't watchin' the [ə] game?* Pixburgh's on. 'How come you (pl.) aren't watching the game? Pittsburgh's on.'
4. Jeez oh [oᵚ] man! 'Jeez oh man!'
5. *Nuh-uh!* 'No!'
6. *Quit jaggin' around [əra:nd]!* 'Quit fooling around!'
7. *Jinz eat jet?* I'm gettin' hungry fer a sammich. 'Did you (pl.) eat yet? I'm getting hungry for a sandwich.'
8. I'm going down [da:n] the Southside [sa:said] to drink some Irons n'at. 'I'm going down to the Southside to drink some Iron City beer, and things like that.'
9. I'm taking the trolley [trɔwi] downtown [da:nta:n]. 'I'm taking the trolley downtown.'

> Figure 13.2: The 'sayings' of the Yappin' Yinzers. (Italics indicate marked pitch or volume; bold text indicates 'directives' and the ᵚ symbol shows frontedness [see discussion following].

sayings', Debbie actually comes with eleven. Figure 13.2 lists and glosses the dolls' utterances. (For non-standard pronunciation, I use conventional respellings where available, International Phonetic Alphabet elsewhere.)

The Pittsburghese word represented most often in both Sam and Debbie's speech is *yinz*, 'you pl.', which is heard eight times in the twenty utterances. Versions of *Jeat jet?* 'Did you eat yet?, Have you eaten yet?' appear in both dolls' repertoires. Other lexical items often associated with Pittsburghese are

Irons 'Iron City beer', *n'at* 'and things like that', *redd up* 'tidy up', and *gumbands* 'rubber bands'. *How's come* 'why, how come' and *nuh-uh* [nʌ ˈʔʌ:], an emphatic 'no!', are also sometimes found on lists of Pittsburghese (Johnstone *et al.* 2002; Johnstone 2013b: 3–40). Both dolls use *ain't*, and there is one instance of negative concord in Nebby Debbie's speech ('I ain't payin' no hundert dowers fer 'at!'). Phonologically, the dolls' speech sounds casual, with numerous elided syllables and sounds. Both voices use Pittsburgh accents, though somewhat inconsistently. Of the many words in the utterances that could showcase the area's characteristic monophthongal /aw/ (*down, out, outside, grounded, around, loud* and *downtown*), not all are actually monophthongized every time. Both speakers use fronted versions of the vowel in words such as *over, going* and *oh*, and Debbie's voice fronts the /u/ in *rooms*. Each script includes a word that showcases /l/-vocalization, *trolley* for Sam and *dollars* for Debbie, and both voices strongly vocalize these /l/s. In *bafroom*, Debbie is represented as using /f/ for /θ/.

The speech acts performed by these utterances lean heavily toward the directive. The bold-faced items in the lists in Figure 13.2 are all things a person could say to get someone else to do something. These include 'Come off it', 'Quit jaggin' around', 'Yinz better settle down' and so on. Of the twenty utterances by the two dolls, eight (arguably nine, if 'What's going on?' is taken as a suggestion that the addressees stop what they are doing) could be used as directives. ('Get out of town' and 'Come off it' could also be used as exclamatives, of course.) Almost half of the time, then, the Yappin' Yinzers tell other people what to do or what not to do. Nebby Debbie's audience is also called up by what she says. *Whutsername* and *whutsisface* could suggest that she is accustomed to talking to people she knows well, people who will be able to identify who is being talked about, or that she does not think it is important for her interlocutors to be able to identify them. All but one of her directives represent instructions that adults (especially mothers) address to children, instructions to tidy up, settle down, put on warm clothes before going outside, get back into the house.

Another attribute of the Yinzer speech style, as it is exemplified in the dolls, is a distinctive tone of voice. This occurs only in the male doll's speech, in the phrases that are italicized in Figure 13.2. In these phrases, the pitch and volume of Chipped Ham Sam's voice are raised. The effect of this higher, louder voice is to make him sound aggrieved and petulant.

As represented via these dolls, the Yinzer character is highly gendered. Male Yinzers, the dolls suggest, go to bars to eat and drink, females to find romance. Male Yinzers like sports; female Yinzers like the fireworks that sometimes follow sports events, and the souvenir bobble-head dolls that are sometimes given away there. Male Yinzers wear an outdated hairstyle from the 1980s; female Yinzers wear a lot of makeup. Males yell at the Steelers; females yell at their children. But there are also many commonalities, especially in how their speech styles are represented.

Who, then, is the prototypical Yinzer, as this character is figured in the Yappin' Yinzer dolls? He or she is a white Pittsburgher who does things in Pittsburgh, a sports fan or at least a wearer of the team colors. A Yinzer dresses casually. A Yinzer uses Pittsburghese words and sounds like a Pittsburgher. A Yinzer has a big mouth, and when he or she opens it, the voice that emerges is casual and sometimes non-standard. A Yinzer is uninhibited, not afraid to tell people what to do. A Yinzer yaps.

Judging from what the dolls look like, how they are described, what they say, and how they say it, we might be tempted to say that the Yinzer character is working class. But what would this mean? Neither Chipped Ham Sam nor Nebby Debbie is explicitly identified as working class. Sam is not assigned a job, a trade, or a profession in the biography that accompanies him. Debbie is identified as a nail stylist, which means that she may be an independent operator, not a salaried worker. Neither doll is dressed in work clothes (although Sam wears what might be work boots). The dolls' income is not specified. Nothing they say has explicitly to do with socio-economic class. And yet there are reasons to claim that consumers are meant to think of the Yinzer figure, as it is represented in the dolls, as working class. One of these reasons is their communicative style.

5.   Social Class and Communicative Style

Scholars continue to debate about how to define social class, and this is not the place to rehash the entire debate. The view I take here is similar to that of other ethnographers of the post-industrial 'working class' (Weis 1990; Foley 1990; Dunk 1991; Fox 1997; Lindquist 2002). According to scholars like these, the social identities associated with class result from the material circumstances of work (one's relationship to the means of production, whether as hourly wage-earner, on one end of the spectrum, or as owner and/or investor, on the other) as well as the ideology that shapes how a person makes sense of those circumstances. Social class is thus both a material and a cultural phenomenon. People's understanding of their own place in the economic system – and what that entails when it comes to how to act, talk and think – is shaped by models that circulate as people perform class identity in interaction with others. People have various ways of talking about this aspect of social identity, some of which do not involve using the term 'working class' at all, and 'working-class culture' can take a wide variety of forms. Still, the concept of class is useful, even if the people we study may not overtly orient to it. In a capitalist economy, the need to work (or not), along with the kind of work one does, shapes how people think and talk about identity just as biology shapes how people understand gender and sexuality, and physical appearance shapes how people understand race. As Julie Lindquist (2002: 5) explains it in the introduction to an analysis of working-class rhetorical practices, 'implicit in my claim to take as my subject "working-class culture" is the assumption that shared cultural experiences (and the narrative processes and products of these experiences) are linked to material conditions'.

One aspect of the working-class experience is opposition. As Thomas W. Dunk (1991: 27, emphasis mine) puts it in a study of a 'working man's town' in Ontario, Canada, 'Class happens because of the common experiences of a group of people whose interests are different from *and usually opposed to* the interests of another group'. This may be opposition rooted in competing economic interests, as in the classical Marxist account. This is the sort of opposition that leads to labor unions, to negotiations over wages, hours, and working conditions and to strikes. Or it may be opposition rooted in struggles against the hegemonic ideology circulated in bourgeois institutions and practices like schooling, as in more recent interpretations of Marxism (Thompson 1966; Gramsci 1971; Williams 1982). This is the sort of opposition that leads working-class teens to reject school culture (Weis 1990; Eckert 1996, 2000, 2004) and adults to value low-culture activities like team sports that involve group physical activity over high-culture intellectual ones like theater or ballet (Dunk 1991: 90–1). It is the sort of opposition that leads working-class arguers to value the 'common sense' that arises from lived experience over 'formal, theoretical knowledge that is not immediately applicable to work and to action' (Lindquist 2002: 99).

Linguistic anthropologist Douglas Foley (1989) takes this argument a step further, suggesting that class differences in post-industrial settings are fundamentally differences in expressive style. Foley combines Jürgen Habermas' (1984) insights about how communication is affected by modern economic life with Erving Goffman's (1959, 1981, 1986) analyses of 'the performance of self'. Goffman claimed to be describing how social interaction always works, everywhere, and was apparently uninterested in how inequality could be created and perpetuated in interaction. Foley, however, sees Goffman as 'an ethnographer of communication in late capitalist society, despite [Goffman's] claims to universality' (Foley 1989: 149). Foley points out that 'Goffman's empirical descriptions of communication look very like what Habermas calls instrumental action'(152). Habermas' work critiques modern, bureaucratic, knowledge and service economies, where ways of speaking have become increasingly regimented. What Habermas calls 'instrumental rationality', geared toward efficiency, productivity and profit, requires people to perform elaborately constructed identities in highly staged, instrumental interaction, where 'traditional normative ideals about doing what one says and being sincere and truthful become less of a constraint on communicative action'

(Foley 1989: 155) than the ability to manage one's identity by playing the kinds of language games Goffman describes. For Foley, working-class social identity is 'stigmatized', in Goffman's terms, because traditional working-class expressive norms are different from and opposed to those of the 'normal' social actors Goffman focuses on. As Foley (1989: 151) describes it:

> Two generalized class roles are routinely enacted in recurring everyday situational speech performances. Bourgeois/petit bourgeois actors typically assume they are leaders with 'normal' identities and superior speech, who have the right to speak often and in an official manner. Standard, official speech is authoritative and proper. Proper, polite speech and etiquette become a strategic weapon in their everyday communication. . . . Conversely, working-class actors assume they are outsiders and subordinates with 'stigmatized' identities and inferior speech. . . . Unofficial speech is often non-standard, informal, and lacking in politeness forms. Impolite speech becomes an unstrategic form of expressiveness that either meekly enacts the subordinate, stigmatized role of outsider, or openly, hostilely rejects it. These more open, dialogic speech practices help preserve the dual role and identity of an uncultured, inferior outsider and rebel.

The communicative style of the 'working class actor' Foley describes here maps almost exactly onto that of the Yinzer persona. Located outside the new economy and its regimented modes of speech, the Yinzer can speak freely, using casual, non-standard, regionally marked speech forms, speaking directly, telling people off, gossiping and yelling. But the Yinzer is also frustrated, petulant and sometimes whiny. Her kids misbehave; his team makes idiotic plays on the football field. Yinzers have big mouths and are unafraid to open them, but when they do, they yap powerlessly, like miniature dogs that think they are bigger than they are.

As enregistered in artifacts like these dolls, Pittsburghese is not just a set of words and phrases, but an expressive stance. The dolls embody a stance that is both oppositional and powerless, embedded in a specific set of consumption practices, communicative needs and vocal styles. While Pittsburghese t-shirts and other such artifacts link words and meanings with place and to a certain extent with local practice (Johnstone 2009), the dolls much more explicitly invite their consumers to enregister Pittsburghese with a specific stance toward the world, the stance of the Yinzer, limiting the possible meanings of speaking Pittsburghese in a way that other artifacts do not. The Yappin' Yinzers help focus and standardize not only what counts as Pittsburghese but who speaks it, what they say, and how they sound when they say it.

6.   Discussion

Why, then, would anybody buy one of these dolls? Foley's analysis suggests a way to answer this question. As noted, working-class expressive culture is oppositional. According to Foley, working-class actors like the Yappin'

Yinzers resist the expectations of lifestyle and speech style that are tied to the kinds of non-physical labor that are increasingly the only option: the expectations that one finish school, speak properly and politely, and so on. They resist the commodification of speech in the form of the scripts that a call-center employee has to read, the put-on friendliness of mall-store employees, the carefully managed speech style of the well-trained teacher or manager, the untrustworthy identity performance of lawyers. They resist what Foley refers to as the 'theft of communicative labor' in 'an overly administered world of manufactured symbols and identities' (Foley 1989: 156). Working-class expressive style makes a claim to authenticity, to the realness of people who are not putting on elaborate performances of self.

But 'such expressions of cultural resistance may also become commercialised' (Foley 1989: 156). This happens when the Yinzer persona, once linked causally with the experience of being working class, gets de-linked from the actual conditions of labor and appropriated as a second-order symbol of local authenticity. Once this happens, people start to use the term *Yinzer* for anyone from or even just living in Pittsburgh. TV reporters and teachers – members of the speech-regimented new economy – now adopt elements of a Yinzer persona when they perform Pittsburghese, leaning forward, raising their voices, speaking in a higher pitch, complaining, giving orders, calling people *jagoffs* (a Pittsburghese word derived from the verb *jag* that traditionally meant 'idiot' but has come to have obscene overtones). The Yappin' Yinzer dolls represent a way of life that their consumers, participants in the post-industrial economy, would not choose for themselves. But the dolls also evoke nostalgia for an imagined time when people could speak their minds and sound like whoever they were, an imagined time when there was no need for the kind of persona management that is now required.

However, neither Sam nor Debby is represented as having a traditional working-class job, and this leads to another way of interpreting the Yinzer figure's meaning. Sam's work, if any, is not specified, and Debby is an independent entrepreneur at the bottom of the cline of prestige when it comes to careers. The dolls act working class in some ways, but their actual work is not the skilled labor, protected by union contracts and paid a comfortable wage, that people think of when they think of the American working class of the twentieth century. They are 'working-class without work' to use Lois Weis's (1990) term, exemplars of a post-industrial stereotype that exists not only in Pittsburgh, but also in other places where people whose forebears were proud of their labor are now marginal and often struggling. This means that the dolls can be seen not just as representations of former working-class Pittsburghers – ideologically linked with 'us', even by people whose forbears were not miners or steelworkers – but also as representations of a pathetic, marginalized class of contemporary Pittsburghers, who are ideologically 'other'.

To summarize, the Yappin' Yinzers enregister Pittsburghese, along with other modes of action, appearance and taste, with a characterological figure that can be evaluated in at least two ways. The first is as a positively valorized reminder of working-class Pittsburghers of the past, and the second is as an image of the stigmatized post-working-class Pittsburghers of the present. They complicate the semiotic value of Pittsburghese in a way that is more and more typical, as Pittsburghese moves from being a representation of a way of speaking that people remember, to being an icon of a persona linked with a way of life.

REFERENCES

Agha, Asif 2003. 'The social life of a cultural value'. *Language and Communication* 23: 231–73.
    2007. *Language and Social Relations*. New York: Cambridge University Press.
Babel, Anna M. 2011. 'Why don't all contact features act alike? Contact features as enregistered features'. *Journal of Language Contact* 1: 56–91.
Beal, Joan C. 2009. 'Enregisterment, commodification, and historical context: "Geordie" versus "Sheffieldish"'. *American Speech* 84: 138–56
    2012. '"By those provincials mispronounced": The strut vowel in eighteenth-century pronouncing dictionaries'. *Language & History* 55: 5–17.
Bennett, Joe 2012. '"And what comes out may be a kind of screeching": The stylisation of chavspeak in contemporary Britain'. *Journal of Sociolinguistics* 16: 5–27.
Biber, Douglas and Edward Finegan 1994. 'An analytical framework for register studies', in Biber, Douglas and Edward Finegan (eds.) *Dimensions of Register Variation*. Cambridge: Cambridge University Press. pp. 31–56.
Campbell-Kibler, Kathryn 2012. 'Contestation and enregisterment in Ohio's imagined dialects'. *Journal of English Linguistics* 40: 281–305.
Cramer, Jennifer 2013. 'Styles, stereotypes, and the South: Constructing identities at the linguistic border'. *American Speech* 88: 144–67.
Donaldson, Coleman 2013. 'Jula Ajami in Burkina Faso: A grassroots literacy in the former Kong Empire'. *Working Papers in Educational Linguistics* 28: 19–36.
Dong, Jie 2010. 'The enregisterment of Putonghua in practice'. *Language & Communication* 30: 265–75.
Dunk, Thomas W. 1991. *It's a Working Man's Town: Male Working-Class Culture in Northwestern Ontario*. Montreal and Kingston: McGill-Queen's University Press.
Eberhardt, Maeve 2012. 'Enregisterment of Pittsburghese and the local African American community'. *Language & Communication* 32: 358–71.
Eckert, Penelope 1996. '(ay) goes to the city: exploring the expressive use of variation', in Guy, Gregory R., Crawford Feagin, Deborah Schiffrin and John Baugh (eds.) *Towards a Social Science of Sanguage: Papers in Honor of William Labov,*

Volume. I: Variation and Change in Language and Society. Amsterdam/ Philadelphia: John Benjamins. pp. 47–68.

2000. *Linguistic Variation as Social Practice: The Linguistic Construction of Identity at Belten High*. Oxford: Blackwell.

2004. 'Variation and a sense of place', in Fought, Carmen (ed.) *Sociolinguistic Variation: Critical Reflections*. Oxford: Oxford University Press. pp. 107–18.

Foley, Douglas 1989. 'Does the working class have a culture in the anthropological sense?' *Cultural Anthropology* 4: 137–63.

1990. *Learning Capitalist Culture: Deep in the Heart of Tejas*. Philadelphia, PA: University of Pennsylvania Press.

Fox, Aaron A. 1997. '"Ain't it funny how time slips away?" Talk, trash, and technology in a Texas "redneck" bar', in Ching, Barbara and Gerald W. Creed (eds.) *Knowing Your Place: Rural Identity and Cultural Hierarchy*. New York and London: Routledge. pp. 105–30.

Frekko, Susan E. 2009. '"Normal" in Catalonia: Standard language, enregisterment and the imagination of a national public'. *Language in Society* 38: 71–93.

Gibson, Andy 2011. 'Flight of the Conchords: Recontextualizing the voices of popular culture'. *Journal of Sociolinguistics* 15: 603–26.

Goebel, Zane 2007. 'Enregisterment and appropriation in Javanese-Indonesian bilingual talk.' *Language in Society* 36: 511–31.

2008. 'Enregistering, authorizing and denaturalizing identity in Indonesia'. *Journal of Linguistic Anthropology* 18: 46–61.

Goffman, Erving 1959. *The Presentation of Self in Everyday Life*. Garden City, NY: Doubleday Anchor Books.

1981. *Forms of Talk*. Philadelphia: University of Pennsylvania Press.

1986. *Frame Analysis: An Essay on the Organization of Experience*. Boston: Northwestern University Press.

Gramsci, Antonio 1971. *Selections From the Prison Notebooks*. New York: International Publishing.

Habermas, Jürgen 1984. *The Theory of Communicative Action* (translated by T. McCarthy). Boston: Beacon Press.

Hall, Joan H. (ed.) 2012. *Dictionary of American Regional English, Volume V: Si-Z*. Cambridge, MA: Harvard University Press.

Henry, Eric S. 2010. 'Interpretations of "Chinglish": Native speakers, language learners and the enregisterment of a stigmatized code'. *Language in Society* 39: 669–88.

Jaspers, Jürgen and Sarah Van Hoof 2013. 'Hyperstandardisation in Flanders: Extreme enregisterment and its aftermath'. *Pragmatics* 23: 331–59.

Johnstone, Barbara 2009. 'Pittsburghese shirts: Commodification and the enregisterment of an urban dialect'. *American Speech* 84: 157–75.

2011a. 'Dialect enregisterment in performance'. *Journal of Sociolinguistics* 15: 657–79.

2011b. 'Making Pittsburghese: Communication technology, expertise, and the discursive construction of a regional dialect'. *Language and Communication* 31: 3–15.

2013a. 'Ideology and discourse in the enregisterment of regional variation', in Auer, Peter, Martin Hilpert, Anja Stukenbrock and Benedikt Szmrecsanyi (eds.)

Space in Language and Linguistics: Geographical, Interactional and Cognitive Perspectives. Berlin: Walter de Gruyter. pp. 107–27.

2013b. *Speaking Pittsburghese: The Story of a Dialect*. Oxford, UK: Oxford University Press.

Johnstone, Barbara, Jennifer Andrus and Andrew E. Danielson 2006. 'Mobility, indexicality, and the enregisterment of "Pittsburghese"'. *Journal of English Linguistics* 34: 77–104.

Johnstone, Barbara, Netta Bhasin and Denise Wittkofski 2002. '"Dahntahn Pittsburgh": Monophthongal /aw/ and representations of localness in southwestern Pennsylvania'. *American Speech* 77: 148–66.

Johnstone, Barbara and Scott F. Kiesling 2008. 'Indexicality and experience: exploring the meanings of /aw/-monophthongization in Pittsburgh'. *Journal of Sociolinguistics* 12: 5–33.

Lindquist, Julie 2002. *A Place to Stand: Politics and Persuasion in a Working-Class Bar*. Oxford: Oxford University Press.

Madsen, Lian M. 2013. '"High" and "low" in urban Danish speech styles'. *Language in Society* 42: 115–38.

Managan, Kathe 2011. 'Koud Zye: A glimpse into linguistic enregisterment on Kreyol television in Guadeloupe'. *Journal of Sociolinguistics* 15: 299–322.

Marzo, Stefania and Evy Ceuleers 2011. 'The use of Citetaal among adolescents in Limburg: The role of space appropriation in language variation and change'. *Journal of Multilingual and Multicultural Development* 32: 451–64.

McCool, Sam 1982. *Sam McCool's New Pittsburghese: How to Speak like a Pittsburgher*. Pittsburgh, PA: Hayford Press.

Newell, Sasha 2009. 'Enregistering modernity, bluffing criminality: How Nouchi speech reinvented (and fractured) the nation'. *Journal of Linguistic Anthropology* 19: 157–84.

Podesva, Robert J. 2011. 'The California vowel shift and gay identity'. *American Speech* 86: 32–51.

Remlinger, Kathryn 2009. 'Everyone up here: Enregisterment and identity in Michigan's Keweenaw Peninsula'. *American Speech* 84: 118–37.

Romero, Sergio 2012. 'They don't get speak our language right: Language standardization, power and migration among the Q'eqchi' Maya'. *Journal of Linguistic Anthropology* 22: E21–E41.

Silverstein, Michael 1992. 'The indeterminacy of contextualization: When is enough enough?', in Auer, Peter and Aldo Di Luzio (eds.) *The Contextualization of Language*. Amsterdam/Philadelphia: John Benjamins Publishing Co. pp. 55–76.

1993. 'Metapragmatic discourse and metapragmatic function', in Lucy, John A. (ed.) *Reflexive Language*. Cambridge: Cambridge University Press. pp. 33–58.

2003. 'Indexical order and the dialectics of sociolinguistic life'. *Language and Communication* 23: 193–229.

Slotta, James 2012. 'Dialect, trope, and enregisterment in a Melanesian speech community'. *Language and Communication* 32: 1–13.

Squires, Lauren 2010. 'Enregistering internet language'. *Language in Society* 39: 457–92.

Thompson, Edward P. 1966. *The Making of the English Working Class*. New York: Vintage Books.

Weis, Lois 1990. *Working Class without Work: High School Students in a De-Industrializing Economy*. New York: Routledge.

Wilce, James M. 2008. 'Scientizing Bangladeshi psychiatry: Parallelism, enregisterment, and the cure for a magic complex'. *Language in Society* 37: 91–114.

Williams, Quentin E. 2012. 'The enregisterment of English in rap braggadocio: A study from English-Afrikaans bilingualism in Cape Town'. *English Today* 28: 54–9.

Williams, Raymond 1982. *The Sociology of Culture*. New York: Schocken Books.

14 Enregisterment, Indexicality and the Social Meaning of *Howay*
Dialect and Identity in North-East England

Julia Snell

1. Introduction

In this chapter, I consider the relationship between regional dialect and identity by focusing on a single salient dialect form, *howay,* as it is used in the UK print media and in face-to-face interaction. By salient, I mean that *howay* is 'in some way perceptually and cognitively prominent' (Kerswill and Williams 2002: 81). This prominence is attributable to at least two factors. First, *howay* is unique to the north-east of England and is widely recognised as a marker of north-east identity, in particular a working-class identity. Second, *howay* tends to be foregrounded in interaction because of the important functions it fulfils. Referentially, it means something like 'come on' and it is used generally as a directive (e.g. 'Howay, let's go'), but the precise social and pragmatic meanings associated with *howay* are context dependent and, thus, variable. This flexibility in meaning first became apparent to me during a linguistic ethnographic study I conducted in two socially differentiated primary schools in Teesside, north-east England (Snell 2009). In Section 5 of this chapter, I present some examples of the children's spontaneous use of *howay*. However, I begin my analysis by investigating the ways in which *howay* has been used in the UK print media (Section 4). The newspaper data allows me to broaden the scope of my analysis beyond the urban conurbation of Teesside to the north-east region as a whole. This is important because the identity of Teesside is very much bound up with a wider north-east regional identity. By comparing these two datasets I will show that *howay* is tied to geographical location and to social class, but in no straightforward or fixed way. I begin with an account of the developing perceptual prominence and 'enregistration' of the north-east dialect.

2. Enregistration and Commodification of the North-East Dialect

Joan Beal and colleagues have pointed out that, to outsiders, 'the north-east is perceived as a single, homogeneous entity dominated by Newcastle and the figure of the "Geordie[1]"" (Beal *et al.* 2012: 10; see also Wales 2006: 205). Newcastle is a city in the urban conurbation of Tyneside, which is around 60 kilometres north of Teesside (see Figure 14.1). While there are important differences between the dialects of Teesside and Tyneside (or 'Geordie'), they do share a repertoire of regional dialect forms, including the feature that is the focus of this chapter, *howay* (for a full description of the Teesside and Tyneside dialects, see Beal *et al.* [2012]). Moreover, outside the north-east, dialect differences are often erased in public consciousness. Recent perceptual dialectological studies have shown that Geordie is one of the most recognisable dialects in the United Kingdom, but that people associate it with the north-east region as a whole, not specifically with Newcastle (Montgomery 2007).

Joan Beal's work (e.g. Beal 1999, 2000, 2009, forthcoming) allows us to better understand the perceptual prominence of Geordie from an historical perspective. She points to evidence beginning in the nineteenth century of a growing awareness of urban dialects, such as Geordie, and the association of these dialects with the industrial working class and iconic local identities which, for Geordie, include the miner and the 'unemployed Geordie with his flat cap and whippet'[2] (Beal 1999: 44). This linking of linguistic forms with social personae is evocative of the processes described by Agha (2004: 37) as enregisterment, that is, the processes through which a repertoire of linguistic forms (a 'register') 'become differentiable from the rest of the language (i.e. recognizable as distinct, linked to typifiable social personae or practices) for a given population of speakers'. These processes of differentiation work through 'appeal to *metapragmatic models* of speech, that is, culture-internal models of actor (role), activity (conduct) and interactant relationship (social relations) associated with speech differences' (Agha 2004: 25). In order to find samples of a register, a scholar must be able to observe and document as data 'regular patterns of metapragmatic typification' (Agha 2004: 29). An act of metapragmatic typification occurs when a language user makes evaluative judgements about different linguistic forms in a way that points to the metapragmatic models of speech they associate with those forms. Such evaluative behaviour may be explicit, as when an individual assigns an evaluative label to a register

---

[1] 'Geordie' is the name given to speakers from Tyneside, as well as to the variety of English spoken there.

[2] Northerners are often stereotyped as wearing 'flat caps' (a rounded cloth cap with a small brim) and owning whippet dogs. Other scholars have also noted the relationship between urban dialects and iconic working-class identities. In relation to Liverpool, Crowley (2012: 107) refers to the figure of the dockworker, which embodies Liverpool working-class identity. Kiesling and Winosky (2003) draw attention to the cultural model of the male working-class steelworker in Pittsburg (see also Johnstone [2010: 35] on the 'authentic Pittsburgher' and working-class men). These iconic figures are male, reflecting a long enduring association between urban working-class identity and masculinity (Scott 1988).

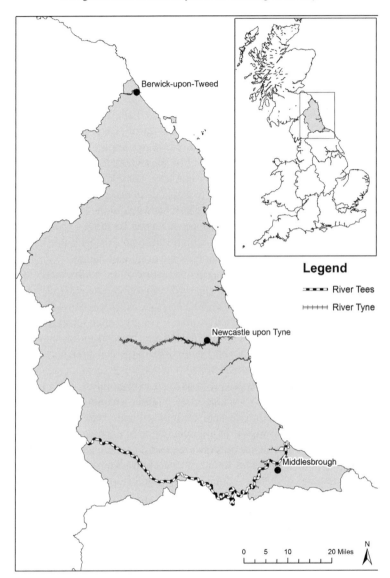

Figure 14.1: Map of the north-east.[3]

---

[3] This map is based on data provided through EDINA UKBORDERS with the support of the ESRC and JISC and uses boundary material which is copyright of the Crown and the Post Office. Location data is © Crown Copyright and Database Right 2015. Ordinance Survey (Digimap Licence).

(e.g. describing someone's speech as 'posh' or 'slang'), or implicit, as when an individual's semiotic behaviour (such as utterances, facial expressions and bodily movements) implicitly evaluate the indexical effects of co-occurring forms in interaction (Agha 2004: 26). Social and cultural information about a register is transmitted across space and time when similar acts of metaprag- matic typification are repeated by multiple language users and linked together into a 'speech chain' (Agha 2003: 246–7).

Beal's (2000, 2009) account of the enregistration of 'Geordie' focuses on explicit metapragmatic discourse, as expressed in proscriptions on language use, dialect dictionaries, songs and cartoons. She shows how features of Geordie were enregistered in the nineteenth century and later 'commodified' in products sold as part of an emerging tourist industry (e.g. folk dictionaries, mugs, tea towels and cookbooks) (see also Johnstone *et al.* [2006] and Johnstone [Chapter 13 in this volume], on 'Pittsburghese', and Cooper [Chapter 16 in this volume] on Yorkshire). She concludes that 'Geordie' has now become a recognisable brand, one which can be exploited in the marketing of the north-east region.

In this chapter, I narrow the focus to just one feature of the north-east dialect and suggest that it has become an 'enregistered emblem' (Agha 2007: 235) of north-east working-class identity. To say that *howay* is an enregistered emblem is to claim that it is widely recognised as marking a particular social persona (Agha 2007: 235). That it is widely recognised can be seen in the way this form has been commodified in novelty items like mugs and greetings cards (Figure 14.2). Evidence that *howay* is linked to a particular social persona can be found in UK newspapers, where it is used to evoke images and figures related to the north-east and to working-class culture. I explore these media images in Section 4. The introduction of interactional data in Section 5 complicates this account, however, by introducing an alternative set of mean- ings for *howay*. I end the chapter by drawing upon linguistic anthropological approaches to indexicality in order to understand the relationship between the media representations of *howay* and its use in interaction. I introduce the notion of indexicality in the next section.

3.   Indexicality and Stance

In using the term indexicality, I am drawing upon Ochs' (1992, 1996) model of direct and indirect indexicality, and Silverstein's (2003) 'orders of indexi- cality'. Ochs (1992, 1996) describes how language has the capacity to index (i.e. 'evoke') a range of sociocultural information, such as affective and epistemic stances, social acts (e.g. commands) and social identities (includ- ing roles, relationships and group identities). These different 'situational dimensions' are related to one another, Ochs argues, through a network of

Figure 14.2: Commodification of *howay*.

cultural associations, norms and expectations, which are shared by members of a community. She refers to these as 'culturally constructed *valences*' (Ochs 1996: 417). It is via these links or 'valences' that, in theory, any situational dimension can help to constitute the meaning of any other situational dimension.

'Stance' is a central component of Ochs' model and has become an important concept in much recent sociolinguistic work (see, e.g., Jaffe 2009). It refers to the processes through which speakers use language (along with other semiotic resources) to position themselves and others, draw social boundaries and lay claim to particular statuses, knowledge and authority in ongoing interaction (see Du Bois 2007: 163). Meanings indexed by interactional stances may be fleeting, but these local social meanings may help to constitute more enduring social identity meanings. For example, tag questions in English have been associated with a feminine linguistic style. But the link between tag questions and the social category of gender is not direct; it occurs only through a series of ideological conventions which associate a stance of hesitancy with female identity (Ochs 1992, see also Moore and Podesva 2009). So we can say that tag questions directly index a stance of hesitancy and only indirectly index a female identity, and '[i]t is in this sense that the relation between language and gender is mediated and constituted through a web of socially organized pragmatic meanings' (Ochs 1992: 341–2). Ochs illustrates her argument in relation to gender, but the model can be applied to social identity categories more generally (including, e.g. class identity).

Whilst Ochs focuses on two levels of indexicality (direct and indirect), Silverstein refers to multiple levels or 'orders' of indexicality. Silverstein's approach makes it possible to conceptualise extended chains of indirect indexicality. The process begins when a particular linguistic form or 'n-th order indexical' becomes associated with social values (e.g. through correlation between the linguistic form and some social characteristic of the users or contexts of use of that form), such that it acquires social meaning. Johnstone *et al.* (2006) use Silverstein's model in their account of the enregisterment of 'Pittsburghese'. They trace how first-order (i.e. n-th order) correlations between the monophthongisation of the diphthong /aw/ (in words like *down*) and demographic identities (such as being from Pittsburgh, being male and being working class) become available for further construal. They map the historical processes by which monophthongal /aw/ becomes a second order (i.e. n+1st) index available for stylistic manipulation, such that individual speakers who use this form variably may 'use it less when they are trying harder to sound educated or cosmopolitan, or more when they are trying harder to sound like - working-class men or like other Pittsburghers' (2006: 83). Johnstone *et al.* (2006: 94) go on to suggest that, in addition to doing second-order indexical work, some regional forms become 'available for self conscious, performed identity work'. They argue that this constitutes a third order (i.e. n+1+1) of indexicality in which variants such as monophthongal /aw/ become even more ideologically laden and are used in self-conscious performances of a person's knowledge about the features that stereotypically constitute a variety such as Pittsburghese (Johnstone *et al.* 2006: 99).

Johnstone and colleagues assign actual values to Silverstein's variable *n* in order to elaborate the historical process through which Pittsburghese has come to be enregistered, but it is not necessarily the case that this process is linear.

As Eckert (2008: 464) points out, Silverstein's n-th order index is always available for reinterpretation because the link between form and meaning is made within 'a fluid and ever-changing ideological field'. This means that n + 1st order indexicality is 'always already immanent as a competing structure of values potentially indexed in-and-by a communicative form of the n-th order, depending on the degree of intensity of ideologization' (Silverstein 2003: 194). The point that the social meaning of a linguistic form is open to continual reinterpretation is significant for the analysis of *howay,* which takes up the remainder of this chapter.

4.   *Howay* and Media Representations of North-East Identity

I have suggested that *howay* is an enregistered emblem of north-east working-class identity. Evidence for this can be found in UK newspapers, where it acts as 'a shorthand' for indexing images of person and place (Wales 2006: 29–30). I investigated these images by using *LexisNexis* to search all UK newspapers for occurrences of *howay.* I focused initially on the fifteen-month period between November 2005 and February 2007, because this is the period during which I conducted the primary school fieldwork discussed in Section 5 and I wanted to explore the kinds of images that were circulating at that time. I then decided to extend my search to include the fifteen-month period immediately prior to my analysis (January 2012–April 2013). Generating two corpora meant that I could compare the use of *howay* over time and, in particular, look for evidence of an increase in the salience of *howay* and the north-east region during this period. I coded each occurrence of *howay* for the main topic of the news article (or section thereof) within which it occurred, the title of the newspaper, and whether it was a regional or national publication (and if national, whether it was tabloid or broadsheet), and whether each token occurred in the headline, photo caption or main body of the text. Summary results for topic can be seen in Tables 14.1 and 14.2.

In the regional newspapers, *howay* occurred frequently in local news stories, which ranged in topic and often included direct quotations from local residents (who used *howay* as part of their quoted speech). There were no equivalent examples in the national press and thus such instances are categorised as 'other' in Tables 14.1 and 14.2. Whilst there was no change over time in the frequency of occurrence of *howay* in the regional newspapers, the number of tokens doubled in the national press from twenty-four in the first corpus (2005–7) to forty-eight in the second (2012–13). This increase occurred in the topic categories of 'football', where references usually involved Newcastle United (e.g. 'Howay the lads!'), and 'celebrity', which in this case meant north-east celebrities (e.g. 'Howay, Cheryl [Cole] is back at last'). In particular, there were many more references in the second corpus to television and

Table 14.1: *Corpus 1 (2005–7) – Distribution of* howay *across topic in national and regional newspapers.*

	National		Regional NE		Regional (other)		Total
Football	8	33%	6	19%	2	25%	16
Celebrity	5	21%	0	0%	2	25%	7
Newcastle/NE	5	21%	1	3%	2	25%	8
Language	4	17%	12	38%	1	13%	17
Other sport	1	4%	0	0%	1	13%	2
Literary	1	4%	3	9%	0	0%	4
Other	0	0%	10	31%	0	0%	10
	24		**32**		**8**		**64**

Table 14.2: *Corpus 2 (2012–13) – Distribution of* howay *across topic in national and regional newspapers.*

	National		Regional NE		Regional (other)		Total
Celebrity	20	42%	2	6%	4	50%	26
Football	19	40%	13	38%	2	25%	34
Newcastle/NE	4	8%	1	3%	1	13%	6
Language	2	4%	2	6%	0	0%	4
Other sport	2	4%	0	0%	1	13%	3
Literary	0	0%	2	6%	0	0%	2
Other	1	2%	14	41%	0	0%	15
	48		**34**		**8**		**90**

popular music stars from the north-east, including the singer Cheryl Cole, television presenters Ant and Dec, the comedian Sarah Millican and the 'reality TV' stars from MTV show *Geordie Shore*.[4] There were no references at all to Cheryl Cole or the stars of *Geordie Shore* in the earlier corpus, but multiple references in the later corpus.

The rise in popularity of north-east celebrities and football teams goes hand in hand with a rise in prominence of the north-east region and dialect. In Montgomery's (2012) terms, the north-east dialect has increasing 'cultural prominence'. In two perceptual studies, one of the north of England and one of the Scottish-English border, Montgomery found that Geordie was the dialect area most commonly recognised by his research participants.

---

[4] This is a British reality television series set in the city of Newcastle. It is broadcast on MTV and is the British adaptation of the American MTV show *Jersey Shore*.

Table 14.3: *Occurrences of* howay *in tabloid and broadsheet newspapers.*

	Corpus 1 (2005–7)		Corpus 2 (2012–13)	
Tabloid	16	67%	41	85%
Broadsheet	8	33%	7	15%
TOTAL	24		48	

It was also the most well-regarded dialect area based on an analysis of the labels and evaluative comments participants used. Montgomery interprets these findings in relation to the cultural prominence of the north-east, which he measures by using the relative exposure of the area in the print media. He searched *The Times* and *Sunday Times* for all mentions of Newcastle-upon-Tyne between 1989 and 2004 (the date of the first study) and then from 2004 to 2008 (the date of the second study). Mentions per head of population were already high in 1989 (0.00404, the highest figure of the ten locations Montgomery investigated), but increased by 128 per cent between 1989 and 2004 and by 222 per cent by 2008 (Montgomery 2012: 659). Montgomery's study provides further evidence for Beal's (2009) point that the north-east region and dialect has become a recognisable brand imprinted in the national consciousness, and it helps to explain the increase in use of *howay* in the national press.

In the regional newspapers, most tokens occurred in the main body of the news articles (88 per cent in Corpus 1 and 74 per cent in Corpus 2), but in the national press just over half of all occurrences were in headlines. Here it was often the case that even the broad referential meaning of *howay* (i.e. 'come on') was lost, being replaced with a splash of north-east colour amidst familiar tabloid wordplay, as when it was used as an alternative for standard English 'away' (e.g. 'Anchor's howay', 'A weekend howay', 'Up, up and howay'). In such examples, *howay* is bleached of its referential meaning ('come on'), leaving indexical meanings related to the north-east region and its associated figures.

Overall, then, *howay* was used in the national press to index the north-east or persons associated with the north-east. As well as indexing regional identity, however, it also seemed to be linked to social class. First, it occurred most frequently in tabloid newspapers (67 per cent in Corpus 1 and 88 per cent in Corpus 2, see Table 14.3), such as *The Mirror* and *The Sun,* which are read by a predominantly working-class audience. The latest figures from the National Readership Survey report that 32 per cent of those who read *The Sun* fall into the category ABC1 and 68 per cent fall into the category C2DE (which equate to middle-class and working-class respectively, based on occupation.)

Compare this with the broadsheet newspaper, *The Guardian*, whose readership is 85 per cent ABC1 (NRS October 13–September 14). Drawing upon a different dataset (the British Household Panel Survey), Chan and Goldthorpe (2007: 1109) find that broadsheets, taken as representing 'highbrow' cultural taste, are read more frequently by individuals in higher-status occupational categories, while the reverse is true for 'lowbrow' tabloids. Second, the topics that prompted the use of *howay* in both corpora were evocative of working-class culture. Football is traditionally associated with the working classes (though this association has recently been challenged, see e.g. Crompton [2008: 4]), as are the other sports that occasioned the use of *howay* in the corpora, darts and pigeon racing (which also have 'a "northern" feel about them' [Townson 1997, reproduced in Dobre-Laza 2003: 2]). Celebrity culture, particularly in relation to reality TV stars, is also perceived stereotypically to be a working-class preoccupation. As Tyler and Bennett (2009: 389) point out, '"celebrity preferences" are now regularly invoked alongside other social cues, such as accent . . . as a way of making class judgements' (see also Bourdieu 1984).

Based on this broad analysis of the frequency of occurrence of *howay* in the newspaper corpora and the topics associated with its use, it is possible to hypothesise that an n-th order indexical model linking *howay* with regional and class identity circulates through the 'mass mediated speech chains and networks' of which these newspapers are a part (Agha 2007: 132). Further evidence for this emerges in the close analysis of specific examples from the newspapers. One example in particular stood out because it did not fit neatly into any of the main topic categories that were part of my coding scheme. (It is categorised as 'other' in Table 14.2). This was a mock letter published by the tabloid newspaper *The Daily Mirror* in February 2012.

The background to the letter is that the Director General of the BBC, Mark Thompson, is preparing to step down. A cartoon character who appears in the newspaper, Andy Capp, applies to replace him. Andy is a working-class figure from Hartlepool, a town in the urban conurbation of Teesside. He was created by cartoonist Reg Smythe (also from Hartlepool) in 1957 and has appeared regularly in a comic strip in the *The Daily Mirror* and *The Sunday Mirror* since that time. By the time of Smythe's death in 1998, the comic had been syndicated to newspapers across the world. As a result of this popularity, Andy has become, to quote Russell (2004: 270), 'one of the great universal figures of amiably dissolute working-class masculinity'. His iconic status has been commemorated in a public statue in Hartlepool, which was erected in 2007 (see Figure 14.3). Andy's application to the BBC is imagined thus by *The Daily Mirror* (this is an abbreviated form of the letter – see the online version of the newspaper [Reade 2012] for the full form):

Figure 14.3: Statue of Andy Capp.[5]

**Extract 1: Excerpts from Andy Capp's letter to the BBC
printed in *The Daily Mirror***

1   Dear Stuck-up Southern Jessies,
2   I've never written one of these types of letters before but the dole says it's the only
3   way I can get me beer money, so here's what they call a job application [...]
4   Let's be honest, it's just not workin' is it? And there's no one with more knowledge
5   about not workin' than me. Except for Flo. Who's studied me not workin' first-hand.
6   But then, being an old lass who's never gonna trouble the Miss Hartlepool judges
7   again, she's obviously barred from top jobs with youse anyway. Which is the one
8   thing you're gettin' right.
9   [...] I'm throwin' me cap in the ring. Well, gettin' Flo to. I don't want to strain me
10 arm as there's a darts match down the pub tonight.
11 Your problem is you've lost touch with the common man. I count meself as a
12 daytime TV expert (apart from between opening time and 3pm when I go back to

13 me couch for me afternoon nap) an' youse are gettin' it all wrong [...]
14 [...] Your football coverage would be much more enjoyable if we could see more
15 action replays of the fights. Especially between the panellists. This is what we
16 want to see our male role models doin' on the telly.
17 Instead what do we see? Dancin'. Every time Flo switches the box on I see some
18 jessie in too-tight trousers and a blouse prancin' around lookin' like they need a
19 pie and 10 pints. [...] BBC3 and 4. Howay, man. What are they aboot? Arty-farty
20 garbage watched by one man and his dog [...]

In this mock letter *howay* appears together with other enregistered north-east forms, such as the vocative *man* (line 19, 'howay man' being a very common collocation), *youse* for second person plural (lines 7 and 13), possessive *me* (which is used here categorically and thus does not reflect real life use – see Snell 2010) and some features of pronunciation represented through non-standard orthography (e.g. 'aboot', 'gettin'). This repertoire of forms is linked with particular social practices and with the kind of person who engages in such practices: a north-eastern man who is interested in drinking beer, eating pies and playing darts, and ultimately hiding all of this from his long-suffering wife Flo. Andy presents himself as a 'real' man, one who enjoys fights, but does not like art or other cultural (and stereotypically feminine) pursuits like dancing, and who stands in stark opposition to soft 'Southern Jessies'[6] (line 1). This news item presents a very overt, distinctive (and arguably negative) metapragmatic stereotype of north-eastern working-class masculinity.[7] Non-linguistic features, such as Andy's flat cap, are part of this stereotype. A picture of Andy accompanies the letter in the online version of the newspaper and this visual image further reinforces the link between linguistic forms like *howay* and a particular social persona (www.mirror.co.uk/news/uk-news/andy-capps-job-application-to-run-680072).

I searched the corpora for other spoofs of this kind, in which a stylised north-east dialect was used for humour. I found one other example, this time in the earlier corpus. The example comes from the *London Evening Standard,* a London-based regional newspaper. It was categorised under 'football' in my original coding scheme because the news item relates to a BBC documentary on corruption in football. In this news item, a columnist parodies the responses of key football figures to the documentary. Amongst

---

[6] Beal (forthcoming) highlights a set of dichotomous stereotypes which have evolved over centuries and 'define the north as cold, harsh, uncivilized, poor, working-class and socialist, and the South as warm, soft, civilized, rich, middle-class and Conservative'.

[7] It is clear that residents of Hartlepool recognise Andy as a embodying a negative stereotype of the region because of the controversy that surrounded the campaign to build the commemorative statue. Although the statue was eventually erected in 2007, some local businesses had initially refused to sponsor the project 'for fear of a PC backlash' should they be associated with 'a flat-cap-wearing wife-beater' (Harris 2002).

these is Paul "Gazza" Gascoigne, former England international footballer from Tyneside who is known for his drinking binges and reckless behaviour in addition to (and often instead of) his sporting achievements. His fictional response is repeated in full in Extract 2.

Extract 2: Paul "Gazza" Gascoigne's imagined response to a question about 'bungs' (i.e. bribery) in football (Curtis 2006)

1 Howay man, I cannet see what the problem is, like. I was regularly offered one
2 before a match, and sometimes at halftime, like. Then, after the match, me and
3 Jimmy Five Bellies, we'd be offered four or five more, like. Then we'd have a
4 few borrels of the broon, purron a pair of plastic breasts, take wor kecks off and
5 run through the toon before hoying it all up in a kebab shop. What's that?
6 Bungs? Why aye, man, I thought yer said BUNS.

As with the previous example, the writer uses *howay* together with other salient features of the north-east dialect to develop the caricature (e.g. sentence final 'like' [lines 1, 2 and 3] and 'wor' for first person plural possessive pronoun [line 4]). This repertoire of linguistic forms is linked with particular social practices – drinking copious amounts of Newcastle Brown Ale (i.e. 'the broon') and engaging in disorderly behavior, like removing one's trousers ('kecks') and being sick ('hoying') in a kebab shop. The result is a negative caricature of Gazza as unintelligent and uncouth.

Analysis of the newspaper corpora suggested the existence of an n-th order indexical model linking *howay* with regional and class-based identities. As discussed earlier, n-th order values are always available for reinterpretation. In Extracts 1 and 2, this reinterpretation appears to be based on cultural values and beliefs (i.e. ideologies) that associate north-east working-class identity with a lack of education and/or intelligence, anti-social behaviour, poor eating and drinking habits, sexism and physical masculinity (Connell 1995). In both cases, then, *howay* comes to index a particular gendered persona – the work-shy sexist or drunken lout. In the Teesside school data, however, there is evidence for a different kind of reinterpretation. I turn to this data next.

5. *Howay* in Face-to-Face Interaction

Between November 2005 and January 2007, I conducted ethnographic field-work in two primary schools in Teesside. These schools were chosen deliberately to highlight a social contrast. Ironstone Primary was situated in a lower working-class area of Teesside, and Murrayfield Primary in a lower middle-class area (all names used in this chapter are pseudonyms). These class designations were based on 2001 Census statistics (taking into account factors such as housing and levels of employment) and government measures of deprivation. Since the pupils were living in the areas immediately surrounding their schools, the two groups of children were broadly classified as 'lower working-class' and 'lower middle-class'. Through ethnographic fieldwork, I began to understand how these demographic differences translated into actual experience (see Snell 2009 for detail).

I made weekly visits to the Year 4 (aged 8–9 years) classroom in both schools and participated in school life as a classroom helper. I followed the same children into Year 5 (aged 9–10 years). Throughout, I spent time with the children in the playground, chatting and playing games. As a result, I was able to develop some knowledge of the children's personalities, interests and friendships, and engage with their activities both inside and outside of the classroom. After seven months, I began recording the children using a radio-microphone. This method produced a rich repository of children's spontaneous speech. The quantitative and interactional analyses presented in this chapter are based on 50 hours of radio-microphone recordings (25 hours from each school), collected when ten pupils from each school wore the radio-microphone for half a day. These recordings were supported by the observations and field notes I made throughout fifteen months of ethnographic fieldwork and informal interviews with the class teachers.

I drew upon the data to investigate grammatical and discoursal variation in the children's speech. Quantitative analyses of the distribution of linguistic variants across the two groups of children revealed familiar class-based differences: the working-class participants used more 'non-standard' and locally marked linguistic forms than their middle-class counterparts (Labov 1966; Wolfram 1969; Trudgill 1974; Macaulay 1977; Reid 1978 – see Snell 2014 for a review). For example, there were only seven tokens of *howay* in the Murrayfield data, three of which were attributable to a single speaker, Craig. In the Ironstone data, there were forty-two tokens from ten different speakers (see Snell [2009] for full analysis). *Howay* was thus linked to class identity in the sense of marking differences in frequencies of use between class-differentiated groups, but analyses of the children's language use in context revealed a more complex picture.

Interactional analyses indicated that *howay* had a range of potential meanings (an 'indexical field' in Eckert's [2008] terms) related broadly to issues of authority, fair play and egalitarianism. These general meanings become more specific in local contexts of use. By way of illustration, I share below an extract from my analysis of one episode involving the repeated use of *howay* (for more detailed analysis, see Snell [2012]). It was recorded when 9-year old Robert was wearing the radio-microphone during a game of 'bulldog' in the Ironstone Primary playground. Bulldog is a 'tag-based' game common across England in which one or two players are selected to be the 'bulldogs' and must stand in the middle of the playground. The other players stand at one end of the playground and try to run to the other end without being caught by the bulldogs. If they are caught, then they must also become bulldogs. Robert used *howay* seven times during the 15-minute game (a much higher rate than any other speaker in the dataset). I present short episodes from this game in Extracts 3 and 4. As Extract 3 begins, Robert is involved in an argument with Sam about whether Sam has been 'tug' (i.e. caught) and should thus 'go on' (i.e. become a bull dog).

Extract 3[8]

1	Robert:	go on
2		you're on
3	Sam:	I'm not
4	Robert:	yea::h
5	Sam:	I didn't know
6	Robert:	yeah you did
7	Sam:	no I never
8	Robert:	[yeah you did
9	Sam:	[(xxxxxxxxxxx)
10	Robert:	she said
11	Sam:	everybody told me [Gemma was on
12	Robert:	[she said
13	Sam:	nobody said-
14		nobody said Clare
15	Robert:	just go on
16		(1.4)
17		I'll get tug in a minute anyway
18	Sam:	so
19	Robert:	howa::y
20		(2.1)
21	Robert:	howay you have to take it
22		(2.3)
23	Robert:	Chris has taken it

[8] Transcription notations (based on the system developed by Gail Jefferson [see, e.g., Jefferson 1984]):

(text)	- Transcription uncertainty
(xxxxxx)	- Indistinguishable speech
(.)	- Brief pause (under one second)
(1)	- Longer pause (number indicates length to nearest whole second)
(( ))	- Description of prosody or non-verbal activity
[[	- Overlapping talk or action
text	- Emphasised relative to surrounding talk (underlined words)
te:xt	- Stretched sounds
>text<	- Speech delivered more rapidly than surrounding speech.
TEXT	- Shouting
(.hhh)	- Audible inhalation
(hhh)	- Audible exhalation

24		he hasn't been tug yet though
25	Sam:	yea:h
26		he doesn't know that
27		(1.5)
28		it's because I didn't-
29		I didn't even know she was on
30	Robert:	yeah but he-
31		he soon goes on
32		((Background noise – 5.2 seconds))
33	Robert:	Sam won't take it
34	Sam:	I wasn't even-
35	Robert:	because he got tugged by Clare
36		(0.8)
37		he should take that though

In line 1, Robert directs Sam to *go on*, but Sam does not accept this (line 3). Over the next six turns disagreement between the two boys is signalled through a series of opposing polarity markers (*yea::h / no*), broken only by Sam's attempt to account for his position in lines 11–14 (see Goodwin 1990, 2006: 128–9). Sam explains that he did not know that Clare was a bulldog and thus cannot legitimately have been *tug* by her. In line 17, Robert changes tactic and tries to cajole Sam into accepting his fate by projecting a stance of camaraderie (*I'll get tug in a minute, anyway*), thus suggesting that the two boys are in it together, but this stance is rejected by Sam (line 18). Robert responds with *howa::y* (line 19), which he articulates with an extended vowel sound in the second syllable and a distinctive fall-rise intonation, a pattern that according to Ladd (1980: 150) may be used to 'do something like a holistic "contradiction" or questioning of [a speaker's] assumptions'. This is exactly what Robert is doing. Moreover, the assumptions being questioned extend much further than the immediate interaction. *Howay* enables Robert to take a stance of authority with regard to the local social and moral order. Fair play and equity are important aspects of these playground games: Sam has been tug and therefore should *go on* just like Chris has done (lines 23, 30–1), and his resistance to do so is deemed unacceptable by Robert. Sam is thus negatively evaluated as someone who flouts the rules of the game and is not a team player. Robert continues with *howay, you have to take it* (line 21, that is, 'you have to accept that you have been caught'). Sam appears to acknowledge the validity of Robert's stance when he offers further explanation for his behaviour (in lines 28–9), claiming again that he did not know that Clare was a bulldog.

Extract 4 occurs around five minutes later. Robert finds himself in a tricky situation because both he and Sam are now being unfairly marked by the bulldog (i.e. the bulldog is standing very close to Robert and Sam with outstretched arms, ready to catch them if they try to run). Robert attempts to negotiate his way out of this situation, again using *howay* to assert his authority with regard to the social order.

Extract 4:

1	Robert:	howay you need to let u::s
2	Sam:	you need to let us out
3		(1.7)
4	Sam:	if I did that-
5		Hannah you're on
6	Hannah:	I know I am
7	Sam:	so you have to let us out
8	Robert:	you can't just stand there
9		(1.2)
10		you need to actu-
11		see what I mean
12		Nathan's just ran
13		(2.7)
14	Robert:	no if you get me here then it doesn't count
15		coz you're just letting everyone go except for me

((1 minute 55 seconds later))

16	Robert:	howay you can't guard
17		*((Background noise – 3.7 seconds))*
18	Robert:	someone at least-

Robert's utterance on line 1 means something like 'come on, you need to move out of the way and at least let us try'. Sam builds on Robert's utterance, repeating *you need to let us out* (line 2) and then *you have to let us out* (line 7); thus Sam, who was previously at odds with Robert, now demonstrates alignment with him. Together they take a collaborative stance against their interlocutor, who is negatively evaluated as flouting the implicit rules and 'spirit' of the game. Robert goes on to explicate these rules in lines 8–15, and makes the authoritative judgement, *no if you get me here then it doesn't count coz you're just letting everyone go except for me* (lines 14–15).

Around two minutes later, the same situation arises again, and Robert again takes action: *howay you can't guard* (line 16, meaning 'you can't stand in front of us'). The use of *howay* here (and elsewhere) marks a change in footing, defined as 'a change in the alignment we take up to ourselves and the others present as expressed in the way we manage the production or reception of an utterance' (Goffman 1981: 128). There is a subtle change in 'production format' in these utterances: Robert remains 'animator' and 'author' of his words, using Goffman's terms, but now speaks on behalf of a wider moral authority (a change in the 'principal' of the utterance), in the name of 'we' not merely 'I'. Robert is appealing to a shared sense of what is considered right, fair and acceptable within this game, and within the local community more generally, and *howay* encapsulates this appeal. So the meaning of *howay you can't guard* (line 16) is actually something like 'come on, don't stand guard over us; it's not fair, **and you know it**'.

This was typical of the way *howay* was used during the rest of this game of bulldog, and also in the data more generally. It indexed meanings related to authority, fair play and egalitarianism, and was often used in situations in which the speaker felt that their interlocutor had somehow infringed upon their rights. The following examples are taken from the data collected across both schools:

1) 'What you eating now then, howay' (Clare, Ironstone Primary, during a lunch-time dispute)
2) 'Aw howay Andrew, you're going to hit me' (Danielle, Ironstone Primary, trying to discourage unwanted attention from a boy in the playground)
3) 'Howay, I haven't put any bit in' (Holly, Murrayfield Primary, who feels she is not being allowed to contribute to a group task)
4) 'Howay, where's Matty man? He supposed to be going in goal' (Daniel, Murrayfield Primary, complaining when his team concedes a goal because they do not have a goalkeeper)

Robert was the most prolific user of *howay* in the dataset. Indeed, across *both* schools, it was the confident outgoing children who used this feature most frequently. The status of these children likely contributed to the indexical meanings of *howay*. At the same time, the use of *howay* also helped to constitute their peer-group status. Although fleeting, the stances taken by Robert in Extracts 3 and 4, and the way that others align with him, reinforce his identity as a confident peer-group leader.

6.   Discussion

Drawing upon my analysis of the newspaper corpora I suggested that an n-th order model linking *howay* with region and class is circulating in public discourse (or at least within the print media) and thus is available for n+1st order reinterpretation. I then presented two different types of metapragmatic data: comedic spoofs appearing in newspapers, which explicitly link *howay* with regional, class and gender-based stereotypes on the one hand, and interactional utterances which implicitly evaluate the indexical effects of this form on the other. These two data points highlight the existence of alternative schemes of value. This should not necessarily surprise us. As Agha (2003: 242) points out:

[t]here is no necessity … that … evaluations [of a register] always be consistent with each other society-internally; in fact their mutual inconsistency often provides crucial evidence for the co-existence of distinct, socially positioned ideologies of language within a language community.

In this case the data suggests the co-existence of two different ideologies related to language, region and class. The comedic spoofs of the Andy Capp job application and Gazza's testimonial reinterpret the n-th order link in terms of an ideology that ties north-east working-class identity to character- istics and practices such as laziness, toughness, propensity to drink and fight and sexism. This ideology likely has most currency for those outside the north-east whose exposure to the north-east register is fragmented, occurring mostly through popular media and fiction rather than face-to- face interaction (see Agha 2003: 242; 2007: 166). The children's inter- actions, on the other hand, involve reinterpretation based in a local ideology about what it means to be working-class in the north-east of England (Eckert 2008: 462). Going back to Ochs' model of indexicality (set out in Section 3), it is possible that components of the meaning of 'north-eastern working-class identity', such as toughness and egalitarianism, help to con- stitute Robert's authority in relation to the local social and moral order and his appeal to fair play in taking corrective action. Robert's stance in Extracts 3 and 4 is confrontational, but some more general sense of solidar- ity attached to *howay* (derived from the association with working-class culture) may serve to mitigate the potential face-threat and thus retain the spirit of camaraderie in the playground game.[9] The highly localised dialect form has acquired this 'indexical potential' through the 'history of usage and cultural expectations surrounding that form' (Ochs 1996: 418). Included in this history are its prominence in the media, its association with Newcastle United Football club and north-east celebrities, and its appearance in novelty items that celebrate the north-east dialect and culture, in particular working-class culture. Meanings related to region and class are thus part of the wider indexical valence of *howay* even though more immediate indexicalities of stance and act may be most relevant for speakers/hearers when they use/interpret this form in interaction (as in Extracts 3 and 4).

The two sets of data appear to evoke contrasting personae: a sexist lout who lacks regard for social decorum versus a reliable peer-group leader who values

---

[9] Compare Bucholtz's (2009) analysis of the Mexican American youth slang term *güey* and Kiesling's (2004) analysis of *dude*.

fair play. It is possible to see these personae as two sides of the same coin, however. Wales (2006: 28) points out that it has historically always been the case that against the negative images of the industrial north of England and northern speakers 'there are the more positive stereotypes ... of the resilient northerners, hard-working and humorous in the face of adversity, blunt speaking and straight-forward, friendly to strangers ... they have "no side": they are what they seem' (see also Beal 1999: 44). Andy Capp might be a work-shy sexist, but he is also straight-forward, down to earth, honest with his views, and humorous – the 'amiable' as well as 'dissolute' of Russell's (2004: 270) description (quoted earlier). This more positive evaluation of Andy and north-east identity helps to explain why working-class north-easterners are able to enjoy the Andy Capp cartoon strips (for a similar argument in relation to the cartoon 'Sid the Sexist' in Newcastle-based satirical magazine *Viz*, see Wales [2006: 31] and Beal [2000]).

7.   Conclusion

In this chapter, I have shown that it can be illuminating to focus on a single salient dialect form in order to explore more general linguistic and social processes. I used my analysis of *howay* to investigate the relationship between language, regional identity and class in the north-east of England, focusing on different kinds of data and different levels of social meaning. Throughout I have described the link between *howay* and regional and class identity as an n-th order indexical link and explored its relationship with other levels of social meaning by considering how different ideologies bring about different n+1st order reinterpretations. This is not to suggest, however, that the link between *howay* and region/class necessarily temporally precedes the link between *howay* and other levels of social meaning, such as the interactional stances described in my analyses of the Teesside school data. Social meanings associated with region and class may help to constitute social acts and stances related to fair play and egalitarianism in interaction, but at the same time, working-class speakers who repeatedly take such stances are constructing a particular kind of working-class identity (Snell 2010: 649; Ochs 1992). In other words, the children's language use informs ideologies of region and class at the same time as it is shaped by them (Bucholtz and Hall 2005: 591). The result is a circular chain of indexicality in which meaning flows from local interactional stances to styles, personae and macro-level identity categories, and then back to local interactional use. Certain types of metapragmatic data may highlight particular points in the chain as being most salient, but it is difficult (if not impossible) to see where the chain begins and ends (Moore and Podesva 2009: 479; Snell 2010: 650). As Silverstein (1998: 128–9; 2003: 196–7) points out, the dialectic nature of indexicality means that 'there is no possible absolutely preideological – that is – zero-order, social semiotic'.

There remain some question marks over my account, however. I have posited the existence of an n-th order model linking *howay* with regional and class-based identities and suggested this may inform speakers' use of *howay* on the ground, but I have not provided direct evidence of uptake of this model by the children who participated in my research. Describing the local inter-actional meanings of *howay* does not in and of itself tell us about the images of person or place that the children themselves associated with this form. Add-itional data is needed. It would be useful, for example, to elicit explicit metapragmatic commentary from the children and other Teesside speakers via interviews, focus groups and questionnaires; matched-guise techniques and other tests of perception would also be valuable. Unfortunately, none of these methods were included in my original Teesside study. I end therefore with a call for future studies of language variation and identity to include multiple data points and an extended analytic tool kit for, as Bucholtz and Hall (2005: 607) point out, 'identity in all its complexity can never be contained within a single analysis'.

REFERENCES

Agha, Asif 2003. 'The social life of cultural value'. *Language and Communication* 23: 231–73.
    2004. 'Registers of language', in Duranti, Alessandro (ed.) *A Companion to Linguistic Anthropology*. Oxford: Blackwell. pp. 23–45.
    2007. *Language and Social Relations*. Cambridge: Cambridge University Press.
Beal, J. C. 2000. 'From Geordie Ridley to Viz: popular literature in Tyneside English.' *Language and Literature* 9(4): 343–59. doi:10.1177/096394700000900403.
Beal, Joan 1999. '"Geordie Nation": Language and regional identity in the northeast of England'. *Lore and Language* 17: 33–48.
    2009. 'Enregisterment, commodification and historical context: "Geordie" versus "Sheffieldish"'. *American Speech* 84 (2): 138–56.
Beal, Joan. Forthcoming. 'Northern English and enregisterment', in Hancil, Sylvie and Joan C. Beal (eds.) *Perspectives on Northern Englishes*. Berlin: Mouton de Gruyter.
Beal, Joan, Lourdes Burbano-Elizondo and Carmen Llamas 2012. *Urban North-Eastern English: Tyneside to Teesside*. Edinburgh: Edinburgh University Press.
Bourdieu, Pierre 1984. *Distinction: A Social Critique of the Judgement of Taste*. London: Routledge.
Bucholtz, Mary 2009. 'From stance to style: Gender, interaction, and indexicality in Mexican immigrant youth slang', in Jaffe, Alexandra (ed.) *Stance: Sociolinguistic Perspectives*. Oxford: Oxford University Press. pp. 146–70.
Bucholtz, Mary and Kira Hall 2005. 'Identity and interaction: A sociocultural linguistic approach'. *Discourse Studies* 7: 585–614.

Chan, Tak Wing and John H. Goldthorpe 2007. 'Social status and newspaper readership'. *American Journal of Sociology* 112(4): 1095–134.

Connell, R. W. 1995. *Masculinities*. Berkeley: University of California.

Crowley, Tony 2012. *Scouse: A Social and Cultural History*. Liverpool University Press.

Crompton, Rosemary 2008. *Class and Stratification*, Third edition. Cambridge: Polity.

Curtis, Nick 2006. 'The reason for bungs is we're all so underpaid'. *The Evening Standard (London), 21st* September 2006.

Dobre-Laza, Mona 2003. *Sport and the Working Classes*. British Council.

Du Bois, John 2007. 'The stance triangle', in Englebretson, Robert (ed.) *Stancetaking in Discourse*. Amsterdam: John Benjamins. pp. 139–82.

Eckert, Penelope 2008. 'Variation and the indexical field'. *Journal of Sociolinguistics* 12: 453–76.

Goffman, Erving 1981. *Forms of Talk*. Pennsylvania: Pennsylvania University Press.

Goodwin, Majorie Harness 1990. *He-Said-She-Said: Talk as Social Organization among Black Children*. Bloomington: Indiana University Press.

  2006. *The Hidden Life of Girls: Games of Stance, Status, and Exclusion Children*. Malden, MA: Blackwell Publishing.

Goodwin, Majorie and Samy H. Alim 2010. '"Whatever (neck roll, eye roll, teeth suck)": The situated coproduction of social categories and identities through stancetaking and transmodal stylization'. *Journal of Linguistic Anthropology* 20:1: 179–94.

Harris, Paul. 2002. Bosses refuse to honour workshy hero Andy Capp. *The Guardian*, 4 August 2002. Available online at www.theguardian.com/uk/2002/aug/04/paulharris.theobserver.

Hughes, Arthur, Peter Trudgill and Dominic Watt 2012. *English Accents and Dialects*, Fifth edition. London: Hodder Education.

Jaffe, Alexandra (ed.) 2009. *Stance: Sociolinguistic Perspectives*. Oxford: Oxford University Press.

Jefferson, Gail 1984. 'Transcription notation', in Atkinson, J. M. and John Heritage (eds). 1994. *Structures of Social Interaction*. Cambridge: Cambridge University Press. pp. ix–xvi.

Johnstone, Barbara 2010. 'Locating language in identity', in Llamas, Carmen and Dominic Watt (eds.) *Language and Identities*. Edinburgh: Edinburgh University Press. pp. 29–36.

Johnstone, Barbara, Jennifer Andrus and Andrew E. Danielson 2006. 'Mobility, indexicality, and the enregisterment of "Pittsburghese"'. *Journal of English Linguistics* 34: 77–102.

Kerswill, Paul and Ann Williams 2002. '"Salience" as an explanatory factor in language change: Evidence from dialect levelling in urban England', in Jones, Mari C. and Edith Esch (eds.) *Language Change: The Interplay of Internal, External and Extra-Linguistic Factors*. Berlin: Mouton de Gruyter. pp. 81–109.

Kiesling, Scott 2004. 'Dude'. *American Speech* 79(3): 281–305.

Kiesling, Scott F. and Marc Wisnosky 2003. 'Competing norms, heritage prestige, and/aw/-monophthongization in Pittsburgh'. Poster presented at New Ways of Analyzing Variation (NWAV) 32, Philadelphia.

Labov, William 1966. *The Social Stratification of English in New York City*. Washington, D.C.: Center for Applied Linguistics.

Ladd, Robert D. Jr. 1980. *The Structure of Intonational Meaning: Evidence from English*. Bloomington: Indiana University Press.

Macaulay, Ronald 1977. *Language, Social Class, and Education: A Glasgow Study*. Edinburgh: Edinburgh University Press.

Montgomery, Chris. 2007. Northern English Dialects: A Perceptual Approach. Unpublished PhD thesis, University of Sheffield.

2012. 'The effect of proximity in perceptual dialectology'. *Journal of Sociolinguistics*. 16(5): 638–68.

Moore, Emma and Robert J. Podesva 2009. 'Style, indexicality and the social meaning of tag questions'. *Language in Society* 38(4): 447–85.

Ochs, Elinor 1992. 'Indexing gender', in Duranti, Alessandro and Charles Goodwin (eds.) *Rethinking Context: Language as an Interactive Phenomenon*. Cambridge, U.K.: Cambridge University Press. pp. 335–58.

1993. 'Constructing social identity: A language socialization perspective'. *Research on Language and Social Interaction* 26: 287–306.

1996. 'Linguistic resources for socializing humanity', in Gumperz, John and Stephen Levinson (eds.) *Rethinking Linguistic Relativity*. Cambridge: Cambridge University Press. pp. 407–37.

Reade, Brian 2012. 'We want Doontoon Cabbie and north-eastEnders': Andy Capp's job application to run the BBC. *The Daily Mirror*. 9 February 2012. Available online at www.mirror.co.uk/news/uk-news/andy-capps-job-application-to-run-680072.

Reid, Euen 1978. 'Social and stylistic variation in the speech of children: Some evidence from Edinburgh', in Trudgill, Peter (ed.) *Sociolinguistic Patterns in British English*. London: Edward Arnold. pp. 158–71.

Russell, Dave 2004. *Looking North: Northern English and the National Imagination*. Manchester: Manchester University Press.

Scott, Joan W. 1988. *Gender and the Politics of History*. New York: Columbia University Press.

Silverstein, Michael 1998. 'The uses and utility of ideology: A commentary', in Schieffelin, Bambi B., Kathryn A. Woolard and Paul V. Kroskrity (eds.) *Language Ideologies: Practice and Theory*. Oxford: Oxford University Press. pp. 68–86.

2003. 'Indexical order and the dialectics of sociolinguistic life'. *Language and Communication* 23: 193–229.

Snell, Julia 2009. Pronouns, dialect and discourse: A socio-pragmatic account of children's language in Teesside. Unpublished PhD dissertation. Leeds, UK: University of Leeds.

2010. 'From sociolinguistic variation to socially strategic stylisation'. *Journal of Sociolinguistics* 14(5): 618–44.

2012. 'Stancetaking and social hierarchies: Using local dialect to construct the pre-adolescent social order'. *Working Papers in Urban Language and Literacies 96*. King's College London.

2013. 'Dialect, interaction and class positioning at school: From deficit to different to repertoire'. *Language and Education* 27(2): 110–28.

2014. 'Social class and language', in Östman, Jan-Ola and Jef Verschueren (eds.) *Handbook of Pragmatics 2014 Installment*. Amsterdam: John Benjamins. pp. 1–24.

Trudgill, Peter 1974. *The Social Differentiation of English in Norwich*. Cambridge: Cambridge University Press.

Tyler, Imogen and Bruce Bennett 2009. 'Celebrity chav: Fame, femininity and social class'. *European Journal of Cultural Studies* 13 (3): 375–93.

Wales, Katie 2006. *Northern English: A Social and Cultural History*. Cambridge: Cambridge University Press.

Wolfram, Walt 1969. *A Sociolinguistic Description of Detroit Negro Speech*. Washington, DC: Center for Applied Linguistics.

15   Indexing Acadian Identities

Ruth King

1.   Background

Acadie is the original name for what is now the peninsular part of the
Canadian province of Nova Scotia. Settlement dates from seventeenth-century
immigration from the centre-west of France (Massignon 1962). The early
settlers were mainly of rural background and members of the lower class, in
contrast to settlers of Nouvelle France (latterly the province of Quebec), who
were of more mixed origins, both geographically (Charbonneau and Guillemette 1994) and socially (Choquette 1997). As Flikeid (1997) has argued, even
more important for the distinctiveness of Acadian French than geographical
origins, are the relatively low levels of normative pressure which have been
obtained in most Acadian communities over the course of more than three
centuries due to isolation from supralocal varieties. This has led to Acadian
French providing linguists with a window on the history of the language (King
2013). Additionally, this low normative pressure has allowed for changes
nascent in colloquial French to become advanced in some Acadian varieties,
such as use of a default singular form of the verb in subject relatives
(for instance, *les pecheurs qui va à la côte*, 'fishers who goes (sic) to the
shore') instead of matching the number of the subject (King 1994, 2005).
A further source of innovation is contact with English, as shown in the
development of English locative *back* into a French aspectual adverb in
several varieties spoken in close contact with English (e.g. *il l'a back fait*
'he did it again').

This chapter is based in part on a paper presented at the Methods in Dialectology XV conference
held in Groningen, NL in August 2014. I thank audience members for their comments. It also
draws on collaborative research with Philip Comeau on Acadieman, Dano LeBlanc's fictional
Acadian superhero. I thank Phil for working with me on the original Acadieman article and for
comments on the present chapter. I have also benefitted from discussions with Patricia Balcom,
Louise Beaulieu and Gary Butler regarding current language attitudes in Acadia. Thanks go as well
to this volume's editors and to an anonymous reviewer for comments on an earlier version of this
text. All errors are my own. This work was supported in part by Canadian Social Sciences and
Humanities Research Council of Canada Insight Grant 435-2012-1195.

An important source of variation in Acadian French involves contact with a variety of Francophone groups, which stemmed mainly from the forced removal of the Acadian people from their lands during the British Expulsion of 1755–8. Of those who escaped the Expulsion, many fled into the wilderness of what is now New Brunswick and Prince Edward Island while others went to the Gaspé peninsula of present-day Quebec. The post-Expulsion dispersal of the Acadian people and subsequent years in exile involved dialect (and language) contact of various sorts, with the return from exile beginning in the 1760s and lasting over a quarter of a century. Ross and Deveau (1992) document the fact that southwest Nova Scotia saw the return of a significant proportion of former inhabitants of the original Acadian colony at Port-Royal, along with a few other pre-Expulsion settlements, to the Baie Sainte-Marie area of Nova Scotia. This area of Nova Scotia has remained the most homogenous of Acadian regions to the present day. On the other hand, the Acadian settlement of New Brunswick, Prince Edward Island, eastern Nova Scotia, Newfoundland and eastern Quebec (including the Îles de la Madeleine in the Gulf of St. Lawrence), all involved complex migration patterns and population movements (Comeau *et al.* 2014). Of no particular importance prior to the Expulsion, the area which is now northeast New Brunswick became home to a heterogeneous group of Acadians whose descendants comprise more than a third of the population of that province and fully 80 per cent of the north-east. Figure 15.1 shows the areas of Acadian settlement in 1750 while Figure 15.2 shows the four Atlantic Provinces and part of neighbouring Quebec today. While the early Acadian colony had taken hold in present-day Nova Scotia by the late seventeenth century, a distinct Acadian identity arguably emerged only in the eighteenth century (Griffiths 1992).

The early years following British takeover were ones in which the Acadian people were concerned with the essentials of survival. Many writers of the time remarked on the extreme poverty in which many Acadians lived. Even so, as devout Roman Catholics, they regarded the lack of clergy, particularly Francophone clergy, as their most pressing concern. Francophone clergy would prove instrumental in the fight for French education, and thus in the fight against assimilation to English culture, whereas Anglophone clergy were not necessarily supportive of the cause. In contrast to the situation in Quebec, there were no schools in New Brunswick, Nova Scotia or Prince Edward Island until the early nineteenth century, and most of the population was illiterate.

One result of widespread illiteracy among the population was its effect on the historical record for Acadian French, since there are very few vernacular texts such as personal letters and journals that date before the late nineteenth century (Philip Comeau, personal communication). The bulk of early texts is correspondence involving members of the clergy and political elites.

The late nineteenth century saw a growth of interest in Acadian culture, with concomitant growth in Acadian nationalism in New Brunswick, Nova Scotia,

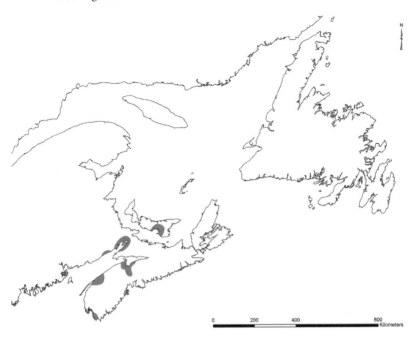

Figure 15.1: The areas of Acadian settlement in 1750.

and Prince Edward Island in spite of being surrounded by an Anglophone majority. This period was marked by the founding of French-language newspapers, such as *Le Moniteur acadien* (Shédiac, New Brunswick) and *L'Évangéline* (Weymouth, Nova Scotia), private colleges such as the Collège Sainte-Anne in Pointe de l'Église, Nova Scotia, and Acadian societies such as the *Société Saint-Thomas d'Aquin*. Acadian National Conventions (held in Memramcook, New Brunswick in 1881, Miscouche, Prince Edward Island in 1884, and Pointe de l'Église, Nova Scotia in 1890) brought together Acadians from all three Maritime Provinces and forged a spirit of nationalism which still resonates. At the Miscouche convention in 1884, the delegation adopted an Acadian flag, a red, white and blue tricolor with a gold star representing the Virgin Mary in its upper left-hand corner. With the coming of Confederation in 1867, article 133 of the Canadian constitution proclaimed French a national language, not just the language of the new province of Quebec. However, the Acadian cause suffered a serious setback with the passing of school acts which established a uniform school system and a uniform curriculum, with English as the language of instruction regardless of native language or religion. Only in privately funded institutions, for which resources were scarce, could French be

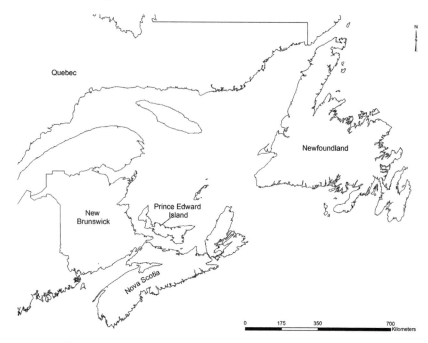

Figure 15.2: The four Atlantic Provinces and part of neighbouring
Quebec today.

the language of instruction. French-language instruction would only come to
many Acadian regions in the late twentieth (and in some cases early twenty-
first) century. As for the Acadian presence in Newfoundland, this former
British colony did not join Canada until 1948. Although there was considerable population migration between its west coast and the islands of Cape
Breton, Nova Scotia, and the Iles de la Madeleine in the eighteenth and
nineteenth centuries, French Newfoundlanders did not become actively
involved in Acadian political and sociocultural interests until the late twentieth
century (Labelle 2002).

As we will see next, this rich and complex history provides the background
for understanding the linguistic indexing of the complex sense of Acadian-ness
which has developed in late modernity.

2.   Traditional and Innovative Language Use

The set of linguistic features typically cited in discussions of the variety
include: for phonology, palatalisation of /k/ and /g/ before non-low front
vowels, as in *guerre* [žɛr] 'war', and *ouisme* (realisation of [u] where Standard

French has [ɔ] or [o]), as in *connaître* [kunet] 'to know' (Lucci 1972; Flikeid 1994) and first-person pronoun *je* metathesis ([əž]); for morphosyntax, preservation of comparatively rich verbal paradigms, including first-person plural *je*+VERB+*-ons* and third person plural *il*+VERB+*-ont* along with use of *point* (instead of *pas*) as the general negator. Also strongly identified with conservative Acadian French is use of the imperfect subjunctive and the homophonous preterite, both of which fell out of use in most varieties of spoken French by the nineteenth century but remain highly productive in the south-west Nova Scotia variety (Comeau *et al.* 2012). The lexicon of Acadian French varieties has typically included, amongst numerous archaisms (*itou* 'too', *astheure* 'now'), semantic extension of nautical vocabulary such as *les hardes* 'everything contained in a sailor's trunk' to use as the general term for clothing (Massignon 1962). As well as being mentioned in the Acadian linguistic literature as far back as the nineteenth century, these features have been enregistered in face-to-face interaction, including the induced natural contexts of sociolinguistic interviews, and in native speaker orthographic choices in personal letters from the late nineteenth century and online language use from the late twentieth century on.

Many twentieth century innovations in Acadian French have their origin in English, such as the borrowing of *back*, mentioned earlier. We also find use of discourse markers *but, so,* and *well* in varieties of Acadian spoken in close contact with English (example from Roy [1979:118] for Moncton, New Brunswick):

So si qu'on fait notre petit party, notre petite soirée, ben on va tous se mettre ensemble.

'So if we have our little party, our little party, well we are going to all get together'.

Roy's work is particularly important because she documents the fact that linguistic features which today are often viewed as recent developments in adolescent Moncton-area speech have a history dating back at least to the mid-twentieth century. We also find code switches involving evidential verbs used with first-person pronominal subjects in matrix clauses, such as *I guess que . . .* (King and Nadasdi 1999).

In recent decades, much attention has been focussed on Chiac, an urban variety spoken in the greater Moncton, New Brunswick metropolitan area, where only a third of the population is Francophone, a situation of long-standing language contact. Features typically discussed in the Chiac literature include those instances of English influence mentioned earlier, along with use of English-origin prepositions such as *about*, phrasal verbs such as *slower down* (-*er* is the French infinitival marker), intensifying adverbs such as *right*, and English cardinal numbers and non-numeric quantifiers such as *last, own* and *anything* (Perrot 1995; Young 2002; along with several papers contained in Brasseur and Falkert 2005). As Gérin (1984) and Pavel (2005) emphasise, such innovations co-occur with traditional features of the sort noted earlier. In a meta-analysis of the burgeoning Chiac linguistic literature, King (2008) shows that usage identified as Chiac is common to young people's Acadian in both Nova Scotia and Prince Edward Island as well and that some of its 'innovations' have long histories in the language. Still, it is important to keep in mind that in the public imaginary such features are strongly linked to the urban Moncton variety.

Today there is considerable interest in those features of Acadian French varieties which have been lost in most modern varieties, such as the preterite-present perfect distinction noted earlier (this particular example is retained fully only in Nova Scotia varieties today), both for the fact that they shed light on changes which happened in other varieties centuries ago and for what they tell us about Acadian identity/ies in the present day. In the latter regard, Beaulieu and Cichocki (2008, 2014) have shown that the north-east New Brunswick variety, on the one hand strongly influenced by long-standing contact with Quebec French, also retains traditional variants, such as *il* +VERB+-*ont*, particularly in the speech of individuals with strong local ties. Beaulieu and Cichocki (2014) show that some such local features are actually on the rise, contrary to what one would expect given their absence from Quebec French and supralocal French generally. Furthermore, Noël (2010) argues that while the *je*+VERB+-*ons* variant is entirely absent from extant sociolinguistic corpora for the same north-east variety, including the speech samples of his own adolescent consultants, it still has discursive value for young north-east Acadians indexing quaintness and/or Acadian French as spoken in other areas.

The previous discussion has presented a number of linguistic forms documented by dialectologists and variationist sociolinguists for Acadian varieties past and present, some highly conservative in terms of their long history in the language and others innovative. We assume that such forms take on social meaning not only in face-to-face interaction (and more recently, in computer-mediated discourse involving Facebook posts and texting, amongst other things), but that social meaning is also constructed in artistic (or, in Coupland's 2007 term, high) performance. As Johnstone (2011) observes, dialect enregisterment in artistic performance involves highly self-conscious linguistic choices. In studying such texts, she argues that the analyst should attend not only to the idealised culturally literate audience member, but to the meaning potential of linguistic forms for diverse audience members. In a similar vein, Coupland (2009: 288) suggests that 'with [mass] mediated acts of identity, analysts need to take their place along with many other interested parties and among a potential welter of interpretive voices'. In the following section, I will consider in detail the use of a number of such features in artistic representations of Acadian French from the late nineteenth and mid-twentieth centuries, and in particular how they have contributed to the stereotypical understanding of the variety. I will then move onto reflecting on the influence such historical representation in examples from the early twenty-first century.

3.   Historical Representations of Acadian French

Historical representations of Acadian French have portrayed it as conservative, as in one of the earliest data sources which is a set of satirical texts, sixteen letters said to have been written by a (stereotypical) late nineteenth-century Acadian housewife named Marichette. The letters were published in the Weymouth, Nova Scotia newspaper *L'Évangéline* between 1895 and 1898. Gérin and Gérin's (1982) annotated edition, *Marichette: Lettres acadiennes*, provides excellent contextualisation of these letters, the community in which 'Marichette' lived, and that particular period in Acadian society. Among the particular linguistic features which figure in these letters, *il*+VERB+-*ont* is near categorical while *je*+VERB+-*ons* is quite robust, occurring in almost 50 per cent of tokens with first-person plural definite pronominal reference (Martineau 2005). Both of these variants are attested for the Old French (ninth to twelfth century) period, undergoing stigmatisation in higher-class speech in the sixteenth century, but surviving in urban European vernaculars until the turn of the nineteenth century and in many rural varieties a century later. Instances of the two variables are presented in bold in the extract below.

J'tenons, moi et mon vieux, une p'tite shop de groceries. Pite est pas content après ceuse qui nous **apportons** des oeufs. Il a envoyé un bill pour faire passer à la chambre, à Halifax, pour finder les femmes qui **apportions** à vendre des oeufs pas lavés. Ah les gambines! **On** veut des oeufs de poules pas mattachés pour le marché de Boston.[1] (March 18, 1897 letter)

'We keep, me and my old man, a little grocery shop. Pete isn't happy with the people who bring us eggs. He sent a bill to be presented at the legislature, in Halifax, to find the women who brought unwashed eggs to sell. Gambines![2] We want clean eggs for the Boston market' (my translation).

---

[1] The author uses the –*ons* ending for both variants, whereas linguists typically write –*ont* for the third person. We do not know if the third-person ending came about through analogy with first-person plural –*ons* or through analogy with high-frequency irregular verbs such as *faire* (*ils font*), *aller* (*ils vont*), and *être* (*ils sont*), or both.

[2] Gérin and Gérin (1982) are unable to find documentation of *gambine* elsewhere in the language and suggest it may be a play on *jambe* ('leg', relating it to *coureuse*, a woman who is said to go out too much). Note as well that *on* here is used with unrestricted reference, referring to a group larger than those known by the speaker while *je* is used with restricted reference, referring only to a group known by the speaker. Prior historical work on this variable has shown that *on* gains ground on *je* in cases of unrestricted reference before it takes over in cases of restricted reference (King *et al.* 2011).

The text is written in eye dialect, with frequent ellipsis of unstressed syllables. Note as well presence of the competing first-person plural colloquial variant *on* (used with definite reference) in the same extract along with an English-origin noun (*bill*) and verb (*finder*, with French infinitival inflection).

Gérin and Gérin's detective work suggests that the 'real' Marichette was in fact school teacher Émilie LeBlanc, born in Memramcook in south-east New Brunswick, that she was educated in a convent school there followed by (English-language) teacher's college in Fredericton, and only then spent several years as a teacher in Nova Scotia. She writes as a poor, uneducated woman who documents, in humorous fashion, the social injustices of the day concerning the treatment of Acadians and other minorities, along with the limited rights of women in society.

A similar text is Pascal Poirier's *Causerie memramcookienne*, also published as a series of (anonymous) satirical letters, in this case in the *Moniteur acadien* between 1885 and 1886. An amateur linguist and historian, Poirier was a career politician who fully embraced the Acadian cause. The first-person plural variant is likewise robust in his letters, and the third-personal plural variant near categorical, as was the case with *Marichette*. Both LeBlanc and Poirier clearly view language as a site of ideological struggle and valorise local language use. Marichette refers to Acadian French as 'note belle langue que j'parlons danpis que j'sont sortis du bois ousque les Anglais nous avions chasé' ('our beautiful language that we have been speaking since we came out of the woods where the English had chased us', my translation). In a similar vein, Pierrichon, one of the rural Acadian characters of Poirier's *Causerie*, describes the variety as 'le point de départ du progrès intellectuel et national des Acadjens, pour lequel j'pouvons sans crainte remercier en grande partie nos bounnes et saintes maisons d'éducation' ('the point of departure for intellectual and nationalist progress for Acadians, for which we can without fear largely thank our good and sacred houses of education (Roman Catholic schools)', my translation), cited by Martineau (2005: 189).

Along with his political and historical writings, Poirier was the author of a treatise on the language entitled *Le parler acadien et ses origines* (1928) and an Acadian dictionary published in instalments in the *Moniteur acadien*, an annotated, full edition of which only appeared several decades later (Gérin 1993). Consider the entry for *je*+VERB+-*ons* (cited by Noël 2010: 28):

[l]e latin *unus* avait aussi quelquefois un sens pluriel: *uni suevi, unae litterae*. On trouve également en vieux français: *un espérons, unes estoiles, unes lettres*. Ceci donne la genèse de *j'avons* et de tous les *je* pluriels. (Gérin 1993: 118)

'Latin *unus* also occasionally was used with plural reference *uni suevi, unae litterae*. One also finds in Old French: *un espérons, unes estoiles, unes lettres*. This is the origin of *j'avons* ['we have'] and all the other *je* plurals' (my translation).

Flikeid (1994: 314) describes Poirier as setting for himself the task of connecting Acadian words and expressions with their origins 'en les rattachant à l'arbre géneologique de la langue française', indeed as Flikeid herself comments 'le plus près du tronc possible' ('by attaching them to the French language genealogical tree ... as close to the trunk as possible', my translation). Indeed, the linguistic features of this renowned language crusader's *Causerie* are quite similar to those of Marichette, with the exception that Poirier deliberately excludes English loanwords (Bonnard 1993: 893).

By the mid-twentieth century the writings of Antonine Maillet put Acadians and their language on the literary map, largely through her celebrated 1971 play, *La Sagouine*, constructed as a series of monologues performed by the titular elderly Acadian cleaning woman. Acadian theatre only dates from the mid-twentieth century and *La Sagouine* remains to this day its most celebrated work. Born in Bouctouche, New Brunswick in 1929, Maillet was educated at the Université de Moncton and at the Université Laval. Her work, spanning more than fifty years, has won critical acclaim in Canada and in France and much popular acclaim as well.[3] Her plays, in particular *La Sagouine*, are widely presented. An entertainment park in Bouctouche is named simply *Au Pays de la Sagouine*; visitors to the park's website are invited to visit and explore Acadian culture.

While Marichette is clearly not a literary masterpiece, its central character and its use of language find clear resemblances in the language of *La Sagouine* several decades later:

Pis les femmes s'**avont** amenées avec des laizes de rideaux et elles vous **avont** doublés la dôré tout en picoté rouge et blanc que ça sentait quasiment pus le poisson pantoute là -dedans. **J**'y **avons** fait un couvert avec la table de la cuisine et j'**avons** accroché de chaque bord les pognées du poêle. Y avait rien qu'une chouse, c'est que **j**'**étions** point sûrs que ça prendrait point de l'eau, cette affaire-là, par rapport que **je savions** toutes que le pauvre Jos passait la motché de ses nuits à bêler sa dôré. (Maillet 1974: 146)

"n the women came over with strips of curtains an' they upholstered the boat all 'n red'n white polka dots so it almost didn' smell of fish at all in there. With the table we made a lid fer it 'n we hooked on each side the stove's handles. Only one thing, we wasn' too sure that ol' boat wouldn' leak, cause we all knew poor Jos use to spen' half his nights bailin' out the water' (Maillet 1979: 117).

---

[3] During the course of fieldwork several years ago in Prince Edward Island, I remember a child bursting into the kitchen of my B&B one day, crying 'La Sagouine s'en vient chez nous!' ('La Sagouine is coming here!'). He was referring to a special performance by Viola Léger, the most celebrated actor to ever play the role. The performance was the highlight of the summer for the local community and for this child and his contemporaries it was as if the character herself was a living person, an Acadian superstar.

As a source for conservative Acadian French, the short extract given above shows many of the features discussed so far: the first- and third-person traditional variants in bold, palatalisation (*moitié > motché*), ouisme (*chose > chouse*), semantic extension (*bord de la table,* from *bord* meaning 'side of a ship'), and use of long-established words of English origin (*dôré < dory*). We also see *point* as the general negator, where most French varieties would have *(ne) . . . pas*, and use of the auxiliary *avoir* with pronominal verbs (King 2013). We find a wealth of vocabulary that make *La Sagouine* a near-essential source for lexicographers wishing to illustrate Acadian usage, including Cormier (1999) and Brasseur (2001). Interestingly, for the north-east New Brunswick adolescents interviewed by Noël (2010: 104–6), traditional Acadian French, including the *je+*VERB*+ons* variant, is linked closely to Antonine Maillet and *La Sagouine*.

The text itself is 'loaded' with Acadian features, with little variation in use. Almost 450 tokens with first-person plural definite reference all have *je+*VERB *+-ons* and almost 550 tokens with third-person definite reference all have *il+*VERB*+-ont* (including subject relative clauses, a context which shows at least some instances of default singular usage in all Acadian varieties for which I have data). As for those cases of indefinite reference, most have *tu* or *vous* subject pronouns as is common in colloquial French, with only thirteen instances of indefinite *on*. This listing is not meant as an evaluation of the 'authenticity' of the text, but rather a commentary on the style of its author. *La Sagouine* has resonated with generations of Acadians for the traditional life and times it creates as well as its artistry.

The earlier examples clearly demonstrate the conservative nature of Acadian French that has been part of popular (as well as academic) discourse on the variety for more than a century. However, by the mid-twentieth century, a second stereotype regarding Acadian French was clearly in play, that the variety is *moitié anglais, moitié français* ('half English, half French'). The texts cited earlier also show long-standing English loanwords such as *traileux* (from English 'trailers', also known as recreational vehicles (RVs) in North America) and *bodrer* (from the English verb 'to bother'), Most of the loanwords found in the nineteenth and twentieth century texts are nouns (e.g. *fun*) or morphologically incorporated verbs (for instance, *finder*) but there is also occasional use of English discourse markers *but* and *so*. Since discourse markers typically occur at the edges of utterances and are less integrated syntactically than, say, nouns or verbs, they would be expected to be among the first functional items to be borrowed.

The *moitié anglais, moitié français* stereotype is the major theme of Michel Brault's largely sympathetic 1969 documentary *Éloge du chiac*, in which Moncton, New Brunswick Francophone high school students debate the use of that variety. Some of the students align themselves passionately with supralocal varieties of French (viewed as more 'pure' forms of French) and others, just as passionately, embrace local language use. The film ends with the students leaving the school grounds, with one young woman crying out, 'Vive le chiac!'. Brault's documentary dealt with a time of social upheaval in both Quebec and in New Brunswick, when local language varieties, Joual in Montreal and Chiac in New Brunswick, were being celebrated by some as a source of pride and decried by others, in the latter case as inferior French. Of course, quantitative sociolinguistic studies such as Flikeid and Péronnet's (1989) study of loanwords in Nova Scotia Acadian varieties and King's (2000) study of Prince Edward Island varieties show that the influence of English tends to be vastly overblown, although the perceptual salience of many words of English origin (apart from very old borrowings) make them seem to be more prevalent than they in fact are in discourse.

Language debates were far less intense in most Acadian locales outside of New Brunswick, where the Francophone population was smaller and, in many cases, lack of access to services in *any* variety of French was still a problem (but see Boudreau and Dubois [2007] for a discussion of recent debates in south-west Nova Scotia). However, over the past decades, more has changed in Atlantic Canada than improved French services. Across Atlantic Canada, traditional employment, centring on the fishery, has been in decline for twenty-five years. Today many residents, including Acadians, seek employment in the western Canadian province of Alberta's oil and gas industries. Some become expatriates, while others commute to their home communities, with several weeks away rotating with weeks at home. While Moncton, New Brunswick has long been an urban centre serving much of Atlantic Canada, traditional employers, such as the national railway, have pulled out or decreased their operations, giving way to a ubiquitous new employer, the call centre industry. French has become a valuable commodity, a workplace skill in Acadian communities where workers are more willing to work for low wages than they would be in larger urban centres in central Canada. Smaller locales have also benefited financially from heritage tourism, which packages rural Atlantic Canada as a nostalgic place out of time (see Heller 2003; King and Wicks 2009 for discussion). Twenty-first century artistic representations, as we will see later, speak to this new reality.

Language debates have continued under a number of guises across the decades, most recently (at the time of writing) in controversy surrounding '2 Faces', an anti-bullying documentary short produced by students of the École Abbey-Landry, Memramcook, New Brunswick. In the fall of 2013, the local Francophone school board refused to have the film shown in other schools in the district (despite support for the film from the Association des enseignants francophones du Nouveau-Brunswick) on the grounds that the young actors spoke Chiac, as opposed to Standard French. The young film makers provided responses such as this one (2 Faces Facebook post, 17 October 2013):

Mon point de vue: un message de Gabrièle Zerb. Moi et mes amis nous ne comprenons pas le point de vue du district et nous sommes totalement en désaccord. Notre but n'était pas de promouvoir le français standard, mais bien de sensibiliser les jeunes contre l'intimidation. C'est vraiment décourageant la reaction du district, car je suis sûre que cela a beaucoup insulté les gens de la région et ce n'est pas une bonne solution. Le Chiaque n'est pas une mauvaise chose, au contraire nous sommes fière d'être acadiens et une grande partie de la population le sont.

'My point of view: a message from Gabrièle Zerb. My friends and I don't understand the district's point of view and we totally disagree. Our goal wasn't to promote Standard French but to educate young people against bullying. The district's reaction is really discouraging since I am sure that [their decision] really insulted local people and it's not a good solution. Chiac isn't a bad thing, on the contrary we are proud to be Acadians as are a large proportion of the population' (my translation).

Perhaps to the chagrin of those opposing its dissemination, the film went on to win awards at New Brunswick film festivals and receive considerable media attention. This is but one of a number of recent incidents which shine a light on language politics in present-day Acadia. These debates often take place in the context of twenty-first century mass media representations of Acadian language use, which draw upon the two stereotypes of the variety: that it is conservative, and that it is 'half English, half French'.

4.   Twenty-First Century Representations

Until quite recently, on national TV and radio, and on regional affiliates in Canada, one did not often hear regional French varieties associated with minority (non-Québécois) Francophone groups. However, late 2005 marked the appearance on cable TV of *Acadieman*, billed as *le first superhéro acadien, sort of* ("the first Acadian superhero, sort of") from the comic book *Acadieman: Ses origines* (2007), the creation of Moncton native Dano LeBlanc.[4] The show aired for three seasons and soon engendered an official Acadieman website,[5] which includes episode summaries, photos, a Chiac lexicon, video clips, cartoons taken from Acadieman *bandes dessinnées*, along with fan postings. While the official diffusion of the TV show was geographically

---

[4] See Comeau and King (2011) for in-depth analysis of the comic strips and TV show.
[5] www.acadieman.capacadie.com, now migrated to www.acadieman.com.

limited, *Acadieman* is embedded in other media: numerous clips are featured on YouTube and there are still Facebook groups devoted to the show and its central character. The Acadieman character is a GenX slacker who speaks *only* in Chiac, whether conversing with his peers, older Acadians, Francophones from other areas, including Quebec and France, as well as unilingual Anglophones. He lives in Moncton and is a call centre worker. The following description of the show's title character is taken from the 2008 *Acadieman* website.

Le First Superhero acadien (ouèlle sort of . . .), le café é à Acadieman ce que le spinach é à Popeye. Un lover of the great indoors, y aime pas prendre dés grandes marches pis y aime pas skier non plus. Y aime hanger out aux cafés pis s'moquer du monde pis de s'faire gâter. Acadieman est l'official Pirate de la langue française. Sa favorite show à la TV cé « Passions » pis y écoute any musique qu'a dés tchuilléres dedans. Cé favorite foods sont dés tétines de souris, la posse-pierre, dés pètes de sœurs, dés poutines à trou, dés poutines (acadiennes), dés fried piss-clams, du houmard, pis du chiar.

'The First Acadian Superhero (well, sort of . . .), coffee is to Acadieman as spinach is to Popeye. A lover of the great indoors, he doesn't like to take long walks and he doesn't like to ski either. He likes hanging out in coffee shops, making fun of people, and indulging himself. Acadieman is the official pirate of the French language. His favourite TV show is 'Passions' and he likes to listen to any music that uses spoons. His favourite foods are samphire, Goose Tongue, Nun's Farts, des poutines à trou, des poutines (acadiennes), fried soft-shell clams, lobster, and rappie pie.' [my translation]

Acadieman, then, draws on a variety of semiotic resources in its presentation of the main character. He is a fan of traditional Acadian dishes (*dés tétines à souris,* also, incidentally a favourite of La Sagouine) and traditional Acadian music (*any musique qu'a dés tchuilléres dedans*). However, he is also a fan of a daytime (English) TV soap opera, *Passions*, and, as we see in the show, American horror movies. Not athletic, he spends his free time hanging out with his friends in coffee shops when he is not working at a local call centre. Thus Acadieman is linked to tradition (e.g. his traditional food and some of his music choices) and to present-day youth (Acadian) lifestyles (his pastimes, the modified Acadian flag on his t-shirt which bears a skull and crossbones rather than the Acadian star) (Figure 15.3).

The narrative commentary found in Figure 15.4, taken from the first issue of the comic book, *Acadieman: Ses origines* (LeBlanc 2007: 15) gives further information on the styling of Acadieman. This extract comes from a conversation with a new friend, Coquille, another Moncton resident and Chiac speaker, when Acadieman first moves to Moncton.

Figure 15.3: Acadieman (LeBlanc 2007), Rogers TV 2007 and Productions
Mudworld 2007.

Figure 15.4: Acadieman: Ses origines (LeBlanc 2007), Rogers TV 2009 and
Productions Mudworld 2009.

NARRATIVE
   COMMENTARY: Yes, Acadieman is a superhero (sort of) but the only problem is
                 that there isn't much for a superhero to do in Acadie.
ACADIEMAN: I guess I have to find a job now!?
NARRATIVE
   COMMENTARY: The difference between Acadieman and other superheroes is the
                 fact that he has no money and no powers as such.

COQUILLE: Me, I work in the call centre of the universe. Them, they change
                            personnel all the time. They are always looking for
                            someone. You will be able to support your superhero stuff
                            with that money . . . and pay your rent, too.

Once again we see traditional Acadian features represented at the phonological level: they include the opening of /ɛ/ before /r/ (*charchont*), palatalisation of /k/ before non-low front vowels (*tchequ'un* 'someone'), and traditional
pronunciations involving metathesis (*je* > *ej*) and epenthesis of an initial
consonant (*eux* > *zeux*). At the morphological level, *il*+VERB+*-ont* is in robust
use. Traditional lexicon is represented by *astheure* ('now') and *itou* ('also').
The text in Figure 15.4 also includes established borrowings from English (for
instance, *la rent*), code switches such as *le call centre of the universe*, and an
example of code switching involving a main clause first-person singular
evidential verb (*I guess . . .*). Particularly interesting is the juxtaposition of the
traditional (archaic) features with English borrowing and code switching: traditional features are recontextualised in the late modern context which the TV
show and comic books represent. The mere fact of speaking Chiac on TV makes
Acadieman a superhero: it has value in Acadieman's world and communicates
this same value to those in non-fictional Acadian society. Although online
discussion makes it clear that Acadieman has Francophone fans outside its
target audience (and Anglophone fans as well), it is clear that the show was
made by and for Acadians. Each episode opens with the Acadian saying *Il fait
beau dans la cabane!* (literally, 'It's nice in the cabin!' which would be rendered
in English by 'Everything's great here!'). As Comeau and King (2011) note, this
opening line would be opaque to non-Acadians, at least on initial hearing. We
suggest that *Il fait beau dans la cabane!* serves as a contextualisation cue
(Gumperz 1992), indexing group membership. It bears keeping in mind, though,
that the show has fans who simply find it entertaining, without necessarily
understanding, or agreeing with, the linkages between language use and social
meaning(s) that enculturated audience members may hold.

Acadieman was wildly successful from the outset, reaching well beyond its
initial target audience of young adults to a wide age range of Atlantic Canada
residents and to the Acadian diaspora as well. It became a powerful resource
for re/creating a sense of the local for Acadians, an imagined community in the
sense of Anderson (1983). However, it was and still is not without its detract-
ors. In 2008, Comeau and King surveyed attitudes towards the show expressed
on approximately thirty-five websites, including online newspapers, personal
blogs and Facebook discussion groups, finding a range of opinions from the
overwhelmingly positive (e.g. that *Acadieman* represented the 'true' voice of
Acadia) to the quite negative (that the show presented a 'bastardised' version
of French due to its inclusion of English loanwords and code switches, along

with non-standard French morphology and lexicon). For a time, *Acadieman* became the centre of language debates as discussed earlier in Section 5.

Boudreau (1996: 152) has suggested, in the New Brunswick context, that there has been a shift from *chiac mépris* ('chiac scorn') to *chiac fierté* ('chiac pride'). Gammel and Boudreau (1998) also highlight this, discussing the role of Chiac in discourses of resistance in recent Acadian poetry. Further, Boudreau and Dubois (2003) consider a re-evaluation of Chiac, an urban variety, to be part of a modernist discourse of Acadian identity, at odds with an older discourse centring on a rural, 'folkloric' identity associated with conservative language use and other aspects of traditional culture. However, *Acadieman* does not entirely fit this characterisation, as it does not so much reject tradition as inject it with modern sensibilities.

Acadieman arguably opened the door for new representations of Acadian identity in mainstream media, such as the TV sketch comedy show *Méchante soirée*, airing since 2013 on the national public network's New Brunswick affiliate (sketches may also be viewed on the show's Facebook page and on YouTube). An October 2013 sketch parodied the 2 Faces controversy aforementioned by having a scene from the documentary enacted by the show's adult actors speaking in highly formal, European French, with subtitling in Chiac. The incongruity of the Standard French dialogue with Chiac subtitles is the source of the sketch's humour; it also presents a strong political stance. Also relevant for new discourses of Acadian identity is Moncton indie band *Les jeunes d'asteure*, whose debut album appeared in 2012 and whose name includes the traditional lexical item *asteure* 'now'. The band's web page states that their work is informed by a contemporary Acadian aesthetic. A rather different aesthetic is found in the music of Acadian rappers Radio Radio, active since 2007, which will be the focus of the remainder of this section, since language use is typically front and centre in discussion of the group's appeal (or lack thereof).

The genesis for Radio Radio was the duo Jacobus (Jacques Doucet) and Maleco (Marc Comeau), two south-west Nova Scotia natives, who began recording under the name Radio Radio in late 2007. They were joined by Moncton natives Gabriel Malenfant and 'Timo' Richard. Radio Radio's first full album, 2008's *Cliché Hot*, met with immediate success throughout French Canada and subsequent albums have been successful in Louisiana and in Europe as well. I concentrate here on the first album since it was made by the group's original line-up before they began playing to international audiences; it was made for Acadian audiences although it soon received wide airplay and fan following in Quebec. As music writer Paul-Emile Comeau (2014: 91) puts it:

Radio Radio is a nationally known rap band whose rappings are at least as much acadjonne [label for the south-west Nova Scotia variety] as they are chiac. The group has no qualms about putting the Baie Sainte-Marie way of speaking on full display. It is an unusual and bold move because most apostles of non-standard expression have only a local platform.

Comeau characterises their language use as 'contentious', noting the publication of a negative article in 2012 in Montreal's newspaper *Le Devoir* which engendered huge debate among the readership. Radio Radio were not the first Acadian musicians to use local language in their music, but they are arguably the first to consistently use English loanwords and code switches in line with young people's Acadian in south-east New Brunswick and Nova Scotia (see King 2008 for a discussion of commonalities between the varieties). The following excerpt from one of their early successes, *Dekshoo*, gives a flavour of their lyrical style:

1	Avec mes penny loafer	With my penny loafers
2	Avec mes dekshoo	With my deck shoes
3	Le jour je [əž] faisons rien trop gros [gru]	During the day we don't do a lot
4	Je [əž] marchons pour des causes	We march for causes
5	Mais je croyons rien du tout	But we don't believe in anything at all
6	C'est la new edition	It's the new edition
7	Television	Television

This short excerpt shows a number of traditional features, *je* epenthesis, *ouisme*, and the first-person plural traditional variant. *Loafer* and *dekshoo* do not show English plural morphology and thus fulfil one criterion for having the status of borrowings (versus code switches). Lines 6 and 7 show an unambiguous code switch to English, frequent in their music. A comparison of language use in *Acadieman* comic strips and TV shows and Radio Radio lyrics shows considerable overlap for the linguistic features considered in the present study, with the exception that the first-person plural traditional variant and use of *point* as the general negator is absent from the former. This is understandable since *Acadieman*'s creator is a Moncton, New Brunswick, native and both variants are almost entirely absent from sociolinguistic corpora for that region. Even in the 1970s, for the oldest sociolinguistic corpora, *je*+VERB+*-ons* is restricted to the speech of very old consultants (Roy 1979).

While mid- to late twentieth-century traditional Acadian musicians, such as singer-songwriters Angèle Arsenault, Edith Butler and Donat Lacroix, have enjoyed large audiences in Acadia and in Francophone contexts more generally, their music does not contain the kind of linguistic innovation we find in Radio Radio. While other contemporary performers such as Marie-Jo Thério do use some of the English-origin forms found in Radio Radio's music, they are less prominent. Still, *Acadieman* and Radio Radio also have much in

Table 15.1: *Linguistic features by source.*

Linguistic Features	Marichette	La Sagouine	Acadieman	Radio Radio
/k/ /g/ palatalization	+	+	+	+
ouisme	+	+	+	+
ej metathesis	+	+	+	+
Point general negator	−	+	−	+
je+VERB+-*ons*	+	+	−	+
il+VERB+-*ont*	+	+	+	+
Traditional lexicon	+	+	+	+
Old English borrowings	+	+	+	+
English-origin discourse markers	+	+	+	+
English-origin intensifiers	−	−	+	+
English evidentials	+	−	+	+
English (based) phrasal verbs	−	−	+	+
English cardinal numbers and non-numeric quantifiers	−	−	+	+

common with the nineteenth- and twentieth-century artistic representations discussed earlier. Table 15.1 summarises presence or absence of particular linguistic features from *Marichette*, *La Sagouine*, *Acadieman* and Radio Radio, showing both linguistic continuity and a certain degree of linguistic discontinuity.

5.   Conclusion

Traditionally, representations of Acadian language and identity have celebrated the history of the Acadian people, such as the nineteenth-century parodic texts, the widely performed *La Sagouine*, as well as local summer theatre and festivals which typically centre on aspects of traditional culture. To a certain extent, *Acadieman*, *Radio Radio*, and their contemporaries are quite removed from these earlier representations. For instance, while *La Sagouine* was a retired cleaning woman, *Acadieman* is a call centre worker. However, all of the artistic representations discussed here present local language use in a positive light, although what exactly comprises 'the local' has changed over time. A recurring theme throughout all these artistic representations is the treatment of Acadian people as a linguistic minority. In the case of *Acadieman*, this is referenced in part by Acadieman's refusal to speak anything but Chiac to his interlocutors, regardless of their own language use. For an Acadian not to switch to more standard French with a non-Acadian Francophone, and not to switch to English when speaking with an Anglophone, is easily read by encultured audience members as an act of rebellion.

Despite the hand-wringing about the decline of the language, it is clear that for many Acadians (and other young Francophones in Canada) *Acadieman* and Radio Radio are cool. However, they are not entirely at odds with an older discourse centred around a rural 'folkloric' Acadian identity: the new representations reconfigure those older identities, including local language use, in a changing world. Today, the situation is not unlike that described by Beal (2009) for northern British English, where a variety that only a few decades ago typically appeared in media as the butt of comedy, if at all, has now come to index an edgy urbanity.

Some aspects of local language use described here may no longer be part of the everyday discourse of some of its proponents. This is the case of linguistic features found in Radio Radio's repertoire which have disappeared from the Acadian spoken in urban areas of New Brunswick, such as use of first-person plural *je*+VERB+-*ons* and use of *point* as the general negator. Another instance is when, as a part of Arts et Culture du Grand Rassemblement Jeunesse (an Acadian youth congress bringing together delegates from all over Acadia in 2009), fifteen teenagers aged 12–16 made a documentary short on what it means to be an Acadian today. Watching the film it is clear that in this documentary the young participants do not pepper their speech with many of the vernacular variants discussed in this chapter. Yet, the title they chose for their film is the somewhat surprising *J'avons note* [sic] *place et j'la gardons chaude* ('We have our place and we are keeping it warm'). Thus even a traditional feature which has all but disappeared from New Brunswick Acadian varieties, *je*+VERB+-*ons* still has discursive value for these young Acadians. Perhaps this is because its perceptual salience contributes to its availability for linkage to a variety of social meanings, even when it has arguably all but disappeared from language use in face-to-face interaction.[6]

In summary, the present chapter has shown that the identity values of this particular North American French variety have never been entirely uniform: they have been contested across the time periods under study. However, the stereotypical associations of the variety as exhibiting 'old' linguistic features alongside numerous English borrowings have been demonstrated to be important in the popular representations of the variety in twenty-first century mass media. Such stereotypical understandings of what might index Acadian-ness have therefore been recontextualised in these representations with 'new'

---

[6] The first-person Acadian variant is more salient than the third-person one since the first-person plural supralocal vernacular variant, *on*+VERB+-*Ø* (e.g. *on parle* 'we are speaking'), differs from the local vernacular variant in both subject pronoun and inflectional ending (/õ/ vs a phonetically-null ending), leaving the former quite open to social (re)evaluation. King (2014b) discusses this variant's changing indexical field across time and space in French.

features added to the set. This further demonstrates the importance of artistic performance when attempting to understand the social meanings attached to minority language varieties.

REFERENCES

Anderson, Benedict 1983. *Imagined Communities: Reflections on the Origin and Spread of Nationalism.* London: Verso Editions.

Balcom, Patricia and Louise Beaulieu 1998. 'Le statut des pronoms personnels sujets en français acadien du nord-est du Nouveau Brunswick.' *Linguistica Atlantica* 20: 1–27.

Beal, Joan C. 2009. '"You're not from New York City, you're from Rotherham": Dialect and identity in British indie music'. *Journal of English Linguistics* 37: 223–40.

Beaulieu, Louise and Wladyslaw Cichocki 2008. 'La flexion postverbale -*ont* en français acadien: une analyse sociolinguistique'. *Revue canadienne de linguistique* 53: 35–62.

　　2014. 'Les formes comme / comme que en français acadien du nord-est du Nouveau-Brunswick: variation synchronique et variation diachronique'. Paper presented at the annual meeting of Canadian Linguistic Association. St. Catherines: Brock University.

Bonnard, Henri 1993. 'Archives du mouvement'. *Francophonie acadienne* 57: 5–8.

Boudreau, Annette 1996. 'Les mots des jeunes Acadiens et Acadiennes du Nouveau-Brunswick', in Dubois, Lise and Annette Boudreau (eds.). *Les Acadiens et leur(s) langue(s) – Quand le français est minoritaire: Actes du colloque.* Moncton: Éditions d'Acadie. pp. 137–55.

Boudreau, Annette and Lise Dubois 2003. 'Les espaces discursifs de l'Acadie des Maritimes', in Heller, Monica and Normand Labrie (eds.). *Discours et identités: La francité canadienne entre modernité et mondialisation.* Belgium: Cortil-Wodon. pp. 89–113.

　　2007. '*Français, acadien, acadjonne*: Competing discourses on language preservation along the shores of the Baie Sainte-Marie', in Duchêne, Alexandre and Monica Heller (eds.). *Discourses of Endangerment: Ideology and Interest in the Defence of Languages.* London: Continuum. pp. 99–120.

Brasseur, Patrice 2001. *Dictionnaire des régionalismes du français de Terre-Neuve.* Tübingen: Niemeyer.

Brasseur, Patrice and Anika Falkert 2005. *Français d'Amérique: Approches morphosyntaxiques.* Paris: L'Harmattan.

Brault, Michel 1969. *Éloge du chiac.* [Motion picture]. Montreal, QC: Office national du film du Canada.

Brunot, Ferdinand 1966. *Histoire de la langue française.* Paris: Librairie Armand Colin.

Charbonneau, Hubert and André Guillemette 1994. 'Les pionniers du Canada au 17ᵉ siècle', in Mougeon, Raymond and Édouard Beniak (eds.). *Les origines du français québécois.* Québec: Presses de L'Université Laval. pp. 59–78.

Choquette, Leslie 1997. *De français à paysans*: *Modernité et tradition dans le peuplement du Canada français.* Québec: Septentrion,

Cichocki, Wladyslaw 2011. 'Retention of traditional phonetic features in Acadian French'. Paper presented at York University, Toronto, March 2011.

Comeau, Paul-Emile 2014. *Acadian Driftwood: The Roots of Acadian and Cajun Music*. Kingston, Ontario: Quarry Press.

Comeau, Philip and Ruth King 2011. 'Media representations of minority French: Valorization, identity and the Acadieman phenomenon'. *Canadian Journal of Linguistics* 56: 179–202.

Comeau, Philip, Ruth King and Gary R. Butler 2012. 'New insights on an old rivalry: The passé simple and the passé composé in spoken Acadian French'. *Journal of French Language Studies* 13: 323–37.

Comeau, Philip, Ruth King and Carmen LeBlanc 2014. 'Dialect contact and the sociolinguistic history of Acadian French'. Paper presented at Methods XV, Groningen, The Netherlands.

Cormier, Yves 1999. *Dictionnaire de l'acadien*. Quebec: Éditions Fides.

Coupland, Nikolas 2007. *Style: Language Variation and Identity*. Cambridge: Cambridge University Press.

2009. 'The mediated performance of vernaculars'. *Journal of English Linguistics* 37: 284–300.

Flikeid, Karin 1994. 'Origines et évolution du français acadien à la lumière de l'étude de la diversité contemporaine', in Mougeon, Raymond and Édouard Beniak (eds.) *Les origines du français québécois*. Québec: Presses de L'Université Laval. pp. 275–326.

1997. 'Structural aspects and current sociolinguistic situation of Acadian French', in Valdman, Albert (ed.) *French and Creole in Louisiana*. New York: Plenum Press. pp. 257–86.

Flikeid, Karin and Louise Péronnet 1989. 'N'est-ce pas vrai qu'il faut dire 'J'avons été'?: Divergences régionales en acadien'. *Français moderne* 57: 219–28.

Gammel, Irene and J. Paul Boudreau 1998. 'Linguistic schizophrenia: The poetics of Acadian identity construction'. *Journal of Canadian Studies* 32: 52–68.

Gérin, Pierre M. 1984. 'La création d'un troisième code comme mode d'adaptation à une situation où deux langues sont en contact, le chiac'. *Papers from the Seventh Annual Meeting of the Atlantic Provinces Linguistic Association*, 31–8.

1993. *Le glossaire acadien de Pascal Poirier (Édition critique de Pierre M. Gérin)*. Moncton: Éditions d'Acadie/Centre d'études acadiennes.

Gérin, Pierre and Pierre M. Gérin. 1982. *Marichette: Lettres acadiennes*. Sherbrooke: Éditions Naaman.

Griffiths, Naomi 1992. *The Contexts of Acadian History, 1686–1784*. Montreal: McGill-Queens University Press.

Gumperz, John J. 1992. 'Contextualization and understanding', in Duranti, Alessandro and Charles Goodwin (eds.) *Rethinking Context: Language as an Interactive Phenomenon*. Cambridge: Cambridge University Press. pp. 229–52.

Heller, Monica 2003. 'Globalization, the new economy, and the commodification of language and identity.' *Journal of Sociolinguistics* 7: 473–92.

Johnstone, Barbara 2011. 'Dialect enregisterment in performance.' *Journal of Sociolinguistics* 15: 657–79.

King, Ruth 1994. 'Subject-verb agreement in Newfoundland French'. *Language Variation and Change* 6: 239–53.

2000. *The Lexical Basis of Grammatical Borrowing*. Amsterdam & New York: John Benjamins.

2005. 'Morphosyntactic variation and theory: Subject-verb agreement in Acadian French', in Cornips, Leonie and Karen Corrigan (eds.) *Syntax and Variation: Reconciling the Biological and the Social*. Amsterdam: John Benjamins. pp. 199–229.

2008. 'Chiac in context: Overview and evaluation of Acadie's Joual', in Meyerhoff, Miriam and Naomi Nagy (eds.) *Social Lives in Language*. Amsterdam: John Benjamins. pp. 137–78.

2011. 'The linguistic trajectory of an old borrowing', in Martineau, France and Terry Nadasdi (eds.) *Le français en contact: Hommages à Raymond Mougeon*. Québec: Presses de l'Université Laval. pp. 193–216.

2013. *Acadian French in Time and Space: A Study in Morphosyntax and Comparative Sociolinguistics*. Durham, NC: Duke University Press.

2014a. 'Convergence, divergence and the recent history of Acadian French'. Paper presented at The International Conference on Methods in Dialectology XV, Groningen, The Netherlands, August 2014.

2014b. 'The life cycles of a vernacular variant'. Plenary paper presented at New Ways of Analyzing Variation (NWAV) 43, University of Illinois at Urbana-Champaign, October 2014.

King, Ruth, France Martineau and Raymond Mougeon 2011. 'The interplay of internal and external factors in grammatical change: First person plural pronouns in French'. *Language* 87: 470–509.

King, Ruth and Jennifer Wicks 2009. '"Aren't we proud of our language?": Authenticity, Commodification and the Nissan Bonavista Television Commercial.' *Journal of English Linguistics* 37: 262–83.

King, Ruth and Terry Nadasdi 1999. 'The expression of evidentiality in French-English bilingual discourse'. *Language in Society* 28: 355–65.

King, Ruth, Terry Nadasdi and Gary R. Butler 2004. 'First person plural in Prince Edward Island Acadian French: The fate of the vernacular variant *je...ons*'. *Language Variation and Change* 16: 237–55.

Labelle, Ronald 2002. 'Le monde tourne et je tourne avec', in pp. 165–83.

Magord, Andre (ed.) 2002. *Les Franco-Terreneuviens de la Péninsule de Port-au-Port: Évolution d'une Identité Acadienne*. Chaire d'études acadiennes, collection Mouvange Université de Moncton.

LeBlanc, Dano. *Acadieman – Le First Superhero Acadien*. See www.acadieman.com.

2007. *Acadieman: Ses Origines*. Moncton, New Brunswick: Les Éditions Court Circuit.

Lucci, Vincent 1972. *Phonologie de l'acadien*. Montréal: Didier.

Maillet, Antonine 1974. *La Sagouine*. Montreal, Québec: Leméac.

1979. *La Sagouine* (English edn). Toronto, Ontario: Simon and Pierre Co.

Martineau, France 2005. 'Perspectives sur le changement linguistique: aux sources du français'. *Canadian Journal of Linguistics* 50: 173–213.

Massignon, Geneviève 1962. *Les parlers français d'Acadie: Enquête linguistique*, vol 2. Paris: Klincksieck.

Noël, Hubert 2010. Le 'je collectif' dans la grande région de Shippagen: Entre image et usages. Unpublished M.A. thesis, Université de Moncton.

Pavel, Maria 2005. 'Régionalismes grammaticaux en 'chiac'", in Brasseur, Patrice and Anika Falkert (eds.) *Français d'Amérique: Approches morphosyntaxiques. Actes du Colloque international grammaire comparée des variétés de français d'Amérique*. Paris: L'Harmattan. pp. 49–56.

Péronnet, Louise, Wladyslaw Cichocki and Patrice Brasseur 1998. *Atlas linguistique du vocabulaire maritime acadien*. Quebec: Université Laval.

Perrot, Marie-Eve 1995. 'Aspects fondamentaux du métissage français/anglais dans le chiac du Moncton (Nouveau-Brunswick, Canada)'. Unpublished PhD thesis, Université de la Sorbonne.

Poirier, Pascal 1990. *Causerie memrakcookienne*. Moncton: Chaire d'études acadiennes.

Ross, Sally and J. Alphonse Deveau 1992. *The Acadians of Nova Scotia Past and Present*. Halifax: Nimbus Publishing.

Roy, Marie-Marthe 1979. 'Les conjonctions « but » et « so » dans le parler de Moncton'. Unpublished MA thesis, Université du Québec à Montréal.

Young, Hillary 2002. '*C'est either que tu parles français, c'est either que tu parles anglais:* A cognitive approach to Chiac as a contact language'. Unpublished PhD thesis, Rice University.

16   'Turtlely Amazing'
The Enregisterment of "Yorkshire" Dialect
and the Possibility of GOAT Fronting as a
Newly Enregistered Feature

Paul Cooper

1.   Introduction

In this chapter, I discuss the enregisterment of the Yorkshire dialect. Agha (2003: 231) defines enregisterment as the 'processes through which a linguistic repertoire becomes differentiable within a language as a socially recognized register of forms'. Johnstone *et al.* (2006: 82; see also Johnstone, Chapter 13 in this volume) expand upon this definition, stating that a feature has become enregistered when it has 'become associated with a style of speech and can be used to create a context for that style'. Enregistered features can be associated with particular social values, including social class or geographical region, but also more abstract concepts like 'authenticity' or 'friendliness'. My focus in this chapter is on the enregisterment of Yorkshire dialect and how a new feature seems to be becoming part of the enregistered repertoire.

The county of Yorkshire is located in the north of England, as shown in Figure 16.1. It is organised into four major administrative areas: North Yorkshire, West Yorkshire, South Yorkshire and the East Riding of Yorkshire.[1] Most of modern North Yorkshire once belonged to the North Riding, whereas West and South Yorkshire were in the West Riding (Kellett 2002: xxi). As discussed later, North Yorkshire and the East Riding are largely more rural and sparsely populated than the urban areas of West and South Yorkshire.[2] The former region includes areas like the Yorkshire Dales, and cities like York and, as discussed below Hull. The latter includes larger cities like Sheffield, Leeds, Halifax, Huddesfield, Bradford, Wakefield, Rotherham and Barnsley.

Following Beal (2009) and Johnstone *et al.* (2006), I discuss the fact that speaker awareness of language variation is reflected in the production of dialect dictionaries and glossaries. Consequently, as Beal (2009: 142) states,

---

[1] See www.ons.gov.uk/ons/rel/regional-trends/regional-trends/no–41–2009-edition/portrait-of-yorkshire-and-humberside.pdf.
[2] See www.ons.gov.uk/ons/rel/regional-trends/region-and-country-profiles/key-statistics-and-pro files—august-2012/key-statistics—yorkshire-and-the-humber.html.

This work is based on data provided through EDINA UKBORDERS with the support of the ESRC and JISC and uses boundary material which is copyright of the Crown, the Post Office, and the ED-LINE Consortium. Further elements of the map made use of data provided by the Historic County Borders Project.

Figure 16.1: *Geographical location of Yorkshire showing historic country boundary*

these kinds of texts can highlight 'progressive enregisterment and reification' of dialects (Beal 2009: 142). In many cases these texts provide overt commentary on language use, which creates and reinforces links between language features and social values. In their study of a variety of U.S. English, 'Pittsburghese', Johnstone *et al.* (2006) highlight how these kinds of sources can contribute to features' enregisterment. They state that:

People … link the regional variants they are most likely to hear with Pittsburgh identity, drawing on the increasingly widely circulating idea that places and dialects are essentially linked (every place has a dialect). These people, who include Pittsburghers and non-Pittsburghers, use regional forms drawn from highly codified lists to perform local identity, often in ironic, semiserious ways. (Johnstone *et al.* 2006: 82–3)

Therefore, I consider data from Yorkshire dialect dictionaries and examine the correlation between textual representation of 'Yorkshire' features and speakers' perceptions of them. Features which are frequently and consistently represented in dialect literature, defined by Shorrocks (1996: 386) as 'works composed wholly (sometimes partly) in a non-standard dialect' and literary dialect, which is 'the representation of non-standard speech in literature that is otherwise written in standard English', are strongly indicative of the enregistered repertoire of Yorkshire dialect . I discuss the comparison of these features with metapragmatic judgments about Yorkshire dialect features elicited from speakers who are both from and not from Yorkshire in an online survey, following Johnstone *et al.* (2006: 99), who elicited similar judgements from Pittsburgh speakers about 'Pittsburghese'. They conducted interviews in order to ascertain speakers' perceptions of the variety with specific regard to certain language features. Their results highlighted that there is a repertoire of features enregistered as 'Pittsburghese'.

Finally, I consider written representations of Yorkshire features which appear on commodities. Beal (2009: 148) has noted that commodified features can also be seen as evidence for their enregisterment, because the social value of the language features is illustrated by their being available for purchase. I present examples here of commodified Yorkshire features including definite article reduction [henceforth DAR], which is the tendency for Yorkshire speakers to reduce the definite article to either a glottal stop or, more rarely, a [t] (see Tagliamonte and Roeder 2009), as in the examples [ɪ ʔ ʊvən] and [ɪ t ʊvən] for 'in the oven' respectively (Jones 2007: 61). DAR is also very strongly associated with Yorkshire (Wales 2006: 187) and can be stereotypical of the county 'in spite of its more widespread distribution in other Northern regions such as Lancashire and parts of the North-Midlands' (Richards 2008: 87–8). I also discuss the lexical items *owt* 'anything', and *nowt* 'nothing', and compare these examples with the results of the aforementioned online survey (see also Cooper 2013) which investigates speakers' perceptions of which features index Yorkshire dialect. This illustrates the extent to which speakers are aware of these features and associate them with Yorkshire. As I discuss elsewhere (see Cooper 2013, 2014), DAR, *owt* and *nowt* have been enregistered as Yorkshire since at least the nineteenth century, so it is perhaps unsurprising to see them represented on commodities. However, we can also see evidence for a relatively recent feature becoming part of the enregistered 'Yorkshire' repertoire. This takes the form of a Yorkshire t-shirt which displays the non-standard spelling of the word 'totally' as *turtlely*. This appears to be an allusion to a specific variety of Yorkshire English spoken in Kingston upon Hull (hereafter Hull), which is a port city situated in the East Riding of Yorkshire.

The Hull dialect was included in the BBC Voices dialect survey (2004–5). This survey aimed to capture 'the variety and richness of accent and dialect' throughout the United Kingdom. It also involved recordings of speaker interviews, an accent recognition survey, and an online survey where informants were asked to submit examples of regional dialect lexis.[3] As part of its 'Guide to Hull dialect', the Voices survey states that it is 'impossible to live in Hull and not hear words such as *err nerr* meaning "oh no"'. They go on to present a word list designed as a guide to some of the most 'commonly used words' in Hull, and list the example *curlslur* for 'coleslaw'.[4] These examples suggest a pronunciation of [ɜː], known as GOAT fronting (Watt and Tillotson 2001). This relates to the GOAT lexical set (Wells 1982) in English English, which in many southern varieties has a pronunciation of [əʊ]. This is not the case in some northern varieties where the pronunciation can be [oː] (Watson 2009: 350). This pronunciation is extremely salient in representing Hull dialect and Hull speakers are aware that it is associated with them (as noted by Watt 2013: 217), almost to the point that the feature distinguishes Hull dialect from the rest of Yorkshire. However, as I shall discuss later, there is evidence to suggest that the phenomenon of GOAT fronting is spreading out of Hull into other areas of Yorkshire. What is particularly interesting about this feature is that it seems to be in the process of becoming enregistered as Yorkshire dialect, despite its occurrence in a limited area within the county.

2.   The Enregisterment of Yorkshire Dialect

2.1   Textual Data: Dialect Commentary

There are many dialect dictionaries and folk texts which discuss Yorkshire and provide overt commentary on features of the dialect. These texts (listed in

---

[3] See www.bbc.co.uk/voices/yourvoice/voices_recordings.shtml.
[4] See www.bbc.co.uk/humber/content/articles/2005/02/14/voices_hullspeak_glossary.shtml.

Table 16.1: *Yorkshire dialect commentary texts.*

Author	Year	Title
Markham	2010	*Ee Up Lad! A Salute to the Yorkshire Dialect*
Collins	2009	*The Northern Monkey Survival Guide*
McMillan	2007	*Chelp and Chunter How to Talk Tyke*
Battye	2007	*Sheffield Dialect and Folklore since the Second World War: A Dying Tradition*
Johnson	2006	*Yorkshire-English*
Kellett	2002	*The Yorkshire Dictionary of Dialect, Tradition and Folklore*
Whomersley	1981	*Sheffieldish a Beginners Phrase-Book*

Table 16.1) mostly take the form of popular books aimed at a non-specialist audience and give an insight into how the Yorkshire dialect is portrayed and viewed in the late twentieth and early twenty-first centuries. They are predominantly word lists, which in some cases include general descriptions of the Yorkshire accent and dialect.

There are several features which are frequently and consistently discussed in these texts. These include: DAR, orthographical representations suggesting alternate pronunciations of certain diphthongs, and Yorkshire lexical items including *owt*, *nowt* and *summat*.

According to Johnstone *et al.* (2006: 96), practices like this enable features of varieties 'to acquire legitimacy', as the same features are consistently used in similar constructions and with similar representations time and again. For instance, DAR is discussed frequently; there are comments like 'You'll also hear t'definite article begin to contract as you head for the Yorkshire border' (Collins 2009: 135) and 't' (the) which is not actually sounded, but replaced by a brisk opening and shutting of the glottis at the top of the windpipe' (Kellett 2002: xxviii). The orthographical rendering of DAR as <t> is also especially consistent. In addition, we can observe frequent discussion of word-initial /h/-dropping. Battye (2007: 29), for instance, states that all of the words listed in the 'H' section of his glossary would 'almost always' be pronounced without the initial /h/.

Two variant pronunciations of PRICE words are also represented consistently in these texts. A suggested pronunciation of /ɛɪ/ can be seen in *reight* (Whomersley 1981; Kellett 2002; Battye 2007; McMillan 2007), and /iː/ is indicated in *reet* (Johnson 2006; Markham 2010). The former variant is more common, and can also be seen in words like *feight* (Whomersley 1981, Battye 2007) or *feyt* (Kellett 2002: 59) for 'fight'. However, the latter vowel can be also be seen represented in words like *leet* for 'light' (Kellett 2002; Battye 2007; McMillan 2007), and *toneet* for 'tonight' (Whomersley 1981: 24) – even

Table 16.2: *Corpus of Yorkshire Dialect Literature and Literary Dialect texts sampled for quantitative analysis.*

Author	Date	Title
Dialect Literature		
Kellett	2007	*Ee By Gum, Lord! The Gospels in Broad Yorkshire*
Hague	1976	*Totley Tom: Tales of a Yorkshire Miner*
Hirst	(2011)	*A Coil Fire; Adam An' Eve An' T' Apple; A Deep Grave; A Mucky November Neet; A Pain I' T' Neck*[6]
Greensmith	(2011)	*Christmas Party; Len Wilde; Mi Secret Luv; Robin Hood Wor a Yorkshireman*[7]
Alden	(1933) 2011	*T' Concert Party Ride*[8]
Literary Dialect		
Smith	1998	*Plaintiffs, Plonkers and Pleas*
Taylor-Bradford	1981	*A Woman of Substance*
Herriot	1977	*Vet in a Spin*
Hines	(1967) 2000	*A Kestrel for a Knave*
Holtby	(1935) 2011	*South Riding*

though these writers give *reight* or *reyt* for 'right'. This suggests that the use of this variant diphthong is perceived to be restricted to a small number of words, and that its use is not presented as consistent across every PRICE word.

Finally, *owt, nowt* and *summat* ('something') appear in every commentary text considered here. Most texts, as those cited above, simply give the definitions for these words; some give etymologies which date back to Old English, such as Kellett (2002: 125), for instance, who states that *nowt* derives from OE 'na-wiht'. The OED also gives this etymology, stating that *nowt* represents 'a variety of English regional, Scots, and Irish English pronunciations of nought',[5] and that 'nought' derives from the Old English form also given by Kellett. The majority of these texts give the orthographical forms <owt>, <nowt> and <summat> for these words, highlighting a consistency in their written representations.

2.2   Textual Data: Dialect Literature and Literary Dialect

The majority of the dialect literature texts discussed here (listed in Table 16.2) take the form of dialect poetry. The works of Hirst, Greensmith and Alden come from the website www.yorkshire-dialect.org, which states that it is dedicated to 'Yorkshire verse'. This site also contains glossaries and word lists, as well as examples of Yorkshire recipes. In addition, the

---

[5] See www.oed.com.

site also encourages contributors to submit their own Yorkshire poetry. Tom Hague's *Totley Tom: Tales of a Yorkshire Miner* (1976) is also a collection of poetry written in Yorkshire dialect, but published as a book rather than online. Kellett (2007) describes his text as a 'retelling' of the gospels in Yorkshire dialect and is essentially a 'translation' of them written entirely using non-standard orthography.

The literary dialect texts listed in Table 16.2 all feature dialogue from Yorkshire characters. Some even have parts of the story which take place in Yorkshire. For example, some of Smith's *Plaintiffs, Plonkers and Pleas* takes place in Rotherham and features characters who speak in Yorkshire dialect; these characters' speech is represented using non-standard orthography. A similar case can be observed in *A Kestrel for a Knave*, which features Barnsley as a location.

As with the commentary material discussed earlier, similar features of Yorkshire dialect were frequently and consistently represented in the dialect literature and literary dialect. For instance, definite article reduction is extremely common. In the dialect literature we see constructions like (1)–(5) below:

(1) *thru t'door* 'through the door' (Greensmith 2011)
(2) *For t'thing was mare an horf full then* 'For the thing was more than half full then' (Alden 2011)
(3) *Its wahrm glow penetrated all t'corners o' t'room* 'Its warm glow penetrated all the corners of the room' (Hirst 2011)
(4) *All t' pleasure went frum aht o' t' day* 'All the pleasure went from out of the day' (Hague 1976)
(5) *T' Babby Born in a Mistal* 'The baby born in a mistal' (Kellett 2007)

Wales (2006: 187) discusses the use of <t> for the reduction of the definite article, stating that it is one of the most 'salient features of traditional Northern English . . . conventionally represented in writing and stereotypes as <t>'. The orthographic form <t> is also frequently and consistently employed in literary dialect. For instance, we can see constructions like:

Well me mother 'ad a big pot a stew ont' cooker like, ready to cook for tea. It must 'ave been some bugger wi' a grudge 'cos the dirty bastard did 'is business int' pot. (Smith 1998: 3)

In the example above we can clearly see <t'> used to represent a reduced definite article, although the reduced form is not exclusively used for every

[6] www.yorkshire-dialect.org/authors/fred_hirst.htm.
[7] www.yorkshire-dialect.org/authors/bert_greensmith.htm.
[8] www.yorkshire-dialect.org/authors/gertie_alden.htm.

instance of the definite article, as we can see the full un-reduced form *the* in 'the dirty bastard'.

Several examples of Yorkshire lexical items occur frequently in the dialect literature. These include *sen* meaning 'self'; *owt, nowt* and *summat*; and the use of archaic pronouns such as *thee* and *tha* in the second person. These words are also consistently discussed in the commentary material, as mentioned earlier. We can see examples like: *An wy dint a gu an luk fer missen*, meaning 'And why didn't I go and look for myself' (Greensmith 2011), *Ah dooan't suppooase the' thowt 'at this lad wor owt aht o' t' ordinary*, meaning 'I don't suppose they thought that this lad was anything out of the ordinary' (Kellett 2007), *Why, nowt ti fuss aboot*, meaning 'Why, nothing to fuss about' (Alden 2011), and *A coil fire wor a must, summat that ivvrybody 'ad*, meaning 'a coal fire was a must, something that everybody had' (Hirst 2011). These lexical items can also be seen in several of the literary dialect texts. Holtby, for instance, gives 'D'ye hear owt, lad?' ([1935] 2011: 146), and Hines has 'I've never taken owt o' yours, have I?' ([1967] 2000: 8). Taylor-Bradford also makes use of this item in character dialogue such as 'Yer can't stop me if I runs away and run away I will, out of this godforsaken hole, here there's nowt but misery and poverty and dying' (1981: 101–2). With regards to *summat*, Herriot has his characters employing constructions like 'Yes ah thought ah'd better take 'im to somebody as knows summat about dogs. He's a vallible dog is that' (1977: 61).

It should also be noted that the features discussed above have been observed in Yorkshire dialect in the late twentieth and early twenty-first centuries. The SED records DAR, /ɛɪ/ and /ɪː/ in certain PRICE words, and the lexical items *owt, nowt* and *summat* in Yorkshire (see Orton and Dieth 1962, 1963). These features were similarly recorded by Hedevind (1967), Tidholm (1979) and Glauser (1984) in Dentdale (Yorkshire Dales), Egton and Grassington (both North Yorkshire) respectively. More recently, Roeder (2009: 117) records DAR in York and notes that it is being used to maintain local identity. The representations of these features in textual data therefore index Yorkshire dialect in part due to their presence in the dialect in reality.

2.3   Elicited Metapragmatic Judgements

Johnstone *et al.* (2006: 99) note that awareness of the Pittsburgh accent on the part of the non-Pittsburghers is evidence of the enregisterment of certain features as 'Pittsburghese'. As I have discussed elsewhere (Cooper 2015, 2016), I conducted an online survey of speakers in order to investigate similar awareness of Yorkshire dialect over the period of a month. For the purpose of illustrating the efficacy of this methodology in highlighting enregistered "Yorkshire" features including GOAT fronting, I will also briefly recount the details of this survey here. There were 410 respondents; 56% of the

Table 16.3: *Common Yorkshire features provided by both Yorkshire and non-Yorkshire respondents (arranged in decreasing order of frequency for Yorkshire respondents).*

Yorkshire Feature	Definition	Non-Yorkshire Respondents		Yorkshire Respondents	
		n	%	*N*	%
DAR	Definite article	32	53	27	45
Reight	Really	26	43	19	32
Thee	You/your	25	42	39	65
Terms of endearment	For example 'love', 'duck'	20	33	8	13
/a/ and /Y/	Northern BATH and STRUT vowels	16	27	9	15
h-dropping	Lack word-initial of [h]	15	25	16	27
Nesh	Susceptible to cold	14	23	8	13
Gennel	Alleyway between houses	14	23	14	23
Nowt	Nothing	13	22	24	40
Ey up	Hello	10	17	18	30
Aye	Yes	9	15	8	13
Owt	Anything	8	13	16	27
Sen	Self	7	12	14	23

Table 16.4: *Enregistered Repertoire of Yorkshire dialect.*

Feature	*Definition*	Examples
DAR	Definite article	*Watch out for 't boggarts in 't snug o 't Red Lion*
Nowt	Nothing	*Nowt o 't' sooart*
Owt	Anything	*Doin' owt this evening?*
Summat	Something	*Tha nesh or summat?*
h-dropping	Lack of word-initial [h]	*Nah lad, put t' wood in t' oil*
Reight	Really/right	*Ah'm reight glad*
Sen	Self	*Missen, thissen*
Tha/thee	You/your	*Can't tha fit us in somewheeare?*

respondents stated that they were from Yorkshire (230), 44% said they were not from Yorkshire (180). Overall, 33% of respondents were male (135) against 67% female (275). Respondents were categorised according to the age groups 18–29, 30–39, 40–49, 50–59 and 60+. Of the 410 respondents, the group with the smallest number was female Yorkshire speakers aged 60 and over, six of whom completed the survey. As a result, twelve respondents were chosen from each age group for analysis (six male and six female), giving a total of 120 respondents that were analysed. The non-Yorkshire respondents from each age group were chosen to represent as broad a geographical range as possible across the whole country (see Cooper [2013] for a full list of locations). The responses to the survey questions did not vary significantly according to gender, hence, one respondent from each location was deemed to be representative thereof. The respondents from Yorkshire were also chosen to represent as broad a range as possible across the county, however, there was a notable bias towards South Yorkshire. This is likely due to the fact that, according to the 2011 census, the combined population of South and West Yorkshire is almost 2.5 times larger than the combined population of North Yorkshire and the East Riding.[9] The survey asked respondents to list language features they thought of as 'Yorkshire' dialect. They were also asked to rate features that were frequent and consistent in the textual data on the strength of their association of those features with Yorkshire.

Table 16.3 shows that there are thirteen Yorkshire features that were commonly listed by both groups of respondents. Furthermore, the lexical items *owt* and *nowt* were both frequently listed and showed a strong association with the region. This illustrates a consistency in the results for the textual data versus the survey, insofar as features which are frequent and consistent in written representations of Yorkshire dialect were similarly frequently and consistently listed as, and strongly associated with, 'Yorkshire' dialect by the survey respondents.

Comparison of the survey results with the textual data highlights a repertoire of Yorkshire features, set out in Table 16.4 (see Cooper 2013 for a full account of this comparison). This repertoire can be seen frequently and consistently in the textual data listed above. These features were also among the most commonly listed and those most strongly associated with Yorkshire in the online survey. We can therefore see that there is a correlation between written representations of Yorkshire dialect and speakers' perception of it. Thus, written representations give a strong indication of the features which index Yorkshire dialect.

As I discuss in the following section, several of the features in Table 16.4 appear on Yorkshire commodities. These commodities also display written representations of Yorkshire dialect and represent, as Johnstone (2009: 159) states, 'naturally occurring evidence of dialect awareness'. Therefore, following Beal (2009) we can use commodities as evidence for the enregisterment of Yorkshire features.

2.4   Commodification of Yorkshire Dialect

Johnstone (2009: 161) states that a 'linguistic variety or set of varieties is commodified when it is available for purchase and people will pay for it'. This

---

[9] Adapted from data from the Office for National Statistics licensed under the Open Government Licence v.1.0 at www.ons.gov.uk/ons/rel/mro/news-release/census-result-shows-increase-in-population-of-yorkshire-and-the-humber/censusyorkandhumbernr0712.html.

has the effect of directly linking linguistic features to a non-linguistic quality, in this case, regional location. The commodities then serve to maintain the enregistered status of the language features they display, as their social value is illustrated by their availability for purchase. Indeed, there is a limited amount of commodification to be observed with Yorkshire dialect features. For example, the website of the pottery manufacturers Moorland Pottery features a section called 'Yorkie Ware', www.moorlandpottery.co.uk/moorland-pot tery-ranges/yorkie-ware-mugs, where one can buy coffee mugs, coasters, teapots and also a small selection of bags and aprons. The majority of these products feature examples of Yorkshire dialect, such as the use of definite article reduction (in slogans such as 't' best place in t'world'). DAR, *owt* and *nowt*, as discussed earlier, are three of the most frequently occurring dialect features in written representations of Yorkshire dialect. They were also frequently listed as 'Yorkshire' dialect by respondents to the online survey.

Further examples of the 'Yorkie Ware' range feature such slogans as *Yorkshire born and bred, wi' nowt teken out*, displaying parallels with the Geordie[10] *Borth Sortificat* 'birth certificate' discussed by Beal (2009: 147), who states that 'these artefacts are selling "authenticity"'. The "authenticity" here is to by the statement that the owner was 'born and bred' in Yorkshire and has not had any of that 'breeding' removed over time (*wi' nowt teken out* – 'with nothing taken out'). The latter half of this logo seems to refer to the advertising slogan for Allinson's bread, which, since the 1980s, has declared their bread to be made with 100 per cent wholemeal flour: *bread wi' nowt taken out*, and has appeared in several television commercials.[11] Wales (2006: 28) discusses the above slogan, but incorrectly states that it appeared in an advertisement for Hovis bread; she is possibly here referring to a 1994 advert for Hovis which features a voice-over in a Yorkshire accent telling the story of a young boy in a flat cap on the screen.[12] Wales goes on to state that the use of phrases like this in advertising also demonstrates the exploitation of 'positive stereotypes' of Northerners. These stereotypes can include qualities such as 'resilient Northerners, hard-working and humorous in the face of adversity, blunt speaking and straight-forward, friendly to strangers ... they are what they seem' (Wales 2006: 28). As a result, the phrase *wi' nowt teken out* on Yorkshire commodities also indexes the more general 'northern' qualities described by Wales above, as well as simply 'authentic Yorkshire'. This illustrates that notions of a Yorkshire identity are also embedded in a broader northern one, similar to Beal's (2009: 153) discussion of Sheffield and

---

[10] The variety of English spoken in Newcastle-upon-Tyne, in the north-east of England (Beal 2009: 138).

[11] www.youtube.com/watch?v=raJRe7J5m6g.

[12] www.youtube.com/watch?v=BvhpD9XsrsE.

Yorkshire, and Wales' (2006: 30–1) discussion of 'different 'types' of Northerners' such as 'Yorkshire *tykes*,[13] Scousers[14] and Geordies[15]'.

A further method of linking language and place is to include the name of the region in question on the commodities. Johnstone (2009: 169) discusses examples of 'Pittsburghese' on t-shirts, where orthographic representations of Pittsburgh lexis and pronunciation are presented, often alongside the words 'Pittsburghese', or 'Pittsburgh'; in some instances, images of the Pittsburgh skyline appear also. This has the effect of directly linking linguistic features to a non-linguistic quality, in this case, regional location. This occurs in Figure 16.1 and other items of ware that see dialect features appear with the term 'Yorkshire'. Johnstone (2009: 170) goes on to states that commodities like these 'link dialect and place by juxtaposing local words on images of the city, sometimes directly, as when local words are enclosed in speech balloons emanating from downtown windows'. This occurs in a similar manner with Yorkshire t-shirts. For instance, the website www.cafepress.co.uk features a shirt with the phrase *Tha can allus tell a Yorkshireman* on the front below an image of the white rose of Yorkshire, and *but tha can't tell him much!* on the back.[16] This slogan is also similar to one noted by Beal (2009: 147) on a 'Geordie' coffee mug, which bears the slogan: *How to tell a genuine original Geordie. Divvint. He canna be telt.* The intended joke here being the dual meaning of the word 'tell' in both the Yorkshire shirt example and in Beal's; in the first instance, *tell* is used in the sense of 'discover', whereas in the second instance, *tell* means 'inform' or 'instruct', and 'alludes to the stereotypical intransigence of the '"Geordie"' (Beal 2009: 147), which also appears to extend to the stereotypical 'Yorkshireman'.

The previous discussion illustrates that the social values associated with particular language features (such as the geographical location of Yorkshire), and with particular speakers (such as 'intransigence') can be highlighted by their appearance on commodities. In the next section, I will turn to the case of one specific commodity, which, if we continue to assume that commodities serve to enregister language features and then to reinforce their enregistered status, we can take as evidence for the enregisterment of an additional feature of Yorkshire dialect in the form of GOAT fronting. Speaker awareness of this feature is reflected primarily in the feature's appearance on a t-shirt and, as with the rest of the Yorkshire repertoire discussed earlier, we can see a correspondence between the appearance of written representations of this

---

[13] A label given to Yorkshire speakers which, according to Wales (2006: 133, note 19), is of Scandinavian origin.
[14] From 'Scouse': the variety of English 'spoken in Liverpool, in the north-west of England' (Honeybone & Watson 2013: 306). Speakers of this variety are referred to as 'Scousers'.
[15] Applied to speakers of Geordie (see note 2 in this chapter).
[16] www.cafepress.co.uk/mf/4126811/tha-can-allus-tell-a-tshirt-_tshirt.

Figure 16.2: 'Yorkshire It's Turtlely Amazing' t-shirt.

feature and its perception and use by certain speakers. Therefore, I suggest that this commodity is indicative of GOAT fronting becoming part of the enregistered Yorkshire repertoire.

3.   GOAT fronting and Yorkshire

Figure 16.2 shows a representation of a fronted GOAT pronunciation in the word *turtlely* ('totally') printed on a t-shirt, available from the website www.balconytshirts.co.uk. The t-shirt highlights an explicit link between pronunciation and Yorkshire. The pronunciation of 'totally' as *turtlely* appears to be an allusion to 'Hull English, in which GOAT is characteristically [ɜː] (as in RP *bird*)' and is a stereotypically 'Hull' pronunciation (Watt and Smith 2005: 109). Further examples of this feature can be seen on a guide to the area, produced for students studying at the University of Hull. On the back cover of this guide there is a page entitled 'How to Speak "Hullish"', which contains a short list of dialect features, most of which are lexical items. The phrases 'I need to make a phone call' and 'I'm going shopping on the high street' are 'translated' as 'A need t' mekka fern curl' and 'Gurn on rerd'. Both of these 'translations' suggest a fronted GOAT pronunciation; 'phone' as *fern* in the former case and 'high street' (or 'road') as *rerd* in the latter. Indeed, Watt (2013: 217) states that in Hull itself, GOAT fronting is 'sufficiently far above the level of conscious awareness that it is overtly commented upon and represented in joke spellings'.

Evidence for the association of this feature with 'Hullish' can also be seen on some internet sites, notably www.thehullshop.co.uk, which states that it is 'promoting Hull to the world'. Interest in such promotion appears to be a reaction to Hull being named the UK City of Culture 2017.[17] Many of the items for sale at www.thehullshop.co.uk include examples of Hull dialect, and shoppers may purchase the Hull Dialect Pack, which includes a t-shirt, mug, fridge magnet and postcard. Three of these four items includes *Err nerr* 'oh no', and two of them feature *Goin on rerd*.[18] Additionally, the website www.codalmighty.com presents a 'Hull to Grimsby[19] dictionary', which lists *Nerth perl* as 'the most northerly point on Earth' (the North Pole) and *Perler* as a 'small white mint with a herl';[20] the latter example describing the *Polo* mints – which are famous for having a hole in the centre of them.

Examples of this feature being associated with a Yorkshire variety outside of Hull are somewhat less common, although evidence of this can still be seen. For instance, the discussion forum www.utdforum.com dedicated to Manchester United includes a discussion entitled 'Stupid Words Said in a Leeds Accent'. One post gives 'I don't know' as *I duuuuuuuuurrrrnttttttttt knnnnnneeeeeeeeer* although this is contested later in the discussion and is stated to be specifically a 'Hull' pronunciation rather than Leeds.[21] The earlier post does suggest that some speakers associate GOAT fronting with other areas of Yorkshire, though. This was also highlighted in the online survey, discussed further below.

We can also see sociolinguistic evidence which suggests GOAT fronting is not confined to Hull. For example, Watt and Smith (2005: 109) state that this feature is also found in West Yorkshire English, and that this can be linked to pronunciations found in Hull. Watt and Tillotson (2001) record this feature in the speech of younger speakers of Bradford English. Khattab (2007: 398) states that GOAT fronting has been 'informally observed in Leeds and York,

---

[17] See www.hullcc.gov.uk/2017hull.   [18] www.thehullshop.co.uk/hulldialectpack.html.
[19] The town of Grimsby in north-east Lincolnshire is situated approximately 16 miles to the south-east of Hull.
[20] www.codalmighty.com/site/ca.php?article=249.
[21] www.utdforum.com/forum/showthread.php?t=12411.

which indicates a change in progress', and that this fronted GOAT pronunciation is a relatively new feature of Yorkshire dialects. Furthermore, Finnegan (2011: 239) states that there is evidence of 'early stages of a change towards the central GOAT monophthong [ɵː]' in Sheffield.

Additionally, respondents to the online survey displayed some evidence of an association of GOAT fronting with Yorkshire dialect. When compared with the data for features like DAR, *owt*, or *nowt*, though, the numbers of respondents who listed fronted GOAT pronunciations were considerably smaller. Only four respondents in the whole survey listed this feature as Yorkshire dialect and, of those four, three were not from Yorkshire. There was also a tendency for these respondents to state specifically in Yorkshire where they thought this feature occurred. For instance, a female respondent aged 30–39 from Rochdale, Greater Manchester listed *fern curl* for 'phone call' as being a 'Hull' pronunciation, but also listed *can er kirk* for 'can of coke' as 'Leeds', which tallies with Khattab's (2007) data and the post in the 'Stupid Words Said In a Leeds Accent' online discussion, noted earlier. Furthermore, a female respondent in the 60 and over age group from Bradford in West Yorkshire listed *there's nerh snerh on the frehm rehrd* for 'there's no snow on the Frome Road' and stated that this pronunciation was 'specific to Hull'. The final two respondents to list this feature were somewhat less specific in their geographical locations. The first, a male respondent in the 40–49 age group from Wilmslow in Cheshire listed 'oh no (both pronounced to rhyme with 'her')' as being used in the East Riding of Yorkshire, and also the Wakefield area. The former location is consistent with Hull as the city is contiguous with the East Riding; the latter is consistent with Leeds as Wakefield is also in West Yorkshire. Finally, a female respondent in the 30–39 age group from Sutton in Surrey was no more specific than 'Yorkshire' in listing a location for GOAT fronting, as she simply gave 'O sounds more drawn out to "errrrr" e.g. Roses becomes Rerrrrrrses'. These perceptions, combined with the linguistic data, provide some explanation as to why the t-shirt in Figure 16.2 associates GOAT fronting with 'Yorkshire' more broadly, rather than Hull specifically.

An additional explanation for the apparent inconsistency in the association of GOAT fronting with either Hull or Yorkshire may be found in Beal's (2009) discussion of 'Sheffieldish'. She states that the stereotypical identity of a Yorkshire speaker is shared with many towns and cities in the county. In the case of Sheffield, she goes on to state that 'the identity of Sheffield and the Sheffielder seem at all times to be interchangeable with those of Yorkshire and the Yorkshireman' (Beal 2009: 149–50). A similar scenario was noted by Montgomery (2010: 594) in his study of the perceptions of northern English dialect areas. He discusses how informants from Hull also identified a 'Hull' dialect area, embedded within a larger 'Yorkshire' area. This corresponds with Watt's data discussed earlier, which suggests that Hull speakers see themselves as having their own distinct variety. The GOAT fronting data presented here indicates that the term 'Yorkshire' dialect is indeed interchangeable with the dialect of Hull.

However, despite indications from the above sources, which suggest some speakers are aware of GOAT fronting and associate it with Yorkshire, there is little evidence of this association in dialect dictionaries or other textual data. Indeed, some writers refer to alternate pronunciations of GOAT words that do not include a fronted variant. For instance, Kellett (2002: xxvii) discusses the Yorkshire pronunciation of words like 'bone' and 'stone' and states that these words would be pronounced as *booane* and *stooane*, suggesting that the diphthong in these words would be [ʊə]. He goes on to discuss the differences between pronunciation in the historical West Riding and the North and East Ridings (which, as noted earlier, roughly equate to modern West and South Yorkshire, North Yorkshire and the East Riding of Yorkshire respectively). With regards to 'don't', he lists the pronunciation above for the West Riding, but for the North and East Ridings, he gives *deeant*, suggesting [ɪə]. No reference to a fronted GOAT pronunciation is made throughout Kellett's text. This is similarly the case with the other texts listed in Table 16.1.

4.   Conclusions

In this chapter I have illustrated that the study of written representations of language features, specifically those which occur frequently and consistently, highlight an enregistered repertoire of Yorkshire dialect. Moreover, the consistency between the textual data and the results of the online survey shows that there is a correspondence between speakers' perceptions of 'Yorkshire' dialect and representations of it in writing. Thus, the textual material discussed here reflects speaker awareness of this repertoire. In addition, the consistency and repetition of orthographic representations allows them to be marketed on commodities. These artefacts therefore highlight overt links between language and place. However, as Johnstone (2009: 160) states, the 'same feature can be enregistered in multiple ways', and so we can see that Yorkshire dialect on commodities also indexes more abstract social values such as 'authenticity', 'intransigence', 'humorous' and 'friendliness', as discussed earlier.

I have also shown that we can use commodities to discuss the enregisterment of language features which are not necessarily frequent and consistent in written representations. This is illustrated by the case of GOAT fronting and Yorkshire dialect. This particular pronunciation is stereotypically associated with Hull, as noted by Watt and Smith (2005); however, the t-shirt in Figure 16.2 illustrates that this feature is also associated with Yorkshire. Following Johnstone (2009), I argue that this t-shirt is evidence for GOAT fronting becoming enregistered as Yorkshire dialect in addition to its existing association with Hull. The locations given for this feature by respondents to the online survey are consistent with areas where linguistic research highlights sound change in progress. This suggests that speakers are aware of this feature and are beginning to associate it with the wider area of Yorkshire as well as Hull specifically. The relatively small number of speakers who listed this feature in the survey, combined with the lack of frequent and consistent evidence for this feature in textual data regarding Yorkshire dialect, also implies that GOAT fronting is in the early stages of being enregistered. It therefore appears that, if the sound change recorded by Khattab (2007) and Finnegan (2011) continues, we will see GOAT fronting more widely recognised as a Yorkshire feature. As Beal (2009: 151) states, 'awareness of dialectal differences' can lead to enregisterment, meaning that the addition of GOAT fronting to the enregistered Yorkshire repertoire may occur in the near future.

Finally, Beal (2009: 154) has observed that the commodification of the Yorkshire variety 'Sheffieldish' is not as advanced as with 'Geordie'. I argue that this is also the case more broadly with 'Yorkshire' dialect. But, due to the strong correlation between the limited examples of Yorkshire commodification, the frequent and consistent dialect representations in textual data, and speakers' perceptions of what 'Yorkshire' dialect is, we can conclude that where a 'Yorkshire' feature is commodified, it represents a wider awareness of that feature. Similarly, we can state that such a feature is enregistered due to its appearance on the commodity itself. I have shown here that the potential for increasing awareness of one particular Yorkshire feature as a result of ongoing language change may be reflected in its appearance on commodities. As in the case of GOAT fronting in Yorkshire dialect, this illustrates two things: firstly, that enregistered repertoires change over time as a result of changes in progress. Secondly, that the social values indexed by individual features alter because of the same processes of language change. Thus, the Yorkshire repertoire appears to be gaining a new feature in the form of GOAT fronting, and GOAT fronting appears to be gaining a new indexical link with Yorkshire. Agha (2004: 25) states that registers are 'historical formations caught up in in-group relative processes of valorization and counter-valorization, exhibiting change in both form and value over time'. The Yorkshire data I have discussed in this chapter is an example of what appears to be the early stages of such a change in both form and value, highlighted in the commodified description of "Yorkshire" as *turtlely amazing.*

REFERENCES

Agha, Asif 2003. 'The social life of cultural value'. *Language and Communication* 23: 231–73.
　　2004. 'Registers of language', in Duranti, Alessandro (ed.) *A Companion to Linguistic Anthropology.* Oxford: Blackwell Publishing Ltd. pp. 23–45.
Alden, Gertie 2011. 'T'concert party ride by Gertie Alden'. Available at: www.yorkshire-dialect.org/authors/gertie_alden.htm.

Atomclub37 2006. 'Allinson's "Bread wi' Nowt Taken Out"'. Available at: www.youtube.com/watch?v=raJRe7J5m6g.

Balcony Shirts Ltd 2006. 'Yorkshire – It's Turtlely Amazing'. Available at: www.balconyshirts.co.uk/media/catalog/product/cache/1/image/640x/ 9df78eab33525d08d6e5fb8d27136e95/m/b/mbtc-33-bk-thumb_1.jpg.

Battye, David 2007. *Sheffield Dialect and Folklore since the Second World War: A Dying Tradition.* Sheffield: ALD Design and Print.

BBC Voices 2005. 'Guide to Hull Dialect'. Available at: www.bbc.co.uk/humber/ content/articles/2005/02/14/voices_hullspeak_glossary.shtml.

  2005. 'About Voices'. Available at: www.bbc.co.uk/voices/yourvoice/voices_ recordings.shtml.

Beal, Joan C. 2009. 'Enregisterment, commodification and historical context: "Geordie" versus "Sheffieldish"'. *American Speech* 84: 138–56.

Collins, Tim 2009. *The Northern Monkey Survival Guide: How to Hang on to Your Northern Cred in a World Filled with Southern Jessies.* London: Michael O'Mara Books Limited.

Cooper, Paul 2013. Enregisterment in Historical Contexts: A Framework. Unpublished PhD thesis, University of Sheffield.

  2014. '"It takes a Yorkshireman to talk Yorkshire": Towards a framework for the historical study of enregisterment', in Barysevich, Alena, Alexandra D'Arcy and David Heap (eds.) *Proceedings of Methods XIV.* Frankfurt am Main: Peter Lang. pp. 158–69.

  2015. 'Enregisterment in historical contexts: nineteenth century Yorkshire dialect', *Dialectologia* 14: 1–16.

  2016. 'Deregisterment' and 'fossil forms': the cases of *gan* and *mun* in "Yorkshire" dialect. *English Today* 33: 1. 1–10.

Finnegan, Katie 2011. *Linguistic variation, stability and change in middle-class Sheffield English.* Unpublished PhD thesis, University of Sheffield.

Greensmith, Bert 2011. 'Christmas Party by Bert Greensmith'. Available at: www.yorkshire-dialect.org/authors/bert_greensmith.htm.

Glauser, Beat 1984. *A Phonology of Present-day Speech in Grassington (North Yorkshire) A.* Francke AG Verlag: Bern.

Hague, Tom 1976. *Totley Tom: Tales of a Yorkshire Miner.* Kineton: Roundwood Press.

Hedevind, Bertil 1967. *The Dialect of Dentdale in the West Riding of Yorkshire.* Uppsala: Uppsala University.

Herriot, James 1977. *Vet in a Spin.* London: Pan MacMillan, UK.

Hines, Barry [1969] 2000. *A Kestrel for a Knave.* London: Penguin Books Ltd.

Hirst, Fred 2011. 'A Coil Fire by Fred Hirst'. Available at: www.yorkshire-dialect.org/ authors/fred_hirst.htm.

Holtby, Winifred [1935] 2011. *South Riding.* Reading: BBC Books.

Honeybone, Patrick and Kevin Watson 2013. 'Salience and the sociolinguistics of Scouse spelling: Exploring the phonology of the Contemporary Humorous Localised Dialect Literature of Liverpool'. *English World-Wide* 34: 305–40.

Hull City Council 2014. 'Hull UK City of Culture 2017'. Available at: www.hullcc.gov.uk/2017hull.

Johnson, Edward 2006. *Yorkshire-English.* London: Abson Books.

Johnstone, Barbara 2009. 'Pittsburghese shirts: Commodification and the enregisterment of an urban dialect'. *American Speech* 84: 157–75.

Johnstone, Barbara, Jennifer Andrus and Andrew E. Danielson. 2006. 'Mobility, indexicality and the enregisterment of "Pittsburghese"'. *Journal of English Linguistics* 34: 77–104.

Jones, Mark 2007. 'Glottals and grammar: Definite article reduction and morpheme boundaries'. *Leeds Working Papers in Linguistics* 12: 61–77.

Kay, Ian 2014. 'Portrait of Yorkshire and the Humber'. Available at: www.ons.gov.uk/ons/rel/regional-trends/regional-trends/no–41–2009-edition/portraitof-yorkshire-and-humberside.pdf.

Kellett, Arnold 2002. *The Yorkshire Dictionary of Dialect, Tradition and Folklore*, Second edition. Otley: Smith Settle Ltd.

2007. *Ee By Gum, Lord! The Gospels in Broad Yorkshire*. Skipton: Smith Settle.

Khattab, Ghada 2007. 'Variation in vowel production by English-Arabic bilinguals'. *Laboratory Phonology* 9: 383–410.

Markham, Len 2010. *Ee Up Lad! A Salute to the Yorkshire Dialect*. Newbury: Countryside Books.

McMillan, Ian 2007. *Chelp and Chunter: How to talk Tyke*. Glasgow: Harper Collins.

Montgomery, Chris 2010. 'Sprachraum and its perception', in Lameli, Alfred, Roland Kehrein and Stefan Rabanus (eds.) *Language and Space: An International Handbook of Linguistic Variation, Volume 2: Language Mapping*. Berlin: De Gruyter. pp. 586–606.

Moorland Pottery 2010. 'Yorkie Ware'. Available at: www.moorlandpottery.co.uk/moorland-pottery-ranges-yorkie-ware-c-1_47.html?zenid=c958aa1786bc358cc105c5290cebedf7.

Office for National Statistics 2012. 'Census result shows increase in population of Yorkshire and the Humber'. Available at: www.ons.gov.uk/ons/rel/mro/news-release/census-result-shows-increase-in-population-of-yorkshire-and-the-humber/censusyorkandhumbernr0712.html.

2014. 'Regional Profiles: Key Statistics – Yorkshire and the Humber', August 2012. Available at: www.ons.gov.uk/ons/rel/regional-trends/region-and-country-profiles/key-statistics-and-profiles—august-2012/key-statistics—yorkshire-and-the-humber.html.

Orton, Harold, and Eugen B. Dieth 1962. *Survey of English Dialects: The Basic Materials. Volume 1: The Six Northern Counties and the Isle of Man*, Part 1. Leeds: E. J. Arnold for the University of Leeds.

1963. *Survey of English Dialects: The Basic Materials. Volume 1: The Six Northern Counties and the Isle of Man*, Part 2. Leeds: E. J. Arnold for the University of Leeds.

1963. *Survey of English Dialects: The Basic Materials. Volume 1: The Six Northern Counties and the Isle of Man*, Part 3. Leeds: E. J. Arnold for the University of Leeds.

Oxford University Press 2014. 'OED Online'. Available at: www.oed.com.

PikerAds 2008. 'Hovis Advert'. Available at: www.youtube.com/watch?v=BvhpD9XsrsE.

Richards, Hazel M. 2008. *Mechanisms, Motivations and Outcomes of Change in Morley (Leeds) English*. Unpublished PhD thesis, The University of York.

Roeder, Rebecca 2009. 'Lexical exceptionality in Yorkshire English'. *Toronto Working Papers in Linguistics* 30: 105–18.

Shorrocks, Graham 1996. 'Non-standard dialect literature and popular culture', in Klemola, Juhani, Merja Kytö and Matti Rissanen (eds.) *Speech Past and Present. Studies in English Dialectology in Memory of Ossi Ihalainen.* Frankfurt am Main: Peter Lang. pp. 385–411.

Smith, Steven D. 1998. *Plonkers Plaintiffs & Pleas.* Barnsley: Neville-Douglas Publishing Limited.

Stilton, Mark 2004. 'Hull to Grimsby Dictionary'. Available at: www.codalmighty .com/site/ca.php?article=249.

Tagliamonte, Sali A. and Rebecca V. Roeder 2009. 'Variation in the English definite article: Socio-historical linguistics in t'speech community'. *Journal of Sociolinguistics* 13: 435–71.

Taylor-Bradford, Barbara 1981. *A Woman of Substance.* Glasgow: Grafton Books.

Tidholm, Hans 1979. *The Dialect of Egton in North Yorkshire.* Bokmaskinen, Göteborg.

The Hull Shop 2013. 'No Place Like Hull'. Available at: www.thehullshop.co.uk/ hulldialectpack.html.

Utdforum.com 2006. 'Stupid Words Said in a Leeds Accent'. Available at: www.utdforum.com/forum/showthread.php?t=12411.

Wales, Katie 2006. *Northern English: A Cultural and Social History.* Cambridge: Cambridge University Press.

Watson, Kevin 2009. 'Regional Variation in English Accents and Dialects' in Culpeper, Jonathan, Francis Katamba, Paul Kerswill, Ruth Wodak and Tony McEnery (eds) *English Language Description, Variation and Context.* Houndmills: Palgrave Macmillan.

Watt, Dominic 2013. 'Sociolinguistic variation in vowels', in Ball, Martin J. and Fiona Gibson (eds.) *Handbook of Vowels and Vowel Disorders.* New York: Taylor & Francis LLC. pp. 207–28.

Watt, Dominic and Jennifer Smith 2005. 'Language change', in Ball, Martin J. (ed.) *Clinical Sociolinguistics.* Oxford: Blackwell Publishing Ltd. pp. 101–19.

Watt, Dominic and Jennifer Tillotson 2001. 'A spectrographic analysis of vowel fronting in Bradford English'. *English World-Wide* 22: 269–302.

Wells, John C. 1982. *Accents of English Volume 2: The British Isles.* Cambridge: Cambridge University Press.

Whomersley, Derek 1981. *Sheffieldish: A Beginners Phrase-book.* Sheffield: City of Sheffield Publicity Department.

Index

Acadian French, 325–8
AISEB (Accent and Identity on the Scottish/
    English Border), 196–204, 207–10
Annotation, 113, 117–18, 122
artistic performance, 330
aspiration, 199, 202
attitudes, 7, 178, 193, 196, 198, 209, 216, 228
authenticity, 109, 175, 218, 229, 267, 296, 348,
    358
    local, 296

BATH lexical set, 42, 261, 263–6
Berwick-upon-Tweed, 15, 89, 91
big data, 123
border(s), 191–2, 194, 197, 209–10, 241
boundaries
    administrative, 192, 196, 238
    dialect, 156

Canadian English, 69, 84
characterological figure, 8, 285, 289
class, 23, 81–2, 200, 221–2, 260, 285, 293–7,
    301–4, 306–7, 309–10, 312–14, 318–21,
    348
collaborative research, 130, 135–6, 138–40,
    142
commodification, 8–9, 296, 301, 305, 357, 364
communicative style, 285, 290, 293, 295
commuting, 162–5, 184
contact zone, 132, 134, 140–1
Cornish English, 261
corpora, 3–4, 107, 117, 120, 312–13, 318
counterurbanisation, 182
cultural heritage, 128, 130–4, 140, 142
Cumbria, 159, 162

definite article reduction, 15, 18, 350, 354, 358
derhoticisation, 59–61, 221–2, 228
dialect areas, 151–6, 158–62, 164–5, 362
dialect contact, 2, 7, 60, 180, 234–5, 243, 246,
    248–9, 254, 262

dialect death, 99, 101
dialect dictionaries, 304, 350–1, 363
dialect elicitation methods, 92, 99, 139
dialect levelling, 2–3, 7, 66, 69, 71, 74, 78, 84,
    99, 101, 254
dialect literature, 9, 350, 353–5
dialectology, 4, 19, 98, 137, 147–9, 153–8,
    162, 165–6, 177, 179–81, 325

education, 21, 25, 30, 32, 260, 262–4, 267,
    269–70, 273–6
electronic corpus, 39, 91, 107, 115–16, 137
embodiment, 219, 285, 295, 312
enactive engagement, 128, 132–3, 135–6, 139,
    141–2
enregisterment, 8–9, 84, 90, 184, 217–18,
    251, 302, 306, 330, 351, 355, 357, 359,
    363–4
ethics, 120, 123, 131
ethnography, 129, 235, 293–4, 301, 313–14

farming, 90, 133, 138, 176, 260, 268, 270,
    272–3

gaze, 4, 171–82, 184–5
gender, 7, 23, 28, 32, 110–11, 117, 179, 243,
    258, 263, 273–6, 288, 292–4, 318
GIS, 4, 148, 155–8, 162, 165–6
Glasgow, 2, 38–40, 44–6, 49, 51–3, 58–60,
    159, 219–22
Glaswegian, 7, 38, 40, 42, 56, 60, 216
GOAT fronting, 351, 359–64

H-deletion, 79, 82–3
Holy Island, 3, 88, 90–101, 132
howay, 8, 304–5, 307–10, 312–21
Hullish, 360–1

identity, 6–8, 33, 90, 202–4, 208–10, 229–30,
    250–2, 276–7, 283–5, 302–7, 313–14,
    318–21, 330, 340, 342–3

local identity, 79, 81–2, 84, 101, 235, 249, 266, 269, 285
ideology, 8, 79, 83, 173, 178, 219, 235, 260–1, 293–4, 319
immigration, 183, 262, 325
independent, 22, 65, 73, 110, 219, 293, 296
indexical field, 80, 82, 314, 343
indexicality, 6, 69, 79, 230, 283, 304–7, 319, 321
indicator, 27, 90, 97, 164, 235
indie, 218–21, 230, 340
innovation, 2, 166, 180, 184, 195, 325, 329–30, 341

language ideologies, 38, 61, 171
language variation, 5, 7, 15, 33, 121, 184, 217, 230, 274–5, 321, 348
Leeds Archive of Vernacular Culture (LAVC), 128–9, 134, 136, 139
lenition, 70, 75
linguistic change, 15, 20, 22, 30, 65, 68, 80, 83, 172, 184
linguistic markets, 273
literary dialect, 350, 353–5

mapping, 1, 4, 147, 149, 151–3, 158, 160, 162, 166, 195
maps, 129, 139, 149–56, 158, 160–3, 165, 193, 197, 283, 295
marker, 90, 100
media representations, 9, 304, 307, 336
metadata, 112–14, 120, 138
metapragmatic data, 318, 320
mobility, 3, 49, 110, 131, 171, 182
multiethnolects, 180, 184
museums, 4, 130–5, 139–42
music, 7, 68, 215–21, 223, 229–30, 308, 337, 340–1

Newfoundland English, 3, 66, 68, 83
Northumberland, 3, 6, 18, 87–91, 93, 97–8, 101, 162–4
Northumbrian Burr, 87–90, 93–7, 99–101

obsolescence, 28
oral history, 39, 131, 262, 267

perceptual dialectology, 148, 153–8, 162, 165–6
perceptual prominence, 15, 301–2

performance, 79, 82, 218, 230, 294–6, 306, 330, 333, 344
phonological resistance, 235, 248, 254
Pittsburgh, 6, 8, 266, 285–93, 296, 306, 350, 355, 359
Pittsburghese, 250, 285–9, 291–3, 295–7, 304, 306, 350, 355, 359
place, 32–3, 65, 69–70, 147–8, 209–10, 216–17, 229–30, 249–51, 258, 276, 284–6, 288, 295, 307, 363
plosive, 19, 49
postvocalic /r/, 217, 221–3, 225–30
preterit 'come', 24–8, 30, 32

real-time change, 42, 47, 59–60, 121
regional dialect loss, 65
rhotic, 7, 94, 173, 175, 208, 221–6, 228–9
rural, 4, 68–9, 80–3, 87–90, 148, 221, 258, 276, 331–2
rural idyll, 173–4, 177–8, 182

Scots, 7, 38, 40, 42–3, 46, 56, 59, 90, 196, 207, 215, 220–1, 228–9
Scottish English, 38, 42, 49, 56
Scottish Vowel Length Rule, 49
Scottish–English border, 158, 160, 163
social meaning, 2–3, 5–9, 60–1, 75, 79, 81, 101, 230, 235, 254, 266, 274–6, 283–4, 306–7, 320, 330
song, 175, 215–18, 220–30, 304, 341
South Armagh, 107–8, 113–15
space, 251
    perceptual, 87, 147, 161, 165, 195, 207, 209
    physical, 1–2, 4–5, 9, 45–6, 147, 149, 172–3, 193–4, 209, 258, 276, 283
    social, 130, 134–5, 147, 162, 165–6, 194–5, 209, 258, 277, 283, 304, 343
stance(s), 6, 193, 198, 216, 274, 284–5, 287, 289, 304–6, 317–20, 340
Standard English English, 261
stereotype, 82, 90, 100, 216, 228, 302
style, 7, 222, 229, 258, 267, 274, 290, 292–6, 306, 320, 348
Survey of English Dialects, 89, 96, 129, 137–8, 148–51, 176–7

Text Encoding Initiative, 114
TH-stopping, 79–81
tourism, 68, 90, 174, 181, 260, 274, 335
TRAP lexical set, 7, 42, 244, 261–6, 269, 274–6
Tyneside English, 91, 107, 116, 137

undergraduate research, 130, 139
uvular /r/, 3, 87, 89, 95–100

variable (ing), 15, 18–21, 23, 26, 32–3
variationist sociolinguistics, 3–4, 15, 18, 179
VOT (Voice Onset Time), 6, 199–202
vowel quality, 39, 42–3, 46, 53, 261, 265

word-initial /l/, 39, 42, 56–7, 59, 61

Yinzer, 285–9, 291–3, 295–7
yod-dropping, 175, 184
Yorkshire, 9, 15, 130, 235, 348
  dialect, 246–7, 348, 350
  dialect texts, 352–3